A CULTURAL HISTORY OF THE EMOTIONS

VOLUME 5

A Cultural History of the Emotions
General Editors: Susan Broomhall, Jane W. Davidson, and Andrew Lynch

Volume 1
A Cultural History of the Emotions in Antiquity
Edited by Douglas Cairns

Volume 2
A Cultural History of the Emotions in the Medieval Age
Edited by Juanita Ruys and Clare Monagle

Volume 3
A Cultural History of the Emotions in the Late Medieval, Reformation, and Renaissance Age
Edited by Andrew Lynch and Susan Broomhall

Volume 4
A Cultural History of the Emotions in the Baroque and Enlightenment Age
Edited by Claire Walker, Katie Barclay, and David Lemmings

Volume 5
A Cultural History of the Emotions in the Age of Romanticism, Revolution, and Empire
Edited by Susan J. Matt

Volume 6
A Cultural History of the Emotions in the Modern and Post-Modern Age
Edited by Jane W. Davidson and Joy Damousi

A CULTURAL HISTORY OF THE EMOTIONS
IN THE AGE OF ROMANTICISM, REVOLUTION, AND EMPIRE

Edited by Susan J. Matt

BLOOMSBURY ACADEMIC
LONDON • NEW YORK • OXFORD • NEW DELHI • SYDNEY

BLOOMSBURY ACADEMIC
Bloomsbury Publishing Plc
50 Bedford Square, London, WC1B 3DP, UK
1385 Broadway, New York, NY 10018, USA
29 Earlsfort Terrace, Dublin 2, Ireland

BLOOMSBURY and the Diana logo are trademarks of Bloomsbury Publishing Plc

First published in Great Britain 2019
This edition published in Great Britain, 2022

Copyright © Bloomsbury Publishing, 2019

Susan J. Matt has asserted their right under the Copyright, Designs and Patents Act, 1988, to be identified as Editor of this work.

Cover image: *Egoism personified*. Handcoloured engraving from Pierre de la Mesangere's Le Bon Genre, Paris, 1817. (© Florilegius / SSPL / Getty Images)

All rights reserved. No part of this publication may be reproduced or transmitted in any form or by any means, electronic or mechanical, including photocopying, recording, or any information storage or retrieval system, without prior permission in writing from the publishers.

A catalogue record for this book is available from the British Library.

A catalog record for this book is available from the Library of Congress.

ISBN: HB: 978-1-4725-3575-7
        PB: 978-1-3503-4526-3
        Set: 978-1-3503-4769-4

Series: The Cultural Histories Series

Typeset by RefineCatch Limited, Bungay, Suffolk
Printed and bound in Great Britain

To find out more about our authors and books visit www.bloomsbury.com and sign up for our newsletters.

CONTENTS

LIST OF ILLUSTRATIONS		vi
GENERAL EDITORS' PREFACE		x
	Introduction: What Were Emotions? Definitions and Understandings, 1780–1920 *Susan J. Matt*	1
1	Medical and Scientific Understandings *Rob Boddice*	17
2	Religion and Spirituality *Julius H. Rubin*	33
3	Music and Dance *Wiebke Thormählen*	55
4	Drama *Aileen Forbes*	75
5	The Visual Arts *Kerstin Thomas*	95
6	Literature *Gregory Eiselein*	121
7	In Private: The Individual and the Domestic Community *Peter N. Stearns*	137
8	In Public: Emotional Politics *Ute Frevert*	157
NOTES ON CONTRIBUTORS		175
NOTES		177
REFERENCES		179
INDEX		209

ILLUSTRATIONS

CHAPTER 1

1.1	Charles Bell, Muscles of the Face, 1806 (Wellcome Library, London).	20
1.2	Duchenne de Boulogne, Facial Expression of Terror, 1862 (Wellcome Library, London).	22
1.3	Cesare Lombroso, Six Figures Illustrating Types of Criminals, 1888 (Wellcome Library, London).	25
1.4	George John Romanes, Mental Evolution in Animals, 1883 (Wellcome Library, London).	26
1.5	W.M. Bayliss (right) and E.H. Starling (left): experimentation on hormones in a dog, 1903 (Wellcome Library, London).	31

CHAPTER 2

2.1	J. Maze Burbank, "Religious Camp Meeting"—Or An Old Time Camp Meeting (1838) no. 1910.1.2. Courtesy of New Bedford Whaling Museum.	34
2.2	Jarena Lee.	43
2.3	Religious Dancing of the Blacks Termed Shouting.	43
2.4	Possibly Harlan Page. Courtesy of National Gallery of Art, Washington.	49

CHAPTER 3

3.1	Musical Union. Photo by Hulton Archive/Illustrated London News (27 June 1846) Getty Images.	60
3.2	J.J. de Momigny, Cours complet d'harmonie et de composition, Paris, 1810. Planche 30. © The British Library Board. Hirsch 5303.	62
3.3	Caricature depicting Franz Liszt (1811–86) playing the piano (c.1845). Photo by Leemage/Corbis via Getty Images.	69
3.4	Liebig card, advertising meat extract, featuring Walther von Stolzing in R. Wagner's opera_Die Meistersinger von Nürnberg—, c. 1910. Photo by Chronicle/Alamy Stock Photo.	72

LIST OF ILLUSTRATIONS vii

CHAPTER 4

4.1 "An expression of horror." From Henry Siddons' *Practical Illustrations of Rhetorical Gesture and Action; Adapted to the English drama* (1822). Courtesy of the Brander Matthews Dramatic Library, Rare Book and Manuscript Library, Columbia University. 79

4.2 "Melodramatic expression." From Henry Siddons' *Practical Illustrations of Rhetorical Gesture and Action; Adapted to the English Drama* (1822). Courtesy of the Brander Matthews Dramatic Library, Rare Book and Manuscript Library, Columbia University. 80

4.3 (a) "Terror." (b) "Jealous Rage." (c) "Despondency." From Henry Siddons' *Practical Illustrations of Rhetorical Gesture and Action; Adapted to the English Drama* (1822). Courtesy of the Brander Matthews Dramatic Library, Rare Book and Manuscript Library, Columbia University. 89

CHAPTER 5

5.1 Charles Le Brun, *Horror* (La Frayeur), c. 1688, ink and pencil on paper, 19 × 25.6 cm, Paris, Musée du Louvre. © bpk/RMN—Grand Palais/Gérard Bolt. 97

5.2 Jacques-Louis David, *Lictors Returning to Brutus the Bodies of his Sons* (*Les Licteurs rapportent à Brutus les corps de ses fils*), 1789, oil on canvas, 323 × 422 cm, Paris, Musée du Louvre. © Getty images. 98

5.3 Daniel Nikolaus Chodowiecki, *Natural and affected Attitudes* (*Natürliche und affectirte Handlungen des Lebens*), 2nd series, plate 3 and 4: *Sentiment* (*Empfindung*), 1779, etching, 87 × 50 cm. © bpk | Hamburger Kunsthalle | Elke Walford, 99

5.4 John Constable, David Lucas, *Old Sarum*, 1830, Mezzotint, first state of two, 14.9 × 17.8 cm. © Victoria & Albert Museum. 101

5.5 Caspar David Friedrich, *Monk by the Sea.* (*Mönch am Meer*), c. 1809, oil on canvas, 110 × 171.5 cm, Berlin, Alte Nationalgalerie. © Getty images. 103

5.6 Camille Corot, *View of Riva* (*Vue prise de Riva*), 1865–70, oil on canvas, 73 × 123 cm, Marseille, musée des Beaux-Arts. © bpk/RMN—Grand Palais/Jean Bernard. 104

5.7 Francisco de Goya, *Saturn*, 1820–23, oil on canvas, 146 × 83 cm, Madrid, Prado.© Getty images. 106

5.8 Jean-Baptiste Carpeaux, *Ugolino and his Sons* (*Ugolin et ses fils*), 1865–67, marble, 197.5 × 149.9 × 110.5 cm, New York, The Metropolitan Museum of Art. © Getty images. 107

5.9 Théodore Géricault, *Mazeppa*, 1823, lithograph, 15.9 × 20.7 cm. © bpk/RMN—Grand Palais/René-Gabriel Ojéda. 108

5.10 Eugène Delacroix, *The Death of Sardanapalus* (*Mort de Sardanapale*), 1827, oil on canvas, 392 × 496 cm, Paris, Musée du Louvre. © Getty images. 110

5.11 Pierre Puvis de Chavannes, *The Poor Fisherman* (*Le pauvre Pêcheur*), 1887–92, oil on canvas, 105.8 × 68.6 cm, Tokio, National Museum of Western Art. © Getty images. 112

5.12 Fernand Khnopff, *The Abandoned City* (*Une ville abandonnée*), 1904, pastel and pencil on paper, glued on canvas, 76 × 69 cm, Brussels, Musées royaux des Beaux-Arts de Belgique. © Royal Institute for Cultural Heritage, Brussel. 113

5.13 James MacNeill Whistler, *Nocturne: Blue and Gold—Old Battersea Bridge*, 1872–75, oil on canvas, 68.3 × 51.2 cm, London, Tate Gallery. © alamy. 115

5.14 Carlo Carrà, *Railway Station in Milan* (*La stazione di Milano*), 1911, oil on canvas, 50 × 55 cm, Stuttgart, Staatsgalerie. © Staatsgalerie Stuttgart/VG Bild-Kunst, Bonn 2017. 117

5.15 Georges Seurat, *Chahut*, 1889–90, oil on canvas, 171.5 × 140.5 cm, Otterlo, Kröller-Müller Museum. © Getty images. 119

5.16 Ferdinand Hodler, *Lake Thun with Reflection* (*Thunersee mit Spiegelung*), 1905, oil on canvas, 80 × 100 cm, Geneva, Musée d'art et d'histoire. © alamy. 120

CHAPTER 6

6.1 Goethe's *The Sorrows of Young Werther* epitomized the *Sturm und Drang* movement's commitment to the representation of powerful emotion. Image: Tony Johannot ["Werther and Charlotte"], illustration from *Werther par Goethe*, trans. Pierre Leroux (Paris, 1845), opposite p. 162. 125

6.2 Stowe famously deployed moving portrayals of the suffering of her enslaved characters to generate support for the antislavery movement in the United States. Image: George Cruikshank, "Eliza Crosses the Ohio on the Floating Ice," illustration from Harriet Beecher Stowe, *Uncle Tom's Cabin, or Life Among the Lowly* (London: 1851), opposite p. 51. 126

6.3 Little Nell's death in *The Old Curiosity Shop* is perhaps the most well-known example of Dickens' mastery of sentimental literary art. Image: George Cattermole, ["At Rest (Nell dead)"], illustration from Charles Dickens, *The Old Curiosity Shop*, with introduction and notes by Andrew Lang, 2 vols. (London, [1897]), vol. 2, p. 340. 130

6.4 Darwin's theory of natural selection and his naturalistic understanding of emotion, which juxtaposed human with animal expression of emotion, had an enormous impact on literary realism. Image: T.W. Wood, "Cat, savage, and prepared to fight," illustration from Charles Darwin, *The Expression of Emotion in Man and Animals* (London, 1872), p. 58. 131

6.5 Dada cultivated forms of literary surprise and startle, in part by refusing the traditional hermeneutical association of poetry and art with meaning and interpretation. Image: Paul Eluard and Tristan Tzara, *Dada ne signifie rien*, broadside leaflet, 1919. The International Dada Archive, Special Collections, University of Iowa Libraries. 135

CHAPTER 7

7.1 Mother love. Courtesy of Library of Congress. 145

7.2 Courtship in the early nineteenth century. Courtesy of Library of Congress. 146

7.3 The new poignancy of grief. Courtesy of Library of Congress. 148

7.4 A husband's grief. Courtesy of Library of Congress. 149

7.5 The happy family. Courtesy of Library of Congress. 151

7.6 Relative frequency of obedience references in the United States. Source: Google Books (American English) Corpus. http://googlebooks.byu.edu 151

7.7 Cheerful obedience: U.S. data. Source: Google Books (American English) Corpus. http://googlebooks.byu.edu 152

7.8 Cheer combined references: U.S. data (cheerful, etc.). Source: Google Books (American English) Corpus. http://googlebooks.byu.edu 153

CHAPTER 8

8.1 Queen Victoria's Jubilee, 1887, Queen's marriage to Prince Albert of Saxe-Coburg and Gotha, February 10, 1840, royal family in 1846. Photo by DEA PICTURE LIBRARY. 162

8.2 Photomontage postcard showing William II in front of the Berlin Cathedral. Courtesy of Eva Giloi. 165

8.3 Political meeting, sketches, agitation in Ireland (1879). Photo by DEA PICTURE LIBRARY. 167

8.4 SPD banner commemorating the 10th anniversary of the General German Workers' Foundation, May 23, 1873. Courtesy of Archiv der sozialen Demokratie/Friedrich-Ebert-Stiftung. 169

8.5 Claude Monet, Rue Saint-Denis, Celebration of June 30, 1878. Source: The Yorck Project on Wikimedia Commons. 172

GENERAL EDITORS' PREFACE

The General Editors, volume editors, and individual authors of this series have many organizations to thank for helping to bring it into existence. They gratefully acknowledge assistance from the Arts and Humanities Research Council (UK); the European Research Council Project, The Social and Cultural Construction of Emotions, University of Oxford, and its Director, Professor Angelos Chaniotis; the Leverhulme Trust; and the Wellcome Trust. Above all, the series has depended on support from the Australian Research Council Centre of Excellence for the History of Emotions (CE110001011). The project was conceived as a key part of the Centre's collaborative research work and has benefited greatly from the generous help of its academic and administrative staff.

The General Editors also express their deep gratitude to the volume editors and authors for their time, expertise, and gracious willingness to revise essays in the light of readers' comments. Many other people helped in reading, tracing images, and advising in various ways. Our thanks go to Merridee Bailey; Jacquie Bennett; Sophie Boyd-Hurrell; Frederic Kiernan; Mark Neuendorf; Fiona Sim; and Stephanie Thomson; and to the patient staff at Bloomsbury: Dan Hutchins; Claire Lipscomb; Beatriz Lopez; and Rhodri Mogford. We especially acknowledge Ciara Rawnsley, who as Editorial Assistant for the entire series has tirelessly helped authors and done indispensable and meticulous work on all aspects of the volumes' preparation.

This series is dedicated to the memory of Philippa Maddern (1952–2014) who was an original General Editor, and an inspiring friend, mentor, and colleague to many of the contributors.

Introduction

What Were Emotions? Definitions and Understandings, 1780–1920

SUSAN J. MATT

What were the emotions during the period 1780 to 1920, an era marked by revolutions, sentimentalism and romanticism, imperial politics, the rise of psychology and the emergence of psychoanalysis? These relatively few years witnessed radical changes in how people conceived of their feelings—changes that continue to resonate in the modern age. Indeed, it was during this period that many of our current conceptions of emotion first emerged.

Bookended by the American and French Revolutions in the eighteenth century and the end of World War I in the twentieth, the era witnessed dramatic transformations in how philosophers, scientists, theologians, artists, politicians, and ordinary men and women came to define what an emotion was. During these years, the role of emotions in public life was also hotly debated. And during that century and a half, new emotions and emotional styles emerged, as well. While there was significant variation across cultures, by the early twentieth century a new view of emotion was dominant across America, Europe, and their imperial holdings.

NEW WORDS, NEW MEANINGS

Between 1780 and 1920, a dramatic change occurred in the terminology and definition of emotional life. Feelings changed from being considered moral, and at least to some extent mental and volitional, to being regarded as physical, bodily experiences that were involuntary. The language used to describe inner life shrank as well, and the word *emotion* came to dominate discussion, replacing a richer and more varied vocabulary.

At the start of the era, in the late eighteenth and early nineteenth centuries, there was an array of terms which Europeans and Americans used to describe their inner lives. Of this rich vocabulary, historian Ute Frevert has written, "The sheer diversity of concepts of emotion that can be documented for this period was unprecedented, existing neither before, nor after it. . . . What made the eighteenth and nineteenth centuries so special was the parallel existence of different systems of thought, each of which defined its own concepts and differentiated them from others" (Frevert 2014: 17).

For instance, there were *passions, appetites, sensibilities, sentiments, affections*, to name a few of the English terms. *Appetites* and *passions* were often grouped together, and were seen as strong feelings that might lead to vice. Medieval theologians identified the appetites as "hunger, thirst, and sexual desire"; historian Thomas Dixon describes them as "movements of the lower animal soul." Similarly, in keeping with longstanding Classical and Medieval Christian views, passions were often regarded as unruly and potentially sinful—key passions included "love, hate, hope, fear and anger" (Dixon 2006, 21–22; Dixon 2012: 339). While traditionally passions were seen as selfish feelings, by the late eighteenth century some Americans and Europeans were beginning to accord them new legitimacy in political life, and in the nineteenth century Victorians endorsed them, as well (Eustace 2008; Stearns 1994: 52).

Appetites and passions stood in contrast to *affections* and *sentiments*, which were seen as more socially productive feelings that could benefit the public good. The term *affections* gained currency as a result of the Scottish Enlightenment, and the works of David Hume and Adam Smith, in particular (Frevert 2014: 13). Affections were virtuous, social feelings which all humans possessed; they arose from cognitive appraisals of the world. *Sentiment* similarly denoted admirable feelings, and, like affections, "bridged the gap between thinking and feeling" (Dixon 2006: 17; Dixon 2012: 339; Reddy 2001: 216; Eustace 2008: 482–485).

There was also *sensibility*, which denoted sensitivity, refinement, and compassion (White 2017: 275; Knott 2004; Eustace 2008: 483). The *Pennsylvania Magazine* described sensibility in 1776, claiming it "expands the mind—it awakens every noble sentiment of pity and compassion—and arouses every tender and human feeling, in the breast" (*Pennsylvania Magazine* 1776: 176–177; Knott 2004: 27). Sensibility became a central concern of many mid- to late- eighteenth-century Enlightenment writers, poets, and philosophers, who characterized it as a state based on sympathy, which allowed one to develop feeling for one's fellows (Ferber 2010: 15–16).

However, over the course of the nineteenth century, these words and their meanings changed radically. At the start of the period, feelings, passions, appetites, and the like were seen as the realm of philosophers and theologians; they were cognitive, moral, subject to volition, and connected to the soul (Frevert 2014: 20–31; Dixon 2006: 3; Dixon 2012: 341–342; Scheer 2014). Thomas Dixon has noted that, in the eighteenth century, feeling words were embedded in a religious view of the world. He writes, "the words 'passions' and 'affections' belonged to a network of words such as 'of the soul', 'conscience', 'fall', 'sin', 'grace', 'Spirit', 'Satan', 'will', 'lower appetite', 'self love' and so on" (Dixon 2006: 5). However, by the end of the nineteenth century, the religious web of meaning had disintegrated, and the rich array of words had been replaced by the single term *emotion*, which became the province of natural science rather than theology and philosophy (Dixon 2006).

There were other changes that happened to conceptions of feelings during this era of transformation, as well. One significant change was that emotional life was gradually differentiated from rational thinking and intellectual activity. As William Reddy has noted of France, "In the late eighteenth century, reason and emotion were not seen as opposed forces; in the early nineteenth they were" (Reddy 2001: 216). Although it happened at different times across Europe, gradually thinking and feeling came to be seen as two separate activities.

Emblematic of all of these changes was the rise of a relatively new word in English: *emotion*. Dixon, who traced the word's history, noted that it originated in France and first began to circulate in English in the seventeenth century; it initially signified "physical disturbance and bodily movement. . . . Increasingly during the 18th century, 'emotion' came to refer to the bodily stirrings accompanying mental feelings" (Dixon 2012: 340). Its evolution continued in the nineteenth century, when the word came into wide circulation in English, publicized by Scottish physician and moral philosopher Thomas

Brown, who used it in his *Lectures on the Philosophy of the Human Mind*, published in 1820 (Dixon 2006: 109–110). Brown defined emotion rather vaguely. He wrote, "Every person understands what is meant by an emotion, at least as well, as he understands what is meant by an intellectual power.... Perhaps if any definition of them be possible, they may be defined to be vivid feelings, arising immediately from the consideration of objects, perceived, or remembered, or imagined, or from other prior emotions." As he employed the word, he also delineated its meaning, asserting that the powers of the mind could be divided into two categories: intellectual states and emotions. In his view, then, emotions were not cognitive (Brown 1822: 252; Dixon 2012: 340).

As emotion became the dominant category to describe feeling, theorists began to further articulate its key features. One quality of emotion that many dwelt upon was its alleged physicality. Charles Bell, who, like Brown, was a Scottish philosopher and medical doctor, claimed that something was an emotion if it produced what he termed an "outward sign"—a facial expression or bodily movement. Another Scottish philosopher, Alexander Bain, suggested in a similar vein, "Every feeling has its PHYSICAL SIDE" (Dixon 2012: 341; Bain 1865: 13). In his 1872 work, *The Expression of the Emotions in Man and Animals*, Charles Darwin likewise explored the relationship between physical expression and inner feeling, arguing that the two were inextricably linked and that emotions were automatic reflexes (Gendron and Feldman Barrett 2009; Dixon 2006: 159–168).

Other significant figures who elaborated on the idea of the physical nature of emotion included philosopher William James, who, in an 1884 article, argued that emotions were the result of physical bodily changes rather than the cause of them. He wrote,

> Our natural way of thinking about these standard emotions is that the mental perception of some fact excites the mental affection called the emotion, and that this latter state of mind gives rise to the bodily expression. My thesis on the contrary is that the bodily changes follow directly the PERCEPTION of the exciting fact, and that our feeling of the same changes as they occur IS the emotion.

In short, it was the perception of one's bodily physical changes that precipitated an emotion. As James explained, "we feel sorry because we cry," rather than the reverse (James 1884: 189–190; Dixon 2006: 208). A Danish physician, Carl Georg Lange, came to much the same conclusion a year later, arguing "Take away the bodily symptoms from a frightened individual; let his pulse beat calmly, his look be firm, his color normal, his movements quick and sure; his speech strong, his thoughts clear; and what remains of his fear?" (quoted in Plamper 2015: 177).

While a growing number of scientists agreed that the emotions were physical, not all believed they were visible in facial or outward physical expressions, however. Otniel Dror, for instance, has shown that nineteenth-century physiologists, such as Angelo Mosso, tried to exclude "any and all linguistic, overt behavioral, gestural, or facial expressions of emotions" in their research. Instead they "assumed and demanded an immobile, catatonic, and incommunicative overt body, which was juxtaposed to an animated and expressive viscera." In his view, it was "the internal actions of the viscera" that were the essence of emotion (Dror 2014: 125).

Although there were many variants, this new view, that emotion was physical and non-cognitive, gradually took hold across Europe. However, it spread unevenly. It emerged in Britain earlier than in some other European cultures. As ethno-historian Monique Scheer notes of Germany, "in the eighteenth century, body and soul were closely connected with each other and with the outside world.... After 1800, some kinds of emotions were removed from the willful part of the soul and transferred to the (newly discovered) 'emotive faculty' (*Gefühlsvermögen*)." For much of the nineteenth century, German philosophers differentiated between *Gefühl*—feeling associated with the soul—and *Affekt*, which described "superficial emotions located primarily in the body: fast, reactive, and quickly dissipated" (Scheer 2014: 34–35). Gefühl, with its linkage of mind and feeling, remained popular throughout the nineteenth century. Ute Frevert explains that the word's continued popularity "reflected the high regard for philosophers" in Germany, and the concomitant "distrust of the body and its relegation to a lower animalistic sphere" (Frevert 2014: 22). However, Germany, too, eventually came to embrace the idea of feeling as a physiological rather than cognitive process, though at a much slower pace.

Yet despite slower lexical changes, there was transformation in the way some began to study feeling in Germany that became influential across the continent. It was the German psychologist Wilhelm Wundt who created the first experimental psychology lab, dedicated to the idea that emotions might be measured as physical and physiological processes (Frevert 2014: 22). Wundt was one of the pioneers of scientific psychology, a field which emerged in the late nineteenth century; he was soon joined by psychologists as well as physiologists across the world who espoused a shared faith in the new science of emotion. As historian Jan Plamper observed, these scientists believed that emotions "could not be studied through the verbal description of subjectively felt feelings. Instead, emotions were to be made physically measurable in the laboratory or clinic, using animals and humans as test subjects and a new, specially developed apparatus." Physiologists and psychologists endeavored to arouse subjects and measure their pulse, their saliva, their urine, in order to gauge their emotions. Plamper notes that their goal was to replicate and reproduce emotions in the lab and to graphically represent them (Plamper 2015: 180, 184–185).

A separate development which reinforced the idea of emotion as something involuntary rather than cognitive and volitional, was the rise of Freudian psychoanalysis at the end of the nineteenth century and start of the twentieth. As Plamper has noted, Freud's position was that "feelings often arise, but they are only epiphenomena of a psychic condition" (Plamper 2015: 195). Psychic conditions and conflicts—hysteria, the Oedipus complex, narcissism—were hard-wired into humanity; their manifestations as particular emotional states were of only secondary interest to analysts. Ute Frevert observed that this psychoanalytical perspective "reduc[ed] the emotional system to a handful of innate drives" (Frevert 2014: 4).

The combined effect of these intellectual trends was to change the European and American ways of thinking about feelings, transforming them from mental, moral, volitional experiences into physical, involuntary, and innate qualities. As this change occurred, and psychologists and scientists began to conceive of emotions as part of the standard physical make-up of humans, they also began to regard them as universal to all humanity (Frevert 2014: 31; Dixon 2012: 341–342). Darwin claimed emotional expressions in our ancestors had once been voluntary but had become hereditary and involuntary, and were now part of the biological equipment of humans (Darwin 1872: 357). William James likewise claimed that "surprise, curiosity, rapture, fear, anger, lust, greed, and the like" were "*standard* emotions" (James 1884: 189).

As they became physical entities, emotions were also primativised, for scientists of the late nineteenth century seized upon this idea of standard, innate emotions and wove them into evolutionary theories about human development. As Fay Bound Alberti explains,

In the 1880s and 1890s, the English experimental physiologist John Hughlings Jackson adapted Darwinian evolutionary theory to build a conception of brain function as a series of layers, each of which was progressively more advanced than that which preceded it. In ways that remain influential today . . . the emotions became associated with the most primitive functions of the brain. Certain emotions, like anger, were believed to be more "primitive" than others, most notably love.

—Bound Alberti 2010: 151–152

By the early twentieth century, then, emotion had become the dominant way to think about feelings. The word was freighted with meaning, implying a physical, innate, involuntary, non-cognitive, irrational experience. Gone was the web of moral meanings that had surrounded feeling; gone too was the possibility that thought informed and shaped feeling.

This was the way that intellectuals—first theologians and philosophers, then physicians, biologists, physiologists and psychologists—conceived of, defined, and redefined emotions over the course of 150 years. However, ordinary men and women were often unaware of the academic categories that were reshaping conceptions of their inner lives. Indeed, they themselves rarely used the word emotion, continuing to rely instead on many of the eighteenth-century terms. They were probably less concerned by the question of whether their feelings were mental or moral or physical than were theologians and psychologists. Yet they too experienced changing emotional norms, and encountered new words and types of feelings, more as a result of the rise of capitalism and romanticism than as a consequence of the rise of scientific psychology. Yet nevertheless, by the early twentieth century, the changing academic conceptions of feelings began to seep into the population at large and subtly altered how many perceived their own emotional lives.

EMOTIONS IN POLITICS AND ECONOMY

Ordinary men and women involved in the revolutionary movements of the late eighteenth century helped reshape expectations about emotional expression as they asserted that their feelings were a source of virtuous action and political order. Several historians of Europe and colonial America have noted that in the early part of the eighteenth century, feelings that aligned with communal needs were more legitimate than were individualistic longings which countered the larger social order (Stearns 1988: 57). As Nicole Eustace noted, in colonial America, there was "continued emphasis on communal solidarity, and the accompanying need for social stability," which "made individual assertions of emotion seem as much threatening as promising, particularly to members of the elite." By the end of the eighteenth century, however, a growing number of Europeans and Americans felt newly empowered to express longings that defied established power (Eustace 2008: 439, 105; Matt 2011: 21).

Their belief in the legitimacy of their own feelings found support and encouragement from Enlightenment philosophers. While the Enlightenment has long been described as the age of reason, that characterization misrepresents the era, for philosophers, particularly those associated with the Scottish Enlightenment, often asserted the value of sentiment, sensibility, and sympathy. Indeed, many historians have now come to regard the era of the Enlightenment as also the Age of Sentiment. As a result, feeling gained new significance in eighteenth-century social and political life (Bolufer 2016: 21–24). The faith in feeling as a guide for action was evident in both the American and French Revolutions. In

America, the struggle for independence relied not just on abstract discussions of natural rights, but on new views of emotionally liberated individuals, entitled to act on their feelings. Whereas earlier in the eighteenth century, passionate anger had been discouraged in colonial Philadelphia, by the middle of the eighteenth century, such emotions were far more legitimate, and regarded as a vital social resource for political change. Colonists deployed other emotions as well to support their rebellious fervor. In *Common Sense*, for instance, Thomas Paine argued that the fight against British oppression should be "the Concern of every Man to whom Nature hath given the Power of feeling." According to Eustace, Paine believed "it to be simple common sense to regard 'the passions and feelings of mankind' as 'the touchstone of nature,' the best basis on which to form judgments on any matter, even the vexed choice between reconciliation and Revolutionary rebellion that faced Americans in 1776" (Eustace 2008: 151–181, 439–440; Knott 2004).

This was the case in many countries, as Ute Frevert has noted: "To feel and be moved was in the eighteenth century perfectly respectable . . . . everywhere in (Western) Europe this song was sung. Literature and poetry described it as the supreme value, and sought to cultivate it in their readers. Fulsome feeling was extolled, and said to be a condition of the ability to make moral judgements" (Frevert 2014: 13–14; Mandell 2017: 270). Likewise in France—William Reddy has noted that "in the late eighteenth century, natural sentiment was viewed as the ground out of which virtue grew . . . political reform was deemed best guided by natural feelings of benevolence and generosity" (Reddy 2001: 216).

While revolutionaries on both sides of the Atlantic shared a deep faith in feeling as giving legitimacy to their cause, after the revolutions were over there was more division between those who had witnessed the French Revolution and the rise and fall of Robespierre and Napoleon, and those living in the new, relatively stable, American Republic. William Reddy suggests that in the wake of the Terror and the rise of Napoleon, the French came to believe emotion should have little role in politics (Reddy 2001). Similarly, in Spain, after the unsuccessful uprising against Napoleon's invasion, there were signs that many there were abandoning their faith in sensibility as a source of political wisdom (Bolufer 2015: 21). In contrast, in the United States, emotion continued to be an acceptable force in the polity—many orators asserted that it was the bonds of affection which united the nation, and claimed that passions, balanced by reason, should guide civic life (Woods 2014: 14–20). In England, too, in the nineteenth century, a discussion of sympathy, affections, sentiment, benevolence, and trust flourished, reflecting the emotional tenor of a constitutional monarchy and parliamentary system. Frevert notes that "there was a unanimous belief that society functioned only if its members fostered public affections, treating each other with sympathy, friendliness, and benevolence. . . . There was a conviction that such feelings flourished to their greatest extent in states whose governments respected the freedom and equality of their citizens." In Germany, in contrast, the possibilities for public participation and political actions were more limited, and bourgeois Germans were encouraged to focus on domestic and private emotions rather than political ones (Frevert 2014: 24–25).

While the role of feeling in political life was contested across Europe and America in the nineteenth century, a new consensus about its role in economic life was gradually gaining strength and influence. Emotion was a driver of economic life, but increasingly many observers came to argue that the impulses that motivated trade, commerce, getting and spending, were not feelings at all—instead they were the reflection of careful reasoning and intellect. As capitalism spread, many came to picture it as a cool, rational, and unemotional form of economic relations and denied the role of feeling in markets.

In reality, capitalism and the industrialism it spawned did not do away with emotion; rather the economy encouraged new emotional styles and behaviors, oriented around individualism, acquisitiveness, and selfishness (Appleby 2010: 19). However, as capitalism spread, and these practices gained acceptance, they were naturalized and labeled rational. For instance, Albert O. Hirschman has demonstrated that feelings such as envy and avarice, which had once been regarded as passions, came, in early modern Europe, to be regarded as the essence of benign self-interest (Hirschman 1997: 9). And while interests and reason were not conceived of as identical categories in the seventeenth and early eighteenth centuries, that conflation had occurred by the nineteenth.

By the mid-nineteenth century, economists were coming to regard rationality and self-interested economic activity as interchangeable. In 1844, John Stuart Mill described economic man in the capitalist world, "solely as a being who desires to possess wealth, and who is capable of judging of the comparative efficacy of means for obtaining that end." Political economy, he wrote, "predicts only such phenomena of the social state as takes place in consequence of the pursuit of wealth. It makes entire abstraction of every other human passion or motive; except ... aversion to labour, and desire of the present enjoyment of costly indulgences" (Mill 1844: 137–138; Matt 2015). Mill himself admitted that his depiction of humanity was limited and that indeed nobody had ever acted exclusively upon such a constrained set of motives. Yet his description of economic man and his behavior gained popularity over the course of the nineteenth and twentieth centuries, particularly among English-speaking economists who came to define the pursuit of wealth (and its motivating and attendant feelings) as rational, natural, and inevitable.

ROMANTIC REACTIONS

It was largely in response to this emerging economic and emotional style, which celebrated cool "reason," that many in Europe and America embraced Romanticism, which, in one scholar's words, stressed "the primacy of individual feelings and the creative imagination over coercive reason and authority" (White 2017: 274). Some historians have suggested that Romanticism represented an extension of the late eighteenth-century Age of Sensibility; rather than being a rejection of earlier intellectual movements, Romanticism was instead a continuation of them (Ferber 2010: 15–17). Others, such as William Reddy, make a greater distinction between the cultural movements, arguing that eighteenth-century sentimentalism allowed emotion to play a significant role in public life while nineteenth-century Romanticism attempted to contain emotion to the aesthetic sphere (Reddy 2001: 259).

These labels and periodizations are open to debate, but what is clear is in the late eighteenth and early nineteenth centuries, there flourished across Europe and America a popular belief in the power and truth of intense, overwhelming feeling. It was during this era that the idea of a distinction, and even an opposition, between reason and emotion began to solidify. Some romantics began to look back to the Enlightenment and describe it—inaccurately—as a movement based solely on reason, and contrasted it to their own sense of liberated feeling. In their mischaracterization of the past, they helped to establish the idea that there was a chasm between thought and emotion (Reddy 2001: 216).

The Romantic tendency, visible in religious revivals, symphonies, landscape paintings, poetry, novels, gardens, and architecture, celebrated the display of spontaneous, deep feeling, supposedly unmediated by rational evaluations, and best provoked by encounters with nature. As Dolores Martín Moruno has written,

> Romantic writers, artists, and scientists believed that industrialization had not only transformed the natural environment into an urbanised landscape, but also human life that had been turned into a new type of artificial existence by means of introducing technology into the most intimate areas of human experience. Thus, the Industrial Revolution represented . . . a broader cultural transformation concerning the affective experience of one's self in one's relation to nature, a new awareness that was aroused by the painful separation of human being from its natural origins.
>
> —Martin Moruno 2014: 196

Romanticism promised to return individuals to a purer, more natural, integrated state of being.

Many in nineteenth-century Europe and America found this promise appealing. They embraced romantic emotional styles because they offered a counterpoint to the demands of capitalism and industrialism. Romantics believed liberal individualism had estranged people from traditional communities and weakened organic bonds (Levinger 2000: 98). The Romantic self they envisioned arising from their movement would find communion, and new, more authentic, modes of self-expression. Ironically, however, many—but not all—of the new feelings that Romantics celebrated also bore the imprint of individualism, for they emphasized the uniqueness of individuals and their right to display autonomy and choice.

A central emotion during the nineteenth century was love and, in particular, romantic love. Romantic love was founded on the idea of unique selves making choices based on individual desire rather than communal imperatives (Lystra 1989; Coontz 2006). One reason romantic love took on new importance during this era was that it offered a private, shielded refuge, separate from markets which increasingly stressed the fungibility of people and products. In contrast, romantic love affirmed the singularity of individuals, asserting that the beloved was irreplaceable and certainly not interchangeable (Lystra 1989: 30). Yet while it may have offered a counterpoint to these market relations, romantic love also enabled them, in that it helped to nurture a sense of individuality. Karen Lystra writes,

> The experience of romantic love among the middle class in nineteenth-century American life was closely intertwined with a cultural commitment to individual differentiation from the group. Though romantic love was only one segment of a complex cultural and social matrix that nourished this individuality, evidence of nineteenth-century middle-class courtship clearly shows that romantic love was a powerful factor in the formation of identity . . . romantic love was a ready-made incubator of the romantic self.
>
> —Lystra 1989: 31

This new form of love also reflected the growing secularization of western societies. Whereas in the seventeenth and eighteenth centuries, spouses were to love each other, but to love God and Jesus even more, by the nineteenth century, many couples were regarding each other in a distinctly different light. In a poem she wrote her husband, a nineteenth-century American woman confided, "Thou art my church and thou my book of psalms," while another told her suitor "Your love is worship—that an angel in Heaven might envy me" (Lystra 1989: 248–249).

In many cases, the rise of romantic love altered family structures, as it blunted, though did not eradicate, the power of patriarchy. As men and women confided their feelings to one another in romantic letters, they often came to identify with each other's needs, and created a "blended" sense of self. As James Blair wrote in 1847 to his wife, love had altered the power relations between them: "There is even about me a melancholy pleasure in feeling my heart and mind so entirely usurped by you and yours—I have not a thought that does not aim at some pleasure happiness or comfort for you, indeed my whole happiness now is in contemplating something that will tend to give you pleasure and happiness" (Lystra 1989: 237). Under such circumstances, patriarchal hierarchies came under assault, and a new belief in companionate marriage emerged.

It was not just romantic love that gained new importance; so too did expressions of family love. In the nineteenth century, private, domestic life came to be widely celebrated and described in terms of affectionate coziness. Architect and cultural critic Witold Rybczynski, has suggested that homey ideals of privacy, comfort, and feeling began to take root in Europe in the seventeenth century, and came into full bloom in the eighteenth and nineteenth centuries. Houses were transformed into homes, and their floorplans changed. New ideas about domestic life governed even the smallest details of architecture – from broom closets to window sashes – for these were essential for creating rooms in which private, familial affection might be displayed and experienced. New styles of emotional life depended in part on new spaces (Rybczynski, 1986).

An example of this new style of domestic affection was visible in America, where, beginning in the 1820s, the bourgeoisie emphasized the centrality of love to family life (Stearns 1994: 20). Mother love was enshrined as particularly sacred, as the touchstone of family morality and stability. Members of nineteenth-century families probably did not love each other more than previous generations had, but they were much more expressive on the subject. They created a new imagery and vocabulary to describe the feeling's sacred joys and wonders. One of the most influential exponents of affectionate family life was Horace Bushnell, a Congregationalist minister born in 1802. In his 1847 book *Christian Nurture*, he worried that "the tendency of all our modern speculations is to an extreme individualism." To strengthen family bonds, he tried to moderate individualism, suggesting that it was, to some degree, a myth. He claimed that rather than being independent and autonomous, people were formed by, and dependent on, their parents. The person to whom children and later adults were most attached was their mothers, with whom they shared an intense, emotional, and naturally arising bond. That connection should be fostered and treasured, for it was the basis of all morality. If parents worked to make domestic attachments stronger, "the family quality of our piety, living itself into our children, will moisten the dry individualism we suffer." Then, "purity" would come to replace "bustle and presumption." Suffused with moral mother love, households would become Christian spaces, leading their inhabitants to salvation and virtue, and inoculating them against the temptations and restlessness of market society (Bushnell 1904: 26, 31, 91–95, 251–252; Hulbert 2003: 25–26). As many historians have noted, this cult of domesticity idealized the notion of an emotional, love-suffused home, which supposedly stood outside of market pressures. However, as scholars such as Mary Ryan have shown, those households often also proved to be incubators for capitalism, as they became nurseries in which mothers instructed their children in market-oriented virtues like delayed gratification, piety, and thrift (Ryan 1983). Romantic emotional styles, which supposedly stood in opposition to capitalist practices, nevertheless often sustained them.

While love was supposed to be a private and domestic feeling, it also took on new significance as a model for political and social bonds. In an age of growing nationalism, many invoked love to encourage loyalty to nation. Nicole Eustace has shown that in the

United States romantic love became the dominant metaphor for American patriotism in the early republic, espoused by statesmen and poets eager to increase the size and power of the nation through reproduction. She writes of early nineteenth-century politicians who "tied American fertility and American freedom directly to the ability to marry. . . . Making marriage and reproduction central to the pursuit of personal and national 'happiness' relocated the site of Americans' most basic inalienable rights from the public to the private realm" (Eustace 2012: 18). Here, love served both individual and national needs. In Prussia in the early nineteenth century, Romantic nationalists "portrayed the nation in those breathless tones usually reserved for descriptions of a lover" (Levinger 2000: 98). In Denmark, in the early nineteenth century, Frederick VI depended upon love among his subjects in order to sustain his absolute monarchy (Martinsen 2015). That emotional connection between citizen and nation was one that N. F. S. Grundtvig, the influential theorist of Danish nationalism, articulated when he wrote, "imagination and feeling . . . have created our social relations." He believed that shared emotions, and particularly love, were essential to national unity, writing, "A State . . . is a real life expression of the heart-relation" (Jonas 2015: 173–75).

If love was a central emotion during the nineteenth century, there were other feelings that gained in significance, as well. One was nostalgia, *heimweh*, or homesickness, which was a feeling that grew out of domestic affections, striking those who traveled too far from the family hearth. A reaction to the development of a shifting, capitalist society, where social and geographical mobility were both possible and encouraged, homesickness became a much discussed emotional problem. The feeling was first given a formal medical label—*nostalgia*—in 1688 by the Swiss doctor Johannes Hofer, who suggested it could turn fatal if wanderers were not quickly returned home. The diagnosis took off during the late eighteenth and nineteenth centuries, with an initial burst of publicity coming from reports of French soldiers in Napoleon's armies afflicted by the condition. French medical treatises were translated into many tongues, and discussions of the dangers of nostalgia began to spread. While the English were thought to be immune to it because they were a commercial and sea-faring people long accustomed to travel, other populations, including the French, the Swiss, and the Americans, documented significant outbreaks of nostalgia, some of them fatal (Matt 2011; Starobinski 1966).

Grief, too, became an emotion that was more acceptable to display during the nineteenth century, for it was a sign that one loved one's friends and families well. This stood in contrast to seventeenth- and eighteenth-century prohibitions against the feeling, which had been based on the worry that one might love one's family and fellows *too* well—at the expense of a pious devotion to God (McMahon 2012). A sign of these new emotional norms was changing funeral practices. Historian Peter Stearns has shown that, on both sides of the Atlantic, Romanticism gave new legitimacy to mourning; as a result, "copious weeping at funerals" came into vogue at the start of the nineteenth century (Stearns 2007: 52).

Related to this was the rise of what Stearns has termed "tearful sadness," an emotional style evident during much of the nineteenth century. Popularized in such late eighteenth-century sentimental works as Henry Mackenzie's *The Man of Feeling* and Goethe's *The Sorrows of Young Werther*, tears remained acceptable (within limits) into the nineteenth century. A new emotion, *Werthersfieber* (Werther's fever), was briefly the rage among young people who emulated Werther's soulful, intensely sorrowful, suicidal feelings, and often donned blue coats modeled after the one Werther wore in Goethe's work. There were other sufferers, first in Germany and then across Europe, who complained of *Weltshmerz* (world suffering) or the pain of existence; it was a widespread complaint in the nineteenth century, an era during which many celebrated their sadness. For instance, the Romantic writer and philosopher Pierre-Simon Ballanche in 1808 declared, "Only sorrow matters in life, and there is no reality beyond tears" (Dixon 2015: 99; McMahon 2006: 275–276). Even the British, who are today remembered for their "stiff upper lips," were, in reality, frequent weepers throughout the first half of the nineteenth century (Dixon 2015). Associated with extreme sensitivity during the Age of Sensibility and the Romantic era, weeping also could be open to mockery when taken to extremes, and began to fall out of fashion in the middle of the nineteenth century (Dixon 2015: 99, 138–139).

As intense sadness gradually fell out of vogue, happiness became a central concern in many liberal, capitalist states, the result of Enlightenment philosophies which suggested it was the entitlement of all humans. Poet Alexander Pope wrote of the feeling, declaring, "Oh, happiness, our being's end and aim!", joining a host of other eighteenth-century celebrants of the emotion (McMahon 2006: 200). However, not all could agree on just what happiness meant or who was entitled to experience it. In America, for instance, the Declaration of Independence had presented it as an inalienable right, but there was a divergence of opinion between Northerners and Southerners as to what constituted true happiness and who could pursue it. As historian Michael Woods has shown, many Northerners, living in states that had outlawed slavery and embraced the market revolution, believed free labor afforded individuals the greatest opportunity for happiness, for an open labor market offered independence, hope, and economic mobility. As Abraham Lincoln observed, "Free labor has the inspiration of hope; pure slavery has no hope. The power of hope upon human exertion, and happiness, is wonderful." Yet not all were seen as entitled to this type of independent, unbounded happiness. Southerners maintained that rather than expect happiness, their slaves should embrace the virtue of contentment, and recognize that their bonded state offered them this. They argued that slaves' basic needs—for food and shelter—were met by their masters; consequently, they had everything they needed and experienced no anxiety. In 1861, the Alabama politician William Russell Smith explained, "In nine cases out of ten, in positive contentment, the Alabama slave is happier than his master," sleeping peacefully with "blissful dreams that are undisturbed by the knowledge of coming necessities" (Woods 2014: 62, 42, 35–74). Happiness grew in importance in the nineteenth century but according to some observers of the era not all could achieve the same kind—some could hope and aspire for more prosperity and even greater joy, others would have to accept their circumstances and be contented.

There were other emotions that were newly important in the nineteenth century, as well. One was boredom. While the French word "ennui" had circulated in English since the seventeenth century, the word "bore" entered the lexicon only in the eighteenth century, and "boredom" only emerged in the mid nineteenth century (Spacks 1995: 12–14). The German equivalent, *Langeweile*, probably first appeared in the eighteenth century (Dalle Pezze and Salzani 2009: 10). Of the English term, Patricia Meyer Spacks suggests that it was an outgrowth of the introspective mood that took hold in Protestant societies, which prompted men and women to explore and evaluate their inner lives. She points out that the word "interesting" likewise was introduced to English in the late eighteenth century, offering new conceptual tools for individuals to assess the quality of their inner experiences (Spacks 1995: 15). Barbara Dalle Pezze and Carlo Salzani have likewise identified boredom as an intrinsically modern emotion, noting, the "demon of modernity is *ennui*, boredom, '*ce monster delicat*' . . . which swallows everything . . . into the great yawn of indifference." They describe boredom as a kind of defeat "of the modern subject, of the yearning for meaningfulness, self-realisation, self-fulfillment, generated by the Enlightenment utopia and the dreams of Romanticism." The Romantic movement had promised "self fulfilment." Boredom was what one felt when that promise went unfulfilled (Dalle Pezze and Salzani 2009: 7, 13–14; Spacks 1995: 15).

From love to boredom to homesickness, many of the emotions central to social life in the eighteenth and nineteenth centuries revealed a new interest in individual choice and desire rather than an adherence to community norms and imperatives. These feelings helped individuals to define themselves, to sketch out the contours of their identity, to show what they affirmed and what they disdained. They were often inward looking, reflecting what some historians have identified as a new focus on interior experience that blossomed during this period (Spacks 1995: 23–24; Lystra 1989). Significantly, during these years, ordinary men and women often described such feelings as moral and mental experiences, feeling states they could actively cultivate. This view of feeling flourished into the late nineteenth century, even while physiologists and psychologists were redefining emotion, transforming it into a physical category, rather than a mental one. Such new academic conceptions only slowly penetrated popular discourse, only slowly transformed felt experience.

Eventually, however, the academic theories came into wider circulation, and new ways of discussing and identifying emotions became popular. Increasingly, lay people adopted academic notions about feelings and described their emotions in more physical terms. An example of this trend was visible in the rise of *neurasthenia*, a supposedly new condition that affected Europeans and Americans in the late nineteenth century. Discussed as a product of industrial, urbanized society, its victims were primarily members of the middle and upper classes, especially those engaged in taxing mental work. Its symptoms included anxiety, sadness, and listlessness. Doctors on both sides of the Atlantic presented it as a condition that developed when individuals' nervous energies were exhausted by the unnatural and unprecedented rapid tempo of modern, urban life. Nerves became strained and weakened; brains became incapable of processing information; physical breakdown ensued (Beard 1881; Kern 1983; Schuster 2011; Lutz 1991). This assessment represented a sea change from earlier experiences of emotions. Now it was nerves and synapses which affected inner life, not intellectual and spiritual forces or moral choices.

EMOTIONS AND DIFFERENCE

Emotions were categories for assessing one's own, inner experiences; they also were essential to nineteenth-century individuals' assessments of the outer world, for feelings became a way of differentiating between the self and others, tools for asserting power. They were used to justify gender roles within the household; when bourgeois and elite Europeans and European Americans encountered members of other racial, ethnic, and economic groups, they often also relied on emotional styles as a means of sorting peoples and establishing social hierarchies.

In Europe and America, moralists, writers, and psychologists used emotion as a way to differentiate between the sexes, arguing that some feelings were the natural province of men, others the realm of women. The authors of an 1835 German encyclopedia, for instance, opined that "female sensibility" was "more vivid and refined than the male," and argued that women were endowed with "excitability, sympathy, patience, and noble weakness," which stood in contrast to the struggling and ambitious nature of men (Bailey 2014: 208). As a result of such views, certain emotions were less accepted in women than men; for instance, many regarded anger as legitimate and natural for free men in public—but not domestic—life; however, the feeling should be completely absent from the emotional lives of women (Stearns 1994: 23–25, 29–31). By the late nineteenth century, in America, women were presumed to be more susceptible to homesickness than men, for the former were allegedly designed for domestic life, while the latter were, by nature, expected to seek out new opportunities (Matt 2011: 125–129). Emotional expectations helped establish and define men's and women's social roles within a household and demarcate what they could do outside of it, as well.

If emotion was used to define gender roles, it also served as a way to separate the races within a society. For instance, white Americans justified slavery on the basis that African and African-American slaves had feelings completely different from their own, and they used this supposed difference to defend the slave system. As escaped slave Harriet Jacobs said of her mistress, "It had never occurred to Mrs. Flint that slaves could have any feelings" (Jacobs 1861: 121). It was not just Southerners who nursed this belief. John Ball, a Vermont native, traveled to Georgia in the early 1820s, and described the slaves he had observed: "Saw much that satisfied me that the African and Caucasian are constitutionally unlike, and cannot by an education be made, even to fully understand each other, any more than the ox and the horse. The negro docile or he could not be enslaved, cheerful under all circumstances, never committing suicide" (Ball 1925: 19).

Emotions were also used as a gauge of economic fitness and a means of establishing class identities. For instance, middle-class moralists in nineteenth-century American cities often judged working-class women's style of mothering as inattentive, unnurturing, and insufficiently loving, and used this purported difference as a way to justify removing poor children from their parents (Stansell 1987: 193–216). Roy Rosenzweig, in examining working-class men, likewise found that their expressions of sociability and friendship were often perceived as wasteful and deviant. Treating fellow patrons in a saloon was a way of creating sociability, reciprocity, mutuality, and countering individualism; however middle-class reformers saw such an emotional style of generous spending on alcohol as sinful, impulsive, and profligate (Rosenzweig 1985: 35–64). To broadcast one's economic fitness and acumen one had to display self-interest and individualism, not generosity and reciprocity. Likewise, by the end of the nineteenth century, middle-class men who did not show sufficient discontent with their lot in life were regarded as maladapted to the conditions of market society; they were seen as innately unsuited for the competitive, ambitious world of business (Matt 2003: 57–95). And in the late nineteenth century, men who felt homesick and would not leave home in search of economic opportunity were deemed provincial, plodding, and incapable of adapting to the competitive, Darwinian conditions of economic life, which required movement, change, and adaptability (Matt 2011: 122–123). Their emotional makeup doomed them to failure and justified their poverty.

Assessments of emotional style also were essential to eighteenth- and nineteenth-century conceptions of difference in the world at large. As European and American powers established empires, emotional norms came to be seen as central tools for evaluating the levels of civilization of foreign peoples. Historians Margrit Pernau and Helge Jordheim have noted that, in the eighteenth and nineteenth centuries as a new global order emerged, European powers began to assert that there were set stages of civilizations and used these stages "for mapping out historical development." Philosophers believed that these stages were "characterized not only by their economic and political development, but also by their particular ways of feeling. Love experienced and expressed by a hunter is a different emotion, the moral philosophers claimed, from the romantic love of a merchant in eighteenth-century Edinburgh—observing how people love is, in turn, a good indicator of how civilized they are" (Pernau and Jordheim 2015a: 4).

While initially many colonizing powers had justified their imperialism by arguing that they would educate those they regarded as uncivilized, and teach them new, more advanced emotional styles, by the mid to late nineteenth centuries, the belief that all could possess the same types of feeling was falling into doubt. According to evolutionary theorists, different races had far different emotional capacities and styles, which were extremely difficult—if not impossible—to change. As Pernau and Jordheim note, "Being able to control one's temper or being prey to violent passions now belonged as much to the racialized body as the colour of the skin or the shape of the skull" (Pernau and Jordheim, 2015a: 9; Bailey 2014: 222).

Such beliefs shaped life and power within imperial holdings. For instance, as Emmanuelle Saada points out, in Algeria and other French colonies, "At the end of the nineteenth century, jurists and administrators justified the exclusion of indigenous people from citizenship on the basis of civility; they argued that there was an organic link between private norms of behavior and public participation in the polity, that is, between civility and citizenship." Those who lived in French territories could try to apply for citizenship, but that required a "long administrative and police enquiry to verify the 'morality' and the 'feelings' of the applicants—and it led to only a few dozen subjects being granted citizenship in the entire empire." In one of the rare cases where an applicant prevailed, officials praised him for his "good French feelings." However, Saada notes, "The vast majority had to remain subjects because they could not change civilizations, any more than they could change their race, or their 'feelings'" (Saada 2015: 77–78).

Whereas earlier in the century colonial powers had held out the proposition that one could change feelings, that imperial powers might in fact "civilize" the emotions of other cultures, by the late nineteenth century such an idea was losing support. With the rise of scientific psychology—which preached that emotions were physical, located in the brain rather than the mind or the soul—and Social Darwinian ideas about race and evolution, emotions seemed to be beyond individual control, the mysterious product of biological forces rather than will and cognition (Bound Alberti 2010; Dixon 2006; Dixon 2012).

During World War I, these views became even more widespread, and were visible in the ways the warring nations viewed each other and themselves. Notions of emotional civility and incivility, ideas about ingrained, innate, racially differentiated feelings, and a new conviction that these feelings were the result of physical difference all affected soldiers' and civilians' inner lives.

During the War, national propagandists played upon the idea that the enemies were racially and emotionally different. While throughout the nineteenth century many had portrayed Western Europeans as exemplars of civility, during the conflict the European opponents began to draw lines between themselves and those they fought. The French and British pictured the Germans as more aggressive, impulsive, and primitive in their feelings (Frevert 2017). In 1916, for instance, a French newspaper described the Germans this way: "They have perfected the most barbaric and cowardly tortures; Faced with such horror, civilized people have to resign themselves and exclaim 'Oh, the monsters!'" (Audoin-Rouzeau 1992: 168). The Allies sometimes presented these notions of German savagery visually in now iconic propaganda posters, which invoked "the rape of Belgium." Some posters imagined the Germans as apes, as an American recruiting sign did, with its message "Destroy this Mad Brute—Enlist" (Library of Congress). An Australian poster likewise referred to Germans as unevolved, offering two images of savage warriors, one dated AD 451, the other dated 1915. The caption read "Always Huns-Protect our Women and Children" (Museums Victoria Collection). Such propaganda suggested that what separated the enemies were not merely different views on Central European borders but fundamentally divergent emotional styles and values.

The new consensus on emotions was also apparent in how warring nations responded to the feelings of their own soldiers. World War I has frequently been portrayed as an end of innocence and Victorian idealism; it also marked the disintegration of an older notion of the self, an idea based on the belief that men's and women's emotions were signs and signals of who they were, that they reflected moral choices and codes. This view, which had already been under siege by scientific psychologists before the war, was undermined further during the War, in the writings of military officials, psychologists, and physicians, which stressed the physicality of emotions.

An example was visible in the way soldiers' emotional complaints were understood and treated. During nineteenth-century wars, homesickness and nostalgia had been among the most common complaints of soldiers far from home. American and French army doctors compiled statistics about the large numbers who grappled with the feeling and they generally regarded sufferers' complaints with some sympathy, given that men were supposed to love their homes and families, and be saddened by their absence from them. By World War I, however, cases of nostalgia had become rare. A far more common diagnosis was a newly identified nervous disorder: shell shock. The condition gained legitimacy after an article about it appeared in the British medical journal, *The Lancet*, in 1915 (Jones and Wessely 2014: 1708). Shell shock was described as a disorder related to a peacetime condition, neurasthenia. Drawing upon the idea of nervous exhaustion and disorder, many on the front believed that "a particularly close hit by a heavy shell or a prolonged barrage produced mysterious transformations in the soldier's nervous system, which damaged his self-control. Sudden flight, hysterical weeping, a refusal to go forward" were all symptoms of the new condition (Leed 1979: 163, 166). Doctors and psychologists regarded these symptoms as signs that primitive emotions had conquered reason. As Tracey Loughran notes, this view reflected many psychologists' belief that "intense emotion" was "a primitive, animal response to danger which worked through the body to overwhelm every other function." She notes, "All theories of the war neuroses were formulated within this evolutionary model of mind, with emotion usually invoked as one of the crucial primary etiological factors in shell shock. The emotion most frequently singled out was fear—fear of threat to life and limb, fear of failing in duty, or even fear of being afraid." The common perception was that "emotion could only gain the upper hand at the expense of the 'higher' faculties." Soldiers' experiences of shell shock and other "war neuroses" were moments when, in the words of a member of Royal Army Medical Corps, "emotions have taken the place of a forceful will-power" (Loughran 2012: 111–112).

Shell shock encapsulated the transformed view of emotion that had gradually taken shape during the nineteenth century. It had become irrational, physical, and primitive—a view that would continue to hold sway for most of the twentieth century.

CHAPTER ONE

Medical and Scientific Understandings

ROB BODDICE

The long nineteenth century witnessed the birth, in English, of "emotions" as a signifier for all those affective states, internal movements or motions, passions, feelings, and sentiments that had come before.[1] This was not mere semantics, but a substantive and fluid alteration of knowledge about the nature, function, and meaning of emotions and how they are experienced. It was mirrored all along the scientific avant-garde, throughout Germany, France, Italy, and North America. This compound shift went together with the emergence of "science" as a pursuit distinct from natural philosophy, and the raft of increasingly professionalized "scientists" that came with it.[2] A recognizably modern science, defined by increasingly controlled experimentation, the rise of mechanical objectivity, positivism, materialism, and a novel biological cosmology (evolution), was instrumental in categorizing and defining emotions anew. This was complemented by an analogous shift in medical knowledge and practice, away from humoral categories of temperamental imbalance toward emerging knowledge of nerves and viscera, with emotions becoming the province of biomedical research in two rapidly evolving scientific disciplines: psychology and physiology.[3] These developments were contemporaneous with insights on the nature and function of emotions from other new scientific disciplines, such as anthropology, criminology, biometry, and psychiatry. By no means do all of these different threads come together in the period in question. On the contrary, a plurality of diverse notions of what emotions were, how they worked, and what they did emerged in this period. As scientific and medical disciplinary boundaries hardened, the range of approaches to the study and interpretation of emotions became increasingly incommensurate with one another. Although the rapid explosion of physiological, psychological, and anthropological work seemed at one point to find common ground and common purpose in the work of Darwin, by the beginning of the twentieth century there were large chasms between distinct epistemologies of emotions.[4] This chapter surveys these developments thematically.

EMOTIONAL UPHEAVAL, OR THE LOST SENSE OF HUMOR

Galenic humoral categories endured throughout the eighteenth century, surviving and informing the emergence of nerves, sensibilities and vapors, and undergirding the principal "emotional" category of the age: passions. The essential quality of the passions is indicated in the word itself. They occurred *passively*, happening to a person rather than emanating from a person. In this fundamental regard, passions were the opposite of emotions, which literally project movements (from inside the body) outward. Passions could be generally understood as afflictions of the viscera, imbalanced mixtures of bodily humors (the word "temperament" comes from the Latin *tempere*, to mix), or exposure to noxious elements.

Prior to a raft of physiological and psychological innovations that would put emotions variously in the body, in the mind, and under the control of the civilized individual, a person was more likely to be a victim of their passions. The disorders arising from ill humor were heavily gendered as female in the decades immediately preceding and following the turn of the nineteenth century. Insofar as they fell under the province of medicine to administer, they were nevertheless not diseases or pathologies per se, and were rooted in the simple fact of being a woman. Attacks of the "vapors," which saw women swooning and languishing in melancholic torpor, were particularly common among the more well-to-do and associated with a delicacy of body/mind, susceptible to over stimulation or affectation. Hence the dangers of education and reading and, in particular, the sentimental novel.[5]

Female maladies were part of the structure of gender dynamics that medical opinion helped to support. The hysteric—afflicted in the original sense of the word with a wandering womb—was necessarily female.[6] The affliction, which manifested in all manner of affective disorders, was still fundamentally physical in origin and was marked by physical signs.[7] In rare cases of male hysteria (Micale 2008), which increased toward the end of the nineteenth century, new physical theories had to be constructed for the obvious disruption of medical epistemology. The need to ground affective disorders in bodily trauma was reaffirmed as new technologies threatened to make "nervous" dispositions more widespread. From the 1840s, "railway spine" emerged as a new form of malady directly resulting from a hitherto untried mode of transport (Erichsen 1867). The hysteria-like symptoms of the victims of railway accidents, which also occurred among accident-free passengers, were presumed by some to be linked to some form of lesion in the spine that, at that moment, could not be detected.

As the nineteenth century progressed, hysteria increasingly came to be associated with a disorder of the emotions or, at least, a problem of the mind. This has become forever associated with the work of Freud and Breuer (1974), who sought a "psychichal mechanism" of hysteria based on a suppressed traumatic event. Crucially, "trauma" here was configured emotionally, not physically, and Freud would pursue a course of unlocking the secrets of the unconscious mind in order to explain physical manifestations of emotional pathologies. The rise of urban illumination, electrification, and round-the-clock stimulation led to further new theories of neurosis. The modern city, inhabited by the particularly sensitive, civilized man and woman, was itself destabilizing the emotional balance of citizens.[8] The neurasthenic, overwhelmed by his or her environment, lost emotional control. Moreover, this loss, which manifested in strange postures, seizures, and contractures, as well as headaches and chronic fatigue, seemed to be contagious. The hysteric or neurasthenic individual risked society by example. Sympathetic cases were not uncommon, and were considered especially dangerous when they interrupted factory or office efficiency, or disrupted fragile communities in hospitals, on ships, or, most alarmingly, on the military front line.

The gradual conceptual shift of hysteria from female malady to a pathology of emasculation was emphatically sealed by the First World War. Military politics made justifiable terror into a crime when it led to desertion or malingering. Refusal to fight was a form of hysteria that betrayed a weakness of character in the soldier, or else it was a pathological cowardice in the conscientious objector. The sights, sounds, and experiences of warfare disabled many with "shell shock"—a forerunner of post-traumatic stress disorder—that marked its victims as damaged men. Many who suffered serious injuries, often losing one or more limbs, were treated for their physical complaints but with scant attention to the emotional or psychological consequences of having been through a war and having come out of it damaged in more ways than one (Bourke 1996). The First World War represents a watershed moment in the history of chronic pain, with thousands of men across the world dealing with the long-term consequences of amputation, disfigurement, shrapnel injuries, and so on. Physical torment was inextricably bound with emotional torment, but medical approaches to the long-term care of the war-wounded tended to isolate bodies from minds, downplaying complaints of pain when they seemed to arise from emotional weaknesses in character or disposition (Bourke 2014: 66–89; Moscoso 2012: 203–206). Coupled with only a rudimentary understanding of, for example, phantom limb pain, the medical establishment saw no advantage in providing veterans with emotional succour, and often dismissed chronic complaints of pain in limbs that were missing as hysteria.

THE SCIENCE (AND POLITICS) OF EXPRESSION

At the end of the eighteenth century it was commonly assumed that physical expressions, not just facial expressions, but the whole range of postures and gestures, were a direct representation of inner states. In a sense, these outward signs were themselves literally emotions, *e* (Latin for out of, or from) *motio* (Latin for movement). They described the ways in which people were internally *moved*. If one wanted to find out the secrets of the ways in which feelings were transmitted, communicated, and received in society, the answers were not in internal, physiological investigations, but in structural anatomical studies. The shape and structure of the musculature and skeleton both limited and, by a certain reasoning, universalized human expressions (and therefore human emotions).

Until Charles Bell intervened, however, the emotions were the province of the philosophers and the expressions were the province of painters and sculptors, who operated without the up-to-date anatomical insights of those who worked with the dead, under the mask of the flesh. Bell (1806; 1824) attempted to bridge the gap between art and anatomy, appealing essentially for more realistic depictions of human expressions of emotion. Bell was looking for verisimilitude in artistic representation, but more broadly he was looking for the truth of human expression—a key for accessing how we know how someone else is feeling.

His key contribution, therefore, was not to artistic practice but to a science of human emotions. His work was to be profoundly influential, both in biology and in medicine, and continues to resonate today in the debate over the universality of human expression.

Underlying Bell's approach was an assumption, perfectly in keeping with his time, that the anatomical continuities among humans that delimited the range of emotional expression were put there by *design*. Humans were made in God's image, and if outward signs of passions were readily accessible to all alike, it was because they had been made that way to serve human communication and understanding. A fundamental shift in the science of expression would come with the attempt to remove God from the machine.

FIGURE 1.1: Charles Bell, Muscles of the Face, 1806 (Wellcome Library, London).

Charles Darwin thought that it fell to him to provide an alternative account, and in the process he thoroughly confused his earlier thesis of natural selection.

Darwin ([1871]2004; 1872) came at the emotions from two angles. On the one hand, it was essential that emotions could be accounted for according to his theories of natural selection, sexual selection, and (though this was implied) species selection. Digging for information from colleagues and contacts around the world, Darwin found both striking similarities in the ways in which emotions were represented expressively and gesturally and marked differences in the ways in which emotions were elicited, interpreted, and controlled. Necessary to the narrative of his particular brand of Victorian evolutionism was a natural-historical account of the progressiveness and supremacy of his own civilization, of Victorian politesse and social conscience, of sovereign greatness and imperial ascendancy. Among his own society, Darwin had to account for the apparent gentleness of emotional dispositions among the refined, compared with the rough and immediate outbursts of the laborer, the "savage," and the animal (children and women also both had to fit in this "lower" scheme) both in his midst and elsewhere.[9]

On the one hand then, Darwin found reasons for the primacy of civilized society in the evolution and social reinforcement of sympathy, a social emotion that bound each individual to the community, defining and situating moral action within a natural-historical process.[10] Those communities with the highest degree and most acute refinement of sympathy would prosper. But, on the other hand, Darwin found it necessary to reject the notion that emotional expressions (facial and gestural) were evolved modes of emotional communication. Sympathy, which inevitably involved an appreciation and understanding of the whole range of emotional experiences, was instinctive; but the actions that followed from it in civilized society were always reinforced and shaped by public opinion. In this way, Darwin demonstrated the human capacity for domestication—contriving with nature—at work in human society itself. Whatever nature selected as "fit," humans could isolate to speed up the process of evolution. By such means, Darwin explained the importance of religion, which involved the institutionalization of the sympathetic refinement of an elite so that it could be deployed to shape the conduct of those whose natural state left something to be desired. Darwin clearly saw, in *The Descent of Man* (2004: 118–119), that religion had run its course as the key stakeholder of public opinion, precisely because it had become evident that clerics were not the best arbiters of domestication; scientists were.

That Darwin's biological science was also a proto social science is often overlooked, but domestication runs throughout his principal works as a marker of human distinction. This reasoning also makes Darwin one of the first historians of emotions, since he firmly believed that convention both delimited and prescribed the range of emotions available to a society, which would be passed down both via the inheritance of acquired habit and through selective forces that would have favored certain emotional dispositions and repertoires over others (Gross 2010: 34–59). But here we also see the beginning of an intellectual knot at the heart of Darwin's evolutionary heyday. It is well known that as the decades marched on after the publication of the *Origin of Species* Darwin became increasingly revisionist, allowing more and more play for Lamarckian evolutionary mechanisms centering on the inheritance of acquired characteristics.

The rejection of expression as an evolved form of communication was, for Darwin, necessary because it contained an emphasis on design. Unable to reconcile himself to this element of Bell's manifesto on anatomy, Darwin felt it necessary to reject the entire thing. Expressions were vestiges of structure and movement that once served an evolutionary function, but which had since become useless. That certain expressions were associated with certain emotions was happenstance, the result of old associations long-since disappeared. Facial expressions associated with anger or fear, for example, were perhaps commonly held, but their purpose was not to communicate anger or fear. While the expression certainly registered the presence of this or that emotion, the expression was mechanical, acquired by association and habit, and thereafter bequeathed to subsequent generations. The social element here was denied.[11]

This has been all too frequently misunderstood.[12] Insofar as Darwin argued for a certain uniformity of emotional expression across the mammalian world, he did not see anything inherently emotional in the expression itself. By way of trying to demonstrate the delimited mechanics of expression, he also highlighted the latter point. Darwin had come across the photographic endeavors of Guillaume-Benjamin-Amand Duchenne de Boulogne (1862), who had used galvanic apparatus to stimulate the facial muscles of his sitters and then photographed the "emotions" produced, in his attempt to understand the mechanics of human physiognomy. One sitter in particular was usefully unable to feel any pain from the electrical stimulation, allowing Duchenne to produce in him all manner of grimaces and grins.

Duchenne was mapping the range of anatomical possibilities of the human face, capturing these mechanically produced expressions through photography and then presenting them as depictions of a whole variety of emotions. His emotional categories were determined *a priori*, which lent the investigation an air of tautology. In any case, Duchenne's own analysis of the results of his technique have proven much less historically significant than the use made of his pictures by Darwin and his followers. Including the

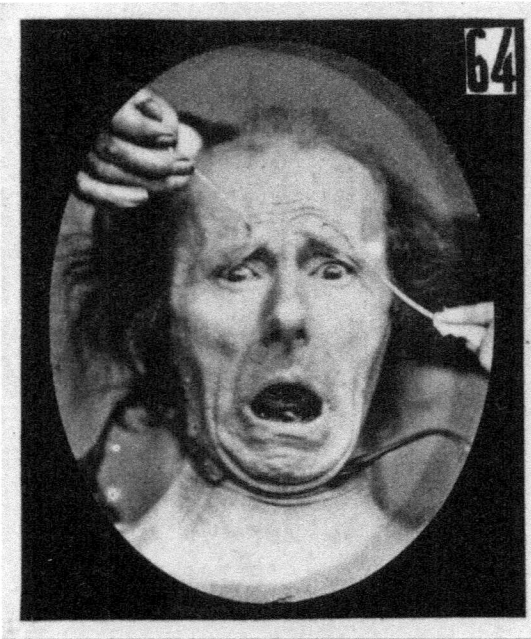

FIGURE 1.2: Duchenne de Boulogne, Facial Expression of Terror, 1862 (Wellcome Library, London).

photographs as woodcuts in his book, *The Expression of Emotions in Man and Animals*, Darwin scrupled to have the evidence of the galvanic apparatus removed. These reproductions were then given as depictions of the emotion itself. But some of the photographs were included with the apparatus clearly visible, and these in the context of other photographs of actors trying consciously to perform this or that emotion. Here Darwin acknowledged that an expression of fear or grief by no means indicated the presence of fear or grief. Duchenne's sitter was contorted into recognizable representations of emotions that were nevertheless absent. The evolutionary science of emotions in the 1870s had therefore demonstrated that appearances could be deceptive: what you saw wasn't necessarily an accurate representation of what was felt; it had also demonstrated that what was felt had as much to do with convention as with "nature." Even William James, about whom more below, had to caution against automatically confounding expression with emotions themselves, for expressions could be "accompanied by a quite cold heart" (1910, vol. 2: 456). There has been a tendency to see in Darwin's treatment of emotions the beginnings of a claim for universality, especially of emotional expression. The reality was rather the reverse.

Part of the problem for Darwin and his increasingly complicated admixture of mechanisms of natural selection, domestication, and Lamarckian inheritance was the general context of analytical essentialism among the sciences that Darwin exploited and which in turn exploited him. Evolutionism, by necessity, ran alongside and often intersected with a burgeoning science of anthropology, which in turn fostered anthropometry, biometry, and criminology (Jann 1994: 287–306). In each of these cases, early proponents worked from a position of assumed racial and intellectual superiority, working to define the "savage," the "degenerate," and the criminal in absolute terms against an equally absolute category of "civilized" man. Darwin's own insistence on the importance of education and public opinion—views forcefully promoted and extended by T. H. Huxley—in refining the emotional and moral disposition of the individual, were all too easily overlooked in a political context of race, class, and gender stratification. Emotional instability or a lack of emotional control came to be handy markers of inferiority for those who were involved, even implicitly, in Victorian programmes of imperial expansion or political exclusion.[13]

Anthropology's study of human difference was, in its Victorian iteration, focused on bodies, brains, and minds, and not so much on culture. Darwin had concretized the notion of a chain of being, which had been a mainstay of Christian philosophy for centuries and which had its roots in Aristotle. Late in the twentieth century, Darwin was interpreted as having ushered in a great note of equality among beings. If everything descended from a common ancestor, then there were no obvious grounds for a preference of one being over another. Humans were as much a part of the grand scheme of life as anything else. But Darwin didn't share this sentiment, and it was only rarely uttered before the First World War. Instead, Darwin used evolution to account for the superiority of some species over others, and, in the case of humans, used evolution in the context of civilization to account for the superiority of some races over others. For Darwin, at least, these were observations meant as justifications for the British civilized order of things. For others, an empirical study of superiority was a call to arms.

Paul Broca had founded the *Société d'Anthropologie de Paris* in the same momentous year that saw the publication of Darwin's *Origin of Species* and Bain's *Emotions and the Will*, 1859. The Anthropological Society of London was founded shortly afterwards, setting out to distance itself from the Ethnological Society that had been founded in 1843. In Paris and London, human diversity was the object of study, and the body was thought to be the key. Built upon fundamentally racist foundations, the study of human types necessarily sought essential differences in the minds and emotions of racial others. Broca set out to weigh and measure a vast collection of skulls and brains, in order to show the greater capacity of civilized crania, and a debate quickly emerged about the mental differences between gentlemen and "savages" or "negroes," between gentlemen and women, and between gentlemen and "lower" types of men. The debate was driven, on the one side, by statistical analysis of comparative weights and measures, physiological commonplaces about male activity and female conservatism, and cultural stereotypes masquerading as scientific observation. On the other side, fingers were pointed at the institutional structures of social, political, and educational exclusion that kept so-called inferiors inferior. The biological determinism of a broad range of anthropologists, physiologists, and evolutionists was shown to be nothing more than the rhetorical gloss of what was in fact a social problem. Still, the biological determinists had the better of the argument.[14]

Their success lay in a scientific tying together of spurious statistical interpretations and extremely old emotional stereotypes recast in the garb of biological novelty. The brains of women and racial others were shown to be smaller, on average, then men's. A number of critics pointed out that the male brains bequeathed to science tended to be of an exceptional nature (often belonging to scientists themselves), whereas the brains of others were picked from a degenerate sample. There were no empirical enquiries that gave clear-cut conclusions as to the average of male and female brains, or civilized and uncivilized brains. But the methodological weaknesses were suppressed by reference to physiological "knowledge." Since Galen, popular belief about the emotional debilitation caused by the womb prevailed. Physiologists no longer believed that the womb traveled around the body, but they did assert that the mere fact of being female led to emotional instability. The relative lack of physical force in women was correlated with a similar lack of mental force, and a greater susceptibility to being swept up by sentimentality. The female's failure to control emotions—a direct result of her sex—disqualified her from being able to attain the heights of abstract reason and invention attained by men. At the same time, this susceptibility was given as a reason *not* to educate her: education might unbalance the delicate woman, leaving her emotionally exposed and risking her essential biological function. Education threatened fertility. The ovum—still, slow, conservative, representing emotion, sensibility, memory—could not be forced to conform to the qualities of the sperm: active, creative, combative, rational.[15]

While the racial other could not be cast low on sexual grounds, Victorian biologists did not scruple against effeminizing the "savage." In the same way, working-class men—particularly the unskilled or unemployed—were framed as underdeveloped from the point of view of the evolution of civilization. The tendency of the "rabble" or the "residuum" to be overwhelmed by emotions, especially violent emotions, was part of the justification for political exclusion. The madness of crowds—a runaway phenomenon of emotional contagion and an abandonment of reason—was part of Parisian lore, and made into science by Gustave le Bon (1895). Essentially, the writers of a science of emotions were white, privileged males at the heart of Metropolitan political discourse. In their analysis of the emotions of lesser beings, all were given the taint of the animal: wild, abandoned to emotional instincts and drives, unchecked by reason. To be sure, there was a scale of animality, with racial others lowest on the list, but only the gentlemen of genius had managed fully to escape the brutal taint.

The urge to justify Victorian lines of exclusion by measurement, both physical and statistical, was developed further by the biometrists and eugenicists who also came in Darwin's wake.[16] At the heart of a concerted effort to institutionalize a science of human typology—from the degenerate to the beautiful—with laboratories, statistical databases, and complex genealogies, was a desire to frame the criminal "type" as emotionally incapable. Photography was again central to a science of emotional expression, designed to capture an indelible appearance of irredeemable criminality. In England from the late 1870s, Francis Galton worked to produce composite photographs, overlaying portraits of different "types" of people in order to arrive at expression archetypes. According to a theoretical supposition that character could be judged by appearances, Galton (1878) produced archetypal images of the criminal, the Jew, the diseased, and the beautiful. While the work has been put to useful purposes, its origins were unquestionably divisive and reductive.

Similarly inspired was the Italian criminologist Cesare Lombroso, whose theories on the heritable embodiment of crime were, even where they were dismissed, influential (Wolfgang 1961: 361–391).

While many scientists decried the notion that a criminal could be adjudged by physiognomy alone, it fitted into a vein of research (Pearson 1909; 1912) that sought to apply Darwin's work to the social and build policy upon it. Moreover, Lombroso's work registered with broad publics who bought his books and who passively consumed his theories via popular fiction, from *Dracula* to Tolstoy's *Resurrection* (Pick 1993: 109–110; Gould 2008: 122–123). Importantly, while both outward appearance and particular details of the brain marked the *look* of a criminal, it was his emotions, or lack thereof, that

FIGURE 1.3: Cesare Lombroso, Six Figures Illustrating Types of Criminals, 1888 (Wellcome Library, London).

allowed the criminal to *act*. The male gendering here is in accord with Lombroso's general scheme, though he made special provision in his thoughts for female criminals, who exercised their degeneracy typically through prostitution. Criminals were, according to Lombroso, less sensitive to pain than the norm. This insensitivity was the result of certain dominant passions that eliminated the fear and unpleasantness usually associated with pain (and which gives it its meaning). The same emotional calibration allowed them a "moral insensitivity," enabling them to commit violent acts without compunction. Essentially, this was nothing more than an inability to feel sympathy with the plight of others, either in pain or anguish, and a lack of sensitivity to the sight of blood. While certain features of the criminal type were absolutely physical—the jaw, the cheekbones, etc.—the general countenance worn by the criminal was, in Lombroso's (2013) scheme, an expression of both emotional excess in some respects and an emotionlessness in others. As part of a general fear that an age of callousness across Europe and North America was dawning, with portents of the moral collapse of civilization, Lombroso was both formed by and formative of the *Zeitgeist*.

MENTAL EVOLUTION AND EARLY COMPARATIVE PSYCHOLOGY

Whereas Darwin – or at least discussion arising out of Darwinism – had dominated the second half of the nineteenth century in terms of biological evolution, Darwin himself felt uncertain about the mind. His work on emotions had focused on expression and on society (or civilization) and not really much at all on the experience of emotions per se. He had to draw on (and somewhat disagree with) experts in the newly emerging field of psychology, and he had to urge on the research of others to map his evolutionary principles onto the mind and therefore the emotions. The early science of comparative psychology therefore pivoted around Darwin, but did not depend on him.

It fell to a young disciple of Darwin, George John Romanes, to fill in the blanks Darwin had left on mental evolution. Romanes took on the enormous task of describing and explaining the evolution of the mind, encompassing the intellect, the morals, and the emotions not just of man, but of all the varieties of animals on land, in the air, in water, and invisible to the naked eye (1883; 1883a; 1888).

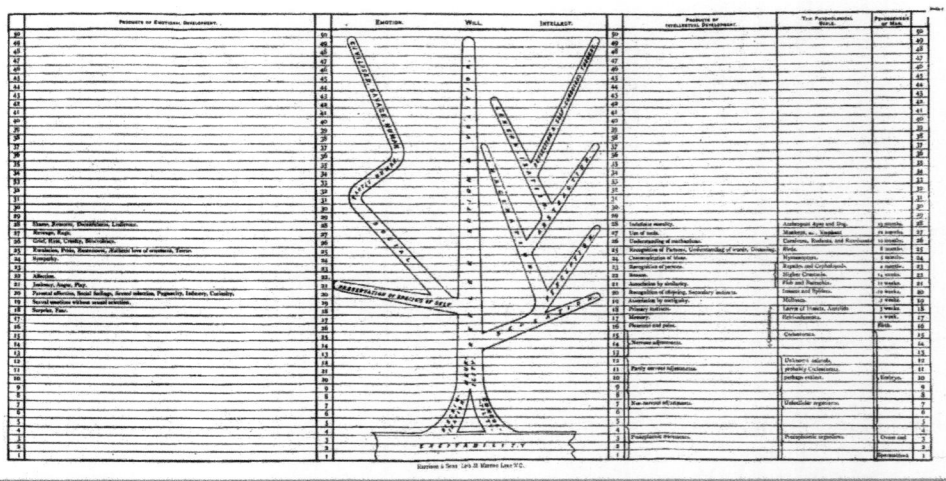

FIGURE 1.4: George John Romanes, Mental Evolution in Animals, 1883 (Wellcome Library, London).

His project remained incomplete at the time of his death, but three weighty volumes had laid the groundwork for a discipline of comparative psychology that had commonality as its defining motif. Whatever differences in mind, intellect, or emotion presented by the varieties in natures, these differences were in degree not in kind. Darwin's core principle of a common ancestor for all life on earth was applied by Romanes also to the mind. The logic here was, of course, undeniable, but in pursuing the mind Romanes was trespassing on the borderlands of the soul. Whereas Darwin's focus on physical features had left room for reluctant skeptics to retain their grip on the notion of immaterial immortality, Romanes collapsed the distance between human and spider, society and bees, and the reason of men (but *not* women) and the sagacity of dogs. Armed with a doctrinaire Darwinism and a pan-species theory of the emotions, Romanes thought it only logical to affirm that what looked like emotions in animals were emotions in fact.

Dogs—Romanes' great passion—received the most treatment. Capable of guilt or remorse, Romanes even ascribed to them a proto-moral conscience. Harvesting anecdotes as scientific data, Romanes built a massive store of folk knowledge about the emotional intelligence of everything from rats to elephants. Though he clearly and deeply understood the ontological problem of defining the emotional experiences of other beings, he assumed that a common ancestry must equate to a commonality of experience, making allowances for differences in forms and functions. Our own subjective interpretations of animal emotions were the best we could do, but they were no less valid for that. A similar dependence on subjective accounts of experience defined the psychological research of Wilhelm Wundt (1874) in Leipzig, who perhaps more than anyone brought the study of the emotions into an academic environment as a specialist field of study under the rubric of psychology.[17]

If Romanes put psychology in evolutionary terms, a contemporary of his and of Darwin set out a science of the mind in its own right. Alexander Bain's (1859) magnum opus, *The Emotions and the Will*, was published contemporaneously with *The Origin of Species*. One of Bain's central premises was that the "fact, or property, named Feeling, is totally distinct from any physical property of matter" (1859: 3). If he had left it at that, Bain's career would have been completely undercut by the Darwinian turn and the coming primacy of materialism. But Bain carefully laid out the body–mind relationship in which emotions prompt actions, and in which there is a "connexion of dependence between it [Feeling] and a material organization" (1859: 4). Bain effectively gave new currency to a Cartesian view: "the physical fact that accompanies and supports the mental fact, without making or constituting that fact, is an agitation of all those bodily members more immediately allied with the brain by nervous communication" (1859: 5). But departing from Descartes, Bain launched a new sophistication in psychological language, combined with a greater understanding of physiological functions, and, most importantly, did not need to account for the soul. Human bodies and human minds were in and of the world and, as such, subject to the world's influence.

Bain identified a "cerebral wave," made in part of "emotional currents." This wave could be reconfigured through the "power of education." In practice, Bain was attempting to account for the cultural differences of emotional expression among different human societies, as well as accounting for the apparent gap between humans and other animals. In a so-called "primitive" state, an astonished man was marked by an "open mouth," "sharp cry," "vehement stare" and a "toss of the arms," but the "civilized" man had the capacity of speech to give "necessary vent to the feeling of the moment." Expressiveness is reined in, modified, artificially represented. Crucially, Bain saw that this change in outward comportment fed back onto the state of consciousness, altering "the nature of the resulting mental condition." Bain thus described an emotional dynamic: a process through which feeling states and expressions were mutually involved and respectively modified each other. The astonishment of the "primitive" man was not only represented differently from astonishment in a "civilized" man, but also experienced differently (1859: 14–15). This gave Bain a clue—echoed by Wundt—that physiology might be the vital key to psychological understanding. The great range of feelings and variations of "mental tone" are, according to Bain, no less variously embodied. What was lacking was a developed science of "tracing the physical outgoings of an emotional wave." Nevertheless, whatever could be described as the physical affect and effect of the diffusion of an emotion would get us to a closer understanding of that emotion. Bodies *talked* the "natural language of emotion," opening up the "character of consciousness" to any observer with the power to understand that language (Bain 1859: 14–15, 28). The basic toolkit of understanding might have been supplied by nature, but changes in emotions caused by civilization necessitated the acquisition of learnt modes of deciphering expressions. This leads Bain to explain the importance of history in understanding changes in emotions over time, which he calls a "constructive process" (1859: 220–221). This idea would burn brightly for a time, before disappearing for a century.

Bain's notion of construction led him to be among the first in a "scientific" community of psychologists to uphold association as a key marker of the discipline. The "alliance" of feelings with the intellect allowed for a relational understanding between feelings sensed and the objects that typically stimulated such feelings: "Thus, we connect the pleasures of repose with an easy chair, a sofa, or a bed, and the pleasures of riding with a horse and carriage."[18] Such material objectification helped explain apparent variability in emotional experience, both in different places and over time. Emotional meaning was tethered to the things that surrounded the individual. Emotional signs were *of* the place in which they were produced. In order to sympathize with the emotions of another, first we had to "acquire the signs of feeling." We had to "learn" the appearances of emotions as well as "the names that describe them" (Bain 1894: 432). Central to this process is a cultivated understanding of emotional expressions of moral disapprobation or approval. For Bain, there was no absolute morality, but only specific contexts of feeling where right and wrong were, long before being rationalized or intellectualized, experienced as part of a social emotional dynamic. As such, Bain echoed Smith, Hume, and Darwin.

The psychology of Bain and the evolutionism of Darwin both pointed science to an historical understanding and interpretation of the emotions and morality. For a brief period, these ideas had great purchase. The last quarter of the nineteenth century was perhaps the last gasp of the scientist as amateur generalist, or the gentleman polymath. New epistemological configurations of the emotions seemed to become possible and necessary, and yet were fleeting and quickly forgotten. One of the clearest and most profound generalist statements on the importance of the emotions for understanding the human condition came from perhaps the most famous of the polymath radicals, George Henry Lewes, life partner of George Eliot.

Lewes is usually labeled a philosopher or critic, but he was deeply immersed in the study of science, particularly biology, physiology, and psychology. He was a close reader of Darwin, an experimentalist in his own right, and influential in transmitting and translating science for large audiences. Rooting philosophy—the "Logic of Signs"—in the "Logic of Feeling," Lewes concluded that a true philosophy had to take account of sentiment as regulative of conduct and knowledge (1874: 455). The moral sense was instinctive but historical, competing with egoistical desires and filtered through conscious judgement. The emotional and the intellectual were mutually involved in the *feeling* of right and wrong. So much had been said, perhaps, by Adam Smith, but the impetus in this case was to take seriously a science of emotions in order the better to understand their nature and the extent to which they were socialized. Lewes' inspired vision was of brains and bodies in the world, moved by moral instincts formed in the crucible of society and culture.

Unusually then, in an age dominated in scientific circles by evolutionism more or less marked by questions of heredity and acquired habit, Lewes foregrounded social construction as the key to the way in which evolution happens in civilized societies. In short, none of the new sciences of mind and body that sought to define and explore the emotions could work without history: "Because Psychology is interpreted through Sociology, and Experience acquires its development mainly through social influences, we must always take History into account." Lewes understood that while insufficient time had passed for a natural evolution of types of human species within the history of civilization, there were nevertheless significant divergences in "the quality of moral feelings and the range of conceptions." Unlike many of his contemporaries he was convinced that a good physiologist would recognize that the "organs and functions" were the same in "the savage and the civilized, in Greek, Hindoo, old German, or modern European," but could not escape the observation that the "thoughts and sentiments" were markedly different. The "brain of a cultivated Englishman . . . compared with the brain of a Greek of the age of Pericles, would not present any appreciable differences," he averred, noting that the continuity of the physical stuff of humanity by no means accorded with a continuity of emotional or moral disposition. These changes were wrought by social influences, effectively defining and delimiting the emotional and moral compasses of humans who, in physiological terms, were the same over time. Lewes put forward a radical scholarly agenda that is only now being picked up: "while the laws of the sentient functions must be studied in Physiology, the laws of the sentient faculties, especially the moral and intellectual faculties, must be studied in History. The true logic of Science is only made apparent in the history of Science" (1879: 153–154). Alexander Bain would concur, noting pointedly that the historian's task involved the interpretation of "extinct modes of feeling." In effect, to understand the strange experiences of the past, or the strange experiences of unfamiliar places, such scholars had to "construct" new emotions from admixtures of their own experience, as best they could (Bain 1894: 619–622).

MEASURED MEASURING, OR PHYSIOLOGICAL EMOTIONS

Why was the work of Romanes, Bain, and Lewes not more influential? These strands of historical psychology, worlded physiology, and the emotional world of animals were all basically dropped at the turn of the twentieth century, being picked up again only comparatively recently. Why? The answer lies within the politics of science itself. As power shifted to new figures, with new dogmas and new practices, so paradigms shifted accordingly. This process was abetted by a cluster of deaths—some timely, some not so much—and a rising tide of both professionalism and specialism within scientific and medical circles. Darwin died in 1882; Romanes in 1894; Lewes in 1878; Bain in 1903. The proto-psychological and proto-physiological investigations of the last generation of amateur generalists was easily swept away as a dusty relic of an old way of doing things. Romanes was supposed to carry Darwin's mantle, but died very young and in his prime.

Romanes' own disciple, Conwy Lloyd Morgan (1894: 59) would, under the veil of honoring his mentor, undo all of his work at a stroke, essentially launching the behaviorist theory that would dominate twentieth-century animal psychology. The work of Lewes and Bain was undermined by psychologists such as William James, whose focus on the primacy of bodily emotions was increasingly supported by a whole host of physiological specialists who could point to the presence of emotions in this organ or that, marking off emotional traces on mechanical graphs. Meanwhile, Darwin's own uncertainty about natural selection and the extent to which Lamarckian evolution was involved in evolutionary processes was washed away by the rediscovery of Gregor Mendel's (1901) work that essentially launched modern genetics (Bowler 1989). The twentieth century began in the vein of the materialist, the positivist, and the anthropocentrist. Both the study and the understanding of the emotions was heavily influenced.

William James' contribution turned psychology on its head and thrust physiology to the forefront of emotions research. His *Principles of Psychology* first appeared in 1890, coincident with a rapidly expanding experimental fervor among physiological specialists. Laboratories were well established across Europe and reaching important new levels of influence in the United States. James' assertion that "the general causes of the emotions are indubitably physiological" was, in effect, a rallying call for physiological experiment. This branch of psychology at least could be subsumed. James gave the physiologists more to go on. His most famous pronouncement on emotions was to reverse what he saw as a central assumption:

> Our natural way of thinking about these coarser emotions is that the mental perception of some fact excites the mental affection called the emotion, and that this latter state of mind gives rise to the bodily expression. My theory, on the contrary, is that *the bodily changes follow directly the perception of the exciting fact, and that our feeling of the same changes as they occur* IS *the emotion*. Common-sense says, we lose our fortune, are sorry and weep; we meet a bear, are frightened and run; we are insulted by a rival, are angry and strike. The hypothesis here to be defended says that this order of sequence is incorrect, that the one mental state is not immediately induced by the other, that the bodily manifestations must first be interposed between, and that the more rational statement is that we feel sorry because we cry, angry because we strike, afraid because we tremble, and not that we cry, strike, or tremble, because we are sorry, angry, or fearful, as the case may be. Without the bodily states following on the perception, the latter would be purely cognitive in form, pale, colorless, destitute of emotional warmth. We might then see the bear, and judge it best to run, receive the insult and deem it right to strike, but we should not actually *feel* afraid or angry.
>
> —James 1910: vol. 2, 449–450[19]

In this configuration, an expression was not a sign of an inner emotion, but the emotion itself. There could be no such thing as a "purely disembodied emotion." James examined himself and found that "whatever moods, affections, and passions" he had, they were "constituted by, and made up of, those bodily changes which we ordinarily call their expression or consequence." The implications were profound. On the one hand, emotions could be made the subject of scientific certainty, for if they were bodily they were presumably also measurable. Blood pressure, temperature, and a host of visceral and glandular secretions could be subjected to the mechanical gaze of the laboratory. The discovery of the first hormone, secretin, in 1902 was followed quickly by a theoretical expression of hormonal functions by the London-based physiologist Ernest Starling (1905). Here was the *stuff* of emotions.

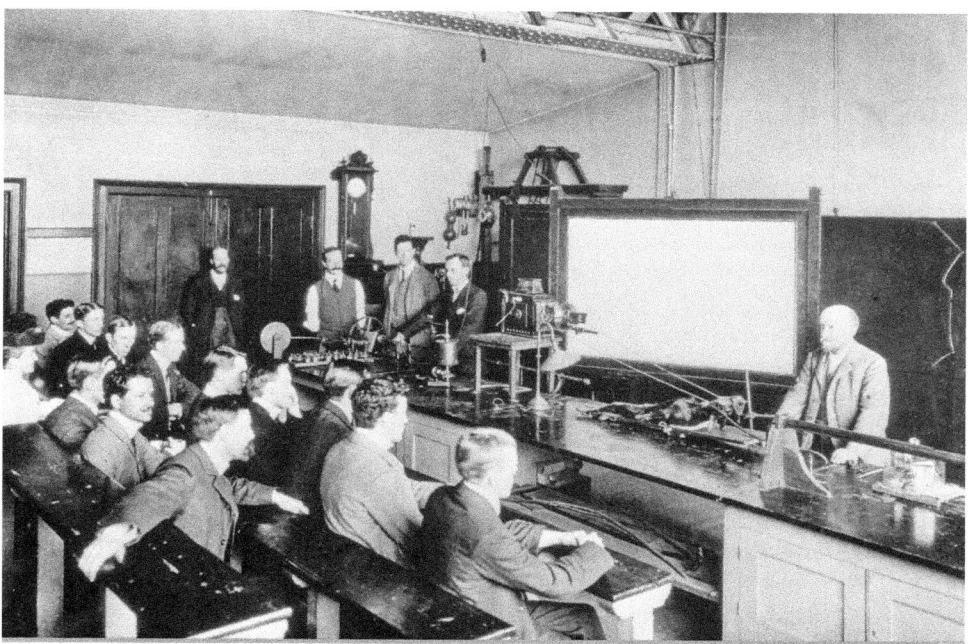

FIGURE 1.5: W.M Bayliss (right) and E.H. Starling (left): experimentation on hormones in a dog, 1903 (Wellcome Library, London).

On the other hand, the possibilities for emotions studies seemed endless. James himself noted the logical consequence of defining an emotion as a reflex action aroused by an object, immediately felt: *"we immediately see why there is no limit to the number of possible different emotions which may exist, and why the emotions of different individuals may vary indefinitely*.... For there is nothing sacramental or eternally fixed in reflex action" [emphasis in original] (1910: vol. 2, 454).

In some respects, this analytical insight returned James to the constructivism of Bain. Physiological mechanics notwithstanding, James knew the influence of custom on instinct, and therefore assumed a highly relativistic position that at once gave a history to emotions and to the body: "*any classification of the emotions is seen to be as true and as 'natural' as any other*, if it only serves some purpose; and such a question as 'What is the "real" or "typical" expression of anger, or fear?' is seen to have no objective meaning at all. Instead of it we now have the question as to how any given 'expression' of anger or fear may have come to exist." In a long line of early psychologists and evolutionists, James too asserted that this was a question for historians to answer, "although the answer may be hard to find" (1910: vol. 2, 454).

The second strand of implications of James' theory did not find any traction among the physiologists who ran with the first strand. On the contrary, if emotions were findable and recordable in the body, then science would discover their true essence. Experimentation would objectively isolate fear, for example, and establish a universal standard for measuring it. Rather than endless possibilities, there would be an endeavor to pare down emotions until the basic foundations for all varieties were discovered.

The experimental impetus behind the search for the physiological constants of emotion came from observations that the emotions of laboratory animals were adversely affecting the results of physiological inquiries with other aims. Qualities of the blood, visceral secretions, responses to injury and disease, and animal behavior in general were the subjects of physiological endeavor, with the aim of finding reliable and repeatable standards or physiological norms. The destabilizing influence of emotions led to great efforts to try to eliminate or control emotions in laboratory animals, with the concomitant need to isolate of what exactly emotions consisted. As Otniel Dror has brilliantly evidenced, the late nineteenth and early twentieth centuries witnessed the attempt to cultivate an emotionally neutral array of "standard" laboratory animals in part through investigations into the visceral nature of animal emotion itself.[20] Agitated emotional states were not mental or immaterial so much as they were physiological. The secretion of adrenalin, or the boost of blood glucose; a rise or drop in blood pressure and so on: these were not signs of emotion but the emotions *themselves*. As such, given the need for control, universal standards and experimental replication, it was possible to conceive of an evolutionary constant of emotional function. James' historical caveat was lost in the noise of the machines that inscribed the emotions being emitted from the viscera of laboratory animals. In the words of Théodule Ribot, who acknowledged the influence of James and Bain, among others, emotions "plunge into the individual's depths; they have their roots in the needs and instincts, that is to say, in movements" (1896: ix).[21] Thus, at the very moment that emotions were being untethered from material considerations by historicists, psychoanalysts, and a certain strain of psychologist, so they were being firmly physiologically grounded in a literal reading of the word "emotion": *outward movement*.

CHAPTER TWO

Religion and Spirituality

JULIUS H. RUBIN

A cultural history of religious emotion and spirituality from 1780–1920, from the American Revolution to the emergence of Modernism, requires the development of an interpretative understanding and empathetic reconstruction of the lived experiences and expressions of believers that can be applied to the immense variety and diversity of piety and religiosity during this period. An examination of religious emotions and spirituality is part of the study of "emotionality" that connects the dynamics of culture and historical change within religious groups and other social institutions to answer the question: what were the mentalities and emotions of believers as they practiced their faith in daily piety, in worship, and in holy days (Stearns and Lewis 1998: 1). Emotionality explores the triumph of evangelical Protestantism that emerged as a national religion and a critical component of the emerging American collective identity as a Redeemer nation, chosen by God as a harbinger of the millennium. The religious effervescence of the century of revivals and evangelical religion was exemplified by the Cane Ridge Rival in Kentucky that harkened the beginning of the Second Great Awakening in August 1801 where possibly 20,000 people attended the combined Presbyterian, Baptist, and Methodist camp meeting, hosted by the congregation of Reverend Barton W. Stone. Participants fell to the ground—weeping, moaning, overwhelmed by religious emotions of melancholy, followed by the experience of grace where many were seemingly possessed by the Holy Spirit as they succumbed to fits, trances, and religious ecstasy in the struggle to redeem themselves from sin and find conversion. Methodist camp meetings and Baptist revivals pervaded both the long-settled eastern seaboard of the United States, and spread throughout the Midwest and south in the antebellum period. The grand revivalist Charles Grandison Finney prosecuted awakenings of New School Presbyterianism in the Burned-Over District of New York that followed emerging cities along the Erie Canal, bringing sinners before the bar of God's law and justice in protracted meetings, praying for sinners by name, segregating the awakened and hopeful on anxious benches and producing outcries of lamentation for sin and the despair of religious melancholy that culminated in the unspeakable joy of grace and rebirth. We also need to inquire what was the nature of religious experience for adherents of African American Protestant churches, the ring-shout ecstatic worship tradition, Phoebe Palmer's Holiness movement, the Businessman's Revival in Boston and New York in 1857, religion and emotion in the Civil War, the Pentecostal Movement of the early twentieth century, and the more secular, non-institutional religiosity of Spiritualism, folk, and "Nature Religion" (Albanese 1990) and the mind-cure movement. Given the complexity, variety, and diversity of religion in America, differentiated by denomination, region, social class, and gender, I will employ the concepts from the sociology of religious emotions, especially religious melancholy and religious ecstasy to help analyze the era under review.

FIGURE 2.1: Maze Burbank, "Religious Camp Meeting"—Or An Old Time Camp Meeting (1838) no. 1910.1.2. Courtesy of New Bedford Whaling Museum.

The religious emotions and experiences associated with melancholy and ecstasy need to be interpreted by the sociology of emotion that investigates the distinctive "emotional regimes" of Protestantism in America. This is a dynamic where religious emotions are constituted by the dialectic of selves who are situated in groups or institutions, and where action and experience are informed by sacred symbols and the performance of ritual and ceremony directed toward the numinous or God. Protestant dogma, ritual, and performance also create "emotional programmes" (Riis and Woodhead, 2010: 8, 47), a repertoire of "religious affections" that encourage the godly to embrace melancholy/ecstasy as preparatory to grace and rebirth. Thus, various Protestant religious regimes and their associated programs placed a premium on inducing religious melancholy/ecstasy among the faithful, prescribing this state as a routinized, expected, and valued religious experience for the believer who traversed the passage to election, healing, and salvation. Protestant emotional regimes formed an affinity that connected the conversion experience and living a godly life with melancholy states of dejection and despair or ecstatic, inner-worldly mystical experiences of possession by sacred pneuma.

Religion provides a roadmap and the cultural directives that define conversion and salvation, sanctification and godly living, and the realization of desired and valued emotional states. Religious culture is a directive system of cues that organize perception, feeling, agenda, belief, what we hold in awe, and what we emulate. Cues "are mediated to individuals with a view to charging and aiding them to define and respond to any possible point of reference—sign, symbol, object, event, person, situation—they might chance to encounter or fancy" (Nelson 1964: 143–144).

Although emotion rules appear to be natural and self-evident to social actors, these rules represent the constitutive power of culture to formulate models of selfhood, interiority, and performance (Pfister 1997: 24). Linking emotions to culture and social structure, Nancy Schnog argues, "emotions are historically contingent, socially specific and politically situated" (Schnog 1997: 7–8).

THE SOCIOLOGY OF RELIGION AND EMOTIONS: RELIGIOUS MELANCHOLY AND PROTESTANTISM

Melancholy associated with religious vocation in Western religion was uncommon to the masses or laity before the Reformation. Melancholy states afflicted medieval monastics and were associated with other-worldly asceticism in a syndrome of sorrow-dejection-despair known as the sin of *acedia* or sloth, regarding a monk's spiritual duties. First identified among the Desert Fathers by John Cassian (ca. 420) as the noonday demon, Stanley W. Jackson explains: "the spiritual authors of the twelfth century and the Scholastics of the thirteenth century had tended to emphasize the state of mind of acedia (weariness, disgust, lack of fervor, sorrow)" (Jackson 1986: 71). The experience of melancholy as the abandonment by God and the absence of the contemplative possession of the holy, also characterized the spiritual lives of Christian and Jewish mystics (Rubin 2008: 297–300).

Unique to England and Europe, by the late sixteenth century there coalesced a set of religious ideas and practices that urged all believers to seek salvation, not just a religious aristocracy of monastics. Known as evangelical pietism, this Protestant belief found its most consistent expression in the nonconformist sects which settled New England. This religiosity emphasized an experiential oneness with God, the spiritual itinerary from sin to conversion and sanctification, a reliance on the Scripture as interpreted by the prepared heart who had been transformed by the infusion of the Holy Spirit. This piety required the religious rejection of the natural man and the fallen world that both were to be remade in the image of God's will. Evangelical pietism fused together inner-worldly asceticism, mystical illuminism, evangelical fervor to convert the masses and transform the world in God's image, and a particularism of grace founded on the doctrine of predestination. Wherever these five elements coalesced, one discovers the propensity of souls to suffer religious melancholy.

Max Weber's sociology of religion assists us in understanding evangelical pietism. He develops a structural phenomenology of religious experience by linking the practical demands of religious ethics and belief that prescribed ways of making a life, with cultivating a distinctive self, identity, and personality that sought religious experience grounded in ultimate values, and directed believers toward the path to salvation. New conceptions of religious personality, personhood, and self were constituted by the ceaseless struggle to achieve ultimate values as an instrument of God's will, as an ascetic warrior, a Christian soldier who engages in *auto-machia* against the "natural man." One must reject the world in order to remake it and refashion one's identity in conformity with divine mandate.

Weber argues that this religious personality possessed an "ethic of inwardness" (*Gesinnungsethik*) distinguishing each person as a unique individual who actively fashioned his or her character and identity as a potter shapes the raw material of clay on the wheel (Goldman 1988: 153). The solitary individual, separated from kindred, neighbors, and religious community, cultivated an inner life, an inwardness and interiority (*Innerlichkeit*) marked by self-examination about sin and grace and election and damnation. And Protestant self and personality were inextricably linked to the distinctive features and burdens of modern identity.

Charles Taylor identifies the genealogy of ideas that account for the emergence of modern identity and the self, peculiar to the West, which included: 1) the quality of inward self-awareness, the hegemony of reason (self-control); 2) vocational asceticism and the elevation of ordinary mundane life in work and family; 3) the uniqueness of each individual and importance of self-expression (expressive individuation) (Taylor 1989: 211). These elements of modern identity crystallized in Calvinistic Puritan sects in England and elsewhere in the transformative breakthrough to modernity in the seventeenth and eighteenth centuries. Both Taylor and Weber argue that modern selves embraced heroic burdens at times bordering on the pathological, as was the case with the obsessional forms of religious melancholy (Taylor 1989: 19). Taylor suggests that the psychopathologies identified by Sigmund Freud at the turn of the twentieth century—hysteria, ego loss, phobia and obsession—reflect the agonies of modern identity in the cultural context of the "loss of horizon," where secularization has stripped the self of ultimate meanings and values that previous religious worldviews had provided. Taylor concludes that:

> the highest spiritual ideals and aspirations also threaten to lay the most crushing burdens on humankind. *The great spiritual visions of human history have also been poisoned chalices, the causes of untold misery* and even savagery. . . . Our link with the highest has been recurrently associated with sacrifice, even mutilation, as though something of us to be torn away or immolated if we are to please the gods.
>
> —Taylor 1989: 519, emphasis added

These highest spiritual ideals or poisoned chalices formed the foundation of evangelical pietist religion in America and Western Europe. The European and English thinkers and ideas—the origins of these ideas of melancholy and ecstasy—informed American Protestant culture from the colonial era through the nineteenth century.

Anyone interested in the origin and definition of religious melancholy needs to begin with John Stachniewski's enduring study, *The Persecutory Imagination: English Puritanism and the Literature of Religious Despair* (1991). He poses C. S. Lewis's question: what did it feel like to be a Protestant in the late sixteenth and early seventeenth centuries? In the spirit of Michel Foucault, Stachniewski attempts to reconstruct the subjectivities, mentalities, and lived experiences of true believers who constituted their selves through the religious discourse of an emerging cultural phenomenon—the persecutory imagination—founded on Calvinist theology.

The theology of Jean Calvin, Theodore Beza, and William Perkins posited the absolute sovereignty of a transcendental and unknowable God who divided creation into an elect predestined to salvation and the masses of reprobates predestined for damnation. "Nothing could coerce, alter, or hinder God's purposes" (Stachniewski 1991: 17).

Although Calvin enjoined the faithful to demonstrate confidence in their election where doubt about salvation was itself evidence of spiritual insufficiency, so many lives foundered on the question of how one could find certainty. How could the believer find assurance that he or she was godly, elect, and the recipient of grace? Was the seeker mired in hypocrisy, a deluded reprobate filled with uncertainty and anxiety regarding the authenticity of religious experience (Stachniewski 1991: 85, 96)?

The Calvinistic Puritan worldview and the terrifying logic of God's law fostered a persecutory imagination replete with souls haunted by insecurity over salvation, obsessed with blasphemous thoughts, fearful of having grieved the Holy Spirit and having committed the unpardonable sin. Stachniewski argues that Calvinism and Puritanism were conducive to widespread despair in England that he substantiates by evidence from the pastoral literature and sermons that addressed these concerns, the 200 diaries and spiritual autobiographies written in this period, medical case histories of religious despair and suicide (Stachniewski 1991: 27), charges of enthusiasm made by Catholic and anti-Calvinist groups, and secular literary texts that reflected the mood of religious melancholy in the popular, collective imagination (Sena 1973: 299).

Robert Burton published *The Anatomy of Melancholy* in 1621 and first identified this spiritual malaise associated with Reformed spirituality as a pathology or malady. "Religious melancholy" was a distinct form of love-melancholy caused by a defect in man's relation to God. Through excesses and religious enthusiasm and through doctrinal error, Satan has polluted individuals' hearts with temptations and sinful obsessions and thus they remain alienated from God's love. Those afflicted with religious melancholy suffered the terrors of conscience, despair, and hopelessness. Only the infusion of faith—the assurance that God's love abides in the soul of the believer—could justify the sinner, and turn the depraved one toward God by renewing his or her mind, will, and heart.

Burton recounts the problems of devotional piety: weakness of faith, misunderstood scripture, the scrupulous conscience, excessive meditations, doubt and despair over one's status of election. His descriptions of the symptoms of "Despair, Fear, Sorrow, Suspicion, Anxiety, Horror of conscience, fearful dreams and visions," derived from the work of Felix Plater, reveal the seriousness of religious melancholy as a mental alienation that frequently resulted in suicide or madness. Plater explains:

> Never was any living creature in such torment before, in such a miserable estate, in such distress of mind, no hope, no faith, past cure, reprobate, continually tempted to make away [with] themselves . . . that they are compelled against their will to harbour impious thoughts, to blaspheme against God, to the committing of many horrible deeds, to laying violent hands upon themselves, &c.
>
> —Burton 1927: II, 948

Burton identified a new form of spiritual desolation among Puritans. He "invented a new name for pathological doubt about one's spiritual state, religious melancholy, and he charged that the Puritans were tearing and wounding people's consciences, so that they were almost mad with fear and sorrow" (MacDonald and Murphy 1981: 64). Religious melancholy reportedly prevailed among Cambridge Puritans in the period from 1580 to 1600. The marrow of divinity in late Tudor England, for divines like William Perkins (1558–1602), Richard Rogers (1550–1618), and Richard Greenham (1535–1594), centered on the question of the assurance of election (*certitudo salutis*). The methodical practice of piety included self-examination, repentance of sin, private prayer, and reading scripture and devotional works. This spiritual itinerary from sin to salvation (*ordo salutis*) provided devotional exercises where the faithful would experience an initial godly sorrow for sin that progressed in severity by means of the "inquisition of self-examination" into despair and the desired state of selfless ecstasy—holy desperation. Peter Iver Kaufman characterizes the assurance of election as a "pious dis-ease" that combined melancholy and vertigo as prefatory to the rapturous reception of grace that signaled the seal of election and salvation (Kaufman 1996: 1, 6). He explains: "The pietists wanted to structure character and desire and took a special interest in the therapeutic value of despair" (Kaufman 1991: 36). This approach envisioned the soul caught in the dialectic between melancholy and hope. Each person needed to lose himself or herself in despair and thus seek redemption and healing as a child of God.

Religious melancholy has three hallmarks: spiritual pilgrimage, spiritual warfare, and spiritual obsession—the seemingly interminable alternation between the assurance of salvation and backsliding into despair. John Bunyan's famous allegory *The Pilgrim's Progress* (1678) and his spiritual autobiography *Grace Abounding to the Chief of Sinners* (1666) offer a clear and precise model of these hallmarks.

The protagonist of *Pilgrim's Progress*, Christian, is dressed in rags, carrying the burden of sin and depravity on his back, grasps a book of Scripture and flees from his wife and children, departing the City of Destruction. He tries to muffle their cries of abandonment. Weeping and trembling in fear, he inquires, "What shall I do to be saved?" as he begins a spiritual pilgrimage guided on the true path by Evangelist. He is joined at times by various companions (Pliable, Faithful, Patience, Hopeful), but throughout this dreamlike, inner journey, the spiritual geography is marked by religious melancholy when he descends into the Slough of Despond or encounters the man in the Iron Cage of Despair, who proclaims: "I have sinned against the light of the Word and the goodness of God; I have grieved the Spirit, and he is gone" (Bunyan 2010a: 45).

Religious wayfarers ventured forth in search of grace, and longed to enter the Celestial City, but invariably encountered the temptation to doubt and the snares of the Devil who urged blasphemy and the devastating realization that a penitent can become a hypocrite. A pilgrim might succumb to enmity toward God's justice and vile thoughts and actions, and thus could have sinned away the day of grace by committing the unpardonable sin.

While traversing the straight and narrow path, the road to salvation, Christian comes upon a Cross, causing the burden of sin to fall from his back. He escapes doctrinal errors and the deadly snares of worldliness in Vanity Fair, only to lose his way and become imprisoned by Giant Despair in Doubting Castle. In the course of the spiritual pilgrimage from sin and guilt to grace, the believer will encounter despair: "An endless roaming in a maze of living death" (Davies 2002: 247). Despair is a cruel torturer who would gouge out the eyes of each captive, blinding them in hopelessness, preventing them from seeing the promises of scripture and recognizing the power of faith in things unseen (Davies 2002: 282). Christian endures torture as the Giant and his wife berate him and Hopeful and urge them to end their lives. But Christian discovers a key in his bosom called Promise (of grace through Christ's redeeming sacrifice) that will open all doors in the castle, and they make their escape.

Grace Abounding is part of the emerging genre of the conversion narrative, the spiritual autobiography and the literature of consolation that provided authoritative guides to authentic religious experience and the itinerary of conversion (Hill 1989: 63). Now every man and woman was called upon to undertake a spiritual pilgrimage, to travel the road to sainthood, to appropriate what William James termed the heroics of the twice-born and morbid-minded, or what Max Weber referred to as religious virtuosity (Rubin 1994: 12–21).

Bunyan records the stages of the soul's passage from the awakening of sin, the terror before divine law, the selfless agony with the realization of human inability to win salvation by the penitent's actions or good works and the obsessive temptations from Satan to blaspheme against the Holy Ghost, to sell Christ as Esau had sold his birthright. After a protracted and torturous journey that lasted more than a decade, Bunyan might enjoy the contemplation of Christ, the reception of grace, and the ecstatic, rapturous belief that Christ's blood and sacrifice remit all guilt. "Now Christ was all, all my wisdom, all my righteousness, all my sanctification, and all my redemption" (Bunyan 2010b: para. 223). He reports enjoying "such strange appearances of the grace of God, that I could hardly bear up under it: it was so out of order amazing" (Bunyan 2010b: para. 262). The joyful assurance of salvation prompted him to exclaim: "I could scarce lie in my bed for joy, and peace, and triumph, through Christ" (Bunyan 2010b: para. 112). However, the contemplation of Christ and the experience of grace proved short-lived, transient, and always punctuated with seasons of doubt and despair (Schmidt 2007: 67). Religious melancholy was his frequent companion: "for my peace would be in it, and out, sometimes twenty times a day; comfort now, and trouble presently; peace now, and before I could go for a furlong, as full of fear and guilt as ever heart could hold" (Bunyan 2010b: para. 205).

The persecutory imagination that developed in England was integral to "the New England Way" that stamped colonial Americans—Calvinist, Separatist, Nonconformist, Puritan and Evangelical Pietist believers—with what John Owen King terms "the iron of melancholy" (King 1983). As I have written:

> From the first settlements in New England until the late nineteenth century, King explores the vicissitudes of the myth of spiritual pilgrimage that has helped shape the American character and experience, which is fraught with psychological anguish, trauma, and desolation. The genre of the American spiritual autobiography, built on the seventeenth-century English tradition of Bunyan, Baxter, Burton, and other theologians of practical divinity, created a myth of the representative Christian life that was branded by the iron of melancholy. The English texts provided exemplars— narratives of successful conversions for New England's visible saints to appropriate. They in turn embraced the iron of melancholy, seeking rebirth in the red-hot travail that was considered the distinguishing mark of Godly affliction visited upon the elect.
>
> —Rubin 1994: 10

The iron of religious melancholy and ecstasy was anatomized in Jonathan Edwards's *A Treatise Concerning Religious Affections* (1746). He wrote the definitive statement on the religious emotions or "high affections" of melancholy and ecstasy. Edwards attempted to provide a theological rationale for the religious awakening that swept New England and the middle Atlantic colonies in the late 1730s through the 1740s. In his writings on religious affections and *A Faithful Narrative of the Surprising Work of God in the Conversion of Many Hundred Souls in Northampton* (1742), Edwards championed the New Light doctrine of the authenticity of sudden conversion for those affected by open field meetings conducted by itinerant evangelists who employed fire and brimstone preaching intended to awaken the stony hearts of slumbering sinners.

In *Religious Affections*, Edwards distinguished true religion that consists in holy affections (emotions) from false religion, error, delusion, Satanic influence, hypocrisy, or bodily states of emotional excitement (Edwards 1821: 16–39). He identified the twelve distinguishing signs of truly gracious and holy affections that began with the new creation and regeneration of the natural or carnal man, who through the seal of grace, enjoyed a spirituality born of the indwelling of the Holy Spirit (Edwards 1821: 123–128, 165). Authentic religious emotions found expression in childlike humility, love to God, and a rejection of self-aggrandizement and self-love and progressive sanctification through godly living. Finally, evangelical humiliation characterizes gracious affections with "a sense that a Christian has of his utter insufficiency, despicableness and odiousness, with an answerable frame of heart" (Edwards 1821: 260).

"High affections" included the terror of a newly awakened sinner before the prospect of an angry God and the prospect of damnation, religious melancholy, and moments of joy approaching ecstasy (Edwards 1821: 50, 293). Edwards argued that religious emotions, inspired by graciousness and the Spirit, were necessarily lively, fervent, and powerful, encompassing a wide range of feeling states from sorrow and brokenheartedness to gratitude, compassion, and, above all, love (Edwards 1821: 20–21, 27). By defending New Light religious affections against the charges of enthusiasm and error, he legitimated the diverse paths to salvation—from moderate to more dramatic affections that included religious melancholy and ecstasy—and set the standard for evangelical religion in America.

Frank Lambert argues in *Inventing the "Great Awakening"* that revivalists like Edwards, William Tennent, George Whitefield, John and Charles Wesley, Thomas Prince's *Christian History* (1743), and many others "invented" the Great Awakening. Here invention refers to the discovery of a hidden phenomenon and the formulation of new measures to promote conversion. Through open field meetings before crowds that exceeded 1,000 people, and by inventing new forms of extemporaneous fire and brimstone preaching, itinerants prosecuted the awakening (Lambert 1999: 9–47). New Lights publicized and promoted their invention through newspapers, broadsides, pamphlets, and tracts. Evangelists acted as mediating elites by articulating and transmitting an "evangelical culture" to the faithful (Rubin 1994: 245–247). They explained how churches had languished and how the godly had grown cold-hearted in apostasy and backsliding. They instructed the laity to expect periodic awakenings and to welcome the special measures designed to hasten the work of the Holy Spirit. The faithful who were enmeshed in this invented tradition of evangelical culture felt the need for a revival, anxiously participating in new measures, and eagerly seeking religious emotions. Souls brought to grace and into full church membership connected local communities with believers in a perceived Atlantic community in England and Scotland. Timothy D. Hall explains how revivals "provided personal representative contact with what was soon to become a vast 'imagined community' of saints that transcended geographical and denominational lines through a common experience of New Birth" (Hall 1994: 33).

Mark A. Noll describes the "evangelical surge" from the early 1800s during the Second Great Awakening until the Civil War. Through the promotion of religious values, print culture, voluntary and reform societies, and Arminian theology that focused upon the will to choose salvation, approximately 40 percent of Americans identified as reborn evangelicals (Noll 2002: 197). The spectacular growth of Methodist and Baptist churches in this period together with the Disciples of Christ and Restorationist movement democratized religion, challenging hierarchy and tradition with the promise of the universality of salvation for all men and women with prepared hearts who might by an act of volition seek God's grace in the encounter with religious melancholy and ecstasy.

R. A. Knox defines the nature of religious enthusiasm—the propensity for religious melancholy and ecstasy—as an "ultrasupernaturalism" where true believers emulate the Apostolic church and seek direct access to God through a theology of grace and conversion founded upon the immediate inspiration of the Spirit. Calvinistic Puritanism, George Fox and Quakerism, Phillip Jakob Spener and German Pietists, Count Zinzendorf and Moravians and Anabaptists, the Wesleys and Methodism; each exemplifies what was first described as enthusiasm and later as an established institutionalized religion, which provided the foundation for religious experience, spirituality, and religious affections in America (Knox 1962: 2–6).

From the seventeenth century in England through the transatlantic revivals in the eighteenth and nineteenth centuries, controversies arose about explaining extremes of melancholy or ecstatic religious experience. Was this true religion or the doctrinal error of religious enthusiasm? Did these states of emotion and spirituality represent the authentic work of the Holy Spirit or deluded imaginations brought about by terror, predispositions to mental illness and bodily or mental weakness (Taves 1999: 23–33)?

RELIGIOUS ECSTASY AND SPIRITUALITY: METHODISM, HOLINESS, AND AFRICAN AMERICAN RELIGIOUS EXPERIENCE

Religious ecstasy forms the second axis of religious emotion that was characterized by extraordinary performances and encounters with the sacred. Weber argues in his developmental history of religion that orgiastic cults and shamanism used ecstatic states as an instrument of salvation through self-deification. Trances and possession induced by alcohol, tobacco, other drugs, music, dancing, and sexuality produced states of self-deification or possession of the godhead. The Greek concept of *ekstasis* was exemplified by the cult of Apollo and Dionysus (Weber 1963: 157–159). However, the development of a transcendental creator deity changed the path to salvation from divine possession or self-deification to the process of an ethical patterning of life (sanctification) and the longing to be spiritually suffused by God—the illumination of the soul by the spirit (*pneuma*) of God. States of religious ecstasy were sublimated by this ethical path to sanctification and were authenticated as integral to the spiritual journey from sin to salvation as evidence of the work of the Holy Spirit. Weber explains: "These phenomena might easily consist in speaking with strange tongues, manifesting hypnotic and other suggestive powers, experiencing impulses toward mystical illumination and ethical conversion, or experiencing profound anguish over one's sins and joyous emotions deriving from suffusion by the spirit of the god. These states might even follow in rapid succession" (Weber 1963: 159). Thus, religious ecstasy served the interests of a methodical striving for salvation from the travails of this world and the promise of the rebirth.

In America, ecstatic experiences helped to democratize religion with an egalitarian appeal that challenged tradition and hierarchy (Malinar and Basu 2008: 241). Ann Taves explains in *Fits, Trances, and Visions* that the experience of ecstasy was characterized by uncontrolled bodily movements such as fits, catalepsy, and convulsions. The ecstatic uttered spontaneous vocalizations by crying out, shouting, and speaking in tongues. Ecstatic experiences also included trances, dreams, visions, auditory hallucinations, possession, convulsions, catalepsy, and out-of-body experiences (Taves 1999: 3). The religious rationale for ecstatic emotions and states attributed these experiences to the power of the indwelling spirit, "Streams of holy fire" for Methodists and Holiness groups or the "baptism of the Holy Spirit" for Pentecostals in the Azusa Street Mission in Los Angeles in 1906.

From 1770–1820, Methodism grew from a small heterodox group of 1,000 to a major denomination of 250,000 adherents drawn largely from "middling people"—artisans, shopkeepers, small planters, the urban working classes, and the dispossessed African American freedmen and slaves. The strategic use of camp meetings and revivals and the canvasing of territories by itinerant preachers and circuit riders who conducted class meetings and love feasts brought Wesleyan teachings to the masses (Wigger 1998: 5). Stressing the importance of an experimental and practical divinity and the centrality of direct religious experiences, believers assumed an ascetic ethic of work, self-control, and individual responsibility. They acknowledged their depravity and need for repentance, and could, through the doctrine of prevenient grace, actively choose to accept grace and eternal salvation. John H. Wigger in *Taking Heaven by Storm* describes this as a "boiling hot religion" that encouraged laymen and women to preach and exhort, sharing with small congregations their powerful testimonies of conversion and urging others to strive toward holiness. Not infrequently, exhorters testified about their experiences of religious ecstasy—prophetic dreams, visions, supernatural events, and healing. Wigger explains the immediacy and communication with God. Methodism "offers a more interactive faith in which the believer and God actively work together to meet life's daily challenge and in which God communicates directly with the believer or community of believers" (Wigger 1998: 110).

The interracial revivals in Virginia and the Middle Atlantic from the 1770s through the early 1800s witnessed the origins of "Shouting Methodists" that combined the importance of preaching the Word with West African influences of spirit possession, the circular dance, polyrhythmic percussion, repetitive singing, call-and-response testimonials, and hand clapping. Mourners "slain by the Spirit" and stricken with a sense of sin, fell to the ground, weeping and shouting for joy as they encountered the ecstatic infusion of grace and proclaimed themselves the New Israelites of Zion (Taves 1999: 68; Rosenbaum 1998: 68; Raboteau 2004: 72–73). The Bethel African Methodist Episcopal Church, founded in 1794 in Philadelphia, crystallized this religiosity of mourners and shouters into the "ring shout" that came to characterize African American Methodism and Pentecostalism. Methodist and Baptist groups effectively evangelized people of color and formed the central institution in African communities both slave and free throughout the nineteenth century (Harvey 2011: 6).

The religious experiences of Jarena Lee (1783–?) illustrate the power of dreams, visions, and ecstatic raptures for African Americans. As a teenager, she came under the charismatic influence of Reverend Richard Allen of Bethel, and after many trials by Satan, found repentance and early conversion. However, Jarena struggled for four years with doubt and religious melancholy bordering on despair. In the midst of this travail, she heard a voice commanding her to ask for sanctification—the final stage of a spiritual quest for holiness and perfection. She exclaimed in her memoirs: "A new rush of the same ecstasy came upon me, and caused me to fall as if I were in an ocean of light and bliss" (Andrews 1986: 34). Jarena devoted her life to work as an exhorter and later Methodist preacher. Zilpha Elaw (c. 1790–?) reports a similar experience of sanctification during a camp meeting in 1817. She fell to the ground and reported this out-of-body trance: "My spirit seemed to ascend up into the clear circle of the sun's disc; and surround and [sic] engulphed in the glorious effulgence of his rays, I distinctly heard a voice speak unto me, which said, 'Now thou are sanctified; and I will show thee what thou must do'" (Andrews 1986: 66).

W. E. B. Du Bois, the distinguished African American sociologist, writing in 1903 in *The Souls of Black Folks*, captured the religious melancholy of the "sorrow song" spirituals of enslaved souls who long to escape despair in the triumph of divine love and salvation.

FIGURE 2.2: Jarena Lee.

FIGURE 2.3: Religious Dancing of the Blacks Termed Shouting.

He described the evangelical and revival tradition of Black spirituality, "the frenzy of Shouting" when the "Spirit of the Lord passed by, and seizing the devotee, made him mad with supernatural joy . . . the stomping, shrieking and shouting, the rushing to and fro and wild waving of arms, the whooping and laughing, the visions and the trance" (Du Bois 2007: 121–127, 91).

Despite the promise of salvation and sanctification for the prepared heart that actively chose to accept the gift of grace through the Spirit, not infrequently, Methodists succumbed to self-accusations of blasphemy, grieving the Holy Spirit, committing the unpardonable sin, and sinning away any hope of salvation. Like Jarena Lee, thousands of participants in camp meetings and revivals succumbed to religious melancholy and protracted spiritual crises. In my study of the first twenty years of operation of The Hartford Retreat in Connecticut from 1822–1843, I discovered that approximately 20 percent of all admissions were diagnosed with religious melancholy/mania, with many patients being admitted directly from protracted and camp meetings and participation in revivals in New England (Rubin 1979). The diagnosis of religious insanity was the most frequently used category in America in the nineteenth century (Bainbridge 1984: 224).

Phoebe Palmer remarked how seekers languished for months and even years. "They feel that their convictions were not deep enough to warrant an approach to the throne of grace, with the confident expectation of receiving the blessing now" (Palmer 1998: 167). She inquired, "is there a shorter way?" and with the assistance of others, founded the Holiness movement to remedy this proclivity with religious melancholy by emphasizing an inner-worldly mysticism, a self-abnegation where the heart was emptied of the self. After decades of personal tragedy and spiritual adversity, she attained an inward sense of holiness, sanctification, and perfect love founded upon the blood of Jesus (Palmer 1998, 175–179). Writing in *The Way of Holiness*, the Altar Covenant on July 27, 1837, Palmer testifies: "The Lord reigns unrivaled in my heart; he has my supreme affections . . . I WILL be holy NOW" (Palmer 1998: 115–118). Offering herself to God on the altar of faith, "her very existence seemed lost and swallowed up in God; she plunged, as it were, into an immeasurable ocean of love, light, and power" (Taves 1999: 149). In this manner, varieties of Methodist evangelical pietism placed a premium upon the ecstatic union with God (*unio mystica*) that directed the faithful in their quest for conversion and the seal of grace.

The late nineteenth century witnessed the continuation of the Holiness movement among Methodists, the emergence of "Holy Roller" sects, radical evangelicals who promoted Holy Ghost Baptism, divine healing, the Fire-Baptized Holiness Church, and later the rise of Pentecostal denominations like the Assemblies of God and the Church of God in Christ. The ideal was to emulate the primitivism of the Apostolic church with a longing for the immediacy and inner-worldly mysticism of the divine through a "third blessing"—following justification and sanctification with the baptism of the Holy Spirit evidenced by speaking in tongues and religious ecstasy (Wacker 2001: 43). Influenced by the teachings of Reverend Charles F. Parham, William J. Seymour, an African American itinerant preacher, prosecuted the Azusa Street mission and revival from 1906–1909 in Los Angeles as thousands of African Americans, whites, Asians, Latinos, and Native Americans participated in what would be known as the American Jerusalem, the beginnings of a national movement that found its greatest strength in the deep south. In the throes of religious ecstasy and mystical transport, "men and women would shout, weep, dance, fall into trances, sing and speak in tongues, and interpret their messages into English" (Synan 1997: 98).

A TYPOLOGY OF PROTESTANT IDENTITY AND RELIGIOUS EXPERIENCE: SELECTED CASE HISTORIES IN ANTEBELLUM AMERICA

Our understanding of individual case histories of religious experiences and emotions of melancholy and ecstasy is aided by a brief discussion of the organization of Protestant temperament and religious personhood in the antebellum period. Richard Rabinowitz's *The Spiritual Self in Everyday Life* identifies three types of Protestant identity: the doctrinalist, the moralist, and the devotionalist. Doctrinalists were orthodox, consistent Calvinists who emphasized the intellect in seeking to understand their place in the divine order, who accepted their innate depravity and inability and longed for a stillness in submission to God. Their conversion narratives eschewed extremes of religious affections. Moralists emphasized an evangelical Arminian dimension of the self-determining will to choose for God and salvation and the active ascetic mastery of self and world through obedience to God's laws and acts of benevolence. Devotionalists made the inner-worldly mysticism of evangelical Pietism the distinguishing mark of religious experience by promoting an intensely emotional, loving, sentimental relationship with God personified as Jesus (Rabinowitz 1989: 49–50, 94, 184). As the case of Martha Laurens that is presented below reveals:

> in the lives of evangelicals in the first half of the nineteenth century, men and women mixed and balanced these various streams of religious experience, shaping the praxis of religion that juxtaposed the seemingly contradictory elements of doctrine, asceticism, and mysticism. In the same conversion narrative one finds the torturous, emotionally harrowing struggle to submit to a sovereign deity (Doctrinalism), the risky venture of making the behavioral self solely responsible to choose holiness, conversion, and Christian activism (Moralism), and the inner search for intimacy and communion with a personal God as the warrant of grace in the heart (Devotionalism).
>
> —Rubin 1994: 127

Martha Laurens (1759–1811) was born to an elite family in Charleston, South Carolina and enjoyed a privileged upbringing and education in French, Latin, literature, and mathematics. In 1770 at age 11, her mother died of puerperal fever; and a year later, her father and siblings left for England. Martha was cared for by a paternal aunt and uncle. At age 14 she became a communicant at Saint Philip's Anglican Church. She wrote "Religious Exercises" and "A Self Dedication and Solemn Covenant with God," which reflected the influence of the English Pietist, Philip Doddridge, *The Rise and Progress of Religion of the Soul*. Absent of a crisis of conversion, Martha found an easy, genteel assurance of salvation (Gillespie 1991: 72–74). She writes this covenant:

> Use me, Oh Lord, I beseech thee, as the instrument of thy glory, and honour me so far, as with doing or suffering that thou shalt appoint, to bring some revenue of praise to thee.... Wash me in the blood of thy dear Son, clothe me with his perfect righteousness and sanctify me throughout by the power of thy Spirit.
>
> —Ramsay 1811: 81

Martha rejoined her father in England in 1775, where they would reside until the family returned to South Carolina after the Revolution in 1785. She married Dr. David Ramsay in 1787. He was twice widowed and ten years her senior. In the first sixteen years of marriage, motivated by the values of "republican motherhood" and pronatalism, she would bear him eleven children, of which eight would survive. Joanna Bowen Gillespie argues: "Martha and David agreed on many things, including grand ambitions about the number of children their union should produce for the new republic. He joked that they would probably never reach the record of twenty-three living offspring achieved by one backcountry family, and she took unabashed pride in being pregnant" (Gillsepie 1991: 77).

During her married life she kept a diary and personal papers that recorded her spiritual trials and attainments, covenant renewals, religious exercises, and affections. Before her death at age 52, her husband explains in the introduction to her memoirs that he published six months after her death: "she then announced the drawer in which they were deposited, and at the same time requested that after they were read they might be kept as a common book for the family or divided among its members" (Ramsay 1811: 2). Martha's published memoir served as a public and enduring document, part of the growing religious intelligence of the diaries of missionaries and evangelical women and an exemplar of the lived experience of those committed to the emerging American Synthesis of evangelical religion, republican ideals, and Scottish moralism (Noll 2002). And Martha's life provides a cautionary tale of a family under severe economic distress and the burdens of maternal depletion from childbearing. It is against this backdrop that we understand her spiritual journey and religious affections.

Martha suffered two episodes of religious melancholy, the first during the summer and fall of 1791 and the second during an eleven-month period extending from 1795–1796. She reveals in her diary entries the methodical practice of self-examination, looking inward for evidence of sanctification and or sin. Writing on July 16, 1791, Martha reports her self-loathing for spiritual pride, an unbroken heart that was the source of an unending obsession that she terms "my easily besetting sin" (Ramsay 1811: 139). Mourning the death of her third child, the family's deteriorating financial situation, and the burdens of republican motherhood, she considered these worldly afflictions as a special chastisement from God. The diary records this lament on July 20: "O day, blackened by sin and spotted by transgression! How long, O Lord! How long; when shall I advance in the spiritual life, and not thus wound my peace and disgrace my profession" (Ramsay 1811: 129–130). Despair and hopelessness marked the diary entries:

> Truly, the pressure of guilt is upon me, and I feel astonished that my bed has not been made in Hell. O Wretched me! When shall I be delivered from the body of this death and from the power of this sin. Oh, how it cleaves me, how it besets me, how it conquers me and leave me almost in the depths of despair. . . . Oh! vilest and most complicated of sinners that I am! Terror and dismay take hold of me. O if men knew me as I am known to God, I should be trampled under foot, the church would disown me; the greatest sinners would abominate me.
>
> —Ramsay 1811: 143

During her early thirties, Martha's spiritual trials coincided with making the transition to womanhood: marriage, motherhood, and the burdens of true womanhood; religious conversion and the struggle to achieve a deepening piety and relationship with God and the traumatic death of her infant son in 1790. Martha Tomhave Blauvelt argues, in *The Work of the Heart*, that the passage to adulthood in the period 1780–1830 necessitated reconstructing the heart as women negotiated the demands of multiple emotional communities that included family and extended kin, and church and residential communities

(Blauvelt 2007: 147). For women in this era, parenting and child rearing became an increasingly maternal concern as mothers shaped the religious and civil character of their children and thus helped instill republican virtues for the next generation of Americans. "Convinced that the stability of the new republic depended on a virtuous citizenry, the post-revolutionary generation called for more intensive styles of childrearing and more prolonged and systematic forms of education. Primary responsibility for instilling republican virtues in childhood rested with mothers, who required better education to meet this high responsibility" (Mintz 2004: 54). Not infrequently, wives and mothers expressed deep anxiety and concern about their ability to meet the increasing cultural and familial demands of true womanhood—piety, purity, and domesticity (Degler 1980: 52–55).

The experience of religious melancholy proved indispensable to the spiritual attainments so cherished by this generation of American women. Like Martha Laurens Ramsay, Sarah Connell Ayer struggled with the burdens of marriage and motherhood, losing her first four children in their infancy. She was filled with anxiety and dread over the burdens of motherhood and the heightened cultural expectations of shaping the moral character of her family and husband. She converted in May 1811, in Concord, Massachusetts, assisted by the Reverend McFarland consistent with the orthodox Calvinist doctrine of human depravity and the reliance upon the mercy and grace of the savior to redeem believers. However, Sarah's emotional and spiritual itinerary later embraced the heart work of devotionalism when she came under the influence of Reverend Edward Payson of the Congregational Church in Portland, Maine. She had long abandoned the culture of genteel sensibility and self-acceptance exemplified by novel reading and attachment to luxury and worldliness that shaped her youth at the Litchfield Female Academy in Connecticut. Now, Sarah strived to wean herself from attachment to this world and become sensible only to God by adopting forms of evangelical humiliation. Here the penitent employed self-examination to uncover evidence of sin that produced feelings of guilt and self-hatred (Blauvelt 2007: 167–175). Through the cultivation of religious melancholy, the penitent sought to vanquish the carnal self and achieve a selfless, ecstatic surrender to Jesus, a heart ravished by the Holy Spirit. Here religious melancholy was preparatory to the experience of joy and acceptance as a child of God.

Martha Laurens Ramsay, like Sarah Connell Ayer, would make a spiritual pilgrimage from religious melancholy to devotionalism during a protracted emotional crisis in 1795. One commentator writes: "To all outward appearances, Martha had everything conducive to contentment: the heritage of a respected name, a growing bevy of promising children, a fond husband who was a leader in civic affairs, and a secure place in Charleston society" (Gillespie 1991: 78). However, Martha suffered numerous afflictions. Her husband David was a ne'er do well who failed to earn a living as a physician, author, or statesman. Martha considered him an "unpolished jem," lacking in piety and social graces. He invested, and lost, in a bankrupt canal venture, the $25,000 dowry and inheritance that Martha brought to the marriage. He owned unproductive farmlands that were a tax liability. He mortgaged their town house and the family lived in straitened circumstances. She reports a heart "bursting with grief" from domestic travails that were compounded by the scandalous elopement of her niece (Gillespie 1991: 83–84).

Martha languished in religious melancholy, embracing a self-imposed regimen of evangelical humiliation that included self-examination, meditation and prayer. However, spiritual assurance eluded her as she succumbed to the slough of despair over her easily besetting sin of spiritual pride and attachment to worldliness. She wrote at the beginning of her crisis in June, 1795: "Wo is me, for fear I have sinned away God's mercy, and am fearful about the manifestation of his power.... I can no longer say the skies are darkening for they are so darkened that I see no light; and I am ready to call my self desolate, forsaken, cast off by God" (Ramsay 1811: 162–163).

Consistent with the logic of religious melancholy, Martha reflected that "the Christian life is a warfare" against extravagance, self-indulgence and the proclivity to sin (Ramsay 1811: 168). In the course of her warfare, Martha found consolation and spiritual direction in *Keeping the Heart* by John Flavel, who prescribed heart-work that included a single-minded devotion to God through the practice of daily piety that augured a renewed communion with God. He advises "the diligent and constant use and improvement of all holy means and duties to preserve the soul from sin, and maintain its sweet and free communion with God" (Flavel, n.d.: 18).

During the summer and fall of 1795, Martha alternated between hope and despair, praying for release from her besetting sin, for the conversion of a friend and for the preservation of her husband in the management of his secular affairs. The diary entry for July 31 reflects her struggles:

> My soul is exceedingly sorrowful and weary because of sin.... I hope that through grace I had walked more carefully, more warily of late, and trusted that, at this season of solemnities, I should be enabled to praise God, for having made a better progress in religion, but alas, within a few days I have fallen off, ceased to resist with vigor the assaults of my easily besetting sin; my soul is full of trouble and darkness.
>
> —Ramsay 1811: 189

Nearly a year of spiritual crisis reached a successful resolution as Martha records the death of her carnal self and the ecstatic surrender and devotion to Jesus, a profound moment of healing that she experienced on January 3, 1796 on Sabbath while partaking of Communion. She offers this account of devotionalism:

> On Sabbath morning, my soul panted after God; and after conformity to him with inexpressible desire; and thus I went to the sanctuary, and there Jesus made himself indeed known unto me in the breaking of the bread.... I felt such an annihilation of self, such a swallowing up of my will in the will of God, that my soul lay, as it were, prostrate at the foot of the cross. It lay meekly and sweetly at the feet of Jesus, saying, Lord, not my will but thine be done.
>
> —Ramsay 1811: 190

These cases of evangelical spiritual pilgrimage mix doctrinal and devotionalist tropes with episodes of religious melancholy punctuated by times of assurance and inner-worldly mystical rapture and ecstasy as the seal of grace. The next example illustrates a more staid, methodical moralism.

The Memoir of Harlan Page was written by William Allen Hallock and published in 1835 by the American Tract Society as a model for making a Christian life. Page (1791–1834) came from modest circumstances, received a "common education," and worked as a joiner and mechanic in the growing factory towns of eastern Connecticut. He spent the last decade of his life employed by the American Tract Society (ATS) in New York City.

He is memorialized by a portrait and published biography that reprinted his many pastoral letters and unrelenting spiritual direction to friends, family, and the urban working classes that he encountered, exhorting them to greater piety, devotion, and conversion. Although he left a wife and four children at the time of his death, he

FIGURE 2.4: Possibly Harlan Page. Courtesy of National Gallery of Art, Washington.

periodically traveled as a domestic missionary, conducting religious meetings, worship services, and Sunday School at the boarding house where he resided or factory floor where he toiled. His diary recounts a life marked by chronic illness and a spiritual pilgrimage alternating seasons of evangelical humiliation and religious melancholy with moments of reassurance. He is cast as a non-denominational "everyman" who made a public profession of faith in 1814, selflessly devoted his life to God's work and piety, marked by seasons of religious melancholy. He writes in June, 1817: "Long have I neglected to record my religious exercises. . . . I have forgotten my Saviour" (Hallock 1835: 41). Page explains his evangelical humiliation on February 1819: "This day I have endeavoured to observe a day of humiliation, fasting, and prayer for the outpouring of the Spirit. I find so much in me that is unhumbled, that I have reason to fear the day has been spent in vain" (Hallock 1835: 65). However, he would frequently record times of joyful assurance: "Never before have I so sensibly felt the presence of the Spirit, or the force of those words, 'stand still and see the salvation of the Lord'" (Hallock 1835: 149).

The memoir provides a model of exemplary dying: deathbed exhortations to friends, holy self-denial, the practice of piety in psalm singing and scripture reading, and an abiding sense of the love to Christ. He could state as the Saint's everlasting rest, the final words that complete his journey from doubt to hope and assurance: "What I want now is a sense of the presence of Christ; and I think he is with me, and sustains me" (Hallock 1835: 224).

The spiritual biographies of exemplary believers like Ramsay and Page provided models of and models for making an authentic Christian life that elucidated the emotion rules and inward experiences of piety (Geertz 1973: 90). These works, together with countless other tracts, devotional literature, and pastoral theology and book-length memoirs of missionaries and epigones of conversion and godly living, forged an unending chain of religious intelligence that reached a national and international audience. During the first three decades of the nineteenth century, the rise of literacy, the market revolution, the new technologies of publishing, and the efforts of national, not-for-profit publishing societies, America entered an era of mass media publication and the systematic distribution of printed material (Nord 2004: 5–9). During the 1820s to 1830s the American Bible Society, the American Tract Society (ATS), and the American Sunday School Union pursued the goals of distributing bibles and religious literature to the newly settled regions of the south and west, motivated by the millennial idea that books and the printed word would foster conversion and the Kingdom of God in America. Page worked for and was memorialized by the ATS, founded in New York in 1825 as a nondenominational outreach of Congregational and Presbyterian supporters, who created by 1841 a national distribution system of salaried *colporteurs* who by the 1850s had visited more than 2 million homes and sold or gave away 2.4 million books (Nord 2004: 86). The ATS published inexpensive editions of "evangelical classics": Jonathan Edwards, *Treatise Concerning Religious Affections* and *The Life of Brainerd*, Richard Baxter, *The Call to the Unconverted*, John Bunyan, *The Pilgrim's Progress*, Philip Doddridge, *The Rise and Progress of Religion of the Soul*, and John Flavel, *Touchstone of Sincerity* (Nord 2004: 114). Mass media publications aided by the growth of literacy, especially among women, fostered a growing national understanding about spirituality, making a godly life, and experiencing authentic religious emotions.

THE BUSINESSMAN'S REVIVAL AND EVANGELICAL RELIGION IN THE CIVIL WAR

The Businessman's Revival in the fall and winter of 1857–1858 in Boston occurred during a season marked by brutally cold weather, shortages of food, a credit crisis, and financial panic. The economic crisis dramatized a perceived decline in social order given the precipitous population growth, the expansion of poverty in the Sixth Ward, growing inequality, crime, political corruption, and vice (Corrigan 2002: 48–52). Led by Charles Grandison Finney in December of 1857, businessmen, sailors, merchants, clerks, and apprentices, together with young women and matrons, prayed each noon and evening in chapels, churches, theaters, homes, and outdoors in the spring. As John Corrigan argues in *Business of the Heart*, "The religious revival that broke out on the heels of the crash developed in conformity with a century of thinking about revival that balanced the wish for a mass stirring of affections against the hope that such a movement could be disciplined" (Corrigan 2002: 80). Through petitionary prayer, emotion became a public performance of masculinity, an objectification of feeling, and a contract that petitioned God. By giving up one's heart to God, through utterances that demonstrated courage by tears of repentance, participants engaged in pleading and weeping and promised morally upright conduct in exchange for divine favor (Corrigan 2002: 207, 221). Religious affections were expressed through the idioms of moralism and an effusive devotionalism.

The religious emotions and experiences associated with evangelical religion pervaded the diaries and letters of soldiers who fought in the Civil War. An estimated 10 to 25 percent of the Union army and one third of the Confederate forces identified as Christian soldiers (Rable 2010: 127). They participated in revivals and camp meetings during the protracted military campaigns and viewed personal salvation as essential to preparing for a good death, assured of reunion with loved ones in heaven (Woodworth 2001: 40–48). Death was ubiquitous as soldiers died in accidents, from epidemic illnesses, and in battles where the godly and ungodly lost their lives in disordered chaos. Soldiers feared dying without the hope of salvation, without having resigned themselves to providence and divine will (Rable 2010: 167). Drew Gilpin Faust in *This Republic of Suffering* writes: "Their Victorian and Christian culture offered them the resources with which to salve these deep spiritual wounds. Ideas and beliefs worked to assuage, even to overcome the physical devastation of battle" (Faust 2008: 81). Chaplains recorded the seemingly formulaic accounts of the gravely wounded and dying soldiers who reported the presence of the Lord and the assurance of the infusion of saving grace (Rable 2010: 171). A Confederate soldier who believed that he was dying recorded these religious emotions:

> "Immediately there came over my soul such a burst of the glories of heaven, such a foretaste of its joys as I have never before experienced. It was rapturous and ecstatic beyond expression. The new Jerusalem seemed to rise up before me in all its beauty and attractiveness.... My all-absorbing thought, however was about the Divine Redeemer, whose arms were stretched out to receive me. So completely overwhelming and exclusive was the thought of heaven, that I was wholly unconscious of any tie that bound me to the earth."
>
> —Woodworth 2001: 195

"NATURE RELIGION," MIND-CURE, AND THE SECULARIZATION OF SPIRITUALITY

Religious experience, emotions, and spirituality also flourished in America in secular, non-institutional settings that were not tied to Protestant denominations. Through a seemingly inexhaustible variety of folk religion and popular religion, in Transcendentalism, healing cults like Mesmerism, the water cure, Grahamism, and Spiritualism, people sought answers to the vexing existential questions of bodily and mental suffering. Catherine L. Albanese argues in *Nature Religion in America* that believers encountered the divine and the numinous in nature, which served as a model of cosmic and social harmony. By bringing the mind and body into balance with the pre-established harmony in nature, nature religion promised a this-worldly salvation through self-mastery and control and freedom from suffering (Albanese 1990: 9). John Muir (1838–1914), who helped establish Yosemite National Park and the Sierra Club as a champion of wilderness preservation, likened the "wilderness experience" to conversion, finding a mystical unity, an ecstatic rapture with "King Sequoia." He writes: "I'm in the woods, & they are in me-ee-ee. The King tree & me have sworn eternal love ... & I've taken the sacrament with Douglass Sqiurrell drank Sequoia wine, Sequoia blood, & with its rosy purple drops I am writing this woody gospel letter" (Albanese 1990: 100).

William James examines nature religion in *The Varieties of Religious Experience* in a chapter devoted to the religion of healthy-mindedness. The once-born conceived of God as kind and benevolent, as an animating spirit of a beautiful, harmonious world (James 1961: 80). James termed this "mind cure" or New Thought that relied upon Transcendentalism, Berkeleyan idealism, evolutionary ideas of progress, and Hinduism. He explains the contributions of Phineas Parkhurst Quimby or Mary Baker Eddy's *Science and Health* (1875) and Christian Science by arguing:

the leaders in this faith have had an intuitive belief in the all-saving power of healthy-minded attitudes as such, in the conquering efficacy of courage, hope and trust, and a correlative contempt for doubt, fear, worry, and all nervously precautionary states of mind. Their belief has in a general way been corroborated by the practical experience of their disciples; and this experience forms to-day a mass imposing in amount.

—James 1961: 90

James provided numerous detailed case histories of those treated by mind cure. One married woman who seemed to suffer from a combination of spiritual crisis, psychological depression, and bodily disorders, consistent with the diagnosis in the 1870s of neurasthenia and invalidism, recounted her spiritual passage from illness through a mystical union and cure:

I cannot express it in any other way than to say that I did "lie down in the stream of life and let it flow over me." I gave up all fear of any impending disease; I was perfectly willing and obedient. . . . The creative life was flowing into me every instant, and I felt myself allied with the Infinite, in harmony, and full of the peace that passeth understanding. There was no place in my mind for a jarring body, I had no consciousness of time or space or persons; but only of love and happiness and faith. I do not know how long this state lasted, nor when I fell asleep; but when I woke up in the morning, I was well.

—James 1961: 109

Like the secular mind-cure movement, numerous healing cults known as faith healing arose in the late nineteenth and early twentieth century that were associated with the Holiness movement, perfectionism, and homeopathic medicine such as the one championed by Charles Cullis of the Boston Faith Work in the 1880s. In addition to weekly prayer meetings for the sick, Cullis established annual summer Faith Conventions in New England that resembled holiness camp meetings (Cunningham 1993: 4). While faith cure did not attract a mass following, it did create controversy by attributing cures to the miraculous intercession of Jesus and found resistance from physicians who doubted that organic disease could be cured through prayer. The movement attracted sufferers who sought relief when medicine and religion failed them. James Buckley, writing in the *Christian Advocate*, identified the access to the supernatural and the rapturous, ecstatic experiences of believers afflicted with diseases of the nervous system. He explained, "it is not improbable that a certain exaltation and intense exercise of faith and the religious faculties generally have contributed largely to the effects which have been produced, and which are so confidently ascribed to supernatural or special divine interposition" (Buckley 1883: 343).

The Emmanuel Movement, begun by Reverend Dr. Elwood Worcester of the Emmanuel Episcopal Church in Boston, brought together the strains of New Thought, psychotherapy, medicine, and the concept of the "healing ministry of Jesus" in Social Gospel outreach to slums, settlement houses, and the urban immigrant poor. Allied with Reverend Samuel McComb, the movement served those afflicted with tuberculosis and later alcoholism. By 1909, the movement had spread to Brooklyn, Buffalo, Detroit, Philadelphia, Baltimore, and Seattle as Worcester effectively publicized his ideas in five articles in 1908 in the *Ladies Home Journal*. Dr. Cabot, a physician working at Massachusetts General Hospital, reported that the alliance with medicine and auto-suggestion was successful in providing a medically informed religious pastoral care, "in assisting a large body of sad, dispirited men and women to face the problems of life and bear their burdens more cheerfully, in consoling the distressed, in guiding the doubtful, in counseling the despondent and in deterring persons meditating suicide from the accomplishment of this purpose" (Green 1934: 514). Reverend Lyman P. Powell of St. John's Church, Northampton, Massachusetts published *The Emmanuel Movement in a New England Town*, recounting his work in the church clinic treating those with depression, neurasthenia, religious melancholy, and "psychasthenia"—obsessional and anxiety disorders. Explaining that Northampton was a college town of predominately female students numbering 20,000 inhabitants, he treated 105 patients in 1907. Seating them in a comfortable Morris chair before the fireplace in his study, Powell instructed these sufferers in relaxation techniques, becoming one with God, the power of prayer, and positive thinking (Powell 1909: 35, 74–75).

The religious experiences, emotions, and spirituality associated with melancholy and ecstasy have provided the interpretive and heuristic constructs to understand American religiosity from the Revolution to the first decades of the twentieth century. During this 140-year period, America was predominately a Protestant culture area dominated by varieties of evangelical religion, secular healing cults, and Nature religion. The limitations of this chapter have precluded detailed and comprehensive considerations of Protestant evangelical culture. Excluded are considerations of Catholicism, urban immigrant religion, Judaism, and the panoply of spirituality and piety in the utopian and communitarian movements, small sects, Mormonism, and the seemingly innumerable forms of religious association. Nevertheless, the spectrum of melancholy and ecstasy characterized American religiosity and provides useful concepts for future research and to explore the groups not examined in this chapter. Wherever believers sought conversion, relief from mental or bodily suffering, the path to salvation from the travails of this world and the promise of heaven, they encountered religious melancholy and religious ecstasy on their spiritual pilgrimage.

CHAPTER THREE

Music and Dance

WIEBKE THORMÄHLEN

> On the one hand it is said that the *aim* and *object* of music is to excite emotions – i.e., pleasurable emotions; on the other hand, the emotions are said to be the *subject-matter* which musical works are intended to illustrate. Both propositions are alike in this, that one is as false as the other.
>
> —Hanslick ([1854] 1986: 17)

The story of the relationship of music to the emotions in the nineteenth century is best begun in the middle of the century, at the very moment when a dagger is pierced through the emotional heart of music, the rug pulled out from under the feet of those worshipping at the temple of music's ineffable expression, and the wool peeled from the eyes of the swooning concert goers. Eduard Hanslick's *Vom musikalisch Schönen* cut across long-held and celebrated assumptions about music's emotional content and purpose, and it earned the music critic and aesthetician a barrage of insults, articulated not least in one of music history's most pertinent musical caricatures, the figure of Sixtus Beckmesser, town clerk of Nürnberg in Richard Wagner's opera *Die Meistersinger von Nürnberg*, first performed in 1868. Beckmesser, the cantankerous guardian of the old rules for the construction of a master's song worthy of the name and the guild, is pitted against the young and impetuous, love-fueled knight, Walther von Stolzing. Both seek to woo Eva, the daughter of the town's goldsmith, yet their means of expressing their passion for her through music are diametrically opposed. Beckmesser's representational penchant for tradition, decorum, and most prominently strict rules is set against Walther's improvisatory, seemingly free-flowing expressions. Form is juxtaposed with inspiration, learning with true feeling, as Beckmesser marks each of Walther's mistakes on his marker's board in their first poignant encounter in Act I Scene II; a scene which clearly ridicules the idea that music's innermost expression could possibly be compressed into and assessed by the strictures and regulations of form.

Wagner engaged in what is perhaps the most profound and deliberate factionalization in music aesthetics in reading Hanslick's text as an attack on his own aims to stir the emotions through a music that sets its own rules and boundaries. Hanslick was making a point about the *aesthetic* assessment of music, and with that about the all-to-oft unquestioned relationship of beauty to the emotions. Wagner and Hanslick, pitted against each other in the annals of music history, were less distant than either of them would have admitted with regard to their assessment of a particular piece of music's power: Hanslick would not have refuted that Walther's song has a more profound effect on Eva and on Wagner's opera audience, and would therefore sway her—she who already loves Walther, not Beckmesser—further in her leanings towards Walther. Yet, if we transferred his theories into practice, Hanslick argued that the profundity of this effect would be determined less by the song's make-up than by its set-up within the opera as a whole. In other words, the song was constructed as an *interested* object and its affect was directly linked to this interest; works of art, however, according to Hanslick ought to be disinterested: "the beautiful, strictly speaking, *aims at nothing*, since it is nothing but a *form* which, though available for many purposes according to its *nature* has, as such, no aim beyond itself" (Hanslick [1854]1986: 18).

In writing his controversial treatise, Hanslick attempted to illuminate the inherent problems of the all-pervasive celebration of music as the language of the emotions, a celebration that during the nineteenth century took on the reverent qualities of a religious ceremony, in which audiences, critics, and composers alike worshipped music as an art religion. In a Kantian move that separated the aesthetic appreciation of the object from the judgment of the perceiving subject, Hanslick addressed—wrongly or rightly—both pre-Kantian and post-Kantian music aesthetics. In his view, the fact that "beauty in music is still as much as ever viewed only in connection with its subjective impressions, and books, critiques, and conversations continually remind us that *the emotions* are the only aesthetic foundation of music, and that they alone are warranted in defining its scope," obscured people's clear view of music as a form of art, replacing it instead with an existence as a cheap emotion-monger (Hanslick [1854]1986: 17). In contrast to Kant, who in his *Critique of Judgement* of 1795 had deemed music the lowest of the art forms, if an art at all, Hanslick held on to music's position as the highest form of art precisely by divorcing its value from the rather loose circumlocution of music as the "language of emotions."

The many formulations of music's relationship to the emotions developed, revered, dismissed, and discarded in the nineteenth century all centered around the question of language: was music a language of emotions; was music related to the emotions in other pre-linguistic or metaphysical ways, or was music perhaps emotion itself? These debates were conducted across disciplines as varied as aesthetics, education, historiography, physics, and psychology and were manifest in a variety of social and political discourses. Theorists, composers, performers, choreographers, music-lovers, philosophers, and those with political agendas across the nineteenth century and across Europe argued from the inside out and the outside in, establishing in the process the terms of reference that have pervaded the discussion on music until today. In one form or another music remained what it had been formulated as in the eighteenth century: a tool for education, yet both the understanding of emotions and the idea of education changed considerably over the course of the nineteenth century. Still, for all the differences in explication and explanation, the myriad theories all relied on one thing: via its relationship to the emotions, music was at once profoundly individual, focusing inward onto the mind and soul, yet also profoundly communal and universal, establishing an emotionology by which and through which groups and societies would identify and define themselves. This chapter touches on key debates and key moments in which the understanding of music's representational, narrative, expressive, or essential characteristics were framed and employed.

ART, MUSIC, EMOTION, AND MORAL EDUCATION

The description of music as the language of the emotions was coined in the late eighteenth century as music was reformulated from a mimetic to an expressive art (Neubauer 1986).

Since the departure from the belief in cosmic harmony in the later seventeenth century, music's relationship to the emotions had been the central tenet of discourse on music and dance (Gouk 1999; Clark and Rehding 2001). The relationship between a composer/performer (in the widest sense), the music as act or as text, and the audience/perceiver became central to the debate on music's powers to "move the passions" and to be expressive; music's relationship to the emotions, therefore, became synonymous with music's meaning. In a conflation of the moral, the good, and the beautiful rooted in the Enlightenment reception of the Ancient Greeks, art's purpose came to be defined by its ability to educate the moral and sociable senses, a job that was easier for the conceptual arts of literature and painting than it was for music.

"The primary purpose of the arts must reside in awakening a lively feeling for the beautiful and the good, and a strong repulsion towards the ugly and the evil," Sulzer declared in the preface to his *Allgemeine Theorie der schönen Künste* (Sulzer 1771, XIII). His grand tome to art indeed served no other purpose but to explore how the different arts could fulfill this primary social and political function of the education of one's moral sentiment and "societal virtues" (*gesellschaftliche Tugenden*) and to implant in the soul (*Gemüth*) "the feeling for moral order through the beautiful and the good" (Sulzer 1771, XII). This feeling was based on inner senses and manifest in physical reactions to art that were variously described as passions and affections, feelings, and eventually emotions. Music's powers were adumbrated through a variety of models in which music mimicked nature, mimicked the emotions in their manifold undulations, and represented these emotions. The purpose remained the same: music's powerful relationship to the emotions had to be steered, so that music—like the other arts—could aid in the education of the individual as a worthy member of a civil society. Yet, the overwhelming majority of theorists in the eighteenth century maintained that instrumental music was inferior to vocal music—a view that persisted till late in the century (Hosler 1981; Neubauer 1986). Robbed of words, instrumental music was seen to be either overly mimetic—as in those instances in which it imitated bird calls or thunder storms—or simply pleasant banter, yet not valuable for the important job of moral education. Wordless music seemed at best too ephemeral—here one minute, gone the next—and at worst it represented a dangerously unmonitored agitation of the body and the senses.

In fact, proclaiming music as the language of the emotions was one way of dealing with the potential dangers of music's visceral effects, caused variously by the acts of making music, receiving music, or dancing to music. The dichotomy between the physicality of music's effects on the one hand and its conceptualization on the other led some writers to describe the relationship of music to emotion in quasi-medical terms by focusing on the effects felt and manifest in the body and their relationship to the body's nerves and fibers; here, the emotions were still defined as material processes and sensory perceptions (Bound Alberti 2006). Others, like Jean-Jacques Rousseau, couched explanations in anthropological terms by focusing on the relationship between music and natural utterances. Choreographers, most prominently Jean-Georges Noverre, tied dance to pantomime defined as physical gesture ordered into a narrative, so as to channel music's visceral effect through a concomitant physical display (Dahms 2010). Pantomime communicated passions from the soul of the performer to the spectator's heart and therefore, like music, did not rely on cognition to stir the passions.

The question of music's precise relationship to its perceived stimulation entered a new phase in the early nineteenth century as the emotions themselves were re-conceptualized as essentially mental rather than physiological entities (Dixon 2003; Bound Alberti 2010).

Questions surrounding music's ability to inspire collective and unified emotions came to a head with the rise of instrumental music as its ineffable qualities led many to praise it as the highest of the arts. The formulation and justification of its effects, however, inevitably pulled at the understanding of music's ontology.

LISTENING TO MUSIC

Taking the passions as manifest in a person's physique as his starting point, Sulzer had rationalized the relationship of physical effects to musical parameters. He posited passions as absolute emotional states, which could be strategically induced in the listener by mimicking their natural sounds' effects on the body in music. Despite this mimetic understanding of music, Sulzer already conceded that "nature has established a direct connection between the ear and heart" (Sulzer, III, 421). He continued that "hearing is . . . the most effective sense for awakening the emotions," thereby giving new significance to listening and the listener. In this small move, Sulzer allowed the idea of music as *making* an impression to be replaced with music *being* an impression, thereby sowing the seed for the replacement of mimesis with expression.

Moving the sense of hearing center-stage paved the way for music's elevation beyond the limits of reason. Music's non-conceptual nature, its biggest disadvantage so far, now emerged as its biggest asset. Sounds, not words, were now "the universal and natural utterances and characteristics of life, and of its changes," explained Wilhelm Heinse in his novel *Hildegard von Hohenthal* published in 1795 in which he embedded the music theoretical thinking of the last fifty years into an unusually sensuous plot with a morally disreputable ending (Fuhrmann 2015). W.H. Wackenroder, in his *Phantasien über die Kunst für Freunde der Kunst* (1799), developed this notion by proclaiming that "between the individual, mathematical tonal relationships and the individual fibers of the human heart an inexplicable sympathy has revealed itself, through which the musical art has become a comprehensive and flexible mechanism of the portrayal of human emotions." The key word in his formulation was "inexplicable": music was now not lamentably but ideally beyond reason, rationality, and explanation. Wackenroder, along with other early Romantics such as Ludwig Tieck and E.T.A Hoffmann, presented a new way of accounting for music's effects in which textless, purely instrumental music was heralded as the highest not only among the musical arts but among all the arts. In Wackenroder's idea of a *Seelenlehre* (knowledge of the soul), art's value was transplanted from the conceptual to the unknowable, from that which is clearly defined and present to that which remains a mere *Ahnung* (premonition), as life itself could not ever be grasped by reason. *Ahnung* for the early Romantics was a supersensible notion—an emotion that was at once profoundly present and beyond one's reach.

Music's physiological impact—the mere sense perception—that was relegated to the status of a tool as meaning was now seen to reside in the supersensible realm. Music was divorced from earthly emotions and moved instead into a world of ideals (Evan Bonds 2009; Kennaway 2012). It was experienced with a new enthusiasm: the emotional state of the overwhelming, all-consuming feeling of the sublime. For the early Romantics, individual perception dictated the value of art, yet this perception superseded the mere sense perception to involve the inner sense of feeling. Both music and emotions were seen as dynamic processes and therein lay their analogy, yet music was no longer an expression of moments of emotion—fear, love, anger—but the whole soul and the whole "quality of our existence" (Hosler 1981).

Listening itself was now formulated in such a way that only proper listening would yield the higher truth that the new metaphysics of music promised. "I no longer hear then the feeling that dominates the piece, but my thoughts and fantasies are, so to speak, carried away by the waves of the song and often lose themselves in distant corners," Wackenroder explained (Wackenroder 1797). This intense listening focused on music's structural elements as through their contemplation the higher truth might reveal itself.

Aestheticians in Germany had begun to describe different modes of listening to music in the late eighteenth century, separating them into two main types: *attentive listening* was accompanied by reflection, while *natural listening* described an immediate, unthinking, involuntary, or even compulsive reaction to the sounds of music, which was mixed with wonder (Riley 2004). These ideas reflected contemporary compositional practices, as composers had begun to write music with the intention of engaging the listeners in two particular ways: one targeted an intellectual engagement with the music and was centered around building up and then playing with and defying conventions. It demanded a level of complexity in the music that stretched the listener's imagination and concentration. A different manner of writing brought forth music that could appeal to the sense of hearing as a physical process itself through melody, harmony, timbre and richness of tone, and tonality. While a symphony must inspire the first, dance music naturally inspired the second. Noverre and later the critic Francois Castil-Blaze built their ideology of dance as an art that conveys passions around this duality: dance music had to have accessible melodies and simple harmonies so as to accompany the temporal unfolding of a series of emotions, understood through aural and visual means. According to Sulzer, both modes of listening were valuable, if they stimulated the understanding, i.e. if they inspired cognitive processes to follow on from the initial sense perception; for the early Romantics, in contrast, only the intensity of the first could yield music's higher truth, now located beyond both the physical and the rational.

The resulting notion of silent, concentrated listening has been much discussed in relation to the emergence of a new concert culture: audiences were silenced into reverent attention and contemplation as they were expected to engage in acts of aural exegesis of great works of art (Evan Bonds 2009; J. Johnson 1995). Listening experiences were described with reference to the aesthetic terms of the sublime, the beautiful, and the "pleasurable." The sublime experience assumed a quasi-religious status, framed as a moment of revelation in the act of listening. In a paradigm shift that stretched beyond music to a wider understanding of the location and formulation of subjectivity and, with it, creativity, in German aesthetic writings the sublime musical experience was elevated beyond all others (Evan Bonds 1997). Further, through this act of listening, divorced from the individuality of the physiological experience, emotional communities were formed. As audiences sat in reverent silence the concert hall began to function like the church and the experience of listening to music was couched into language borrowed from the emotions associated with religious enthusiasm (Wackenroder 1797). The "religion of music" was based on a willing adoption of the listening practices that might yield such enthusiasm, together with a desire to become part of the emotional community which exercised this religion.

Impresarios, composers, and performers alike embraced this ideology. In London, for instance, the Italian opera had been the prominent musical entertainment for the upper classes for a century, yet its aims and objectives were viewed critically under the influence of recent German music aesthetics. In 1813, the Philharmonic Society was formed with the purpose to further attentive listening (Elkin 1947). Those wishing to partake in the project had to listen and behave in certain ways in order to do justice to the music, and they had to attend to the task with a particular state of mind. Described as "the highest class" of music, reports of the Society's concerts time and again stressed that their choice of music demanded "exertion," "nourishment," and "support." In fact, the whole enterprise was one of deep involvement—organizational and emotional—yet also one of exclusivity.

The idea of attentive listening and the exclusive binding of social groups through and in this act of engaging with music remained pervasive across the nineteenth century. John Ella's founding of the Musical Union in 1845, an elite series of chamber music concerts, pandered as much to the ideology of attentive listening as did George Grove's endeavors at the Crystal Palace Concerts in the second half of the century even though they were aimed at widely different audiences (Bashford 1999; Bower 2016). The ability to listen actively was trained as much as the correct sensibility for the music itself was educated in written discourse. Emotional investment was coupled with detailed study, thereby enhancing the emotional experience of the concert through the initiation into the music's rites: Ella expected his listeners to read his illustrated, analytical program notes before listening to the music and he encouraged the listener to experience the music through the ears and the eyes at once, as the latter wandered along the printed miniature score of the work.

Grove adopted a similar format for his analytical concert programs but he also included references to the type of social community and its self-understanding that the listener entered into emotionally by partaking of the concerts in this serious manner. Here, a particular aesthetic comprehension was mapped onto social, political, and gender identity and was enshrined through the emotions.

The idea of a community united in the religion of the musical art was perpetuated in specialist journals—The *Harmonicon* and the *Quarterly Musical Magazine and Review* in England, the *Allgemeine Musikalische Zeitung* and the *Neue Zeitschrift für Musik* among

FIGURE 3.1: Musical Union. Photo by Hulton Archive/Illustrated London News (27 June 1846)/Getty Images.

others in Germany, and the *Revue Musicale* in France—in a variety of printed scores designed for the large amateur market and produced in a format that could fit easily into one's pocket to be taken along and perused at any time, and in the emerging composer biographies and collected editions. In this print culture, the musical work was celebrated, and through this conscious building of a musical canon a community of listeners was built along which society could be stratified. This danger was acerbated by the internalization of values which the printed material allowed as each individual could immerse him- or herself in the intimacy and interiority of the ideas of the musical art, indulging at once in the affective world of the music and in his or her own sentimental attachment to the higher truth promised therein.

MUSIC ANALYSIS

The emotionology of art music, then, was conducted across various disciplines, which emanated largely from the turn to musical form in an attempt to rationalize the ideas of *Geist* and interiority. The perceived powers of the *Geist* were sublimated into the printed medium, which would awaken and kindle the true emotions that resided in the imagination, not in any physical experience of music. E.T.A. Hoffmann, in his analysis of Beethoven's Fifth Symphony, had enshrined music's ability to carry expression through a belief in the inherent expressiveness of music's material components, independent of words and circumstance (Hoffmann 1810). Hoffmann's review presented a substantial exegesis including music examples, occupying twenty-one columns of the *Allgemeine musikalische Zeitung*, but his writing like that of Wackenroder remained mostly discursive, rather than analytical. Some sought to digest the musical works of the past and those of the present that had been deemed greatly effective—Beethoven's first and foremost, but also Mozart's, Haydn's, Handel's, and Palestrina's—seeking the key to music's power in their form parameters. The new discipline of music analysis was born out of the desire to receive the truth and the emotion through a deep contemplation of the musical form, a contemplation and exegesis that moved from the quasi-religious tone of the early Romantics to the ultra-scientific; music analysis emerged as a prominent voice in determining music's emotional powers in a series of treatises that were no longer written as composition treatises—so as to codify for composers how to construct a musical narrative intra-textually—but as treatises for the proper reception and understanding of musical meaning, aimed at educating the listener into the sacred realms of perceiving the high art of music (Christensen 2006).

In writing his *Versuch einer Anleitung zur Composition* (1782–93), Heinrich Christoph Koch had already veered away from traditional compositional treatises by including a series of musical analyses which were designed as models for the relationship between form and content, between a piece of music's construction and its expressive effects. The Czech-born Viennese resident Anton Reicha in his *Treatise on Melody* presented a systematic study of melody as the formative element of a composition which generated the overall form and, crucially, the music's expressive meaning, codifying a motivic-thematic coherence that infused every element of a composition and would thereby grant coherence to the piece; understanding this would reveal the music's *Geist*. Though Reicha pointed at the idea of universally pleasing patterns, it was the French music theorist Jérôme-Joseph de Momigny who formulated the first theory of composition that posited the unity of art beyond reality, found in the imagination and accessed through silent, inner listening aided by scores. Here Wackenroder's *Geist* became the *goût absolut*, a

FIGURE 3.2: J.-J. de Momigny, Cours complete d'harmonie et de composition, Paris, 1810. Planche 30.

concept that stretched across the whole of music and the whole of art to encapsulate the universal value and higher truth of the inherent expression of true art. In an analytical reading of Mozart's string quartet K 421, Momigny clarified his position that *Geist* is no longer born of the emotions of the individual composer, but rather is the defining feature of art itself. By equating the art of poetry of the ancient world with Mozart's art of music, he sought to illustrate that true art is unified by a universal spirit that will determine its form, so that all works that possess this true spirit can be brought into relation with each other (Momigny 1810). Momigny equated Mozart's Allegro moderato from K 421 to the drama of Dido and Aeneas, yet he was certain to point out that the word underlay was motivated not by the linguistic character of the music, but that it served to illustrate the arch of dramatic tension that was inherent in the music and that unified the composition.

In his composition treatise, Momigny mirrored Hoffmann's exegesis of Beethoven's fifth Symphony, in which the latter had adhered to the Romantic notion of relationships that went deeper than language and spoke only "from the heart to the heart," inaccessible to reason despite using copious amounts of technical language to expose the symphony's structures. For both Momigny and Hoffmann, the music conveyed something beyond its structures, yet this something was profoundly emotional and, as such, bound humans together without their rational understanding of the process itself or its mechanics.

Adolph Bernhard Marx, in *Die Lehre von der musikalischen Komposition*, promoted an idealist unity between content and form, a unity that he also explored with particular reference to Beethoven's works (Marx 1837; Burnham 2006). In contrast to Hoffmann, however, Marx dissected the works into their germinating parts only to put them back together and show their organic unity. Musical works now had to be considered in their entirety to grasp their content through their full form—any less would mutilate the *Geist* into a series of sense impressions that might appear as single emotions yet without displaying the true force of the music's meaning (Pederson 1994). Form itself was necessarily mutable and historically conditioned as it morphed into and together with content. In listening to music, the individual would experience a journey of musical perception from a titillation of the senses via incipient feelings to specific and recognizable thoughts, a journey that mirrored the progress of music itself. Across his writings, then, he had an agenda beyond explication of works as his goal was profoundly educational: as chief editor of the *Berliner allgemeine musikalische Zeitung* from 1824–31, he endeavored to educate the listening public. It was their "duty to devote to art the purest and noblest feelings, and to prepare ourselves for its service as diligently and carefully as possible" (Marx 1852, here at ix). Music, for Marx, was an ideal tool to grow the individual and a society at large by educating their sensibilities and their ability to move from inchoate emotion to definite thought. Music as a teaching tool would assure a move from the enthusiasm of the heart in which the effects on the soul remained without specificity to the enthusiasm of genius in which the *Geist* revealed itself in the unity of expression.

Like Marx, Hanslick was primarily concerned with the role of music in society. Yet, whereas Marx's formalism sought to educate feeling into thought, Hanslick's sought to extricate music from the shackles of assessment against the emotional yardstick. Music was no longer supposed to be understood as the expression of a composer's emotion, nor should its primary aim be to elicit emotions in the listener; Hanslick rebelled against the generalizing equation of the emotional with the beautiful as much as he resisted the idea that each emotion has a musical instantiation, still prominent in writings in the 1830s. His objection was based on a similar understanding of historicity in music as Marx had displayed: Hanslick believed that any attempt to transfer emotions into music must necessarily lead to a music that would become hackneyed within a few years. Even though he granted that emotions had dynamic properties which music might resemble, this was not enough to qualify as proper representation of emotions in music. As such, a listening practice that was indulgent of emotions, that presumed the emotional representation in music yet let the self be swept emotionally by it, was dangerous, even pathological. Only proper contemplation could advance the individual. As a result, it also had to be recognized that music's essence and beauty were entirely independent of the performer, but were also independent of the acoustic stimulus of the sound per se—which in itself was not a matter of aesthetics but of physics; music's essence resided in its form.

Around the same time, a different school of theorists reformulated the idea of music's interiority by focusing on its material element: sound itself. In an attempt to provide a scientific basis for music's effects, they turned to the nature and perception of sound to explain the relationship between physical stimulation and emotional sensation. Universal properties of sound and of sound perception were combined with the aesthetic perception in the discipline of psychophysics, which attracted much attention among musically literate scientists in the second half of the nineteenth century (Hui 2013). Hugo Riemann attempted to mediate between the individual perception of music and the universality of music aesthetics, holding onto the fusion of emotion and aesthetics, by examining the process of musical hearing in relation to the physical properties of musical sounds. As such, he circumvented the emotions as the primary means of assessing music's quality and effect. In his work, as in that of Hermann Helmholtz and Arthur von Oettingen, the aesthetic perception was reformulated through the physical perception, thereby taking Marx's idea of active listening and examining it from a scientific angle. Riemann retained an aesthetically powered speculative angle in his idea that all music in its physical properties relied on a weak–strong pattern which formed its basic unit; this fundamental unit was a unit of energy—*Lebenskraft*—which he borrowed from the early nineteenth-century vitalists and which was in essence a reformulation of the idea that passions function as catalysts. His main objective—along with others arguing from a psychophysical perspective—was less that music is not the subject and object of emotions, but that these emotions did not function in linguistic terms, but in physical terms. The equation of music *as language of* the emotions was finally replaced with music *as* emotions.

Riemann, like Marx and Hanslick, was steeped in the tradition and the belief that listening had to be educated and his scientific theories served to give backing to this cultural idea, where Hanslick had turned to form. In Britain, the theorist Ebenezer Prout produced two volumes on musical form just before the close of the nineteenth century (*Musical Form* in 1893 and *Applied Form* in 1897), followed in Germany by Hugo Leichentritt's *Musikalische Formenlehre* in 1911 (English translation in 1951). Following Marx's historicist trajectory in music, Prout's work narrated an implicit trajectory from the small scale in music to the large scale, starting with motifs and phrases, then sentences and then on to simple formal structures (where emotional expression was rooted in the folk-like small elements of a musical construction but which also built an image of emotional and expressive sophistication with dance forms as its lowest manifestations), traversing vocal forms and the sonata to arrive at the grand scale of the symphonic poem. Leichentritt revealed a not dissimilar agenda in his inclusion of the analysis of full works so as to argue for a music-internal logic but also for an aesthetics of ideas as fundamental to musical styles and forms, in other words for an expressive ambition to give coherence to styles not at the level of the individual composer or piece but at a meta-level of musical forms that therefore possess inherent expressive meaning.

ENGAGING WITH MUSIC

No matter what theorists and composers concocted in their aesthetic idealization of music, musical construction, the phenomenology of musical parameters, and of narrative, for the public the notion that music somehow stirs and—by extension—expresses emotions physiologically as well as mentally never lost its sway. This rift between musical construction (or composition) and its reception was in part caused by the increasing professionalization within the musical world and a resultant "other": amateur music-making culture. Music was produced for domestic consumption at a breath-taking rate— the parlour song, the four-hand piano arrangement of the symphony, and the countless ditties for violins, pianos, guitars, harps, and other domestic instruments. While advertised and discussed in the musical press, which also brought philosophical essays on the high art of music and concert reviews, this repertoire was placed in stark opposition to that high art of music, which was considered capable of delivering music's powerful and superior message. At the level of emotional reception, however, these ditties fulfilled a separate but similarly potent function in the emotional civilization of the individual through education. This repertoire, more than the high art of Brahms's, Mahler's, or Strauss's symphonic works, shaped the social self-consciousness of the individual and functioned as the Foucauldian civilizing tool (Gramit 2002; Weber 2008), as the individual engaged in and through it with an emotional canon dictated by the great master works. Here, the physical experience of engaging with the music complemented the deep engagement with music per se. The two forms of engagement with music reliant on the nature of the experience itself—the one on the sense of listening alone, the other on the haptic sense as much as the sense of listening—differed in their latent assimilation of narrative content and affective power. The emotional meaning of the four-hand piano arrangement of Verdi's arias relied less on the music's melodic and harmonic content or its linear construction but on the physical act of engaging with one's partner at close proximity at the piano. Affect emerged from the liminal space in between, independent of any narrative other than that of two bodies interacting.

A second emotionally potent manner of engaging with music was manifest in the developing choral culture in both Germany and England. Eighteenth-century choral festivals had engaged few amateur singers and were a spectacle to attend and observe rather than to participate in. The communal listening experience was granted emotional force by the increasingly large-scale performances of G.F. Handel's oratorios, which formed the center-piece of choral festivals. By 1784, these performances reached their zenith in the Handel Commemorations in Westminster Abbey with 253 instrumentalists and 257 singers; the correspondent for the *European Magazine* noted that the "immense volume and torrent of sound . . . was almost too much for the head or the senses to bear," and even Charles Burney in his skepticism of the Handelmania that was sweeping across British lands, had to admit to his passions being stirred by "I know that my redeemer liveth" to the point that he—along with everyone else present—was reduced to tears (Burney 1785). That Handel's music was endowed with this power of the sublime was part of a larger national and political project, which endured into the nineteenth century and was revived after the hiatus brought by the Napoleonic wars (Weber 1989). In the nineteenth century, choral festivals and with them choral societies emerged, which attracted a large number of a rising middle-class public to come together and sing (Pritchard 1968; Drummond 2011; Minor 2012). In England, a full performance of the *Messiah* was customarily the three-day festival's crowning glory. The powers of Handel's music were here combined with a religious sentiment that celebrated worship through active participation. The individual could feel religious fervor and fulfillment in the act of singing, while tying him- or, crucially, herself, emotionally to a group through the communal activity and the celebration of a particular cultural canon (Thormählen forthcoming).

Provincial festivals were also a site for the development of social dancing in the early nineteenth century. Along with assemblies, balls, masquerades, and *ridottos*, the festivals offered space for the physical exploration of music's emotive qualities. While here the high art music of each era was placed in close proximity aurally to simpler dance music, the most popular melodies from operas by Rossini, Bellini, Donizetti, Verdi, Auber, and Meyerbeer were borrowed as the basis for dance arrangements. The emotional associations of the opera itself and that of the occasion of attending the opera were physicalized on the ballroom floor as men and women twirled like choreographed moving paintings. Even though, or perhaps because, the social dances of the first half of the century were still highly stylized and carefully studied pre-event—the earlier *cotillions*, *quadrilles*, and *lancers* were all taught by dancing masters before the ball and dance cards showing the sequence of dances to be played on a particular night were distributed beforehand—these events were nevertheless important sites for the negotiation of particular male and female socio-emotional behaviors (Faulds 2015; Helme 1985; Franks 1963). Deportment was physically practiced and emotionally internalized through dance etiquette; the decorum of dance shaped particular forms of femininity, while the choice of dances, events, and manners of engagement was laden with the anxieties of social class structures that had to be negotiated and upheld (Engelhardt 2009).

As much as social dancing trained and entrained particular socio-political emotions, watching social dancing was a matter of romantic and carnal fantasies; here, men in particular were offered a vista onto the gracefully moving female body, which would offer momentary glimpses of a usually hidden physicality that allowed the imagination to conjure the undulations beneath the elegant folds of bodice and dress (Richardson 1960). The pleasures of visual sensation were titillated in the fleeting glances across the room as one turned to hold a gaze only briefly before turning back to the inside of the circle as the quadrille in particular facilitated changing sightlines and foci across the four-couple formation and out towards the audience. The audience spectated the dancers as much as the dancers spectated the audience in this game of visual tag (Rendell 2002).

The waltz broke this convivial play of desires by focusing two dancers inwards; the close embrace as much as the frequency of the revolution of the dance pattern brought the dancers' attention onto each other, onto the liminal space between their two bodies and onto the unity created of these two bodies. It is not surprising that the perceived sexual tension inherent in this new form of dancing raised ire of such heat that it exceeded the carnal pleasures of dancing themselves. "National morals depend on national habits," *The Times* pontificated in July 1816, advising parents to shield their daughters from the contagion of this lascivious dance.[1] Now that the dance had moved, according to the reporter, from the brothel to the respectable classes, "the modest reserve which has hitherto been considered distinctive of English females" was threatened by "the voluptuous intertwining of the limbs, and close compressure of the bodies" in the waltz (Aldrich 1991; Yaraman 2002).

A significant part of this narrative lay in a new middle-class anxiety as the waltz was "forced on the respectable classes of society by the evil example of their superiors," in the wake of which it becomes the press's duty to step in as the warning voice and potential saviour of middle-class morals (*The Times* 1816). Both, the self-conscious delineation of the middle class with its own set of morals which had to be imbibed and embodied—felt internally to be displayed and upheld externally as flags of a newly self-conscious and distinct social group—and the concomitant anxiety over physicality were topics equally discussed in the discourse on music. This anxiety came to a head in the reception of the cult of virtuosity in the early nineteenth century as in the aesthetics of staged dance.

Noverre had already grappled with the balance between raising only the emotions of astonishment in the audience through the sheer virtuosity of physical control and unnatural physical comportment of dance and the possibility that dance could incite a narrative of true passions in the spectator (Ruprecht 2011). The onset of ballet criticism in the nineteenth century by Castil-Blaze, Théophile Gautier, and later Jules Janin betrayed this very anxiety over the physicality of dance as it sought to complement the art form's central character—the performer's body—with a second protagonist—the perceiving critical mind. The rationalization of dance in the pages of the French press in particular presented an aesthetic of dance designed to de-sexualize the art of dance with its female stars. In these aesthetics, however, opinions varied and Castil-Blaze argued for the need to follow a narrative along the lines of Noverre's *ballet d'action*, while Janin—his successor at the *Journal de débats*—believed that the physicality of dance in and of itself could be transfigured to express emotions beyond the body. For either, though, ballet began to be played out as a symbiosis of the onstage physicality and the off-stage spectacle, imagination, and enthusiasm disseminated in writing (Hibberd and Wrigley 2014). Concomitantly, focusing on the nature of ballet music and interpreting the physical gestures as a way to accompany the meaning that resided in the music, diffused the anxiety over ballet's physicality. Indeed, composers used a variety of techniques here to convey particular emotions: short passages from famous operas would put words and feelings back into the audience's minds; the use of particular solo instruments would conjure the human voice, the rhythm could follow that of speech rhythm and together these two devices could express a character's emotional development; recurring musical motifs would build a web of association within the ballet itself, thereby bringing back particular emotions at various points (Smith 2011). The attempts to claw back aesthetic meaning via musical expression rose in proportion with the increasing revelation and sexualization of the body on stage and its mechanization, particularly in the form of the virtuoso Marie Taglioni, who fused the ethereal appearance of a spirit with the revealing Romantic ballet costume that drew attention to her calves and even thighs, and with the distortion of the body extended by pointe shoes (Kant 2011).

Both Nicolo Paganini and Franz Liszt made their fame through a highly visual display of musical performance in which the performing body moved center-stage. The performer had long since been the star of that embattlement of the aristocracy holding forth at the King's Theatre, the Italian Opera. As such, instrumental virtuosi became an extension of this upper-class entertainment that celebrated spectacle, while the press and countless aesthetic pamphlets propounded the new middle-class seriousness. Caricatures of Liszt portrayed the pianist with a head that exceeded the size of his grand piano.

This head as symbol for the inspiration of the genius operated an infinity of stick-thin limbs, which pounded the piano like a frenzied machine. The display of a mental state riven with madness coupled with a pathologically distorted body mirrored a profound anxiety over the physicality of performer and performance. Emotions were frequently recorded as somatic experiences: diaries and letters composed in the early to mid-nineteenth century betray the common articulation of emotions as physical states rather

FIGURE 3.3: Caricature depicting Franz Liszt (1811–86) playing the piano (*c*. 1845). Photo by Leemage/Corbis via Getty Images.

than pure mental states; the idealized notion that subjectivity was a matter of the mind, not the body, in practice was highly problematic (Thormählen 2014). In Liszt's performance, the mind remained indeed the head of the operation, yet the emotions were externalized through the body, thereby giving a visual voice to the all-too-tangible concept of the emotions as residing in the body's physiology. His performance, then, was problematic and beloved at once because it cut across the re-conceptualizations in medical and aesthetic writings of the emotions as a higher order of the mind, independent of the body, a formulation which audiences adopted rationally yet struggled with emotionally.

Virtuoso performance in its physicality denied the idealist, metaphysical notions of art. It epitomized the larger battle of the values and virtues that pitted the German instrumental music with its concomitant attentive listening practices against Italian opera (Dahlhaus 1989; Mathew and Walton 2013). Formulated as an insurmountable opposition by Raphael Kiesewetter in his *Geschichte der europäisch-abendländischen oder unserer heutigen Musik* of 1834, the "twin styles" of Rossini and Beethoven marked a lasting rift between music as text and universal truth versus music as event and experience. While Beethoven's music according to his followers—not least of them Marx and

Hanslick—had to be studied for its layers of truth, Rossini was consumed as a series of pleasurable sense impressions. The types of emotions seemingly enshrined in both were fundamentally different.

Hermann Helmholtz delivered a quasi-scientific rationale for his own ardent anti-virtuosity. In *Die Lehre der Tonempfindungen als physiologische Grundlage für die Theorie der Musik* of 1863, he attempted to put his own middle-class penchant for German instrumental music and attentive, exegetical listening on a scientific footing by providing the basis for music's validity in sound sensation, divorced from the inevitably subjective perception theories of the time (Hui 2013; Rehding 2000). While he acknowledged the relevance of physicality in the appreciation of music—he himself preferred to play rather than solely listen—he nevertheless claimed scientific grounds for his dismissal of overtly physical, i.e. virtuosic, music by claiming that the plethora of notes obscured the universal physical laws of tone sensation (Hui 2013). Virtuosity masked nature, where nature should be audible.

This virtuosity was not just a problem in and of performance but of compositional styles as well. Helmholtz had merely given a scientific basis for a debate that had raged alongside the text versus performance debate since the 1830s. Particular sound sensations to Helmholtz were natural to man's sensation of sound while others obscured these, rendering music incomprehensible and its emotional effects false. Natural sounds were present in music that remained true to its own purity; here, form resulted from the natural consonances and dissonances of tones thereby stimulating a meaning that was at once physical yet also subconscious as the ear followed the sounds without the mind having to rationalize these into narratives. So called *absolute music*, defended by the Leipzig composers around Robert Schumann and Felix Mendelssohn, and the performers Joseph Joachim and Clara Schumann, later joined by Johannes Brahms, was based on a rejection of verbal, dramatic, or representational narratives or meanings in music (Evan Bonds 2014; Dahlhaus 1978). Schumann described his own experience of Berlioz's *Symphonie Fantastique* in his famous review of 1830, explaining that external narratives obscure the true vision of the music as "the ear no longer judges independently once the eye has been led to a given point" (*Neue Zeitschrift für Musik* 1835). Narrative became problematic as it dictated visions which obscured the reception of the music's deeper emotional expression (Cone 1971).

Interestingly, Schumann tied the proper sensibility for the higher truth of music to nationalism. "The German," he explained, "with his delicacy of feeling and his aversion to personal revelation, dislikes having his thoughts so rudely directed," whereas Berlioz was, of course, "writing primarily for his French compatriots, who are not greatly impressed by refinements of modesty" (*Neue Zeitschrift für Musik* 1835). However, the "progressives," or so-called composers of the "music of the future," equally appealed to national sentiment for support. Franz Brendel, in addressing a grand convention of musicians in Leipzig in June 1859, suggested that the epithet "music of the future" be replaced with the more apt name "New German School" even though—as he pointed out—two of its main representatives, Liszt and Berlioz, were not German nationals. Yet, these two had "from the first drawn nourishment from the German spirit and grown strong with it," and their music was a powerful display of German mastery and sensibility (F. Brendel [1859]2008). In choosing the name, Brendel also played on the almost subconscious conflation of German nationalism and religious sentiment by presenting the "New German School" as the worthy successor of the "Old German School," the recently keenly revived Protestant church music of Bach and Handel (Applegate 2005).

The religio-national narrative, the hierarchy of the senses in the acquisition of emotional knowledge and spiritual revelation, and the mapping of the senses' proper education onto national sensibilities were key strands in the debate of "absolute" versus "programme music." Rarely has a battle on music aesthetics raised the emotions of its participants to the ferocity with which the two sides accused each other of being morally corrupting and academically decrepit. The defenders of absolute music accused the "music of the future" of indecency and depravity, as narrative emotions allegedly undermined the essence of music itself. The "progressives," however, promoted emotions as powerful driving forces that breathed life into the composer's or performer's inspiration and gave vigor to his material whether on stage or on paper. As a composer, Liszt argued for the inevitability of a program at the inception stage. Imagination and poetic conception were driven by inner feelings, and together these had to give form to the music; he objected vigorously to the idea that music and musical material in and of itself contained a meaning or expression which should determine its form.

If Liszt's performances were pathologized, his compositions received comparatively mild criticism. The vitriol of madness and moral corruption was reserved for the staunchest supporter of the idea that music was not emotion in itself but a tool to express the ingenious composer's access to a higher truth through his own emotions and premonitions. Richard Wagner believed that the higher truth that art must convey comes from the "deepest chambers" of the artist's heart. Beethoven's symphonies—the Fifth and Ninth in particular—were the works that directed the way in this quasi-religious revelatory journey of music "from out her own peculiar element into the realm of universal art" (Wagner ([1849]1895: 123–126). In his overtly flowery language, Wagner claimed that the anchor of Beethoven's ship as he steered it "from the ocean of infinite yearning to the haven of fulfillment" was *the word*; with this Christian allusion, Wagner proclaimed Beethoven's music the "evangel of the art of the future." Schumann and the "formalists" equally claimed Beethoven as their guiding light, but in their eyes the verbal undermined a universal truth as words were too fickle to yield the same meaning to each person. Only the depth of the musical material could achieve such communication.

Wagner claimed a significant place for the modern artist as the redeemer of society. In his ideology of a *Gesamtkunstwerk* Wagner employed the full gamut of musical tools—not least the infinite sonorities of the orchestra—to maneuver music into the center of socio-political life. His music swept away the audience with an emotional fervor previously reserved for religious revelations alone: experiencing his music was described in terms of elation, ecstasy, and exaltation, so strong as to be experienced somatically as well as cognitively, and always steeped in the ideology of Christian religious experiences, not least through the Schopenhauerian virtue of "sympathy" (Borchmeyer 2008).

Friedrich Nietzsche perpetuated this idea of a spiritual emotional stringency and Wagner's music became the tool for his "diagnosis of the modern soul." Yet, *The Case of Wagner* also carried the pathologization of Wagner's music in an interpretation of the *Gesamtkunstwerk's* decadence which was the decay of society. In the years leading up to World War I, Wagner's music—nervous music that over-stimulated in its over-sensualization and conflated physical with spiritual experience—had increasingly become embroiled in a debate about music's threat to health (Kennaway 2012). It was particularly detrimental to female listeners, yet represented the over-stimulation of a modern lifestyle to all in its combination of sense perceptions. Wagner staged the experience of his music carefully as a potent mix of socio-cultural, collective affirmation, and psycho-somatic effects: the pilgrimage to his new theater, the auditorium darkened and built so that the

FIGURE 3.4: Liebig card, advertising meat extract, seaturing Walther von Stolzing in R. Wagner's opera_Die Meistersinger von Nürnberg—, ca. 1910. Photo by Chronicle/Alamy Stock Photo.

audience would not see each other but focus on the stage alone, and the sunken orchestra pit that allowed the mighty musical forces which vibrated the fibers of the audience's bodies to appear to sing from the depth of their own souls, created a heady swirl of physical, mental, national, religious, and collective passions. Here eroticism and sexual desire as the pinnacles of physiological emotions merged seamlessly into spiritual elation and rapture in a hyper-emotionality and interiority which had been set up by the early Romantics' conception of the musical sublime, yet which reached unprecedented heights and unprecedented numbers of citizens in and through Wagner's works.

EPILOGUE: SUBLIMATING NARRATIVE—SUBLIMATING THE VOICE

Wagner himself had no luck with writing for the ballet—a necessary requirement so as to bring his operas to the Paris stage—yet his multimedia approach to emotional stimulation had as many precursors on the dance stage as it did in symphonic music. The most successful fusion of visual stimulation in dance virtuosity (Marie Taglioni) and choreography (Jules Perrot and Jean Coralli), mental stimulation in poetic narrative (Théophile Gautier), and aural simulation in a music that borrowed opera's leitmotif and reminiscence techniques (Adolphe Adam) appeared in *Giselle*, premiéred at the Paris *Opéra* in 1841. What Wagner sought to fuse in a single author to grant coherence, was here brought together by many, yet critics willingly wrote unity and coherence into their reception of the ballet. Its pre-condition was its existence as a *ballet d'action*: it stood alone as a piece of art, independent of the opera which ballet still customarily adorned in

Paris. Ballet in its own right had moved from pleasant emotions—the moments of light relief within the opera—to a fully fledged emotional drama that celebrated its central performer in the double function of virtuoso and dramatic character.

Despite some arguing for an "absolute ballet," ballet remained reliant on linear narratives and the gesture of the dance was but a means to convey narrative structure, characters, and their emotional engagement with each other throughout the nineteenth century. Yet, ballet also built up a web of emotions conjured by stories based around sublimated sexual desires, female identity, exotic or ancient notions of dance's proximity to death (as in the popular display of Paganini dancing a Tarantella to his own music accompanied by witches), the intimate, domestic space, a new industrial mechanization, nationalism, and the supernatural. Tchaikovsky's ballets, perhaps, formed the balletic counterpart to Wagner's operas in their ability to transport the audience into a world of magic, fantasy, and fairy-tale. Tchaikovsky envisaged the ballet as a multi-sensory experience that would present an emotional narrative through the combination of visual and sound effects on stage (Wiley 1985). In his most successful collaboration with the French-born, St. Petersburg based celebrity choreographer Marius Petipa, *Sleeping Beauty*, Tchaikovksy aimed to transcend the linear narrative, the story-telling so dear to Petipa, through a complex web of associations built into the music and the choreography. If Petipa had already perfected the art of varying the dances, juxtaposing characters through realistic physical display, staging transformation scenes that would serve both to embroil the audience in the character development of his drama as well as spark the sensation of astonishment in them, Tchaikovsky sublimated much of this overt spectacle into a psychological drama in the subtlety of his orchestration which pushed beyond the realms of acceptable ballet music at the time (Hurley 2011). Yet, pushing into the symphonic idiom connected his ballets to a different emotional world in the ears, minds, and hearts of his audience. Here, the subconscious reception of musical form with its articulated emotive powers was fused with the powers of the imagination titillated by associational musical and visual devices.

Ballet's emancipation had been viewed skeptically by composers in the second half of the nineteenth century. Rimsky-Korsakov described balletic miming as "extremely elementary," warning at the same time that it "leads to a naïve kind of symbolism." Still, with the Russian ballet school at its helm it developed into the paradigmatic Imperial art at the beginning of the twentieth century in a compositional move that endowed the music with independence from conventional traits of symbolizing emotions through gestures while considering both music and dance's independence from the pragmatism of words as the necessary step towards aestheticized emotions. The increasingly complex musical scores, however, had yet to meet their match in a choreography that engaged with the anxieties of the modern world to the same degree to which the composer adopted and adapted ideologies of modernity in music—a match finally made in Stravinsky, Diaghilev, and Nizhinsky's *Rite of Spring*, premiered to a riotous house in May 1913 (Thormählen, in press). Here, the narrative story of the ballet—the ritual sacrifice of a young maiden in spring—no longer functioned as the emotional narrative; in this function it was displaced by ideologies of an original, primordial, musical expression that borrowed from theories of sound and from Wagner's idea that the orchestra was created by dance itself, while staging the modernist anxiety over mechanization and a decadent fascination with it.

Under the influence of Sigmund Freud, Arnold Schoenberg performed a similar turn away from anything cognitive—readable by the audience according to particular rules— to a sublimation of ideas of expression in music. Art was redefined as belonging to the realm of the subconscious; as human subjectivity was driven by inner impulses that were both emotional and subconscious, art necessarily was an unconscious creation that sought to bring to the surface the result of that which is hidden from the creator. "The music seeks to express all that swells in us subconsciously like a dream," Schoenberg wrote in a program note to the first performance of his "Five Pieces for Orchestra Op.16" (1909). Here, the early Romantic notion of interiority received a new guise as even the composer himself was not fully aware of his own perception and conception. Schoenberg started from the two ideas of form as meaning—giving on the one hand, and of sounds per se eliciting an emotional effect on the other. Yet in combining sounds into a form, intelligibility, accessibility, and comprehensibility had to be avoided as these would only recall musical conventions that by association portrayed particular emotional characters. These, however, were yet they were not true emotions; they remained inauthentic. In his third piece of Op.16, Schoenberg forced his listener into a new type of listening, one that focused on the sound and its inner oscillations reflected through the slow change in timbre achieved through orchestration. That parameter established early in the nineteenth century as the carrier of invention, expression, and emotion—melody—now became the tool towards the exploration of the sound itself in what Schoenberg called his *Klangfarbenmelodie*.

Simultaneously, Debussy focused on the integrity of sounds per se and on timbre, yet he also explored the cross-artistic influence of poetry and painting on music. His sound world was entirely different: the audience was to marvel at its beauty without being enraptured. His emotional intention was molded by the symbolist poets' rejection of "false sentimentality" and their desire for "plain meanings." Exploring the permeability of sound, his music was to be suggestive without reverting to associational meanings. Form was his friend just as it was Schoenberg's, a fact that betrayed the late yet deep influence of the mid-century debates, sparked by Hanslick and taken on board in different ways by both sides of the divide between program music and absolute music. Like Hanslick, Debussy and Schoenberg both defended the beauty of the form per se, of the material independent of associated meaning, while they believed that extra-musical art—poetry, literature, painting—and non-Western music would fuel the form through the composer's subconscious.

The new psychological theories of creativity resulted in an interesting and nearly insurmountable proliferation of different styles of music, different modes of consumption and reception, but also a stark opposition between an engagement in music as leisure time, and a serious reception of music through concentrated listening and study. Here, the idealized system of universal communication of music as a language of the emotions—fought for and formulated by eighteenth-century theorists, philosophers, composers, and musicians, was replaced by a sublimated system of understanding open to only the initiated few, just as the societal strata engaging with music had taken the opposite route from the elite few to the broader middle classes. The ideal of emotional communities shaped through the powers of music, now perceived as utopian as it had always been employed towards nationalism and social control, had given way to a fractionalization into individual experiences which bound particular individuals through the mere ability to be susceptible to these experiences in particular ways; the nature of the experience itself, however, was purely individual. The binding forces of narrative and communication in and through music could not adequately reflect modern anxieties about society; while narrative would remain central to music and emotions for another half century, its reception was already becoming brittle.

CHAPTER FOUR

Drama

AILEEN FORBES

In the final scene of Samuel Taylor Coleridge's *Remorse* (1797), Ordonio is reunited with the brother whom he tried to have murdered three years earlier, prompting his remorse—"My brother! I will kneel to you, my brother! / Forgive me, Alvar" (5.1.151). His shock and guilt at seeing Alvar alive are suddenly subsumed by the grief Ordonio already suffers in response to his most recent misdeed—his murder of his henchman and Alvar's failed assassin, Isidore. Ordonio's ensuing fit captivates his interlocutors:

> TERESA.   O mark his eye! he hears not what you say.
> ORDONIO (*pointing at vacancy*). Yes, mark his eye! there's fascination in it!
>   Thou said'st thou didst not know him—That is he!
>   He comes upon me!
> ALVAR.   Heal, O heal him, heaven!
> ORDONIO.   Nearer and nearer! and I cannot stir!
>   Will no one hear these stifled groans, and wake me?
>   He would have died to save me, and I kill'd him—
>   A husband and a father!—
> TERESA.   Some secret poison
>   Drinks up his spirit!
>
>   —5.1.151

As it culminates in the exhibition of Ordonio's eponymous remorse, Coleridge's play exemplifies how drama in the period is largely consubstantial with emotion. The site of emotion is the origin of theater: Teresa and Alvar become spectators to an ordeal that affects Ordonio in body—Teresa "marks" Ordonio's distracted "eye" and, ostensibly, his paralyzed limbs—and mind—she surmises an affliction of "his spirit," or soul. Beyond his body and mind, Ordonio's emotion also acts upon his onlookers: his distress is communicable to Teresa and Alvar, as their excited responses betray, even as he himself becomes increasingly oblivious to them.

Coleridge's play about remorse illustrates what philosopher Ronald De Sousa calls the "level ubiquity" of emotion. Emotion, as one witnesses in Coleridge's climactic scene, plays out not only on the level of the mind but also on that of the body and society: it constitutes psychological, physical, and social phenomena simultaneously. As it encompasses the dynamics of spectatorship and performance, the public and private, the material and intangible, theater mirrors this level ubiquity, befitting the delineation of emotion. In the nineteenth century, emotion comes to inhabit center stage, stealing the spotlight from what Aristotle had defined as the basis of drama—action. Emotion becomes the crucial element of the period's major dramatic genres, which this chapter will examine: melodrama, romantic tragedy, closet drama, and mental theater.

These four dramatic forms rest on the premise that where there is emotion, there is theater. Not only do they represent emotion as part of a play's content, but the structure of representation shaping each form also illuminates the very structure of emotion. On one end of the spectrum, melodrama emphasizes expression and sensational effects, highlighting the spectacular quality of emotion, the conspicuous behaviors and physical symptomatology that inevitably attract attention. As Peter Brooks argues, melodrama coincides with the theatrical impulse itself (Brooks 1976: xi): the melodramatic representation of emotion reflects the very theatricality of emotion. On the other end, what Byron called "mental theater" focuses on internal psychic struggle, on dramas of consciousness that resist material embodiment. Mental theater is thus a species of closet drama, a category of plays intended for print rather than stage production. The efforts of mental theater to delineate interiority correspondingly reflect the prevalent antitheatricality of the age. In this vein, closet drama negotiates the divide between public and private and hence the place of emotions in society. Romantic tragedy similarly lies between the poles of theatricality and antitheatricality. More radical than melodrama, on the one hand, and entertaining stage pretensions, on the other, romantic tragedy nevertheless incorporates elements of melodrama and mental theater. What distinguishes romantic tragedy is perhaps its affinity for the aesthetic structure of the sublime, a structure of mediation that underpins emotions in situations of extremity characteristic of the era.

In the feverish aftermath of the French Revolution, nineteenth-century theater begins to mime a history saturated with emotion, engendering theaters of emotion in the forms of melodrama, romantic tragedy, closet drama, and mental theater. While these theaters channel historical currents, they also—as this chapter will show—anatomize the nature, structure, and function of emotion across its level ubiquity.

MELODRAMA

In a certain light, perhaps, nineteenth-century theater begins in the late eighteenth-century streets of Paris. Drama and history become mutually implicated: theater shapes revolutionary politics just as revolution transforms history into theater (Buckley 2006: 6). Edmund Burke famously portrays this conflation when he "reflects" on the French Revolution as though he were a spectator in the theater:

> All circumstances taken together, the French revolution is the most astonishing that has hitherto happened in the world. The most wonderful things are brought about in many instances by means the most absurd and ridiculous; in the most ridiculous modes; and apparently, by the most contemptible instruments. Every thing seems out of nature in this strange chaos of levity and ferocity, and of all sorts of crimes jumbled together with all sorts of follies. In viewing this monstrous tragi-comic scene, the most opposite passions necessarily succeed, and sometimes mix with each other in the mind; alternate contempt and indignation; alternate laughter and tears; alternate scorn and horror.
>
> —Burke 2009: 10

For Burke, the events of the French Revolution assume hyperbolic terms—the "most astonishing," "most wonderful," "most absurd," "most contemptible" and "out of nature"—which magnify history to spectacle. He then explicitly invokes theatrical rhetoric when he describes the "tragi-comic scene" that arouses the conventional emotions of classical comedy and tragedy: "laughter and tears." Significantly, Burke associates the Revolution with neither the one nor the other classical dramatic genre but with a mixed form inciting "opposite passions," anticipating the explosive controversy that would arise in England in response to his *Reflections on the Revolution in France* (1790). Exemplifying a central strategy of the *Reflections* as a whole, Burke here criticizes the Revolution as an aesthetic failure. He condemns the "monstrous" juxtaposition of incoherent "modes"— the "chaos" of "crimes" and "follies"—in much the same way eighteenth- and nineteenth-century critics censored the mixed theatrical productions that strayed from the proper spoken dramas intended for the patent houses. Burke's dramatic assessment of the Revolution ultimately hints at the Revolution's impact on dramatic history, which Matthew Buckley formulates: the French Revolution, Buckley argues, "should be recognized not as a background to the history of the drama but as a primary event within that history," such that "in and through the dramatic politics of the Revolution," a new genre developed—*melodrama* (Buckley 2006: 6).

Melodrama arises from censorship, both with regard to content—to the official suppression of explicit dramatic reference to revolutionary history—and with regard to form—to the legislation of classical dramatic decorum in the patent theaters (Buckley 2006: 65; Shepherd and Womack 1996: 194). Instead of direct representation, melodrama translates the violence of revolutionary history into the "shootings, stranglings, hangings, poisonings, drownings, stabbings, suicides, explosions, conflagrations, avalanches, earthquakes, eruptions, shipwrecks, [and] train wrecks" that abound in the plays (Booth 1965: 114). But, perhaps even more crucially, it channels historical violence into the emotional expression characteristic of the genre. In his *Reflections*, Burke's notorious account of the arrest of Marie Antoinette, in this vein, prefigures melodrama:

> I saw [the queen of France] just above the horizon, decorating and cheering the elevated sphere she just began to move in,—glittering like the morning star, full of life, and splendor, and joy. Oh! what a revolution! and what an heart must I have, to contemplate without emotion that elevation and that fall! Little did I dream . . . that I should have lived to see such disasters fallen upon her in a nation of gallant men, in a nation of men of honour and of cavaliers. I thought ten thousand swords must have leaped from their scabbards to avenge even a look that threatened her with insult.— But the age of chivalry is gone.
>
> —2009: 75–76

Burke's histrionic tones rival the exuberance of the stage melodramas that would arise within a decade. Again, as if as a spectator, he "contemplates" the queen's deposition as a tragic *peripeteia*, inciting the emotions of astonishment, pity, and, finally, grief. But in the absence of tragic insight, Burke portrays this "revolution" as a Manichaean conflict, a feature that becomes a hallmark of melodrama. Because Marie Antoinette, cast as the beautiful, persecuted heroine, fails to command "ten thousand swords" in her defense, an incredulous spectator can feel only disdain for the vilified nation.

Burke's *Reflections*, as Buckley argues, "translat[es] the debate over France's political conflict into a question of spectatorial response" (Buckley 2006: 72), calling attention to the emotions ignited by the turbulent events. Burke thus exemplifies the generally charged atmosphere surrounding the Revolution, which for Charles Nodier made melodrama inevitable: "le mélodrame était une nécessité" (Pixerécourt 1841: vi). Nodier, in his introduction to the plays of Guilbert de Pixerécourt, the French dramatist credited for originating melodrama, viewed the French not simply as spectators but as actors in "le plus grand drame de l'histoire":

> Tout le monde avait été acteur dans cette pièce sanglante, tout le monde avait été ou soldat, ou révolutionnaire, ou proscrit. À ces spectateurs solennels qui sentaient la poudre et le sang, il fallait des emotions analogues à celles dont le retour de l'ordre les avait sevrés. [Everyone had been an actor in this bloody play, everyone had been a soldier, a revolutionary, or an outlaw. To these solemn spectators who had smelled the gunpowder and the blood, there was a need for emotions analogous to those from which they had been severed by the return of order.]
>
> —Pixerécourt 1841: vii

Revolutionary violence—"the gunpowder and the blood"—touched the lives of all who lived through the "greatest drama of history," producing a taste for sensational emotions the public would later seek to satisfy in the literal theater.

Melodrama therefore arises in the late eighteenth and early nineteenth century quite literally as a theater of emotion. The term "melodrama" derives from the Greek "*melos*"-drama or "music"-drama, and the French "*mêlée-drame*," or "mixed-drama," signaling the form's integration of multiple media, including music, pantomime, and spectacle (Booth 1965: 44). Thomas Holcroft's "A Tale of Mystery" (1802), the first English play to refer to itself as a "melo-drame" and an adaptation of Pixerécourt's *Coelina, ou l'Enfant du mystère* (1800), relies heavily on music, pantomime, and tableaux to serve the primary function of melodrama: expression. As Brooks argues, "The desire to express all seems a fundamental characteristic of the melodramatic mode. Nothing is spared because nothing is left unsaid.... Everything appears to bear the stamp of meaning, which can be expressed, pressed out, from it" (Brooks 1976: 4, 10). The melodramatic mode fully operates on the level of exteriority; all meaning, by word, gesture, or image, is acted out, made visible. The representation of emotion in this expressionistic, externalized mode highlights emotion's inherent theatricality. Emotion is something that can be seen and, indeed, causes a "scene" where it occurs. Melodrama sheds light on the "publicness" of emotion, on the dimension that makes it accessible and striking to others. In melodrama, the body performs on stage the same role it has in psychic life; as neuroscientist Antonio Damasio argues, "All emotions use the body as their theater" (Damasio 1999: 51).

The physical manifestation of emotion on stage assumes for Brooks a "plastic figurability" (1976: 47) that relates theater to sculpture. In "A Tale of Mystery," for example, Holcroft configures emotion through physical gesticulation and attitude in conjunction with dumb show. Consider the pivotal scene in which the mute Francisco reveals he was the victim of treachery:

> BONAMO. Do you know the traitors?
> FRANCISCO. (*gesticulates*)
> FIAMETTA. (eagerly) He does! he does!
> BONAMO. Who are they?
> FRANCISCO. [*writing*] "The same who stabbed me among the rocks." (*A general expression of horror.*)
> BONAMO. Name them.
> FRANCISCO. (*gesticulates violently, denoting painful recollection; then writes*) "Never!"
>
> —2007: 403

FIGURE 4.1: "An expression of horror." From Henry Siddons' *Practical Illustrations of Rhetorical Gesture and Action; Adapted to the English Drama* (1822). Courtesy of the Brander Matthews Dramatic Library, Rare Book and Manuscript Library, Columbia University.

Francisco's account of violence provokes a "general expression of horror," which the company assumes in tableau. Holcroft repeats this effect when the aptly named villain Malvoglio interrupts a wedding party: "*the company start up; Francisco, Stephano, Selina, and Bonamo, all with more or less terror. The peasants, alarmed and watching: the whole, during a short pause, forming a picture*" (2007: 413). The company's simultaneous postures of fear punctuate the action, throwing the spotlight on the emotion that, with total legibility, acutely forms the substance of the drama.

Beyond the spectacle of petrified emotion, the figure of the mute plays a critical role in melodrama by his reliance on the language of gesture. In a genre that emphasizes expression, the speechless mute expresses the unspeakable through the body: in the above scene, Francisco's frantic gesticulations convey the double trauma of the violent ambush that left him mute and the literally unspeakable identity of his attacker, his brother Romaldi, which he suppresses. When he comes face to face with Romaldi in the penultimate scene, Francisco enacts terrified dismay through pantomime: he "falls back and covers his eyes, with agony" (2007: 422). Melodramatic gesture and pantomime recapitulate Rousseau's association of gesture with the primal emotions, the "cry of nature" in fear, desire, anger, or grief (Rousseau 2011: 58). In its emphasis on bodily representation, melodrama signals the relation of the basic emotions to survival. The characteristic heightened pitch of the genre, indeed, projects life-and-death stakes.

Verbal expression in melodrama can thus also reflect the plasticity of emotion by its virtually tangible intensity. Despite his admiration for Charles Maturin's *Bertram* (1816), Byron nevertheless recommended the "lowering" of its emotional register, since "no performer could support the tone and effort of continual and sustained passion through five acts" (Maturin [1816] 1992: ii). Maturin's heroine Imogine, for example, seems without pause for breath to express a progression of unabating emotion. Forced by necessity to marry her beloved Bertram's rival, Imogine protests her heart's fidelity to her beloved: "I am that wretch—/ The wife of a most noble, honoured lord—/ The mother of a babe whose smiles do stab me—/ But *thou* art Bertram's still, and Bertram's ever! (*Striking her heart*.)" (16). She insists upon her virtue—"I am a wretched, but a spotless wife" (17)—though she longs for the past: "The thoughts of other days are rushing on me, / The loved, the lost, the distant, and the dead, / . . . I will mingle with them" (17). When Bertram unexpectedly returns, Imogine curses first her marriage—"Aye—curse, and consummate the horrid spell, / For broken-hearted, in despairing hour / With every omen dark and dire I wedded—" (32)—and then her temptation: "I'm weary of this conflict of the heart—/ These dying struggles of reluctant duty—/ These potent throes of wild convulsive passion" (45–46). After ostensibly yielding to Bertram in an offstage tryst, Imogine succumbs to remorse—"Oh hang me shuddering on the baseless crag—" (54)—and, in the face of her husband, mortal despair: "Be generous, and stab me—" (58). In accordance with melodrama's expressionistic emphasis, Imogine seems to withhold nothing, to leave nothing unsaid. Her "wild convulsive passion" is in Brooks' terms "pressed out" to the point of her (and the audience's) exhaustion, her outpouring miming the inflated tones of grand opera (Booth 1965: 49). This excess and hyperbole serve melodrama's purpose to convey absolute moral clarity. In the process, they reinforce the notion of the exteriority of emotion, its "publicness," which melodrama squarely enlists in its moral program.

FIGURE 4.2: "Melodramatic expression." From Henry Siddons' *Practical Illustrations of Rhetorical Gesture and Action; Adapted to the English Drama* (1822). Courtesy of the Brander Matthews Dramatic Library, Rare Book and Manuscript Library, Columbia University.

While the physical and verbal expression of emotion can itself constitute spectacle, as Joanna Baillie will argue, melodrama often relies on spectacular stagecraft to achieve emotional effects. In its dependence on "visual excitement and the thrill of the moment" (Booth 1965: 13), melodrama departs from Aristotle's emphasis on drama's narrative action: while, according to Aristotle, tragedy can be heard without being seen, the new form melodrama constitutively resides in its visuality. This emphasis on vision has significance for the production of emotion. Images are keyed into the emotional apparatus such that virtually every image, according to Damasio, is accompanied by emotion (Damasio 1999: 58). De Sousa, moreover, aligns emotion with patterns of attention ([1987]1999: 242). Since the very structure of theater fundamentally defines a field of vision, it plays a role in shaping emotional responses. The invention of limelight technology, in the late 1830s, advances this basic theatrical function to spotlight and hence to focus attention (Booth 1995: 302). Even before the advent of limelight, however, Matthew Lewis capitalized on spectacle for sensational effect. Consider, for example, the conclusion of Act IV of *The Castle Spectre* (1798), in which Angela, contemplating the rescue of her imprisoned father, encounters the ghost of her murdered mother:

> [*The folding-doors unclose, and the oratory is seen illuminated. In its centre stands a tall female figure, her white and flowing garments spotted with blood; her veil is thrown back, and discovers a pale and melancholy countenance; her eyes are lifted upwards, her arms extended towards heaven, and a large wound appears upon her bosom. Angela sinks upon her knees, with her eyes riveted upon the figure, which for some moments remains motionless. At length, the spectre advances slowly, to a soft and plaintive strain; she stops opposite to Reginald's picture, and gazes upon it in silence. She then turns, approaches Angela, seems to invoke a blessing upon her, points to the picture, and retires to the oratory. The music ceases. Angela rises with a wild look, and follows the vision, extending her arms towards it.*]
>
> ANGELA. Stay, lovely spirit!—Oh! stay yet one moment!
> [*The spectre waves her hand, as bidding her farewell. Instantly the organ's swell is heard; a full chorus of female voices chaunt "Jubilate!" a blaze of light flashes through the oratory, and the folding doors close with a loud noise.*]
> ANGELA. Oh! Heaven protect me!—[*She falls motionless on the floor.*]
>
> —4.2.79–80

Lewis floods the scene with emotionally charged imagery: the specter wears white and a veil, perhaps a wedding dress, symbolizing innocence that is tainted by desire—the spots of blood—and corrupted by violence—the "large wound" upon her bosom. Presumably like the theater audience, Angela is "riveted" and agitated by the figure. The ensuing multi-media effects, including the organ and choral music, the flash of light and crashing doors that mark the specter's heavenward ascension, ultimately overwhelm Angela. Spectacle reinforces melodrama's standard of clarity: the audience can make no mistake about what to notice, where to direct attention. Spectacle hinges on the quality of "salience" that for De Sousa coincides with emotion: emotion focuses a frame of vision, which in turn conjures the emergence of emotion (De Sousa [1987]1999: 191, 195–198). The folding and unfolding doors, music, and bright lights signal the appearance of the specter, evoking awe, wonder, and fear, and, for Angela in particular, renewed longing and loss. In melodrama, seeing is feeling.

Salience characterizes melodramatic stagecraft as a whole. From hyperbolic speech, legible pantomime, emphatic tableaux, to arresting spectacle, "depth and subtlety," as Michael Booth argues, "are useless to melodrama" (Booth 1965: 36). Salience focuses a spectator's attention, eliciting emotion that defines the experience. By pointing out that the Greek word *páthe* means both "passion" and "experience," Philip Fisher suggests that passion precisely underpins what "having an experience" means (Fisher 2002: 8). Fisher elaborates that the passions (which, he clarifies, translate to "the emotions" by the mid-eighteenth century), in a sense, articulate time:

> The passions convert pure, featureless, everywhere-the-same stretches of time into something like a temporal landscape, building an architecture into time. . . . The strongest claim that can be made is that the passions do not mark or give evidence about the structure of time, but that they are that structure insofar as it can enter our personal experience.
>
> —78

The passions give shape and structure to time, distinguishing one stretch of time from the next, converting "featureless" time to time loaded with meaning, to an "experience." Emotionally articulated time, in other words, becomes *dramatic* time.

From this perspective, emotions again reflect the substance of melodrama. Successive moments of emotional intensity compress the architecture of time in which drama is happening seemingly without pause. The contours of emotion mime the contours of plot; emotions not only trace but also become conflated with the action. In Holcroft's "A Tale of Mystery," for example, music acts as a prominent vehicle of emotion, which changes tune with each plot twist. During the wedding party, the "humorous dancing of the Italian peasants" ceases as music which "inspires alarm and dismay" heralds Malvoglio's entrance. After Malvoglio presents a letter to Bonamo, the "music expresses confusion and pain of thought" as Bonamo learns the truth of his ward Selina's parentage. The music then yields to Bonamo's exclamation: "Oh, shame! dishonour! treachery!" (2007: 413). These rapid musical transitions mark the play's climax. After Selina learns her true father is the mute Francisco, father and daughter leave Bonamo's patronage in exile accompanied by "music expressing dejection." As the pair comes upon the house of the miller who had once been charitable to Francisco, "cheerful music" attends their steps. When not refuge but the enemy—Francisco's treacherous brother Romaldi—meets them there, "music of hurry, terror, etc." erupts (422). Melodrama constructs itself upon the scaffolding of emotion that confers heightened meaning to each moment. There is no "dead," undefined time in melodrama, since emotion animates every moment of what is consequently perceived as "an experience."

Through its emphasis on expression, melodrama exhibits the physical, exterior, public nature of emotion; through its reliance on spectacle, it further connects emotion to visuality and the mechanics of attention. The intensity of melodramatic time finally reflects the power of emotion to give significant shape to our lives. All of the dramatic strategies melodrama employs to expose the basic emotions—Francisco's terror, Imogine's desire, Angela's grief—serve ultimately to delineate a morally unambiguous universe. As indices of moral significance, the emotions belie melodrama's emphasis on externality and spectacle by their access to, in De Sousa's terms, the "axiological level" of reality (332). Melodramatic emotions in their inflated expression and transparent morality ultimately channel recent history: the violence and return of order in revolutionary France (Cox 1990: 41).

ROMANTIC TRAGEDY

If melodrama sought to satisfy the public taste for the sensational emotion instilled by the extreme events of revolutionary history, William Wordsworth, in his Preface to *Lyrical Ballads* ([1800]2010), indicts "sickly and stupid German Tragedies" in his condemnation of "this degrading thirst after outrageous stimulation" (249). Despite his critique of melodramatic excess, Wordsworth nevertheless appropriates melodrama's focus on emotional expression as the basis of his own poetic project. Regarding *Lyrical Ballads*, he claims, "the feeling therein developed gives importance to the action and situation and not the action and situation to the feeling" (248). Whereas melodrama constructs itself on the external signs of emotion, however, Wordsworth, establishing a cornerstone of early romanticism, shifts concern to the internal dimension of emotion—to "feeling." In opposition to melodrama's publicly observable displays of emotion, "feeling" denotes the private, interior experience of emotion, secluded in the mind. Both Wordsworth and his collaborator Coleridge wrote tragedies, which were (ironically) influenced by their German precursor Friedrich Schiller. Their plays—Schiller's *Die Räuber* (1782), Coleridge's *Remorse* (1797), and Wordsworth's *The Borderers* (1795–1797)—present romantic tragedies that query the psychological dimension of emotion in their common preoccupation with the sublime.

The sublime constitutes an aesthetics of fear (Fisher 2002: 133). Whereas Edmund Burke locates the sublime in an empirical encounter with terrible objects, Immanuel Kant conceptualizes the sublime as a subjective struggle of mind. Burke, for example, argues that "Whatever is fitted in any sort to excite the ideas of pain, and danger, . . . whatever is in any sort terrible, . . . is a source of the *sublime*" and hence "productive of the strongest emotion which the mind is capable of feeling" (Burke 1958: 39). Rooted in the perception of "pain and danger," the Burkean sublime produces the "passions which concern self-preservation" (38). In what he calls the "dynamically sublime," Kant, by contrast, attributes powerful emotions to a cognitive contest: "Bold, overhanging, and as it were threatening rocks; clouds piled up in the sky, moving with lightening flashes, and thunder peals; volcanoes . . . —these exhibit our faculty of resistance as insignificantly small in comparison with their might" (Kant 1951: 100). Kant thus internalizes the sublime as a conceptual crisis.

While empirically overwhelming elements of nature might feature in melodrama as Burkean sublime spectacle, in romantic tragedy, the sublime often comes into play in a more Kantian manner on the level of character, showcasing the emotions that arise at the limits of cognition and the will. For example, in *Remorse*, Coleridge conflates sublime spectacle with Kant's model of conceptual difficulty. Act IV opens onto a sublime landscape, where Ordonio appoints a meeting with Isidore: "*A cavern, dark, except where a gleam of moonlight is seen on one side at the further end . . . cast on it from a crevice in a part of the cavern out of sight*" (4.1.100). The cavern's darkness obscuring his sure footing prompts Isidore to contemplate danger:

>You see that little rift?
>[. . .]
>My torch extinguish'd by these water drops,
>And marking that the moonlight came from thence,
>I stept in to it, meaning to sit there;
>But scarcely had I measured twenty paces—
>My body bending forward, yea o'erbalanced

> Almost beyond recoil, on the dim brink
> Of a huge chasm I stept. The shadowy moonshine
> Filling the void so counterfeited substance,
> That my foot hung aslant adown the edge.
> Was it my own fear?
>
> —4.1.102

The "dim brink" which physically threatens Isidore prefigures the moral boundary that psychically haunts Ordonio: "I know not why it should be! yet it is— / . . . Abhorrent from our nature / To kill a man" (4.1.104–105). Like the precipitous "chasm" for Isidore, the contemplation of murder for Ordonio provokes horror.

As Coleridge's figure of the "chasm" suggests, the sublime traverses the limits of the will. Burke argues that part of the emotional force of a sublime spectacle arises from seeing something happening outside our will:

> We delight in seeing things, which so far from doing, our heartiest wishes would be to see redressed. This noble capital, the pride of England and of Europe, I believe no man is so strangely wicked as to desire to see destroyed by a conflagration or an earthquake, though he should be removed himself to the greatest distance from the danger. But suppose such a fatal accident to have happened, what numbers from all parts would crowd to behold the ruins.
>
> —Burke 1958: 47–48

Although, according to Burke, no one would wish to see London burn, if it were to burn by "fatal accident," the catastrophe would draw crowds of spectators. Burke, on the one hand, refers to exemption from the catastrophe, in terms both of personal safety as well as of responsibility or intention in its cause, as productive of the peculiar sensation of "delight." On the other hand, helplessness or passivity in the face of cataclysm can alternately affect a will that ordinarily strives—in Spinoza's sense of the *conatus*—for unlimited self-extension in the world, conjuring not delight but anger or grief (Fisher 2002: 206). In the case of death, Fisher associates "feeling[s] of responsibility" or "guilt" with a "refusal of the passivity built into losses that happen to us" (209). The "passions" for Fisher are "a sign that passivity, powerlessness, and an attitude of hopeless acceptance of whatever will come are not endemic to our reading of the world" (160). Dramatic villains in Schiller's *Die Räuber* like Francis de Moor or Spiegelberg—to whom protagonist Charles de Moor represents an obstacle, respectively, to lust or ambition—notably exemplify the passions that arise at the limits of the will.

The sublime magnifies this model by tracing the passions ultimately at the limits of mortality. In *Die Räuber*, Charles de Moor's contemplation of suicide touches upon the sublime:

> This little tube unites Eternity to Time! This awful key will shut the prison-door of life, and open up the regions of futurity! Tell me! oh tell! to what unknown, what stranger coasts thou shalt conduct me! The soul recoils within herself, and shrinks with terror from that dreadful thought; while fancy, cunning in her malice, fills the scene with horrid phantoms.
>
> —Schiller [1792] 1989: 163

The soul, whose "faculty of resistance," in Kant's terms, is unable to "match the might" of the thought of death, consequently "recoils" and "shrinks," retracting the will. Terror here emerges from the cognitive crisis within. In the Kantian sublime, cognitive failure is, nevertheless, a necessary stage for the mind's transcendence, to which Charles alludes—"Thou may'st reduce me into nothing—but this liberty thou can'st not take from me" (164)—before dropping his pistol. Charles' aborted suicide foregrounds the material, self-preservative impulses which defeat his mind's striving toward the abstractions of "eternity," "futurity," and "liberty." By the play's climax, however, Charles transgresses all mortal bounds. Pressed to choose between his outlawed life among a band of robbers or domesticity with his beloved Amelia, Charles initially resists his brothers: "Dare but a soul of you to violate this sanctuary!—She is mine! . . . Let heaven and hell combine their powers to force her from this hold!—Love is above all oaths!" (214). When the robbers, however, refuse to release him from their criminal fraternity, Charles rises to the occasion:

> I—am free!—Moor must be free, in order to be great! Now, I would not exchange this triumph for an Elysium of love! (*He draws his sword.*) Poor wretches! your mean souls reach not this height.—Whate'er is great seems frenzy in your eyes.—The spirit of despair outstrips your snail-paced wisdom. On deeds like these we pause not till they are done!—I'll think on this—hereafter! (*He stabs Amelia.*)
>
> —216

Charles conveys his sense of the grandeur of the act he has not yet fully rationalized when he fatally stabs Amelia. Although among the "mean souls" of his immediate spectators—the robbers—the act of killing one's beloved would, as Charles taunts, cause "frenzy," shocking the comprehension, it strikingly exalts Charles himself. As Kant claims, the "sublime prepares us to esteem something highly even in opposition to our own (sensible) interest" (Kant 1951: 108). In his *a priori* capacity to esteem the idea of moral liberty—of freedom from the bonds of sensible interest and lawful community—Charles is capable of destroying that which epitomizes these bonds, Amelia. As the violence of the deed checks cognition—Charles postpones thought until "hereafter"—it provokes sublime feeling, an immensity of "triumph" that outweighs an "Elysium of love." Through its reference to the sublime mechanics of mind, Schiller's climactic scene at once delivers a theatrical spectacle and plumbs emotional interiority.

Even as romantic theater features the sublime, the sublime itself structurally incorporates theater. Burke's portrait of catastrophe in London notes, first of all, the necessity of spectatorial distance from the site of danger. Indeed, he ventures that "at certain distances, and with certain modifications," danger or pain can be "delightful" (Burke 1958: 40). These "certain distances" or "modifications" (40) not only remove the spectator from physical harm but also install the space for representation that enables cognition. By integrating theater into his model of the sublime, Burke connects emotion to cognition: not purely physiological responses, the emotions instead constitute cognitive phenomena that issue as "feeling."

Theater provides the framework for representation at the heart of emotion. Just as Burke theorizes that catastrophe in London would produce spectacle, David Marshall argues that a spectacle of real catastrophe "feels like theater" (Marshall 1988: 24); real suffering must appear as a representation in order to elicit an emotional response (133). Emotions depend on our ability, cites De Sousa, "to picture and understand human situations." They derive from "paradigm scenarios" that "teach us how to feel" (De Sousa [1987]1999: 184, 332). In contrast with melodrama's emphasis on spectacle, romantic tragedies recapitulate Aristotle's association of tragedy with narrative that precipitates an *anagnorisis*. Recalling the cavern scene in Coleridge's *Remorse*, Ordonio amidst the sublime setting prefaces his murder of Isidore with storytelling:

> ORDONIO.   [. . .] But that same over ready agent—he—
> ISIDORE.   Ah! What of him, my lord?
> ORDONIO.   He proved a traitor,
> Betray'd the mystery to a brother traitor,
> And they between them hatched a damned plot
> To hunt him down to infamy and death . . . .
> ISIDORE.   A dark tale darkly finish'd! Nay, my lord!
> Tell what he did.
> ORDONIO. (*fiercely*)   That which his wisdom prompted—
> He made the traitor meet him in this cavern,
> And here he kill'd the traitor.
>
> —4.1.109

Ordonio telescopes the "dark tale" with his and Isidore's present situation, articulating a paradigm scenario that for Isidore crystallizes his fate: "Poor thick-eyed beetle! not to have foreseen / That he who gull'd thee with a whimper'd lie / To murder his own brother, would not scruple / To murder thee' (4.1.110). The narrative and dialogue between the pair prompt the recognition that underpins Isidore's disillusioned regret, grief for a potentially soon bereaved family and self-defensive courage. These complex feelings hence depend on a cognitive processing, distinguishing them from the basic terror that afflicts Isidore in the precipitous cavern where the sublime "void" originally obstructs cognition.

CLOSET DRAMA

Spectacle, on the one hand, and cognitive representation, on the other, both factor into a third level of emotion processing—that of society. Emotions are also social phenomena, which engage the self and other and, hence, language. The paradigm scenarios that, according to De Sousa, make emotions intelligible, constitute social situations "drawn first from our daily life as small children and later reinforced by the stories, art and culture to which we are exposed" ([1987]1999: 182). As melodrama's moral tenor exemplifies, theater in the eighteenth and nineteenth centuries forms a critical medium for the cultural shaping of emotion. Before cultural representations mediate emotion, however, the origin of society, as Rousseau argues in the *Second Discourse* (1754), coincides with the impulse to observe one another:

> [A]s the mind and head are trained, the human race continues to be tamed, relationships spread, and bonds are tightened. People grew accustomed to gather in front of their huts or around a large tree; song and dance, true children of love and leisure, became the amusement or rather the occupation of idle men and women who had flocked together. Each one began to look at the others and to want to be looked at himself, and public esteem had a value.
>
> —Rousseau [1754]2011: 73

By describing the original currency of social intercourse as "looking" at one another, Rousseau characterizes society itself as a theater. In the period's discourse of sympathy, social observation enacts a socially reinforcing function. Rousseau, however, is quick to associate it with dissimulation—or "acting"—in society. With regard to socially creditable qualities, such as "intelligence, beauty, strength, or skill," an individual who seeks to "attract consideration" was "soon forced to have them or affect them. It was necessary, for his advantage, to show himself to be something other than what he in fact was" (77). For Rousseau, social theatricality raises the question of authenticity and sincerity.

These eighteenth-century ideas of social theatricality, encompassing the issues of social observation, sympathy, and sincerity, influence nineteenth-century dramatist Joanna Baillie. Baillie identifies the "spectacle of human nature" as the heart of her project, entitled *A Series of Plays: In Which it is Attempted to Delineate the Stronger Passions of the Mind, Each Passion Being the Subject of a Tragedy and a Comedy*, published in three volumes (1798, 1802, 1812). Aiming explicitly to anatomize human emotion through the theater, she, in her "Introductory Discourse" to the plays, predicates the origin of theater on the display of emotion: "The wild tossings of despair; the gnashing of hatred and revenge; the yearnings of affection, and the softened mien of love; all that language of the agitated soul, which every age and nation understands, is never addressed to the dull nor inattentive" (2001: 73). Baillie recognizes that signs of emotion—"tossings," "gnashing," and "yearnings"—inevitably command an audience. Going beyond a description of the basic structure of melodrama, however, Baillie both pointedly connects this physical language with the internal "agitated soul" and further considers its social context by invoking the discourse of sympathy.

Baillie formulates a theater theory based on what she terms "sympathetic curiosity":

From that strong sympathy which most creatures, but the human above all, feel for others of their kind, nothing has become so much an object of man's curiosity as man himself. . . . Every person, who is not deficient in intellect, is more or less occupied in tracing, amongst the individuals he converses with, the varieties of understanding and temper which constitute the characters of men.

—67–68

In addition to Rousseau, Baillie's attention to the fundamental human impulse to "trace" the "characters of men" is indebted to moral philosophers David Hume and Adam Smith. As empiricists, Hume and Smith predicate relations of sympathy between self and other on the perception and cognition of emotion. In Hume's formula, one's "idea" of what another suffers "is converted into an impression" in the self (Hume 1969: 367). Not only does Hume thereby highlight the communicability of emotions between individuals in society, but he also suggests that emotions may not originate from *within*, as expressions of the self, but, rather, as Adela Pinch argues, they may visit the self as "autonomous substances" from *without* (Pinch 1996: 1). Hume attests that "when we sympathize with the passions and sentiments of others, these movements appear at first in our mind as mere ideas, and are conceiv'd to belong to another person" (1969: 370). This "etiological alterity," in Pinch's terms, reprises the element of distance that Burke locates in the structure of the sublime. Such alienation between the self and the other—the source of emotion—allows for the cognitive representation that brings emotions into being. For Hume, our "ideas of the affections of others are converted into the very impressions they represent" such that "the passions arise in conformity to the images we form of them" (370). Hume thus articulates how ideas drawn from the "images" we represent in the mind necessarily mediate our feeling of emotions.

In Smith's elaboration, sympathy outlines a spectatorial relation through which the emotions engendered by one's observation of an other serve a means of socially reinforcing judgment. Even when another's situation does not upon first sight cause sympathy, an observer must, according to Smith, socially contextualize it in order to train oneself to feel appropriately: "[W]e know that if we took time to consider [a sufferer's] situation, fully and in all its parts, we should, without doubt, most sincerely sympathize with him. It is upon the consciousness of this conditional sympathy, that our approbation of his sorrow is founded" (Smith 2002: 22). Sympathy relies on an experiential bank of socially constructed "paradigm scenarios" to which the mind refers in developing an emotional response. For Smith, these social standards of emotion similarly apply to acts of self-reflection: "We can never survey our own sentiments and motives, we can never form any judgment concerning them; unless we remove ourselves, as it were, from our own natural station, and endeavor to view them as at a certain distance from us" (128). To act as a spectator of one's own emotion depends on an internalization of distance, a movement of self-difference by which "'I divide myself,' as it were, into two persons: the spectator and the agent" (131). By viewing the self as other, the mind installs an internal theatrical structure that enables one to represent, sympathize with, and hence feel one's own feelings.

Founded upon the dynamics of sympathy, Baillie's theater of the passions negotiates both external social as well as internal psychic relations, generating what Catherine Burroughs calls "closet stages." Akin to melodrama, her plays focus on human beings in "extraordinary situations of difficulty and distress," which for Baillie generate "spectacle" (2001: 69). However, instead of melodrama's elaborate stage effects intended to amaze a large-capacity house, spectacle in Baillie's plays centers on character, engaging the audience in a more intimate exercise of "tracing the varieties and progress of a perturbed soul" (73). Baillie thereby critiques melodrama's characteristic bombast in favor of greater subtlety in emotional performance: "With their strong and obvious features, therefore, [the passions] have been presented to us, stripped almost entirely of those less obtrusive, but not less discriminating traits, which mark them in their actual operation. To trace them in their rise and progress in the heart, seems but rarely to have been the object of any dramatist" (91). Baillie objects to the melodramatic compression that limits the representation of passion to the "height of its fury" and its "full-blown strength" (91). She thus indicts the era's codified acting as reductive and unnatural. Baillie resists the purely iconic symbolization of emotion through standard body postures and facial expressions that Henry Siddons, for example, outlines in his *Practical Illustrations of Rhetorical Gesture and Action* (1807). The stylized precision of celebrated actor John Philip Kemble, Siddons' uncle, would yield to what was considered the naturalism of rising rival Edmund Kean's intensity and spontaneity (Burroughs 1997: 111; Burwick 2009: 88). With reference to Kean, William Hazlitt proclaims, "A man of genius is not a machine" who imitates the passions by the book, but one capable of risking "improper liberties with his art" (Hazlitt 1818: 293, 235). This spiritedness can manifest in the physiognomy. Baillie's insistence on intimate dimensions of theater that would bring the human character "to our nearer regard" for "nearer inspection" (2001: 85) calls attention to the role of physiognomy not simply in pictorializing emotion through static postures but in delineating the "rise and progress" of emotional expression—a dynamism indicative of movements of interiority (Burroughs 1997: 113).

For Baillie, the "perturbed soul" becomes legible through the body according to a logic of symptomatology that is essentially theatrical: the body externally manifests something

FIGURE 4.3: (a) "Terror." (b) "Jealous Rage." (c) "Despondency." From Henry Siddons' *Practical Illustrations of Rhetorical Gesture and Action; Adapted to the English Drama* (1822). Courtesy of the Brander Matthews Dramatic Library, Rare Book and Manuscript Library, Columbia University.

internally hidden. Her theater thus rejects the pure exteriority of melodrama to make inroads, in a proto-romantic fashion, into the depths of the human psyche. Her incipient interest in psychology will anticipate Charles Lamb's assessment of melodramatic histrionics as the "counterfeit appearance" of emotion (Lamb 1885: 10). By charging melodrama, in line with Lamb, with the artificial display of emotion, Baillie lends voice to the period's concern for emotional sincerity.

Striving toward interiority and authenticity, Baillie locates the passions, again in a proto-romantic manner, not in society but in the human "closet." Contrary to melodrama, her theater ultimately stresses not the "publicness" but the privacy of emotion, which forms its counterintuitive basis:

> For who hath followed the great man into his secret closet, or stood by the side of his nightly couch, and heard those exclamations of the soul which heaven alone may hear, that the historian should be able to inform us? and what form of story, what mode of rehearsed speech will communicate to us those feelings, whose irregular bursts, abrupt transitions, sudden pauses, and half-uttered suggestions, scorn all harmony of measured verse, all method and order of relation?
>
> —2001: 86

If sympathy attracts one to the spectacle of human nature, its reference to social standards, as Hume and Smith argue, also tends to harmonize and order the emotions in social circulation—a process of distortion that the closet, according to Baillie, would "scorn." Baillie's theater thus manifests a force itself in tension with sympathy—curiosity. As Baillie argues, the human mind desires to behold a man "struggling with those feelings of nature, which like a beating storm, will oft times burst through the artificial barriers of pride" (71). Baillie's theater aims to expose the "feelings of nature" that break through the artificial restraints of society—including pride—that are installed and regulated by sympathy. It would belong to a spirited actor, like Kean, accustomed to venturing "improper liberties with his art," to portray these "natural" emotions with the "irregular bursts, abrupt transitions, sudden pauses" that disrupt sympathetic social decorum.

After Kemble, Kean would, in 1821, assume the title role in *De Monfort*, Baillie's most successfully mounted play from her first volume of *Plays on the Passions* (1798). The play examines hatred: the nobleman De Monfort harbors hostility toward his childhood rival Rezenvelt, an animus ostensibly cemented by Rezenvelt's act of forbearance in a duel to which De Monfort had incited him and in which De Monfort was disgraced. In snatches of untoward conduct, Baillie depicts De Monfort's festering passion: De Monfort nervously rings for a servant he does not want (1.2.181–2), identifies Rezenvelt's "well-known foot" in dread of his approach (3.1.154), is paranoid that his servant Manuel "pin[s] thine ear to holes, / To catch those exclamations of the soul" (3.3.25–26), and falls into abstraction before another servant who lets slip information giving him a fatal advantage over his nemesis (3.3.209–232). The dramatic salience of these exchanges rests less on *éclat* than *curiosity*—they break from socially expected behavior—signaling internal dis-ease to De Monfort's interlocutors. Respectively, Rezenvelt "smiles significantly," Jane "pray[s] pardon" for her brother, Manuel "sulks," and Jacques, in the last instance, is dumbfounded: "His honour heeds me not" (3.3.227).

These moments of passion even in "an infant, growing, and repressed state" (Baillie [1798]2001: 104) illustrate the closet stage. Absorbed by his emotions, De Monfort acts out in a state forgetful of his company, evoking Diderot's theatrical paradox. For Diderot, the unconsciousness of being observed—itself guaranteeing authenticity—is precisely what invites observation (Fried 1980: 103). Fisher similarly argues that despite the intense visibility of the passions, their essence resides in solitude: "The sighs, groans, or tears of mourning take place 'as if' one were alone in the world" (2002: 59). What is private, as Burroughs argues, is what engenders theater (1997: 12).

Baillie's theater hence discloses the closet to her audience when in solitude De Monfort gives full vent to his passion:

> (*Throws himself into a chair, covers his face with his hand, and bursts into tears. After some time he starts up from his seat furiously.*)
> Hell's direst torment seize th'infernal villain!
> Detested of my soul! I will have vengeance! . . .
> I'll do a deed of blood—
>
> —3.3.180–183

The theater audience assumes the position of the unheeded spectators before whom an impassioned individual unselfconsciously displays emotion. If, however, the closet reveals uninhibited and spontaneous gestures and words, Baillie's narrative frame indicates their source in acute cognitive engagement. The heat of De Monfort's hostility above rests on a paradigm scenario supplied by false rumor: he is led to believe that his beloved sister Jane has become betrothed to his enemy. In another solitary moment, after he murders Rezenvelt, De Monfort's aggression turns inward:

> (*Looking steadfastly at* [Rezenvelt's dead] *body.*)
> It moves! it moves! the cloth doth heave and swell.
> It moves again.—I cannot suffer this—[. . .]
> (*Runs to the corps and tears off the cloth in despair.*) [. . .]
> How sternly fixed! Oh, those glazed eyes!
> They look me still.
> (*Shrinks back with horror.*)
> Come, madness! come unto me senseless death!
> I cannot suffer this! Here, rocky wall,
> Scatter these brains, or dull them.
> (*Runs furiously, and, dashing his head against the wall, falls upon the floor.*)
>
> —4.3.82–91

Instead of gratifying his hatred, the image of his victim prompts self-loathing, which he endeavors to dispel by destroying his own "brains." In ghostly sympathy, De Monfort sees himself through the "glazed eyes" of his dead enemy, which inevitably condemns his crime. His invocation to madness nevertheless suggests that his mental faculties remain intact. Therefore, through his imagination of the perspective of the other, he represents to himself the horror that eventually overcomes him. For Baillie, sympathetic curiosity is not satisfied simply with the spectacle of aberrant states; rather, the effort in her plays to assimilate or "naturalize" the passions in narrative highlights the socially implicating factor of language in emotion processing.

MENTAL THEATER

Although Baillie published twenty-seven plays, she ardently resisted the notion that they were "only fit for the closet" and staged seven during her lifetime (Slagle 1999: 277).

Lamb, by contrast, viewed the closet as a privileged space that preserved serious drama from the artificial performance of the passions. During a period shaped by Rousseauvian "naturalism" and Wordsworthian "sincerity," the theater became aligned with the spectacular, inauthentic and excessive (Pascoe 1997: 3). In this antitheatrical light, Lamb found the interest of drama not in the display of the body but in an exposition of the "inner structure and workings of mind" (1885: 6). With specific reference to Shakespeare, Lamb therefore advocated less the acting than the reading of plays: "What we see upon a stage is body and bodily action; what we are conscious of in reading is almost exclusively the mind, and its movements" (22). His insistence on turning inward through language to gain an understanding of character resonates with Byron's project of "mental theater."

In his plays, including *Manfred* (1817), *Cain* (1821), and *Heaven and Earth* (1823), all intended for the closet, Byron seems to reject the material stage precisely to zero in on the workings of the mind. As he explains in an 1821 letter to Lady Byron, his goal is "to introduce into our language—the *regular* tragedy—without regard to the Stage—which will not admit of it—but merely to the *mental* theatre of the reader" (Richardson 1988: 43). Like the sublime, Byron's project encompasses an internalization of theater. But, rather than the internal spectatorial distance that mediates sublime cognition, Byron focuses on the very medium of representation that forms the substance of consciousness: language. As Alan Richardson argues, it is almost exclusively through "rhetorical struggle" that mental theater depicts "intense psychological portraiture" (4, 15). Like romantic tragedy and closet drama, mental theater opposes melodrama in its attempt to delineate the invisible, private, psychical aspect of emotion—the feeling. However, its antitheatrical emphasis on language perhaps most explicitly engages what Damasio designates as the final stage of emotion processing—the "feeling of feeling"—that hinges on consciousness (Damasio 1999: 280). The dichotomy between melodrama and mental theater thus suggests a structural analogy with Damasio's distinction between "having a feeling" and "knowing a feeling" (284). To know that one has a feeling and hence to feel one's feeling is predicated on the mental representations that connect feeling to consciousness.

Byron's *Manfred* portrays a drama of consciousness through the intense absorption of the title character. When he is not alone scaling alpine peaks, he withdraws into the tower of his castle to engage spirits in discourse. One of these spirits, the Witch of the Alps, identifies Manfred as "a man of many thoughts" (2.2.34), one who craves disembodiment, as he professes: "Oh, that I were / The viewless spirit of a lovely sound, / A living voice, a breathing harmony, / A bodiless enjoyment—" (1.2.52–55). He expresses aversion for his fellow creatures, whose sympathy would only "degrade" him back to "clay again" (2.2.78–79), as well as for all emblems of mortality. Specifically, blood for Manfred signifies corruption not only in death—an idea he shares with the chamois hunter who prevents his suicide: "Stain not our pure vales with thy guilty blood!" (1.2.111)—but also in his unnamed, illicit love for Astarte that is ostensibly the source of his despair:

> I say 't is blood—my blood! The pure warm stream
> Which ran in the veins of my fathers, and in ours
> When we were in our youth, and had one heart,
> And loved each other as we should not love,
> And this was shed: but still it rises up,
> Coloring the clouds, that shut me out from heaven,
> Where thou art not—and shall never be.
>
> —2.1.24–30

Manfred's elliptical confession exemplifies his brooding self-consciousness. Like Milton's Satan, Manfred recognizes his mind as a hell of his own making. Although otherworldly spirits assail him in the climactic scene, they perhaps represent mere projections with which his conscious mind contends in *psychomachia*:

> Back to thy hell!
> Thou hast no power upon me, *that* I feel;
> Thou never shalt possess me, *that* I know:
> What I have done is done; I bear within
> A torture which could nothing gain from thine:
> The mind which is immortal makes itself
> Requital for its good or evil thoughts—
> Is its own origin of ill and end—
> And its own place and time—its innate sense,
> When stripp'd of this mortality, derives
> No colour from the fleeting things without;
> But is absorb'd in sufferance or in joy,
> Born from the knowledge of its own desert.
>
> —3.4.124–136

Manfred here articulates a theory of emotion as the product of self-judging "knowledge" that is independent of reference to the external world. The mind itself originates the "good or evil thoughts" that underlie his internal "torture" or "sufferance" or "joy." Although Manfred's bid for the mind's autonomy, as a romantic gesture, might be psychologically tenuous, Byron's central insight remains. Through his verbal representation of mind, Manfred renders the self-consciousness that conveys his (tormented) feeling of feeling. Yet, by the same token, his conscious expression of feeling leaves him—like his author—open to charges of posturing and insincerity.

In mental theater, Byron emphasizes "thought-dependent" emotions realized in language (De Sousa [1987]1999: 184). His conception resonates with Martha Nussbaum's "neo-Stoic" account of emotions as "cognitive-evaluative phenomena" dependent on the mind's assent to perceptions and beliefs about the world. While early nineteenth-century drama therefore strives toward knowing feeling, drama later in the century will destabilize this cognitive ideal. Instead of targeting the consciousness, the inwardness of Victorian melodrama probes beneath it, into what Michael Goldman observes as the subterranean currents of feeling in Ibsen and Chekhov. In line with Freud's theory of the unconscious, these plays recognize that the more intense or profound emotions escape knowledge: Miss Julie's outrage at Jean's butchery of her pet bird in Strindberg's play (1889), Nora's desperate *tarantella* in Ibsen's *Doll's House* (1879), Liubóv Andréyevna's subtle nervousness in Chekhov's *Cherry Orchard* (1903) originate from alienated, incoherent sources. The insistent clarity of eighteenth- and early nineteenth-century melodrama later dissolves into unsettling ambiguity, and all efforts at sentimental declamation fall flat—Chekhov's young scholar Trofímov exclaims, "[M]y heart and soul are always full of feelings[,]" but "I can't even explain them" (1997: 361). By the century's end, the closet stage features not only what lies hidden from others but also the enigma deep within ourselves.

CHAPTER FIVE

The Visual Arts

KERSTIN THOMAS

THE PRE-HISTORY OF ROMANTIC EMOTIONS

European Romanticism was undoubtedly of central importance to the development of a new cultural history of emotions in the nineteenth century. Nevertheless, as is so often stressed in the scholarship, the path was determined by the Enlightenment. In France, it was the major Encyclopaedia project which was the catalyst. Joan E. DeJean stated that at the moment in which the *Encyclopédie* redefined the terms *émotion, sentiment,* and *sensibilité*, the French felt differently, or rather acquired access to previously unknown affective possibilities (DeJean 1997: 93). This view is confirmed by Reinhart Koselleck's definition of the late Enlightenment as a period of transition (*Sattelzeit*) in the *Lexikon zur Begriffsgeschichte und zum Bedeutungswandel von Ausdrücken im politischen Diskurs Deutschlands* (Koselleck, Conze, and Brunner 1972–1997). According to this work, the way terms were used in politics changed radically after the middle of the eighteenth century, when social upheaval caused a drastically different experience of reality. In 1988, Ludwig Jäger consequently suggested research on the "historical semantics of the German language of emotions" for that period (Jäger 1988). Recently, an investigation of the mutual influence of the terminology and the phenomenon of emotional concepts was undertaken by Ute Frevert and others with a large-scale project on the history of emotions (Frevert et al. 2011). The authors conclude that feelings and the corresponding terms were already changing in the eighteenth century and that therefore the Enlightenment can by no means be reduced to an "age of reason." Similarly, David Denby concluded in 1994 that "sentimental narratives occupy a central place in the project of the French Enlightenment" (Denby 1994: 240). Considering this pre-history, it is clear that the French Revolution did not constitute a break, as William M. Reddy shows (Reddy 2001). Rather, it is to be understood as a continuation and more eruptive outbreak of this regime of emotion, which nevertheless brought about a reassessment of traditional role models and values.

An analysis of visual art supports these results. The revaluation of emotion accompanied a revaluation of certain aesthetic procedures which were regarded as particularly suitable for appealing to the viewer's feelings. These new procedures, in turn, led to a change in the aesthetic discourse and the development of completely new artistic strategies. With regard to emotional strategies, we can see a close interaction of art practice and critical discourse in the nineteenth century.

While this interaction is particularly marked in France, it can also be observed in England and Germany. The evolution of the art market that accompanied radical social changes in the middle of the eighteenth century is of central importance and changed the way art was experienced. New possibilities for communication and exchanges about art appeared (Sennett 1977; Kernbauer 2011). These were the salons and their broad audience, informed and guided by salon critics, but also the increased activities of galleries, which now served a new type of buyer (Lobstein 2006). Freer press laws had substantial influence on the production, experience, and evaluation of art. The literati who published in numerous new art and literary periodicals often wrote for a very specific audience and accordingly developed their own terminology. On the other hand, the general public participated in art discourse in a way it never had before.

Due to the increasing specificity of the art public everywhere in Europe, in particular however in France, the canon of art discourse formerly regulated by the Academy was now diversified. As Peter-Eckhard Knabe describes in his handbook on art-theoretical thought in France, in the eighteenth century art terms became active forces rather than remaining fixed constructions (Knabe 1972). The new need for intersubjective communication resulting from the extended field of discourse brought forth a new terminology of emotions, which was both shaped by artistic production and in turn influenced it. An analysis of the emotional register of art in the nineteenth century must therefore keep both factors in mind. The history of terminology cannot do without a detailed analysis of the works of art, and this analysis in turn often relies on the discourse.

SENTIMENT

In the early eighteenth-century Theories of Enlightenment, concepts of emotions were mainly given meaning by reference to reason. But at the same time results of empirical philosophy now entered the discourse of art, and taste and feeling became guidelines for the judgement of art, for example with Jean-Baptiste Du Bos and Immanuel Kant (Du Bos 1719; Kant [1790] 1990; Becq 1994: 243–273). In English and French philosophy of the Enlightenment, for example in the works of Anthony Ashley-Cooper, Third Earl of Shaftesbury, and Jean-Jacques Rousseau, as well as later in the German poetry of Johann Gottfried von Herder, the new value of feelings is closely linked to their moral function. Against John Locke, Shaftesbury emphasized in *Characteristicks of Men, Manners, Opinions, Times* in 1711, that people possess the ability to see moral good through emotions, applying the visual metaphor of the "inward eye" (Shaftesbury [1711]2001: 2, IV: 2, III, 16–21; 2, V: 3, II, 231; Dowling 1996). This connection was also followed in art. The significance of the expression of passions in transmitting examples of virtues was already emphasized in seventeenth-century Academy doctrine, and especially in history painting: Charles Le Brun's schemata of human pathognomics influenced the representation of emotions in art well into the nineteenth century (Montagu 1994; Kirchner 1991).

However, the appreciation of sentiment in the eighteenth century also led to a change in the demands placed on the visual arts. With Jean-Baptiste Du Bos' *Réflexions critiques sur la poésie et sur la peinture* published in 1719, the viewer's emotions became the central criterion of art (Du Bos 1719: 5–40). The ability to stir feelings was, according to Du Bos, the highest goal of art (Dauvois and Dumouchel 2015). The passions were considered to point solely to the action and the agent and his moral standing, thus initiating an intellectual evaluation first and foremost. Sentiment, in contrast, was regarded as immediately causing an empathetic reaction in the sensitive observer. Accordingly, artists searched for more suitable ways to address sentiment directly (Busch 1993).

For the noblest genre, history painting, this demand led to the search for new motifs which emphasized an emotional moment of contemplation rather than a heroic action. In

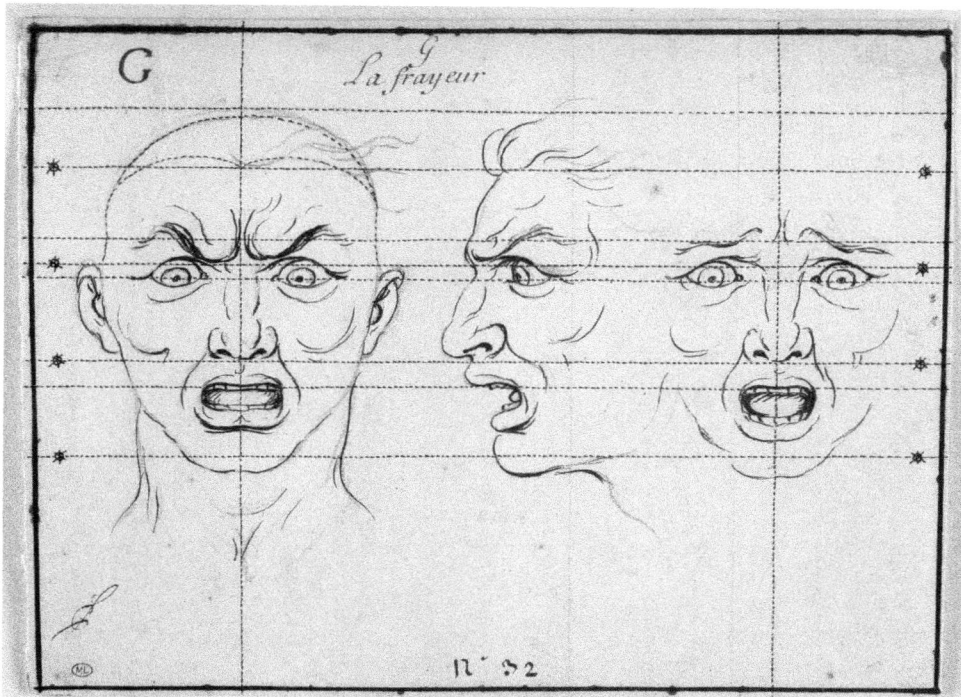

FIGURE 5.1: Charles Le Brun, *Horror* (La Frayeur), *c.* 1688, ink and pencil on paper, 19.5 × 25.6 cm, Paris, Musée du Louvre. © bpk/RMN—Grand Palais/Gérard Bolt.

the 1750s, the Comte de Caylus published *Tableaux tirés de l'Illiade et de l'Odyssée d'Homère et de l'Énéide de Virgile*, which was a source of new motifs for numerous artists (Caylus 1757). In 1754, La Font de Saint-Yenne also proposed a list of new subjects inspired by antiquity with the intention of breathing new life into painting (La Font de Saint-Yenne 1754). Among them was the story of Tarquinius' nephew, Brutus, who had his sons executed for his love of the republic, a story which had already inspired Voltaire to write a play in 1730, and which influenced the republican painter Jacques-Louis David's famous painting.

The hero is motionless in David's painting, shown at the moment of inner conflict, in which he faces his own abyss, while his wife, the daughters, and the nurse openly express their grief at the death of their sons and brothers. The lack of pathos in the main protagonist intensifies the effect on the viewer: a paradox for which Michael Fried introduced the term "absorption," which he contrasted with the "theatricality" of traditional painting, a strategy associated with Denis Diderot (Fried 1980). Diderot had pointed out that it was the restraint of feelings in particular which affected the viewer: "Scenes of violent passion are not those that reveal superior talent in the declaiming actor nor exquisite taste in the applauding spectator" (Diderot 1767; translation in Fried 1980: 117).

Between 1759 and 1781, Diderot acted as a salon critic for Friedrich Melchior Grimm's *Correspondance littéraire, philosophique et critique*, criticizing the traditional forms and subjects of painting on the grounds that they failed to touch and elevate by devoting themselves to the wrong pathos. In the *Encyclopédie*, Diderot distinguished "*sensibilité naturelle*" and "*sensibilité maîtrisé*"—a distinction which he developed further in his *Paradox of the Actor* (de Font-Réaulx 2002). He argues that in painting, honesty and true feelings

FIGURE 5.2: Jacques-Louis David, *Lictors Returning to Brutus the Bodies of his Sons* (*Les Licteurs rapportent à Brutus les corps de ses fils*), 1789, oil on canvas, 323 × 422 cm, Paris, Musée du Louvre. © Getty images.

should be transferred to the canvas. Thus, an artist must be able to experience the feelings himself in order to elicit them. This personalization of feelings leads to a re-evaluation of the different genres, specifically genre painting: regarded as a low form of painting by the academic tradition, genre painting can produce natural emotions, since it is close to the artist's everyday feelings. With regard to the genre painter Jean-Baptiste Greuze, he writes: "If he is thinking about a subject, he is obsessed by it, it follows him everywhere. It infiltrates his own personality. He adopts that of his painting: he is brusque, gentle, guileful, acerbic, flirtatious, sad, gay, cold, serious or insane, depending on the subject he is preparing" (Diderot 1763; translation in: Harrison and Wood 2000: IIIc, no. 12, 607–608). Here, the harmony of the artist's mindset and the emotional expression of his work was regarded as proof of its moral and artistic value (Dassas 2002: 17). The artist's truthfulness brings forth the viewer's emotional response, Diderot explains with regard to a genre painting by Greuze: "When I saw that pathetic, eloquent, old man, I . . . felt my soul moved to pity and I was ready to shed tears" (Diderot 1763; translation in: Harrison and Wood 2000: IIIc, no. 12, 605). Rather than eloquence and pathos, the painting stirs the viewer to tears through gentle feelings. Genuine emotions achieve moral validity by proclaiming truth.

Truthfulness was also the aim of the "expression of the passions," codified by Charles LeBrun. However, this truth was related only to the motif of the painting, not to the truth of a sentient being, namely that of the painter. Art was now understood as the highest

FIGURE 5.3: Daniel Nikolaus Chodowiecki, *Natural and Affected Attitudes* (*Natürliche und affectirte Handlungen des Lebens*), 2nd series, plate 3 and 4: *Sentiment* (*Empfindung*), 1779, etching, 87 × 50 cm. © bpk | Hamburger Kunsthalle | Elke Walford.

moral authority because of its capability of transmitting feelings. This is also very much what Madame de Staël had in mind when in 1810 she wrote: "man has in his soul innate sentiments which objects of reality will never satisfy, and it is to these sentiments that the imagination of painters and poets gives form and life" (de Staël 1810/1813: vol. 3, 140).

The comparison of pathos acquired by rhetorical means and sentiment perceived as genuine remained the topic of discussion in the salon of 1808, where the critic Pierre Jean-Baptiste Chaussard perceived Anne-Louis Girodet's painting *Scenes of the Flood* as exaggeratedly theatrical: "it seems that these paralysed brains could only be stirred by electric and violent shocks; have the gentle tears of the *sensibilité* run dry at the bottom of the withered hearts? Are we damned to shed tears of blood?" (Chaussard 1806: 119; translation by T. and M. Bawden). The distinction between natural and artificial feeling established by Diderot was echoed in a series of drawings entitled *Natürliche und affectirte Handlungen des Lebens* (*Natural and Affected Acts of Life*) by the German artist Daniel Nikolaus Chodowiecki in 1778 and 1779. In the second pair of pictures, he presented a natural and an affected attitude towards nature, by showing a couple lost in contemplation in the one, and expressing their feelings through lively and exaggerated gestures in the other.

ROMANTICISM AND EMOTIONS

It is commonly held that the art of Romanticism in England, France, and Germany presented a stark contrast to the sentimental aesthetic of the eighteenth century. Werner

Hofmann accordingly considered the beginning of the nineteenth century as a period of radical rupture (Hofmann 1972). But with regard to emotions, such a view proves to be too narrow. Quite apart from the fundamental impossibility of defining Romanticism, which Northrop Frye and Isaiah Berlin have pointed out, this view does not do justice to the art of weak feelings and moods, which remained dominant throughout the entire nineteenth century, thus continuing the art of sentiment of the eighteenth century (Frye 1963; Berlin 1999: 1). It is therefore more appropriate to speak of various developments than of a radical change (Jobert 2002). These took different paths in individual European countries, revealing regressions, adaptations, and interdependencies.

Mood

Analogous to the increased importance of genre painting, the appreciation of feeling in art also led to the establishment of landscape painting as a genre in its own right. Departing from the French historical landscapes and the Dutch moralizing landscapes, a new form of landscape painting emerged in England, France, and Germany, the essential elements of which were the feeling of the individual and a natural atmosphere.

England: Constable and Turner In England, the new type of landscape painting was closely linked to the nascent British artistic identity. The rapidly advancing industrialization of the eighteenth century, liberalism, the rise of the middle classes, as well as the geographic and later political isolation of Britain, furthered the genre. The roots of British landscape painting also lie in the establishment of the English landscape garden and in the landscape poetry of early English Romanticism (Hoozee 2007).

John Constable's romantic landscapes are central to this development. Constable, who was born in East Bergholt, Suffolk, sought to provide a true portrayal of British landscapes. He worked on the paintings of his home county outside, so he could look directly at his motif, studying the geographical and atmospheric peculiarities in great detail. Constable also applied contemporary scientific theories in his work. His cloud studies, for example, were based on the classification of the English meteorologist Luke Howard, published in 1803, which was popularized by Thomas Foster in his *Researches on Atmospheric Phenomena* (1813) (Howard [1803]1865; Foster 1813; Clarkson 2010: 156). His series of mezzotints *English Landscape Scenery* (1830) show that feelings are of fundamental importance to the perception of nature (Hill 1985). In the preface of *Landscape Scenery*, Constable explained that he wanted to convey a picture of his native landscape and show atmospheric effects of light and shadow in nature. In his notes on the panels, which were only edited posthumously, there were further indications that Constable saw the sensuous impression and the feelings that the landscapes produced in him as a unit, which he wanted to convey to the viewer through his landscape pictures. In the letterpress to *East Bergholt, Suffolk* he explained: "this work was begun and pursued by the Author solely with a view of his own feelings, as well as his own notions of Art" (Constable [1830]1970: 12).

On *Old Sarum* he noted: "The subject of this plate, which from its barren and deserted character seems to embody the words of the poet—"Paint me a desolation",—is grand in itself, and interesting in its associations, so that no kind of effect could be introduced too striking, or too impressive to portray it" (Constable [1830]1970: 24). Contemplation, feeling, and poetry combine in Constable's landscapes and create suggestive scenes that were meant to affect the viewer.

FIGURE 5.4: John Constable, David Lucas, *Old Sarum*, 1830, Mezzotint, first state of two, 14.9 × 17.8 cm. © Victoria & Albert Museum

The specific combination of nature, science, perception, and feeling is also found in the work of Joseph Mallord William Turner, whose painting *Rain, Steam, Speed—the Great Western Railway* (1844) represents an attempt to capture these phenomena in painting by dissolving them in a vortex of color. The Victorian art critic John Ruskin declared Turner the most important contemporary painter, precisely because he was able to portray this connection by purely pictorial means, which exceeded the power of language. In his five-volume work, *Modern Painters*, Ruskin formulated these two principles as the condition of landscape painting: to truthfully convey nature at the same time as conveying the feelings of the artist who was exposed to this landscape:

> the landscape painter must always have two great and distinct ends: the first, to induce in the spectator's mind the faithful conception of any natural objects whatsoever; the second, to guide the spectator's mind to those objects most worthy of its contemplation, and to inform him of the thoughts and feelings with which these were regarded by the artist himself. In attaining the first end the painter only places the spectator where he stands himself; ... He may follow out his own thoughts as he would in the natural solitude; ... But in attaining the second end, the artist not only *places* the spectator, but *talks* to him; makes him a sharer in his own strong feelings and quick thoughts; hurries him away in his own enthusiasm ..., leaves him ... under the sense of ... having been endowed for a time with the keen perception and the impetuous emotions of a nobler and more penetrating intelligence.
>
> —Ruskin 1860: Part 2: Section I; ch. 1: § 1, 133–134

Here as well, feeling takes the role of vouching for the truth of experience, and is as such closely linked to morality. Constable's and Turner's paintings exerted a strong influence on nineteenth-century French landscape painting.

Germany: Caspar David Friedrich   Jean-Jacques Rousseau's revaluation of the emotions, so closely connected to a renewed interest in landscape, had an enormous influence on early Romanticism in Germany. The notion of Rêverie, which Rousseau expounded on in his *Rêveries du promeneur solitaire*, written between 1776 and 1778 and posthumously published in 1782, had a particular impact (Rousseau [1782]1959). Rousseau described Rêverie as a state in which intuition and feeling connect, in which immersion and wandering, self-indulgence and sensations are combined. Treatises on landscape painting, for example by Christian August Semler, explicitly referred to Rousseau, placing "reveries" or "aesthetic feeling" at the center of the perception of nature (Semler 1800). German landscape painting of the late eighteenth and early nineteenth centuries was also less about picturesque views than about empty landscapes as bearers of mood (Frank 2004: 143–170). The atmosphere was tied to an experience of totality, in which both a mental state and the atmosphere of the surroundings seemed to be present. The twofold designation of "mood" for inner and outer states held a particular interest for poets from the early Romantic era onwards. Landscape turned into a space in which the soul could resonate. Experiencing nature and experiencing self are intertwined, perception and mental stimulation are interrelated. Artists made the important transition from depicting emotions to depicting landscapes as emotionally perceived environments, directly affecting the perception of the viewer. Wolfgang Kemp has described this shift as the replacement of the paradigm of aesthetics of effect with the paradigm of reception aesthetics (Kemp 1983).

Caspar David Friedrich was particularly instrumental in renewing this kind of art. Contemporaries emphasized his ability to move the viewer through his art in a way that usually only nature itself can (Börsch-Supan and Jähnig 1973: 64). Friedrich achieved this by erasing almost all narrative detail, by blurring and extending the field of view, by uniformity of color tone as well as the renunciation of a center. The unbounded gaze which these techniques created is similar to the perception of nature. In his *Nine Letters on Landscape Painting* of 1815–1824, Carl Gustav Carus described mood as one of the main tasks of painting: "The representation of a certain mood of mental life (meaning) through reproduction of a corresponding mood of natural life (truth)" (Carus [1815–24]2002: 91). The emotion of the beholder is evoked through the correspondence between moods and natural states.

Gregor Wedekind points out that contemporaries praised Friedrich's ability to portray landscapes as soft sentimentality almost as much as his ability to portray them in a "gloomy but great" way (Wedekind 2010). In keeping with Carus, mood was not conceived as a homogeneous feeling of sublimity in the presence of landscape, but was also conceived as a trigger of the gloomy, lonely, joyless, even the bleak. If a metaphysical upswing is achieved in the one, the gloomy paintings evoke the pathos of contemplation without hope. Heinrich von Kleist described Friedrich's *Monk by the Sea* as follows: "The painting stands there ... like the apocalypse, as if it possessed Young's *Night Thoughts*, and since in its monotony and boundlessness it has nothing but the frame for a foreground, when one looks at it, it is as if one's eyelids had been cut away" (Kleist 1810; translation in: Harrison and Wood 2000: VIb, no. 15, 1032).

The lonely coast and the view of the blurry distance become a symbol for the impossibility of longed for redemption, and the melancholy that results.

FIGURE 5.5: Caspar David Friedrich, *Monk by the Sea* (*Mönch am Meer*), ca. 1809, oil on canvas, 110 × 171.5 cm, Berlin, Alte Nationalgalerie. © Getty images.

To the accusation of Baron Ramdohr that his art confused aesthetic emotion with pathological emotion, Friedrich retorted:

> The effect [*Effekt*] or rather, to speak in plainer German terms, the way my picture "works" [*die Wirkung*] upon the beholder is enough to justify its worth as long as it works truthfully, as long as its truth is directed towards what is noble. If a picture works feelingly and spiritually upon the beholder, if it inspires a fairer mood within the heart, then it has already fulfilled the first demand placed upon a work of art. . . . If a picture leaves the feeling and responsive beholder cold and the heart untouched . . ., then it can lay no claim to the name of an authentic work of art [*eines wahrhaften Kunstwerks*], although it may well deserve the name of a most beautiful piece of artifice [*einer schönen Künstleley*].
>
> —Friedrich 1809; translated in: Harrison and Wood 2000: VIb, no. 13, 1025

Art, therefore, aimed at the truth through feelings, and Friedrich took up the connection between natural feeling, truthfulness, and morality forged in the eighteenth century. Mood was not the artist's projection onto nature, but rather the landscape was a space of sensibility which the painter actively sought out, in order to be seized by the mood of nature and to reconcile his mood with nature. While Semler spoke of "aesthetic mood," "reveries," or "aesthetic emotionality," Friedrich wrote of the "elevation of the spirit" and "religious upswing" (Friedrich 1999: 115).

France: Corot Henri de Valenciennes was an important figure in French landscape painting who raised its profile significantly. However, the work of John Constable equally impressed French artists with its mixture of the sublime, picturesque, realistic, and naturalistic. Constable became known in France around 1820, and the exhibition of some

FIGURE 5.6: Camille Corot, *View of Riva* (*Vue prise de Riva*), 1865–70, oil on canvas, 73 × 123 cm, Marseille, musée des Beaux-Arts. © bpk/RMN—Grand Palais/Jean Bernard.

of Constable's principal works in the salon of 1824, the so-called *Salon anglais* of the Restoration, as well as the salon of 1827, had a lasting effect on the younger generation of artists (Noon 2003: 192–231).

The new generation based the expression of mood on the natural feeling for landscape. The work of the landscape painter Camille Corot was central to this development (Pomarède 1996).

Even before he actually started painting, Corot's choice of motif was determined by whether or not a landscape appealed to his feelings. In a sketchbook, Corot wrote:

> Let your feelings be your only guide ... follow only that which you can understand and which complements your own feeling. ... Any place I see affects me. However conscientiously I seek to imitate it, I never for a moment lose sight of its first emotional impact on me. ... When faced with nature, begin by looking for form; then values and tonal relations, colour and execution: and subordinate the whole to your original feelings. Our feelings are as real as anything else. ... If we have really been moved, the sincerity of our feeling will be communicated to others.
>
> —Corot 1856; translation in: Harrison and Wood 1998: IVA, no. 1, 535

As contemporary art critics, such as the poet Théophile Gautier, noted, Corot followed Rousseau's aesthetic of the Rêverie (Gautier [1857]1996: 70).

While the role of the artist as a sentient being for Corot was as central as for Caspar David Friedrich, the way these emotions were accessed differed considerably. For Caspar David Friedrich, mood had a metaphysical dimension, while for Corot, feelings were evidence of the livelihood of things: "My goal is to express life," he said (Moreau-Nélaton 1924: II, 36; translation: T. and M. Bawden). With his vitalist understanding of the emotions, Corot was closer to the sensualist tradition in England and France than to Friedrich who was more in line with German Idealism. Corot's paintings became the point of reference for perception-oriented Impressionistic landscapes because of the sense of nature expressed in them. In the art dealer Paul Durand-Ruel's exhibition of Impressionist art in 1899, Corot was hailed as the father of Impressionism. His combination of feeling for nature and dreamy poetics also inspired artists like Pierre Puvis de Chavannes.

STRONG FEELINGS

The sentiments associated with reason and morality, and used in landscape painting as a means of moving the observer, were in stark contrast with the strong feelings and passions of the art of the nineteenth century. However, Theodor Adorno and Max Horkheimer stated in their *Dialectic of Enlightenment* that these strong, "unreasonable" feelings do not constitute a break with the Enlightenment, but merely present another side of it (Adorno and Horkheimer 1947).

Violence, Eros, Agony

This other side of reason was the predominant theme of the Spanish artist Francisco de Goya: stupidity, superstition, and passion and violence. In his graphic cycles in particular— the *Caprichos*, the *Desastres de la Guerra*, and the *Tauromaquia*—low, unregulated, and violent feelings determined the actions of the often grotesquely drawn figures (Wilson Bareau 1993). Goya denounced the madness and absurdity of contemporary society, but his imagination drew on this source. The message of the *Caprichos* was clearly indebted to the Enlightenment climate under the reign of Charles III in 1780s Spain. Goya befriended liberal intellectuals such as the poet Meléndez Valdés, who had translated the poem *Night Thoughts* by the Englishman Edward Young (published between 1742 and 1745), which was so influential throughout Romanticism. In the *Desastres de la Guerra*, which shows the brutality of the Napoleonic Peninsular War relentlessly—the strangled, the stabbed, raped women, and murdered children—the portrayal of emotions was politically motivated. But it also crossed a line of which the art theory of the eighteenth century had been very conscious: Diderot, for example, had excluded images that evoked disgust from the realm of aesthetics (Menninghaus 2002: 125–126).

Goya's pictures were not moralizing, but rather dealt with fundamental human passions, which could be erotic incitement, but which could equally erupt into cruelty and destructive rage.

In his late painting *Saturn*, the God is shown as a raging madman in the process of devouring one of his children whose bleeding neck stump can be seen where his head should be. This scene of cannibalism showcases the cruelty of antiquity, replacing the Neoclassical ideal of noble simplicity and quiet grandeur, which, according to Johann Joachim Winckelmann, manifested itself even in the statue of Laokoon contorted with pain, as it was in accordance with the Greek character (Winckelmann 1754/76: 22). This was a notion upheld by Gotthold Ephraim Lessing, who based it on the necessities of sculpture rather than the Greek character (Lessing [1766]1982: 26–29, 103). In Goya's work, by contrast, there was ardent passion: the face of Saturn is lined with horror and fear; his is an unstable figure overwhelmed by the feelings caused by this gruesome act.

In English art, with John Hamilton Mortimer and with the Swiss artist Johann Heinrich Füssli, who emigrated to England, there were numerous pictures of dreams and sexuality. Füssli's *Nightmare* is associated with sexual desires, symbolized by an ugly incubus crouching on a defenseless woman. At the same time, the image is a feverish delirium of

FIGURE 5.7: Francisco de Goya, *Saturn*, 1820–23, oil on canvas, 146 × 83 cm, Madrid, Prado.© Getty images.

an implied rape, in which the artist's phantasm is masked as the dream of a defenseless woman. Sexuality, violence, and passivity are implicit themes of many of Füssli's pictures. He treated them explicitly in his private erotic series, *Symplegma*.

Mortimer and Füssli were gripped by the fascination with the mysterious and the abysmal, which originated in England and spread through Germany and France, and was characterized in literature by John Milton's *Paradise Lost* (1667), Edward Young's *Night Thoughts* (1742–1745), and by the unfathomable negative heroes invented by Lord Byron—a movement for which Mario Praz coined the term "dark romanticism" (Praz 1930; Krämer 2013).

In the work of the poet, engraver, and painter William Blake, the visionary and the spiritual appeared as torments of passion manifested in the body. In his *Nebukadenzar*, Blake shows the Babylonian king Nebuchadnezzar II from the book of Daniel, who lost his mind due to pride, described by Blake's biographer Alexander Gilchrist as a "mad king crawling like a hunted beast into a den among the rocks; . . . his wild eyes full of sullen terror" (Gilchrist 1998: 408–409).

Suffering, Madness, Death

The most influential picture of suffering, madness, and death was *The Raft of the Medusa*, painted by Théodore Géricault in 1819. Géricault depicted the existential drama of a shipwreck which had taken place on the West African coast on a grand scale. With barely any food, exposed to sun, saltwater, and a struggle for life, which even led to cannibalism, 150 people tried to survive on a timbered raft. Only fifteen survived. The painting of Géricault breaks with the demands of classical history painting and wholly concentrates on the emotions of the dying people, trying to evoke the empathy of the beholders (Wedekind 2014). Géricault emphasized this in a letter of 1819: "neither poetry nor painting possess the ability to communicate with adequate horror all the fears plaguing the people on that raft" (Géricault 1819; translation by T. and M. Bawden). Human suffering is also an issue in Géricault's depiction of the *Monomaniacs*, portraits of women and men with mental illnesses (Wedekind 2007).

Inspired by Géricault's *Raft of the Meduse*, Jean-Baptiste Carpeaux sculpted *Ugolino and his sons* between 1857 and 1861, which aims to "express the most violent passions and blend in the most delicate tenderness," as he wrote in a letter (Carpeaux [1861]1912:

FIGURE 5.8: Jean-Baptiste Carpeaux, *Ugolino and his Sons* (*Ugolin et ses fils*), 1865–67, marble, 197.5 × 149.9 × 110.5 cm, New York, The Metropolitan Museum of Art. © Getty images.

159; Draper and Papet 2014; translation by T. and M. Bawden). The choice of the subject reported in Dante's *Divina Commedia*—of the imprisoned count, starving to death and forced to eat his own children—and its execution with the crouched father, full of anguish, shows the same interest in strong and ambivalent emotions emerging in existential situations as in Géricault's picture.

The fascination with strong feelings generated a new interest in the vulnerable, broken man. Many artists in the French romantic period were inspired to adopt Byron's heroes, who were at the mercy of their passions without gaining understanding from these feelings (Wakefield 2007: 121–130). The figure of Mazeppa, described by Voltaire, and subject of Byron's poem of the same title written in 1818 was a popular subject (Marciuk 1991). It was about the Ukrainian aristocrat, Mazeppa, who entered into a romantic relationship with the young wife of an older count palatine during his time as a page at the Polish court. As a punishment, he was tied naked to his horse and the horse was driven into the wilderness with the intention of killing the horseman. Day and night, Mazeppa was shaken by his horse on its journey through the Ukrainian steppe. Close to death, he was finally saved.

Théodore Géricault's lithograph from 1823 shows the naked, fatigued youth on the horse's back, the straps that tie him to the animal's body cutting deeply into his flesh.

His pose is one caught between martyrdom and heroism. According to the classical ideal, a hero breaks laws to serve a higher morality, whether this was determined by the state-sovereign—as in Jacques-Louis David's *Brutus*—, divine law, or reason (Kirchner 2001). Mazeppa's transgression of the law in his affair with a married woman did not,

FIGURE 5.9: Théodore Géricault, *Mazeppa*, 1823, lithograph, 15.9 × 20.7 cm. © bpk/RMN—Grand Palais/René-Gabriel Ojéda

however, create new rights, nor did he adhere to a higher moral cause, let alone the promotion of the greater good. He was suffering not only his punishment, but his indomitable passions, leading to decline and weakness, like the horse to which Mazeppa was bound, stumbling on the slippery slope. The close binding of the human and the animal body highlights Mazeppa's passionate, animalistic nature; by evoking the motif of the centaur, a negative symbol of libidinal power, Géricault's hero becomes the antithesis of an *exemplum virtutis*. Instead of striking down base instincts, Mazeppa was powerless against his passions, and his action neither disregarded the base nor the selfish, but indeed aimed at both. The suffering which the hero must endure because he followed his nature did not lead to anything great. Rather, he was credited with the recognition of guilt, which in turn increased the suffering (Thomas 2007). The inescapability of the passions also emerges clearly in the closing passage of Byron's poem:

> My undulating life was as/ The fancied lights that flitting pass/ Our shut eyes in deep midnight, when/ Fever begins upon the brain;/ But soon it pass'd, with little pain,/ . . . Dying, to feel the same again;/ And yet I do suppose we must/ Feel far more ere we turn to dust:/ No matter; I have bared my brow/ Full in Death's face—before—and now.
>
> —Byron [1818]1986: 191; 557–568

Romanticism's interest in the ineluctability of passions fostered suffering and broken heroes (Busch 1993).

Romantic passions were destructive, but they did not produce weak heroes. As Charles Baudelaire later pointed out in his *De l'héroïsme de la vie moderne* (1846), the passionate and suffering hero represented a radical individualism beyond morality (Baudelaire [1846]1976: 493–496). Hans Robert Jauß has emphasized that this revolt constituted a new heroic attitude (Jauß 1970: 57–66). Precisely by resisting a divine and protecting nature and by following his own nature, man has the chance to liberate himself from the power of nature over him. Baudelaire's modern hero was of the type that Friedrich Nietzsche paid tribute to in recognizing that Byron's Manfred is "Lord of his virtues, master of his guilt" (Nietzsche [1884–85]1988: 26 [179], 197; translation by M. and T. Bawden). It was his vital, raw, passionate power that made the modern antihero convincing.

Passion of Color

An admiration for this unbridled force can be seen in the animal paintings of Eugène Delacroix. His painting *Young Woman Attacked by a Tiger* (1856) shows that these wild beasts are dominated not only by force, but by impulsive passions. Beauty and eroticism are paired with unbridled passion—this is symbolized by a piece of fiery red fabric at the side of the surrendering woman.

Here, as in Delacroix's important painting *The Death of Sardanapalus*, which is based on a poem by Lord Byron, it is the color, and therefore the painting itself, which expresses the power of passions (Jobert 2004). Gold and red predominate and produce an atmosphere of luxury and violence—notions that contemporaries associated with the Orient (Guégan 2003). The mobile lines and the flow of color merge with the cruel subject of *Sardanapalus*, the mass murder of all the servants and animals of the doomed ruler, and suggest a continuous stream of blood pouring through the image. Delacroix painted wet-on-wet; the color is thin but opaque. He placed small strokes of unmixed paint next to and above one other in order to increase the effect of the color.

FIGURE 5.10: Eugène Delacroix, *The Death of Sardanapalus* (*Mort de Sardanapale*), 1827, oil on canvas, 392 × 496 cm, Paris, Musée du Louvre. © Getty images.

Charles Baudelaire linked Romanticism, Modernity, and the meaning of color in his *Salon de 1846*. In the chapter "De la Couleur," Baudelaire designated color as the most important form of expression in a picture. According to him, color has the role of transmitting emotions. He singled out Delacroix as a colorist: "It is because of this entirely modern and novel quality that Delacroix is the latest expression of progress in art . . . worthy successor of the old masters, he has even surpassed them in his command of anguish, passion and gesture! It is really this fact that establishes the importance of his greatness" (Baudelaire [1846]1981: ch. IV, 66). Due to the commitment to color as a means of expression of passions, Delacroix and Baudelaire were the main points of reference for the generation of young artists at the end of the century.

The Artist

From this perspective, it is clear why Baudelaire's anti-heroes could become bearers of this new concept of the passions: they were also models of the artist, of his creative potential, which Baudelaire later (in the salon of 1859) associated with the imagination, calling it "reine des facultés," the queen of the faculties of the soul (Baudelaire [1859]1976: ch. III, 619–623; Baudelaire [1859]2006: ch. III, 265–87; Baudelaire [1859] 1981: ch. III, 155–158). And this is why the color and the brush stroke of the artist stood to gain the victory of the passions. Delacroix's strong lines, for instance, impart a force similar to that of the animals depicted, conveying the strong feelings of passionate struggle and cruelty, just as the blazing red color expresses life through pulsating blood. The emotions shown in the picture seem to be direct evidence of the artist's energy. The Romantic notion of the artist as a genius driven by strong passions was based on this equivalence of the artist and the artwork. This notion was sometimes promoted by the artists themselves, but also projected onto them. An example of this was one artist's interest in the passions in their most agonizing form: the madness, as in Géricault's *Monomaniacs*. This madness was later attributed to the artist himself, as proof of the topos of the mad genius which led Cesare Lombroso to form his theory in *The Man of Genius* in 1872 (Lombroso 1872/1882). Géricault's interest in madness, however, was motivated by a scientific worldview (Wedekind 2013).

INNER AND OUTER WORLD IN LATE NINETEENTH-CENTURY ART

While in the first half of the nineteenth century the use of emotions in art was aimed primarily at gaining knowledge of the world or of the self, towards the end of the century, artists' interest increasingly turned to the feelings themselves, their specific qualities, and the expression of these in art. The complexity of the interactions between the human psyche and the empirical experience of reality, between the inner world and the outer world, were of particular interest. Two trends were distinguishable, although these were not always strictly opposed to one another: One movement aimed primarily at the expansion of the inner world, while the other aimed at touching the outer world. In the former case, the external became a mirror of a psychological state; in the latter, the artist explored external things through his feelings.

Expansion of the Inner World

Many works of art in the Symbolist tradition systematically foregrounded emotions. The choice of subject was primarily based on its potential for expressing an emotion which viewers should not only identify, but also feel themselves. To this end, the artists dispensed with clear emotional expressions in faces and gestures and alluded to feelings instead, stimulating emotions and ideas, and the viewer's imagination. Stéphane Mallarmé formulated this aesthetic theory in an 1891 interview with Jules Huret:

> I think that [the things] should be presented allusively. Poetry lies in the contemplation of things, in the image emanating from the reveries which things arouse in us. . . . To name an object is largely to destroy poetic enjoyment, which comes from gradual divination. The ideal is to suggest the object. . . . An object must be gradually evoked in order to show a state of soul; or else, choose an object and from it elicit a state of soul by means of a series of decodings.
>
> —Huret/Mallarmé 1891; translation in: Mallarmé 1956: 18–24; 21

Here, Mallarmé stressed the primacy of the images evoked by rêverie and state of the soul for poetry. Only five years earlier, Jean Moréas had still emphasized the importance of idea in terms of language in his symbolist manifesto (Moréas 1886). Mallarmé's definition however was at one with the aesthetic approach chosen by visual artists, that is, creating emotions and imaginings in the viewer with pictorial suggestions. Odilon Redon's charcoal drawings, for example, showed hybrid specters, ambiguous in form and meaning, appearing out of the impenetrable black space, eerie and mysterious (Gamboni 1989). In his diary *À soi-même*, Redon wrote in 1902: "The sense of mystery consists in continuous ambiguity, in double and triple aspects, hints of aspects (images within images). Forms about to exist or existing in the mind of the onlooker. All things that are more than suggestive, since they actually appear to us" (Redon 1867–1915; translation in: Dorra 1994: 54–56; 54).

In aesthetic theory of the late nineteenth century, for example in Paul Souriau's *La suggestion dans l'art* published in 1894, allusion and indeterminacy play a central role, as Dario Gamboni has shown (Souriau 1893; Gamboni 2002). Suggestive art aimed directly at emotions; the motif represented was their result. Thus, the figures painted by Pierre Puvis de Chavannes, who was highly regarded in the 1880s, do not convey a specific content, but act as coded expressions of a "melancholy harmony," as the philosopher and critic Gabriel Séailles put it with reference to the painting *The Poor Fisherman*, "This strange and original work shows us the talent of Puvis de Chavannes in its principle, the suggestion of an image through feeling" (Séailles 1888: III, 184; translation by T. and M. Bawden).

FIGURE 5.11: Pierre Puvis de Chavannes, *The Poor Fisherman* (*Le pauvre Pêcheur*), 1887–92, oil on canvas, 105.8 × 68.6 cm, Tokio, National Museum of Western Art. © Getty images.

Melancholy was one of the most common emotions in nineteenth-century French paintings, and painters liked to present themselves as melancholic (Hauptman 1975; Herding 1990).

In Redon's *Noirs*, in Puvis, but also in Caspar David Friedrich or Corot, the essential means of suggesting feeling was the unification of color, as well as the absence of concrete actions and content. In contrast to its defining role in the work of Delacroix and Baudelaire, color here creates an independent space for meaning, analogous to that which Mallarmé produced with the sound and color of words. This becomes clear in the interiors by Édouard Vuillard, a painter of the artist group of the Nabis, in which spaces and persons without clear outlines and substantive concretization merge into an amorphous whole, whose tonal unity creates a dense emotionally charged atmosphere (Cogéval 2003).

The Belgian artist Fernand Khnopff, member of the group XX., used a uniformly muted color palette in a similar way to create an arena for the emotions (Leen 2004).

In his painting *An Abandoned City*, the gray mist takes on the functions of unification and atmospheric concentration, awarding meaning and intensifying the impression of the melancholic emptiness expressed by the abandoned city with its boarded-up buildings and the surreal advancing sea. In this portrayal of his hometown, Khnopff drew on Georges Rodenbach's symbolistic 1892 novel *Bruges-la-Morte*, which Rodenbach described in his

FIGURE 5.12: Fernand Khnopff, *The Abandoned City* (*Une ville abandonnée*), 1904, pastel and pencil on paper, glued on canvas, 76 × 69 cm, Brussels, Musées des Beaux-Arts de Belgique. © Royal Institute for Cultural Heritage, Brussel.

foreword as "impassioned study, . . . [evoking] in the form of an intangible personality the spirit of a town, endowing it . . . with the power of entering into all the fluctuating conditions of the soul" (Rodenbach [1892]1903: 63). He argued that by looking at the photographs included, the reader should be able to "feel" the city itself. Khnopff, who was a friend of Rodenbach's, designed the frontispiece for *Bruges-la-Morte* and referred to Rodenbach's photographs in various pastel drawings, intensifying its suggestive emotional impact. Bruges became the epitome of the "gray city" to which the protagonist retreated in his grief, and the gray became the epitome of the bleak melancholy which was the actual content of both book and painting, and, moreover, the key sentiment of a whole generation (Thomas 2016).

In the paintings of the Swiss artist Arnold Böcklin, the emotions aimed at a transindividualistic perspective. Here, too, contemporary critics regarded the color of his paintings as "bearers of moods and sensations," which appeal "directly to the sentiment, the potential of the soul to be moved" (Rosenberg 1894: 183; Gaehtgens 2010). Gustav Floerke recalled with regard to his friend Böcklin, that he believed mood was something visible in nature, which the painter could grasp (Floerke 1901: 37). The impression of nature produced pictorial expression of ideas and their connection. Böcklin allowed his motifs to emerge directly from the mood, a view also advanced by Julius Vogel for the *Island of the Dead* (Vogel 1902: 17). The mood was perceived as something essential; thus, Heinrich Wölfflin described Böcklin's *Villa by the Sea* in 1897 as "*Empfindung unseres Jahrhunderts*" (the feeling of our century) (Wölfflin 1897). Accordingly, the Austrian art historian Alois Riegl cited Böcklin in his essay *Die Stimmung als Inhalt der modernen Kunst* (Mood as the Content of Modern Art) (1899) as an example of painting that aims at capturing aesthetic experience and thereby a world view through feelings (Riegl [1899]1929). For Riegl, mood was the promise of Modernism, providing a secure frame in the face of progress and the disintegration of the world.

Nature in the painting provides a space of perception and of sensation for both the artist and the viewer. The barrier between the work of art and the viewer is lifted. He or she is, as it were, in the mood of the picture. The details are suggestive but because their narrative content is left open, the images transcend individual biographies and attest to something more fundamental: crime, decay, death, grief. In the nineteenth century, emotions were illustrated and took on an existential depth at the same time. What was awakened by the art as a fleeting insight into life disintegrated when the aesthetic moment was over. Both sadness and melancholy reside in the pictures.

Touching the Outside World

Several statements by artists, especially from the 1880s onwards, attested to an awareness of the interplay between perception and feeling, between the subject and the object. The Swiss author Henri-Frédéric Amiel, popular in the 1880s and 1890s, wrote in the year 1852 in his diary "Every landscape is, as it were, a state of the soul (état de l'âme)" (Amiel 1894: 30). The passage became notorious, and the art critic Ferdinand Brunetière interpreted it to mean that the *état de l'âme*, the mood, was not a transferal of the artist's feeling onto the landscape, but that the landscapes themselves had emotional expression, which in turn entered into a correspondence with the perceivers (Brunetière 1888: 217).

Even an artistic movement such as Impressionism, committed to achieving the highest degree of precision in the comprehension of reality and the perception of it, did not see this task purely as a matter of the sensory organs, without the involvement of feeling. Claude Monet, for example, combined a highly accurate survey of the perception of nature with an emotionally rich expression. This was particularly true of his paintings from the 1880s and 1890s (Tucker 1989: 17–39; Elderfield 1974; Shiff 1991; Rapetti, Stevens, Zimmermann, and Goldin 2003). In 1889, the Symbolist poet Octave Mirbeau wrote, "Everything seizes him, inspires him; his sensitivity, heightened by study, unfolds itself to the most varied shows of nature.... The need to create, and to give to his unceasing and burgeoning emotions the desired form and colour, rises day by day, simmering, bubbling over, tipping over into an exasperation of conquest, rage of possession" (Mirbeau [1889]1993: I, 380; translation by T. and M. Bawden). Mirbeau portrayed the act of painting as a passionate appropriation of impressions of nature. The resulting landscape paintings testify to this emotional saturation.

The need for an emotionally deepened sensory experience, which is kindled by the vital power of nature, of the world, and of man, can also be observed in the works of Auguste Renoir. Jean Renoir remembered his father's visual and tactile devotion to things and reported him saying, "What happens in my skull does not interest me. I want to touch ... to see at least" (Renoir 1962; translation by T. and M. Bawden). Renoir's urge to touch living creatures and things through the act of painting created an affective relationship charged with meaning. It was this quality of his paintings which led to Renoir's recognition in early Modernism. On the occasion of an exhibition of his paintings in Munich in 1912, German art critics even described the artist as a pioneer of Expressionism (Rohe 1912; Manheim 1986: 100).

The image of the city appears to have been a particularly fruitful source for combining mood and perception, as the paintings of London by William Turner, James McNeill Whistler, and Claude Monet show (Lochnan 2004).

FIGURE 5.13: James MacNeill Whistler, *Nocturne: Blue and Gold—Old Battersea Bridge*, 1872 × 75, oil on canvas, 68.351.2 cm, London, Tate Gallery © Alamy.

In their paintings, as in Whistler's *Nocturne in Blue and Gold—Old Battersea Bridge* (1870–75), the enveloping fog creates a uniform mood. The fog is not only a means of presentation, it also corresponds so precisely to the perceptive reality of London at that time that it becomes a semantic element. Indeed, the dreary fog was a true landmark of the city, and Monet's and Whistler's friend, the poet Stéphane Mallarmé, wrote: "I hate London when there is no mist; in its swathes it is an incomparable city" (Mallarmé [1863]1959: I, 92; translation by T. and M. Bawden). Rather than presenting a specific view of the city, Monet and Whistler let the fog become the bearer of a diffuse, all-encompassing atmosphere that translated the experience of London on an emotional level. In this way, feelings were turned into bearers of meaning. Gernot Böhme has pointed out the effectiveness of such emotional images for the identity of cities (Böhme 2006).

More than in landscape painting, city paintings were clearly not intended to indicate the inner world of the artist alone. Rather, the mood expressed the artist's connection with his surroundings. In line with Monet's and Renoir's approach, this meant that the artist came into contact with the world through his feelings, and perceived the quality of things, not just their outer form. In 1892, in his essay *Art Contemporain*, the critic Georges Lecomte praised the ability of the new art to stimulate both feeling and understanding (Lecomte 1892). He argued that it was precisely through emotion that art expressed the character and the qualitative characteristics of the surroundings, thereby conveying their reality. In his overview, Lecomte referred in particular to the seascapes of the Neo-Impressionist, Georges Seurat.

In the paintings of the time, the distinction between inner sensitivities and external states was abolished. This view reflected contemporary theories of perception. Thus, for example, the philosopher Hippolyte Taine stated in *De l'Intelligence*: "our external perception is a dream from within that is in harmony with things outside; instead of saying that hallucination is a false exterior perception we should say that exterior perception is a *true hallucination*" (Taine 1870/1878: II, 12–13; translation by T. and M. Bawden). His book was well received in artistic circles. In the same way that perception linked inner and outer aspects, it also connected sensory stimuli and emotions, as Taine explained in relation to our emotional memory: "The only thing that reproduces itself in me quite intact and complete is the precise nuance of emotion, violent, tender, strange, gentle, or sad, which once followed or accompanied the external, physical perception" (Taine 1870/1878: II, 70; translation by T. and M. Bawden). Perception and feeling go hand in hand in this view. Théodule Ribot, the founder of the *Revue philosophique*, suggested a comprehensive model of feelings, encompassing physical, sensory, moral, religious, and aesthetic aspects in his book *La psychologie des sentiments* (Ribot 1896). In this, he attempted to combine the leading contemporary physiological and psychological theories from England, France, Germany, and Italy, formulated by, for example, William James, Claude Bernard, Wilhelm Wundt, and Angelo Mosso.

A similar embodiment of perception and feeling was also attempted by the Futurists who aimed at directly expressing the emotional and physical experience of the metropolis through painting: noise, speed, bright lights, the world of advertising, of traffic and technology (Roche-Pézard 1983). In his Manifesto of 1913, Carlo Carrà called for art to capture the simultaneity of impressions in a *pittura totale*, in which all senses were united: one must paint "like the drunks sing and puke: sounds, noise and odours!" (Carrà [1913]1978: 21).

The Futurists used the term "mood" (*état d'âme*) for this physical concept of synaesthesia in their manifestos (Thomas 2014). The state of emotional excitement is turned into the

FIGURE 5.14: Carlo Carrà, *Railway Station in Milan* (*La stazione de Milano*), 1911, oil on canvas, 50 × 55 cm, Stuttgart, Staatsgalerie. © Staatsgalerie Stuttgart/VG Bild-Kunst, Bonn 2017.

principle of art, and the perception of the city was equated with modern perception. In this way, the physical sensation of mood was combined with the social experience of the metropolis, which the viewer was supposed to feel.

SYNTHESIS

The emerging interest in the nature and specific quality of emotions led to new strategies in the art of the late nineteenth century. Viewers were supposed to experience emotions directly, even physically, through suggestive colors and forms. On the one hand, works of art were created that focused entirely on reflecting the inner world. In order to do so, they relied on an enigmatic language, which was "complex and ... obscure" and thus seemed to reflect the entanglement of the subjective inner world, as the symbolist writer Remy de Gourmont pointed out with regard to literature (Gourmont 1892: 323). This led to an individualized cult of the emotional, and created imaginary worlds in the paintings by European Symbolists (Rapetti 2005). Even Symbolist landscape paintings often bordered on the fantastical—for example, in works by Jacek Malczewski, Giovanni Segantini, Walter Crane, Akseli Gallen-Kallela, William Degouve de Nuncques, and Frantisek Kupka (Thomson, Rapetti, Fowle, and von Bonsdorff 2012). Rather than producing emotions, these artworks conjure up images in the mind's eye.

For this reason, in the 1880s and 1890s, a number of artists from very different camps, including those who were among the Symbolists, strove to distinguish themselves from such "symbolistic" pictorial practices. They preferred a more open image able to better affect viewers. The term *synthèse* ("synthesis") was applied to this aesthetic approach, and it was fundamental to aesthetic theory at the turn of the century (Rookmaaker 1959). Synthesis referred to pictorial techniques which dispensed with details in favor of condensing expression.

Paul Gauguin was one of the first artists to use the concept of synthesis programmatically: On the occasion of the presentation of their works in the context of the 1889 World Fair, he referred to the group of artists founded by him as *Groupe Impressionniste et Synthétiste*. By synthesis, Gauguin meant his pictorial method of reducing people and landscapes into expressive ciphers. The contours were closed and all shapes were reduced to dense and distinct areas of color. By means of synthesis, painting developed a language of its own that achieved emotional expression directly, iconically, and not conceptually, as Gauguin put it in 1885 in a letter to his friend the artist Emil Schuffenecker (Gauguin [1885]1984). In a later letter to the critic André Fontainas, Gauguin refined this thought: "Colour which is vibration the same as music is, reaches to what is most general and therefore vaguest in nature: its interior force" (Gauguin 1899; translation in: Gauguin 1946: no. 170; 215–218; 216). Here it becomes clear that Gauguin did not limit the concept of synthesis to formal aspects, but saw it as an adequate means of representing the general expressive powers of nature. While Gauguin followed the Impressionist commitment to the perception of nature, he tried to make clear that perception of nature only brought forth insight when it was synthesized by the sensory organs. And this synthesis was strongest, as Théodule Ribot had stated in reference to *mémoire affective*, when it was emotionally grounded. Painting asserted this emotional synthesis by its own means, as Gauguin argued in a notebook thought to have been written around 1884/85: "Painting is the most beautiful of all the arts; in it all sensations are integrated. Like music, painting has an impact on the soul through the intermediary of the senses" (Gauguin [1884–85]1962: 57; translation by T. and M. Bawden).

In this dual sense, as a formal operation to increase expressiveness and as an emotional quality of perception, the term "synthesis" was prevalent in the art criticism of the 1880s and 1890s (Thomas 2010).

Neo-Impressionist Georges Seurat also combined pictorial synthesis and emotional perception. In a letter to Maurice Beaubourg, he sketched a classification of colors and lines that were "uplifting," "quiet," or "sad" (Seurat [1890]1991). In his later paintings, Seurat applied a scheme of enhancing emotional expression conceived by the polymath Charles Henry, and based essentially on the combination of colors, angles, diagonals, and tones (Zimmermann 1991).

In *Chahut*, the erotic-aggressive mood which prevailed in the Café-Concerts, where the ecstatic and obscene *Chahut* had been performed since the 1880s, is created with angular lines and red color tones (Lebensztejn 1989). As in Gauguin, the synthesis of perception and pictorial means leads to the recognition of reality, even if the object of knowledge is metaphysical in the one case, and social in the other.

The Nabis Maurice Denis also stressed repeatedly in his writings that synthesis could achieve meaning and thus promote knowledge (Bouillon 1993). In his 1907 essay on Cézanne, he wrote: "To synthesize ... means to simplify in the sense of making something intelligible. ... Submit every painting to one rhythm, one dominant feature, sacrifice, subordinate, generalise" (Denis [1907]1993: 147; translation by T. and M. Bawden). In synthesis, the separation of the inner world from the outside world, which the painters were so occupied with, was also resolved, as Denis wrote: "The Synthetism ... implied, however, the belief in a correspondence between external forms and subjective states.

FIGURE 5.15: Georges Seurat, *Chahut*, 1889–90, oil on canvas, 171.5 × 140.5 cm, Otterio, Kröller-Müller Museum. © Getty images.

Instead of evoking our inner state of the soul through the depicted subject, it is the work itself that should mediate the original sensation by perpetuating the emotion" (Denis [1907]1993: 139–140; translation by T. and M. Bawden).

The concept of a connection between perception, feeling, and knowledge through artistic synthesis is also found in the scientific scholarship of the turn of the century. Thus, in his essay *La mémoire affective et l'art* (1909), James Mark Baldwin, co-founder of the *Psychological Review*, developed a model based on Ribot's that analogized the processes of affective memory and the structure of artworks in attributing much importance to the process of synthesis (Baldwin 1909). For him, feeling possessed its own cognitive quality, mediated by a specific form which made no distinction between internal and external factors. Baldwin's interest in the mutual dependence of feeling and form and the empathy of the viewer was reminiscent of the German *Einfühlungsästhetik* of Friedrich Theodor and Robert Vischer, and Theodor Lipps (Vischer 1873; Wölfflin 1886; Lipps 1903–1906). In contrast to them, however, Baldwin did not trace the direct expressive value of forms back to an underlying anthropological structure, but considered it the result of a synthesis of the experiences of a lifetime.

The art of synthesis was contagious for the viewer's feelings where it correlated with perception. This was the case in Paul Cézanne's *petites sensations*, or in the landscapes of Ferdinand Hodler, who attributed emotional impact to painted landscape as it will "grip the spectator without fail and convey to him a deep and lasting impression" (Hodler

FIGURE 5.16: Ferdinand Hodler, *Lake Thun with Reflection* (*Thunersee mit Spiegelung*), 1905, oil on canvas, 80 × 100 cm, Geneva, Musée d'histoire. © Alamy.

[1885–86]1972–73: 112; Gowing 1978). Both artists were convinced of the importance of the sense of nature (*Naturempfindung*), which they attempted to capture and express through the art of synthesis: Cézanne in his construction of the image, divided into *taches*, and Hodler with his symmetrical compositions (Boehm 1988; Bätschmann, Eisenman, and Gloor 1987).

However, if the synthesis resulted in the ornamental, as was often the case with the Nabis, the quality of feeling was lost and a purely decorative value took its place, which produced aesthetic pleasure but no affective contagion. Perhaps it was also due to the application of the concept of synthesis to the aesthetics of the decorative that the term *expression* was increasingly used in the aesthetic discourse after the turn of the century (Vlaminck 1943; Matisse [1908]2009). The term is closely linked to synthesis, but highlights feelings to a greater extent. In particular, it was coined by the French artists of the *Fauves*, such as Maurice Vlaminck, André Derain, and Henri Matisse, who used strong colors and dynamic lines and compositions. It is this notion of expression, which German art criticism widely adopted for the exhibition of the *Fauves* in the *Berliner Secession* in 1911, and which resulted in the transferal of the term "Expressionism" to the German artists (Schmalenbach [1961]1972; Benson 2014). Through Expressionist painting, the concepts and the artistic techniques of the "emotional painting" of the nineteenth century found their way into the twentieth century.

CHAPTER SIX

Literature

GREGORY EISELEIN

INTRODUCTION

When seen with attention to the historicity of emotion, the literary history of the long nineteenth century changes. The period is often understood as the birth of Romanticism followed by an era of realism, and the narrative is about a shift from passionate overflowing emotion to levelheaded detachment, from subjectivity to objectivity, from warm to cool, from idealistic and dreamy to realistic and pragmatic. Within the Romantic era, subjective feelings are valued, but during the realist period emotions become suspect and less significant. If we take an alternative approach, one that emphasizes the cultural history of emotion, a different story emerges, and what seems striking is the enduring impact of sentimentalism. Romanticism continues to be important, though it might be best understood not as a revolution in the representation of affect, but a continuation of earlier ideas and styles. Around the middle of the century, literary trends were shifting, as realism gained traction and Darwin's theory of natural selection redirected Western thought. Yet the place of emotion does not so much diminish as change, with new interest in the observation, recording, and understanding of emotions as something both psychically interior and physiologically exterior. Despite a growing distrust of sentimentality, literary sentimentalism remained a powerful presence throughout the century's literary texts.

SENTIMENTALISM

The eighteenth century witnessed a significant change in literary representations of what we now call the "emotions" but may have been called "appetites, passions, affections and sentiments" in earlier schemas (Dixon 2006: 2). For instance, to illustrate this era's interest in emotional expression and the historical shift from a century earlier, William Reddy turns for evidence to Choderlos de Laclos's epistolary novel *Les liaisons dangereuses* (1782), which "devotes hundreds of pages to minute narration of the means of seduction, means that are emotional in character." One hundred years earlier, such emotions might have been depicted, but they would not have been examined in such detail (Reddy 2001: 142).

Literary studies of the late eighteenth century have carefully documented how emotion is a foremost concern and how the era's sentimental and gothic literary traditions are extensions of and reactions to Enlightenment ideas about emotion. A previously prevailing view that the eighteenth century was dominated by rationalist and neoclassical approaches to writing, which sought to control and subdue the expression and arousal of emotion, has been eclipsed by a more persuasive account of the prevalence and significance of emotion to Enlightenment writing. As Jessica Riskin explains, "if one could name a unifying feature of the Enlightenment as a whole, it would not be rationalism, but instead a pervasive ambivalence about rationalism" (Riskin 2002: 285). Riskin's work demonstrates that the era's interest in empiricism and reason are inextricably tied to its interest in emotion, and the era's most affectively intense literatures helped shape not only culture but also science: "Sentimentalism characterized the methods of what are now considered the hardest sciences, physics and chemistry" (7).

Although eighteenth-century thinking about sentiment had important links to science and medicine (Csengei 2011: 75–118), philosophy is where sentimentalism developed, and literature where it flourished. Rooted in Lord Shaftesbury's work on emotion, in the moral thinking of the Scottish Common Sense philosophers and the empiricism of David Hume, sentimentalism begins with the idea that our ethical decisions are based on our feelings. In *An Enquiry Concerning the Principles of Morals* (1751), Hume explores "the general foundation of MORALS" to ask "whether they be derived from REASON, or from SENTIMENT." He notes that traditional approaches took the view that "virtue is nothing but conformity to reason" (Hume 1998: 73–74). Hume disagreed. As he argues in *A Treatise of Human Nature* (1738–40): "Morals excite passions, and produce or prevent actions. Reason of itself is utterly impotent in this particular. The rules of morality, therefore, are not conclusions of our reason" (Hume 2000: 294). Instead, Hume looked to human feeling as the guide: "morality is determined by sentiment. It defines virtue to be *whatever mental action or quality gives to a spectator the pleasing sentiment of approbation*; and vice the contrary" (Hume 1998: 160).

In *Theory of Moral Sentiments* (1759), Adam Smith builds on these ideas to develop a theory of conscience motored by emotion and imagination and a vision of social relationships reinforced by "*the Pleasure of mutual Sympathy*" (Smith 2000: 10). We cannot truly know what others feel, but we can use our imaginations to put ourselves in others' situations and in an approximate way experience what they experience:

> As we have no immediate experience of what other men feel, we can form no idea of the manner in which they are affected, but by conceiving what we ourselves should feel in the like situation. . . . By the imagination we place ourselves in his situation, we conceive ourselves enduring all the same torments, we enter as it were into his body, and become in some measure the same person with him, and thence form some idea of his sensations, and even feel something which, though weaker in degree, is not altogether unlike them.
>
> —Smith 2000: 3–4

When we make moral judgments, we do so on the basis of imaginative and sympathetic identifications: "When we judge in this manner of any affection, as proportioned or disproportioned to the cause which excites it, it is scarce possible that we should make use of any other rule or canon but the correspondent affection in ourselves" (17–18). Following Hume, Smith sees no basis for ethical judgments beyond emotion, beyond "sentiment or affection of the heart" (17). These are the core ideas of sentimentalism. Emotions guide our moral decisions, and the ability to imaginatively identify with and vicariously experience the pain, pleasures, and emotions of others connects us to them and allows us to feel their suffering and the injustices they have endured.

Hume and Smith were the most important and adept articulators of this perspective on emotion and ethics. Yet sentimentalism was not confined to philosophy and found broad expression throughout Western culture in the long nineteenth century. In an effort to understand sentimentalism "through its longer term origins and effects," Michael Bell makes the valuable point that "much of the important 'thinking' about sentiment was done within the fiction itself" (Bell 2000: 11, 56). In the final decades of the eighteenth century, sentimental thinking shaped the representation of emotion in a wide range of literary texts. These texts aroused sympathy and tears and taught readers about socially acceptable displays of emotion, but they manifested in different forms and under different banners in various countries. Sentimental novels and poems flourished in Great Britain and North America, while the *Sturm und Drang* movement erupted in German literature, and literatures of sensibility appeared in England and France. In all of these styles and movements, the representation of intense or fine emotion was a hallmark of the writing.

For most of the twentieth century, however, the idea of "sentimentalism" was a term of disparagement and condemnation. James Baldwin famously defines it as "the ostentatious parading of excessive and spurious emotion," which he considers "the mark of dishonesty, the inability to feel" (Baldwin 1949: 579). By the late twentieth century, literary sentimentalism began to receive serious scholarly attention. In *Virtue in Distress* (1974), R.F. Brissenden traces sentimentalism's "idealistic and freshly empirical and pragmatic approach to life" (Brissenden 1974: 55) from Samuel Richardson's *Clarissa* (1748) to the Marquis de Sade's *La philosophie dans le boudoir* (1795) and Jane Austen's *Northanger Abbey* (1818). He sees in sentimentalism "the basis for a liberal and a revolutionary political ideology—humanist, anti-authoritarian and compassionate" (55). While his focus on "virtue in distress" as the central theme may seem narrow now, this examination of the literature of tears and its ties to humanitarianism, philosophy, and a range of English, French, and German texts, initiated a reevaluation of literary sentimentalisms, leading to a later explosion of scholarly work on emotion in literature.

Later critics would build on Brissenden's emphasis on tears and suffering to demonstrate sentimental literature's interest in a broad array of affects. For example, in his study of French sentimental writers, from once popular novelists such as Baculard d'Arnauld to Madame de Staël, David Denby expands our understanding of sentimentalism beyond tears. He sees it "as a narrative structure, in which the happiness and misfortune of the represented subject are the primary focus." Yet sentimentality is also always about others, observers, and their emotional responses: "As well as representing a reality, the sentimental text represents the reaction to that reality of an observing subject" (Denby 1994: 4). Just as Denby broadens our understanding of sentimentalism to include suffering *and* happiness, observed *and* observer, Claudia Johnson has drawn attention to the whole range of emotions portrayed in sentimental texts. She characterizes the decade's literary fiction as "bizarre and untidy": "In works by Wollstonecraft, Radcliffe, Godwin, Lewis, and Burney (to name only a few), emotions are saturated in turbulent and disfiguring excess; not simply patently disruptive emotions—such as ambition, greed, anger, lust— but ostensibly gentler ones as well—such as reverence, sorrow, even filial devotion—are always and obviously going over the top" (C. Johnson 1995: 1–2).

SENTIMENTALISM'S LEGACIES

The literary texts that explored emotional excess most famously may have been those we now classify as "gothic." The gothic is often separated from sentimentality because of the kinds of emotions it elicits: fear, terror, horror, and trembling rather than compassionate tears of sympathetic identification. Despite these evident differences, gothic and sentimental literatures are both reactions to neoclassical strictures and Enlightenment certainties. They're both rooted in new understandings of psychology and the affective connections among individuals, and they both aim to stimulate readers' sympathies. As Robert Hume explains, "The literature of the later eighteenth century attempts to rouse the reader's imaginative sympathies; the particular device employed toward this end by the Gothic novel writers is terror, which Burke had stressed as a factor in emotional involvement in his *A Philosophical Enquiry into the Origin of our Ideas of the Sublime and Beautiful* (1757)" (R. Hume 1969: 282). With its outlandish settings and plots, its emphasis on the supernatural and inexplicable, its mysterious atmospheres and insidious suggestions, the gothic invokes what Burke described as the sublime: "Whatever is fitted in any sort to excite the ideas of pain, and danger, that is to say, whatever is in any sort terrible," whatever "is productive of the strongest emotion which the mind is capable of feeling" (Burke 2015: 33–34). Gothic literature is often about repressed feelings and desires (Freud 1919), but it is also a literature that "invokes the pleasures of pain—and the pleasures of being horrified by pain—as a way of constructing identity" (Bruhm 1994: 146).

Although many texts of the period foreground emotional excess, others highlight more nuanced emotional expressions. For example, in her examination of literary, philosophical, and legal texts that represent judges and their deliberative processes, Nicole Wright demonstrates that the era's texts expressed concerns about both overly emotional judges and emotionally detached ones. According to these texts, finer feelings regulated by imagination and self-control are essential to a fair legal process: "Eighteenth-century narratives of criminal justice suggest that by drawing on their own memories of feeling, or imagining passions they may never have experienced themselves, judges can better identify and evaluate motives" (Wright 2015: 347). To cite another example of less extravagant but discerning interest in emotion, Antonina Harbus demonstrates how the language of Jane Austen's *Emma* (1815) reveals "her interest in nervousness, blushing, and other physical manifestations of emotional states." The novel's heroine gradually realizes that she needs to pay attention to the subtle, physical cues that are intrinsic to emotional expression and to "interpret physical signs rather than to attempt to read minds" (Harbus 2011: 779).

Like Austen, and like French and British sentimentalists, German writers were also using Enlightenment discoveries in ethics and aesthetics and the new empirical psychology to expand our understanding of human behavior and emotional expression. Within the German literary landscape, a key development was the *Sturm und Drang* movement. Of the various features of the style, one element seems certain: the spirited representation of human emotion. As Bruce Duncan explains, "Critics may debate when the *Sturm und Drang* began and ended, what political attitudes it espoused, who belonged to it, or even whether it actually constituted a movement at all, but all agree that it evinces strong emotion" (Duncan 2003: 47). While the movement combined elements of German nationalism with Enlightenment trends and a rebellion against neoclassical aesthetic standards, *Sturm und Drang* expressed ardent passions, fervent struggles and what Lesley Sharpe calls a "Promethean longing for release from accepted confines" (Sharpe 1991: 10). The most important and "by far the most widely read text of the tradition" is Johann Wolfgang von Goethe's *The Sorrows of Young Werther* (rev. ed. 1787) (Leidner 1994: 8). *Werther* tells the story of a sensitive young artist who falls deeply in love with Charlotte but later commits suicide when he realizes that Charlotte cannot reciprocate his passion. Werther eventually drifts into melancholy and irrationality:

> Sorrow and discontent had taken deep root in Werther's soul and gradually penetrated his whole being. His mind became completely deranged. . . . The anguish of his heart

FIGURE 6.1: Goethe's *The Sorrows of Young Werther* epitomized the *Sturm und Drang* movement's commitment to the representation of powerful emotion. Image: Tony Johannot ["Werther and Charlotte"], illustration from *Werther par Goethe*, trans. Pierre Leroux (Paris, 1845), opposite p. 162.

>consumed his good qualities, his vivaciousness and his keen mind; he was soon a gloomy companion. . . . A heavy weight lay upon his soul, deep melancholy had taken possession of him. He was pursued by a host of the saddest images and his mind knew no change save from one painful thought to another.
>
>—Goethe 1988: 65–66

This passage manifests Goethe's interest in the susceptible, complex, and emotional psyche of the individual, especially the artist, and it epitomizes the era's deep interest in a range of emotion, including inner conflict, sadness, and despair.

Just as the literature of the *Sturm und Drang* participated in the politics and public discussion of a unified Germany, at a time when "Germany as national state was more aspiration than an actual achievement" (Leidner 1994: 3), the literatures of sentimentalism played an important role in humanitarian reform efforts of the long nineteenth century. Bryccan Carey reveals, for example, the impact that sentimental texts—poems like William Roscoe's *The Wrongs of Africa* (1787) and Hannah More's *Slavery, a Poem* (1788),—had on the British abolitionist movement. These antislavery texts, literary and political, used a language of sentiment to influence and mobilize their audiences, which leads Carey to conclude that "One can think of few other occasions in history at which a literary discourse was so closely allied with a popular political movement" (Carey 2005: 196).

Sentimental rhetoric as a political and cultural force has been an especially important topic within the study of nineteenth-century American women's writing. Countering earlier and more disparaging views of women's sentimental writing (Douglas 1977), Jane Tompkins helped bring positive academic attention to affectively charged women's writing by focusing on the cultural work of novels like *Uncle Tom's Cabin* (1852). Tompkins aimed to re-value the sentimental and demonstrate how it was an expression of women's progressive power in nineteenth-century America (Tompkins 1985). Although the Douglas–Tompkins debate played an important role in drawing scholarly attention to sentimental women's writing, most scholars now have a more nuanced view of nineteenth-century sentimentality. There is no longer the assumption that the sentimental has a single, inherent political perspective. The more typical view now is that "female sentimental discourse is a mode of abstraction that has no a priori political implications for the power of women or other marginalized groups" (Berlant 1992: 270). And a range of critics have been examining the complicated and sometimes volatile relationships among sentimental literary texts and the broader social world. Philip Fisher has shown how "Compassion is . . . the primary emotional goal of sentimental narration" (Fisher 1985: 105), while critics like Glenn Hendler have seen "sympathetic identification as the narrative and affective core of a sentimental structure of feeling" as a way to examine how sentimental writing aimed to use transformative emotion to create changes in the public

FIGURE 6.2: Stowe famously deployed moving portrayals of the suffering of her enslaved characters to generate support for the antislavery movement in the United States. Image: George Cruikshank, "Eliza Crosses the Ohio on the Floating Ice," illustration from Harriet Beecher Stowe, *Uncle Tom's Cabin, or Life Among the Lowly* (London: 1851), opposite p. 51.

sphere (Hendler 2001: 11). Marianne Noble has detailed the ways that sentimental women's writing was not simply humanitarian in its reform ideals but also erotic in its exploration of sadomasochistic forms of desire (Noble 2000). While the diversity and nuance of literary critical work on U.S. sentimentalism can be difficult to summarize, this literature now seems to occupy a central role in the history of American literature and culture. A review of early twenty-first-century work in the field thus confidently asserts that "these studies show that neither American literature nor American culture can be understood without considering the significant role sentiment plays in its formation and definition" (Hoeller 2006: 343).

While it made a lasting impact on reform efforts throughout the long nineteenth century, sentimentality in literature also influenced future literary efforts and movements. For example, "to uncover why the myth of the melancholy female poet continues to have cultural resonance," Claire Knowles returns to the literature of sensibility from 1780 to 1860. What she finds is a template established early:

> in the wake of the phenomenal success of Charlotte Smith's melancholy and introspective *Elegiac Sonnets* (1784), many of the most popular female poets of the era—women like Mary Robinson and Letitia Landon—felt it necessary to exploit the pathos generated by their displays of feminine distress in order to gain entry into a literary sphere that was often overtly hostile to female poetic endeavor.
>
> —Knowles 2013: 2

Knowles' work traces that path from Smith to the twentieth century's confessional poets and our own present.

ROMANTICISM AND REVOLUTIONARY EMOTIONS

Sometimes conceived as a sharp break from the Enlightenment and the Age of Sensibility, the period in Western literary history known as Romanticism is at its core a mode of literary expression that values the expression of individual emotion. The term has been notoriously difficult to define with precision (Lovejoy 1924; Wellek 1949; McGann 1983: 17–20), and many attempts at a standard definition begin with comments about the impossibility of the task (Harmon and Holman 1996: 452; Murfin and Ray 2003: 415–416). Nevertheless, emotion, in author and reader, is undoubtedly a key component in Romantic definitions of writing. In his Preface to *Lyrical Ballads* (1802), for example, the English poet William Wordsworth defines poetry as "the spontaneous overflow of powerful feelings" (Wordsworth 2010: 562). In a similar vein, in an essay "On Goethe's *Meister*" (1798), the German writer Friedrich Schlegel defined the reader's experience in terms of powerful and unscripted emotional responses to the text:

> It is a beautiful and indeed necessary experience when reading a poetic work to give ourselves up entirely to its influence, to let the writer do with us what he will; perhaps only in matters of detail is it necessary to pause and confirm our emotional response with a moment's reflection, raise it into a thought, and where there is room for doubt or dispute, decide and amplify the matter. This is the prime, the most essential response.
>
> —Schlegel 1991: 273

While emotion remains central to the competing definitions of Romanticism, the period is also often characterized in terms of its revolutionary qualities and its break with what came before (Butler 1992; Paulson 1983). The era's ideas and writings are often starkly contrasted with those of the preceding era "in terms of binary oppositions, such as reason *versus* emotion; objectivity *versus* subjectivity; spontaneity *versus* control; limitation *versus* aspiration; empiricism *versus* transcendentalism; society *versus* the individual; public *versus* private; order *versus* rebellion; the cosmopolitan *versus* the national, and so on" (Kitson 1998: 35).

Nevertheless, recent literary historical work on Romantic literature has altered our understanding of the shift from the Age of Sensibility to Romanticism. Indeed, the new consensus might be that "romanticism absorbs rather than supersedes or decisively breaks with Enlightenment culture" (Yousef 2013: 3). In the wake of the American and French revolutions, and in the disappointments and hopes and horrors that followed both, the representation of emotion in Western literatures underwent identifiable transformations. Janet Todd, for example, sees post-Revolutionary British literature as affectively more subdued and more likely to highlight "qualities considered peculiarly British, such as restraint, self-control and stoical, wry acceptance" (Todd 1986: 131; Ablow 1991: 195). Nevertheless, the ongoing influence of sentimental literature is striking, and the changes wrought by Romanticism may be subtler and more nuanced than once imagined.

Often Romantic writers make the representation of emotion complex by adding to it another essential dimension. For example, a common Romantic move is to tie thinking to feeling. Romantic philosophical writers like Johann Gottfried Herder and Georg Wilhelm Friedrich Hegel, for example, did not consider feeling something simple or passive. Instead feeling and thinking were conceived as inextricably linked (Taylor 1975: 21; Oxenhandler 1988: 112). In similar fashion, the French novelist Stendhal theorized that love required self-control *and* passion, seeing self-control as a prelude to the moment when lovers could abandon themselves to passion and loss of self. As Miranda Gill explains in her analysis of this Romantic paradox: "Self-control, for Stendhal, could . . . be compared to a ladder to be dispensed with once the lover attains the final stages of self-surrender" (Gill 2015: 477).

Another way Romantic writers made earlier understandings of emotion more complex was to insist that literary texts represent and evoke emotional responses but also pull back from and observe them. For instance, Alfred de Musset believed that poetry required subjective *and* objective dimensions, emotional elevation, *and* ironic distance: "In order to create truly significant poetry, [the poet] should attain both a state of exaltation and one of detachment from his emotions" (Daemmrich 1973: 6; Beus 2003: 201). In his analysis of Romanticism's Stoic inheritance, Adam Potkay brings to light the Romantic distrust of sensibility, compassion, and pity: "Should anyone be pitied—if not the harassed rich, then the neglected poor? In William Blake's pithy phrase, 'Pity would be no more, / If we did not make somebody Poor'" (Potkay 2015: 1334). Potkay shows that a kind of antisentimentalism informs Wordsworth's poetry, and this "modified Stoic program for poetry" (1345) aimed to make the emotions more rational. Thus, according to Potkay, "we overlook much about Wordsworth's art if we view it about feeling or emotionality without central reference to a standard for evaluating and correcting emotions" (1345).

Romantic writers gave depth and complexity to our understanding of pity and other emotions, and likewise they complicated and expanded our understanding of intimacy and the sympathy on which emotions such as pity and compassion were based. Nancy Yousef's examination of the era's conceptions of intimacy shows us how Romantic writers altered sentimentalism's understanding of sympathy to define intimacy as that which is both "most private" and also "most shared" (Yousef 2013: 119), as a way to show how these writers were trying to come to terms with relationships in which sympathy is not reciprocated, relationships complicated by "the demurral, disappointment, and frustration of the mutual identification and recognition that eighteenth-century theories of sympathy presupposed" (24). Although many of the themes that shaped sentimentalism (emotion, compassion, sympathy) endured, their significance became enlarged, complicated, and sometimes paradoxical during the Romantic era.

REALISM, DARWIN, NATURALISM

One way of interpreting nineteenth-century literary history is that the Romantic era valued emotion more than the Realism of the second half of the century. The Romantics wanted affective intensity, while the Realists preferred affective distance. It is certainly true that some nineteenth-century writers valued a kind of cultivated detachment (Anderson 2001). Moreover, at least one literary analysis has attempted to quantitatively document this decrease in emotional intensity. In her 1942 study, Josephine Miles focuses on a particular kind of literary figuration, pathetic fallacy, the attribution of feelings or emotions to things, to demonstrate a marked decline—"an almost steady downward line of quantity and quality in the device" over the course of the century, from the Romantic poets to the Victorian and modernist poets who would follow (Miles 1965: 108).

Yet another and perhaps more accurate way to understand this change in literary representation is not so much as a shift from more emotional to less emotional but as a shift from intensity and ethics to the observation, description, and analysis of emotions. As Rachel Ablow explains, "The emphasis may have shifted from determining what we should feel to anatomizing what we do feel, but the basic interest in feeling continues unabated" (Ablow 1991: 208). Realism in literature might then be defined as an attempt to observe, describe, and reveal fully the range, intensity, and complexity of human behavior, interaction, and affective reaction and expression. This era also gave rise to a variety of often popular and alternative genres that exploited and amplified the sensationalist or lurid elements of realist fiction to create texts that represented a more extreme range of human feelings and experiences. While sentimentality maintained an impressive influence through the century, developments in science significantly altered the direction of affective representation, beginning around the middle of the century.

New approaches to understanding realist fiction have shown how important sentimental modes of reading continued to be throughout the nineteenth century. Rae Greiner, for example, shows how the realist novel encourages and "enacts sympathetic habits of mind in readers," in which readers both identify with and think along with characters (Greiner 2012: 15). Even writers at the end of the century, such as Joseph Conrad, understood well such readerly habits and "art's affective power" (141). Some realist novelists attempted to use sympathy to humanize what seemed to some an increasingly cold and mechanical social world. As Thomas Recchio argues, Elizabeth Gaskell's *Mary Barton* (1848) turns to sentimental and melodramatic scenes to cultivate forms of affective knowledge in her readers: "By evoking sympathetic feelings in readers, Gaskell's novel produces an experiential sense of shared, 'innate human qualities,' which suggests that individual human volition has some possibility of resisting and reshaping [the] social environment" (Recchio 2011: 298). Thus sympathy becomes in this analysis something that resists the dominant culture. In a North American context, María Amparo Ruiz de Burton's *The Squatter and the Don* (1885) is an example of what Melanie Dawson calls "a hybrid text" that combines realism and sentimentalism (Dawson 2008: 50). Ruiz de Burton's novel

FIGURE 6.3: Little Nell's death in *The Old Curiosity Shop* is perhaps the most well-known example of Dickens' mastery of sentimental literary art. Image: George Cattermole, ["At Rest (Nell dead)"], illustration from Charles Dickens, *The Old Curiosity Shop*, with introduction and notes by Andrew Lang, 2 vols. (London [1897]), vol. 2, p. 340.

rejects the realist emphasis on scenic descriptions, landscapes, and private property to focus instead on emotional descriptions, "affective terrain," and the "multiple and overlapping affective bonds" (71) that link people, families, and both Anglos and Californios (those persons of Spanish ancestry born in what became the state of California following the Mexican–American War [1846–48]).

Many of the greatest writers of the century were deeply indebted to sentimentality's legacy. Charles Dickens, for example, powerfully deployed sentimental conventions, not only in novels like *The Old Curiosity Shop* (1840–41), with its grotesque villain Quilp and Little Nell's heart-rending deathbed scene, but throughout his work. As Valerie Purton demonstrates, Dickens used in "many different, complex and often conflicting ways . . . the rhetoric of sentimentalism," and her analysis is devoted to an effort at understanding "that strange effect, the welling of tears or even the tightening of the throat ('a lump in the throat') which surprises the casual viewer when someone—anyone—weeps in a play or film, or, more specifically, when the mid-Victorian audience read, often aloud and with others, of the death of Little Nell" (Purton 2012: xxvii). As the literary historian Philip Davis reminds us, feeling that sadness or pain is central to Dickens' work: "there is in

Dickens an implicitly Christian defence of memory and emotion, of the moral necessity to feel life whatever the content or even the pain of that feeling" (Davis 2002: 316). Likewise, the great Russian novelist Fyodor Dostoyevsky in early works such as *Poor Folk* (1846) tried to establish himself as "the original creator of the school of 'sentimental naturalism'" (Catteau 1989: 197). Though Dostoyevsky would abandon this mode for psychological realism and the representation of violent emotions, terror, and existential dread in later works such as *Crime and Punishment* (1866) and *The Brothers Karamazov* (1880), readers can see throughout his career an effort to render human emotion intensely and realistically.

While sentimentality persisted well into the nineteenth century and beyond, the literary representation of emotion experienced a sea change around mid-century. These changes might be traced in part to the downturn in idealism following the unsuccessful European revolutions of 1848 or, in the United States, the trauma following the Civil War (Menand 2001: 49–69). Darwin's evolutionary theory, including his functionalist understanding of emotion, had also begun to re-shape literary trends (Beer 1983; Levine 1988; Richter 2011; Gianquitto and Fisher 2014).

In *The Expression of Emotion in Man and Animals* (1872), Darwin studied the observable, physical manifestations of emotion, "the expressions and gestures involuntarily used by man and the lower animals, under the influence of various emotions" (Darwin 1998: 33). He sought a naturalistic explanation of those emotions and expressions, one rooted in his own theory of natural selection, and focused on the functional benefit the expression provides an organism. He theorized that our nostrils flare when we are angry to allow air to fill our lungs readily in anticipation of the exertion required for a physical fight (242). He used the concept of "serviceable actions" (33) to categorize these expressions, movements, gestures, or behaviors that offer some useful benefit to the organism in a particular emotional state.

Not surprisingly, then, Darwin is critical to understanding the transformations in emotional representation that happen from the mid-century on. One of the best accounts of this shift is Melanie Dawson's *Emotional Reinventions* (2015). Dawson's work begins with Darwin's and comparable contemporary attempts to categorize a range of human

FIGURE 6.4: Darwin's theory of natural selection and his naturalistic understanding of emotion, which juxtaposed human with animal expression of emotion, had an enormous impact on literary realism. Image: T.W. Wood, "Cat, savage, and prepared to fight," illustration from Charles Darwin, *The Expression of Emotion in Man and Animals* (London, 1872), p. 58.

emotions. This "practice of isolating and analyzing affective expressions within a larger field" (Dawson 2015: 8) is similar to the efforts of realist writers. *Emotional Reinventions* demonstrates how "realism was, at its heart, an affectively invested mode of writing" (11). Yet, unlike texts written under the influence of the earlier sentimental paradigm, which aimed "to represent emotions *emotionally*," realism took an approach that emphasized instead, following Darwin's lead, "observation and categorization" (11). In her analysis of William Dean Howells's writing, for example, she shows how his realist attitude toward affective representation results in heightened attention to detail and emotional nuance, to the particular and individual, but also to what Dawson calls a "more limited, smaller-scaled version of sympathy" (50), one that subdues idealisms and acknowledges the difficulty of knowing exactly how others feel. Realist fiction also draws our attention to the ways in which individuals might not simply feel an emotion but instead, at times, need to cultivate specific emotions. In her analysis of racial passing narratives, she shows how African American writers such as Charles Chesnutt, Frances Harper, and Pauline Hopkins represented the usefulness of an "emotional flexibility" that "allows a character not only to survive but also to thrive in new environments" (157). The realist novel reveals how "individuals could nurture emotional pathways that could result in real but controlled affective experiences" (199).

Such an analysis of "cultivated emotion" (Dawson 2015: 199) echoes earlier work on literary realism that emphasized how these works often highlight a tension between the social performance of certain emotions and the actual feelings of individuals. Nancy Schnog examines "the transition in women's writing from sentimentality to literary realism—from the conceptual world of the 'true woman' to that of the 'new woman'" (Schnog 1997: 87) to show how realist novels from the second half of the nineteenth century challenged sentimental attitudes about women and "the large prescriptive literature that sought to control them through the social performance of female cheerfulness" (87). Writers like Louisa May Alcott knew that "culturally created ideas about emotion played a key role in underwriting and naturalizing gendered social roles and their accompanying modes of interiority" (104–105). The focus on moods allowed realist writers like Alcott to draw attention to "the scripting of female emotion and . . . the encoding of women's mood" (87), and to highlight a "female interior life beyond sentimentality" (105).

By the 1860s, domestic realism as the dominant mode of fiction had been overtaken by the sensation novel (Pykett 1991: 201). The novels collected under the sensation novel umbrella were "disparate in terms of style and content" and included such different works as Mrs. Henry Wood's domestic *East Lynne* (1860–61) and Mary Braddon's *Lady Audley's Secret* (1861) (Garrison 2001: 1). In all of these novels, however, emotion—the representation of emotion, the exploration of emotional states, the analysis of emotion, the manipulation of emotion and the conjuring of emotional responses in readers—is key. Throughout the genre, "Plots revolve around the effects of characters' emotional, as opposed to rational, behaviour, and the representation of particularly women's strong emotions is a conspicuous feature" (Hansson and Norberg 2012: 154). Sensation novels deployed surprise to engage readers, and they represented and thematized physiological sensation in ways connected to the era's interest in science and the analytical study of emotions: "Descriptions of reflex actions, shock, surprise, and automatic states of action (trance, somnambulism, hallucination, intoxication) are virtually constitutive of the genre" (Dames 2005: 109). Yet these texts also offered readers an intense emotional experience: "The typical sensation plots, more than a hundred years later, are still guaranteed to make the flesh creep and the hair stand on end" (Hughes 2001: 4).

Although sensationalism as a sub-genre would wane, realism's interest in depicting and dissecting emotion would continue throughout the remainder of the century and into the next. The work of Jane Thrailkill, for example, has established "the centrality of feeling to literary realism." She shows how at the height of the realist era, following the work of Darwin and William James, realist writers "conceived of feelings in physiological terms" (Thrailkill 2006: 366). The writers of the period, such as Twain in *Adventures of Huckleberry Finn* (1884), began to imagine the human nervous system, including its emotional expression, in terms of networks, echoing the era's explosion of communication and transportation networks in the form of telegraphs and railways. Literary realism attempted to capture the felt, affective dimensions of living—"*the zest, the tingle, the excitement of reality*," in the words of James (Thrailkill 2007: 41).

A number of late nineteenth-century writers attempted to capture the emotional experience of real life by focusing on their character's interior worlds—their motives, thoughts, and affective states. In *Madame Bovary* (1856), Gustave Flaubert is not merely condemning the sentimental and romantic literary texts that Emma Bovary reads, which have so shaped her emotional life, but he is also deploying free indirect discourse to capture her thoughts, moods, emotions, and speech patterns. Just as Flaubert seems to move back and forth between an objectively described and "'hard-edged' perceptual world" and a more subjective interior world captured in free indirect discourse (Porter 2004: 129), the English novelist George Eliot moves constantly "between consciousness and unconsciousness" (Davis 2002: 196). Eliot is "the great mediator and translator, finding thoughts within feelings, feelings about thoughts" (Davis 2002: 196). Using a stream of consciousness technique (so named by his brother William), Henry James further developed psychological realism by focusing intently on the depth, complexity, and subjectivity of his characters' thoughts and feelings. For critics like Thrailkill and Stephanie Byttebier, James is the novelist who perhaps most profoundly plumbs the human psyche by paying close attention to the ways in which affective responses register on the body (Thrailkill 2007: 201–250). In her examination of empathy in *The Wings of the Dove* (1910), Byttebier shows how James moves away from simple conceptions of empathy but also away from a denial of its existence, arguing: "Rather than showing the impossibility of empathy, then, we might see James as forwarding an understanding of it in *The Wings of the Dove* as a painful, difficult, and revisionary process rather than a natural state or instinct" (Byttebier 2014: 172).

Late nineteenth-century playwrights introduced not only realistic subject matter, as did Henrik Ibsen in *A Doll's House* (1879), but also psychologically and affectively complex characters, such as the protagonist of his later *Hedda Gabler* (1891). Realist and naturalist playwrights made overt explorations of emotional experience the subject of their works. In her discussion of Anton Chekov's *Three Sisters* (1901), Peta Tait notes that "Chekov's plays, depictions of hope, despair, and melancholy, were central to the twentieth-century invention of realistic acting; his characters describe their emotional feelings in the dialogue, and emotions are specified in stage directions" (Tait 2015: 1502). Some of these playwrights were influenced not only by literary realism and naturalism but also by the science of the era. The Irish playwright J.M. Synge used his understanding of Darwin's *Expression of Emotion in Man and Animals* to develop characters in plays such as *The Shadow of the Glen* (1903) whose affective displays were unclear or ambiguous. Rather than "being automatic signs of clearly defined interior states," Michael Bogucki shows these emotional gestures could be read in a Darwinian way as "symptoms of ancient biological inheritances or uncomfortably primal drives" (Bogucki 2010: 516).

Yet Darwin's ideas may have made their most enduring impact on the naturalist fiction writers of France and the United States. One of the most prominent influences might be detected in naturalism's tendency to see humans and animals in a similar light, just as Darwin recognized several kinds of cross-species connections when exploring emotional expression. Émile Zola's notion of the "human beast" from his novel *La bête humaine* (1890) captures well the naturalist view that humans were animals driven by needs and instincts and that writers should objectively and methodically observe their human subjects just as scientists would their objects of study. In 'The Experimental Novel' (1880), Zola makes these comparisons clear: "this dream of the physiologist and the experimental doctor is also that of the novelist, who employs the experimental method in his study of man as a simple individual and as a social animal" (Zola 1964: 25). Later naturalist writers would follow Zola's example. The American novelist Frank Norris represents his protagonist in *McTeague* (1899) "as a kind of human beast" whose "animal-like characteristics" include the fact that he is "huge, dumb, slow, prone to violence, and immensely strong" (Pizer 2000: 21). But for Norris, naturalism and Zola's example are not simply scientific objectivity imported into literature. Instead, what distinguishes naturalism from ordinary or "real Realism" with its "small passions" is its "romanticism," by which Norris means the affective power and magnitude of his work: "Everything is extraordinary, imaginative, grotesque even, with a vague terror quivering throughout.... It is all romantic." He concludes by making an important distinction: "Naturalism is a form of romanticism, not an inner circle of realism" (Norris 2012: 911, 912). And the passions there are large, terrifying, and tragic.

TRANSITION TO MODERNISM

When viewed from a literary history of emotions, the sharp break with the past that characterizes modernism in literature—"MAKE IT NEW," in the words of Ezra Pound's famous modernist slogan, borrowed from Confucius (Pound 1986: 265)—doesn't seem quite as sharp. The deep interest in psychological realism and the attempt to capture the complex and dynamic emotional states of literary characters that is so essential to the achievement of realist novelists like Eliot and James seem simply extended in the stream of consciousness efforts of the French writer Marcel Proust or the Irish novelist James Joyce. As Virginia Woolf notes in her discussion of Joyce in a 1919 essay titled "Modern Novels," modernist fiction attempts to faithfully record a living reality in all of its affective nuance: it "attempts to come closer to life, and to preserve more sincerely and exactly what interests and moves them [young modernist writers like Joyce]" (Woolf 1919: 189). Although Woolf is interested in distinguishing recent modernist innovations from earlier writers and "the conventions which are commonly observed by the novelists," it also seems clear that she is describing an approach to writing pioneered by the realists of the nineteenth century. That literary technique is, in the words of Woolf, to "Let us record the atoms as they fall upon the mind in the order in which they fall, let us trace the pattern, however disconnected and incoherent in appearance, which each sight or incident scores upon the consciousness" (189). Ablow notes that although Woolf may be rejecting the sentimentalism and didacticism of nineteenth-century novelists like Dickens or Stowe, "she is by no means turning away from feeling, per se," but instead extending the exploration and representation of emotion begun in the nineteenth century and carried through modernism (Ablow 1991: 208).

Modernism did take the representation of affect in new directions in certain ways. For example, Dada, like other schools of modernist poetry, cultivated new forms of shock or

FIGURE 6.5: Dada cultivated forms of literary surprise and startle, in part by refusing the traditional hermeneutical association of poetry and art with meaning and interpretation. Image: Paul Eluard and Tristan Tzara, *Dada ne signifie rien*, broadside leaflet, 1919. The International Dada Archive, Special Collections, University of Iowa Libraries.

surprise. Sometimes Dada poets would startle by randomness. As Tristan Tzara explains in his "Dada Manifesto on Feeble and Bitter Love" (1920), the way "TO MAKE A DADAIST POEM" is to cut out words from a newspaper article "of the length you want to make your poem," mix them up, and then randomly select them to assemble the poem (Tzara 1977: 39). Sometimes the surprise is scandalous juxtaposition of ideas or objects in unexpected ways: "the cosmopolitan mixture of god and brothel" (Tzara 1995: 291). And sometimes the shock is the hilarious but unrelenting refusal to mean or to stand for anything. As Tzara insists, "the real dadas are against Dada" (Tzara 1977: 38).

Other forms of modernism expressed an ambivalence, even a distrust, of emotion. In "Tradition and the Individual Talent" (1919), T.S. Eliot offers an "Impersonal theory of poetry" (Eliot 1951: 18), in which the individual feelings of a poet are beside the point in the creation of a poem: "Poetry is not a turning loose of emotion, but an escape from emotion; it is not the expression of personality, but an escape from personality" (21). While Eliot's essay is not a complete dismissal of affective intensity in poetry, his essay would have an enormous impact later in the century on New Criticism and its attempt to exclude emotional response from the critical practice of interpreting poems (Wimsatt and Beardsley 1949).

Nevertheless, despite (or perhaps because of) its embrace of the new and its separation of itself from the past, modernism is also a literature of loss and longing. As Jonathan Flatley explains, the word "modernity" indicates "a problematic sense of anteriority, the sense that the past is lost and gone" (Flatley 2008: 28). Anne Enderwitz has also suggested that to come to terms with modernist writing is to examine its melancholia and the "alienation and disorientation" that seem to characterize so many of its most important works (Enderwitz 2015: 73). Modernism often tries to define itself against a past that it figured as sentimental, popular, and feminine. As Suzanne Clarke explains in *Sentimental*

Modernism (1991): "Modernism excluded whatever was associated with the fatally popular ladies" (Clarke 1991: 16). By analyzing the texts of women writers "for the effects of the modernist revulsion against the sentimental and their strategies for recovering bonds of emotional identity" (13), Clarke constructs an alternative literary history that puts this repressed sentimental past at the very heart of modernism. Although the unconventional sympathies of writers like Emma Goldman and Edna St. Vincent Millay are different from what Hume and Smith had conceptualized a century and a half earlier, this interest in affective connection through writing endured.

CHAPTER SEVEN

In Private

The Individual and the Domestic Community

PETER N. STEARNS

In the century and a half after 1780, various forces in Western society redefined the family in terms of its emotional functions and responsibilities, even as the importance of family-based production activities declined. This was a fundamental change, at least in principle, that in many ways still sets contemporary Western family expectations apart from the norms that had prevailed previously. It brought its own combination of advantages and disadvantages, as the new standards were translated into actual relationships in courtship, marriage, and parenting. It altered the way a number of specific emotions were framed, from love to grief to guilt. It clearly affected gender roles in the family, with women's domestic leadership promoted in part because of women's presumably more benign emotional qualities.

Various observers have commented on the, in some ways, surprising modern success of the family as a traditional unit, despite the pronounced reduction in the economic and productive purposes it served in agricultural societies (Lynch 2003). Obviously, economic criteria for family formation and operation have not disappeared—it's been noted that most people manage conveniently to fall in love with a partner from their existing socio-economic group. And the family has flourished as well, and, increasingly, as a convenient unit for consumer activities. But the emotional definition of the family that emerged from the late eighteenth century onward plays a key role in its ongoing viability, and in fact it links to consumerism directly as well. While there was no clear plan behind heightened family emotionality, no deliberate recasting to help compensate for the historic shift away from home and family as production base, the two changes were clearly related and both were extremely important.

The emotional framework for family life created during the long nineteenth century would be redone in several ways, beginning in the 1920s, but several key elements survive, including the idea of the family as an emotional center. This further highlights the significance of the considerable transformation in domestic emotional priorities.

THE BASELINE FOR CHANGE

Any argument positing a noteworthy shift, as in the rise of the family as an emotional unit, must carefully establish a contrast with what went before. Otherwise the asserted change may be assertion alone. In the case of family emotionality, the need to care is all the greater in that several historians (Shorter 1977; Stone 1983; Trumbach 1978), working in the 1970s and 1980s, exaggerated the novelty of familial emotions, and were appropriately (if excessively) called to task (Pollock 1983). The claim, for example, that one would expect to find, in the premodern Western family, no more emotion than exists in a bird's nest was clearly misplaced, ignoring both the bio-psychological constants in human emotional experience and actual evidence from premodern families themselves.

Families have always been the center of considerable emotional experience, well before the late eighteenth century. While marriages were not usually formed on the basis of previously established romantic love—serving rather as arrangements negotiated by parents of the new couple, with an eye to establishing the appropriate economic basis for the match—love would often develop after the fact (Gillis 1985). Or on another front: while most families would have to expect the deaths of several children, often soon after birth, this did not mean that such common occurrences did not occasion real grief (Rosenblatt 1983). Letters and diaries make it abundantly clear that parents often mourned the loss of a young child as one of the durable and formative events in the family's history (Greven 1972; Demos 2000). Families could also serve as frameworks for anger or other intense emotions.

Granting great variability in the real emotional experience of actual premodern and modern families alike, there were nevertheless two or three significant overall differences between premodern patterns and what was developing by the 1780s. First, several particular emotional criteria were redefined—for example, the idea that it was desirable or appropriate to use anger or fear in parenting. In the new emotional context, guilt came to play a much greater role than had previously been the case. And second, the public emphasis on the family's emotional value, and the many private expectations that were shaped accordingly, were largely novel. In many formulations, as we will see, the family was represented as a desirable emotional alternative to what went on in business or public life (Lasch 1977). Certainly the transformation in definitions of marriage formation—from parental economic arrangement to the formation of romantic attachments by the couple itself—was a crucial indication of the shift in priorities (Lystra 1989). Finally, some legal structures and other public formulations began to reflect the priorities of family emotionality—for example, in the kinds of official publications on good parenting that began to emerge by the early 1900s, or in certain aspects of divorce law. None of this denies important emotional functions of families earlier on, or even certain continuities from premodern ideas, but there were significant transformations.

A second complexity must be noted as well. Some of the bases for the more emotional definition of the family began to be set before the later eighteenth century. As always, important historical changes built to some extent on prior changes. For example, Protestantism, in contesting Catholic beliefs that there were holier alternatives to family life and disputing the idea of separate priesthoods and convents, had already called new attention to the importance of the family (Ozment 2011; 1985). By the seventeenth century, Protestant commentators were discussing the need to promote satisfaction in family life—including favorable relationships between husbands and wives—even as they also urged the role of the family in inculcating religious values (Leites 1995). This reorientation helped set the stage for the more explicit interest in favorable family emotions that developed during the eighteenth century.

Economic changes may have contributed as well, particularly as the West European economy became steadily more commercial. One historian has argued that the increasingly competitive relations fostered by growing commerce, as early as the seventeenth century, helped redirect male emotions from same-sex friendships to marriage, where business rivalry would not apply (Leites 1995). Growing consumerism, by the late seventeenth and early eighteenth centuries, may have contributed as well, though there is a bit of a chicken-and-egg causation question here (Campbell 2005). Certainly much of the new consumer interest focused on household items, like more decorative furniture or fancier tableware, and on clothing. Family mealtimes commanded increasing attention, as wives presided over more elaborate serving vessels; and while this development began in the urban middle classes, it was spreading more widely in Western Europe by 1700 (de Vries 2008). Increasing social interactions within the family, as they resulted, might have contributed to new emotional emphases as well. Clothing was relevant particularly in expressing a new sense of style and self that could apply to more romantic courtships. Various aspects of commercial change, in sum, may have helped drive a new valuation of certain kinds of emotions in family formation and family operation.

The realization that some important family changes were brewing before 1780 does not detract, of course, from an understanding that the fuller flowering of family emotionality was still to come. The importance of earlier emotions in family life, even before the incitements to change, must qualify any excessive claims—basic family emotions such as love, grief, or domestic anger certainly did not have to be invented, though they were open to some serious redefinition. The two points—that serious shifts in family context were already underway, and that family emotion was not a totally new invention—operate in a useful tension, as we turn to the factors that more clearly prompted the characteristic adjustments during the long nineteenth century.

CAUSES OF CHANGE

Two general developments combined to generate new attention to family emotionality. The first, relatively easy to identify though long buried in more formal intellectual history, involved further cultural shifts, associated both with the Enlightenment and with early Romanticism and both taking shape clearly in eighteenth-century Europe. The second involved a series of structural changes affecting the family directly, and broadly speaking linked to the first stages of urban industrialization as it affected a growing middle class. Changes here included the growing separation of work from home and specific reactions such as a reduction of the birth rate.

Culture first. Toward the middle of the eighteenth century, Western readers (particularly European, but there were North American audiences as well, as literacy rates continued to climb) were treated to a steady stream of novels emphasizing emotionality and sensibility (Rosen 1998; Barker-Benfield 1992; Ellison 1999). Love fulfilled, love thwarted, grief at death or departure, tender sorrow—these were the emotions that now received pride of place, and they often surfaced in or around family settings. Richardson's *Pamela*, for example, involved a virtuous maidservant seized by a wealthy man, who resists his advances but gradually falls in love, triggering a corresponding elevation of sentiment on his part: the result, an improbable but clearly love-based match. Tearfulness was a vital part of these "preromantic" novels, which won a wide, substantially female, readership.

It is impossible to know how much these novels responded to changes in emotional signals that had already occurred, but there is no question that they encouraged further change and a stronger focus on the emotional role of courtship and family life more generally. While romance and death were the most obvious emotional triggers in this genre, there was also new attention to the emotions associated with loving motherhood.

Enlightenment contributions to a new emotional agenda must be teased from a movement that was strongly rationalistic, but there were several relevant components developing in the same decades as the flurry of early Romantic sensibility. Redefinitions of childhood played a role here. Building on the earlier work of John Locke, Enlightenment thinkers disputed traditional notions of original sin, seeing children as untainted, open to education, and responsive to loving treatment by adults. Traditional disciplinary measures more appropriate to the sinful child were opened to new scrutiny, particularly the notion of trying to scare children into obedience through references to death and damnation. The figure of the innocent child, cute and lovable, began to emerge from this ideological shift.

A second Enlightenment contribution, clearly taking hold from the middle of the eighteenth century onward, involved the embrace of happiness. As Enlightenment thinkers defined social and personal goals in increasingly secular terms, and envisaged progress on all fronts from living standards to health, they turned against the emphasis on melancholy that had predominated in seventeenth-century Europe. There was every reason for individuals and societies to expect to be happy, and correspondingly cheerfulness should be projected wherever possible (Stearns 2012a; Kotchemidova 2005; McMahon 2006). Enlightenment happiness, to be sure, was not a particularly emotional category, but it certainly could combine with emotional redefinitions when applied, for example, to family life.

The Enlightenment and early Romanticism were different in tone, uneasy bedfellows in principle, but they could coalesce in generating openness to new kinds of emotional signals and a review of more traditional standards. Young people hoping to find love in courtship might be expressing Romantic yearnings along with an Enlightenment-based interest not only in happiness but in personal freedom from parental authority. It could be a heady mix.

Structural changes associated with early industrialization had a number of emotional implications, at least when interpreted through the new lens created by cultural change. Shifts in birth rates, which began with the urban middle class in countries like France and the new United States, were a case in point. Families began to realize that children were more a cost than an economic asset, when they had to make a growing commitment to formal schooling over child labor. Some historians have argued that parents' emotional investment in the individual child goes up when there are fewer children in the family overall, and there are abundant signs of this at least by the later nineteenth century (Zelizer 1985; Wells 1985). Which came first—a new emotional commitment which would encourage lower birth rates to maximize children's well-being, or a shift in family demography first, followed by emotional consequences, can still be debated, but an ultimate connection is highly probable. We will see that during the nineteenth century itself the need for a lower birth rate, and its realization through substantial sexual abstinence, also had an impact on the definition of love in courtship.

Other changes contributed to a new emotional climate within many families. Inheritance remained important, but its priority declined as society shifted from agriculture to industry. Respectable people could now get started in life without waiting for the parental legacy. Gradually, this change in turn operated to reduce tensions between adults and their parents (which had often been severe in preindustrial Europe). The most obvious result, at least in widespread imagery, was the idea of a loving grandparent, particularly grandmother, contributing positively to family emotions rather than serving as a source of tension (Rosenzweig 2005).

The most dramatic overall change in context involved the separation of work from household, the steadily expanding result of the advent of an industrial economy. In the middle class this transition quickly translated into a tendency to remove married women, and often women in general, from the labor force. A French businessman noted in the 1830s how his mother had expected to work, serving as a cashier in the family business (with the family itself living above the shop) (Faucheur 1886). But now that he and his colleagues were new factory owners, they kept their wives at home. Correspondingly, emphasis on the importance of wives and mothers in the family rose steadily, and this proved readily compatible with increasing emphasis on the importance of emotional warmth in the family and, overall, with the family as a vital emotional contrast with the increasingly harsh and demanding world of work (Cott 1997).

Ongoing consumerism continued to contribute to family emotionality, and here too the growing urban middle class was in the lead. A great deal of consumerism continued to be associated with family items, and the mixture could have emotional overtones. By the late eighteenth century, individual wills often specifically granted an item of furniture or clothing to a family member by name—not just children, but cherished nieces or nephews—with the clear implication that the transmission of a cherished object was an expression of genuine sentiment toward the recipient. Family things, in other words, could express love (Stearns 2006; Weatherill 1996). By the early nineteenth century, characteristic family portraits gathered a presumably loving group around a piano—a new but increasingly imperative consumer item for middle-class families, and soon successful artisanal families as well. The object played a clear role in focusing a loving family gathering.

Culture and structure vividly combined. There was no inherent reason for some of the structural shifts accompanying early industrialization to generate greater emphasis on family emotionality; at the very least, the connections can be debated. Moving work outside the home, for example, might simply have reduced the importance of the family (as in some ways it did). But, given the cultural pressures toward seeking love, among other things, a redefinition of family functions toward a greater emotional role made more sense. Courtship shifted still further from making a sound arrangement about property to an effort to find the appropriate emotional basis for marriage. Children, now economically redefined as liabilities rather than assets, gained new functions in contributing to the family's emotional warmth, beginning with their lovable innocence as infants.

COMPLEXITIES

The causes of emotional change did not, of course, bear evenly on all social classes, and they involved important gender differentials as well. Middle-class families, broadly construed, had the greatest access to the cultural underpinnings of this set of emotional changes, and they encountered some of the structures of early industrialization in distinctive ways. They led the charge in reducing birth rates, for example, though gradually other groups would emulate; and while they were hardly alone in experiencing the separation of work and family, they alone, early on, had the resources to respond by systematically withdrawing women from work.

Figuring out domestic emotional changes for working classes and rural groups remains a challenge for historians, because they did not generate separate prescriptive standards and evidence about actual emotional experiences is sketchy at best. Complicating the situation further was the extent to which middle-class observers assumed that lower-class families, or at least urban families, were incapable of living up to the emotional standards which business and professional groups now found essential.

Thus, through the nineteenth century and beyond, middle-class groups and even some trade union leaders bemoaned the lack of appropriately affectionate treatment of children in many worker families. How, one self-serving argument ran, could really loving parents allow their offspring to work in factories? While material and health conditions among the poor drew the greatest attention, the felt need to inculcate appropriate emotional standards was a key motivation in efforts to advise the lower classes (and, in the United States, immigrant groups) about family life in the later nineteenth and early twentieth centuries.

The most blatant illustration of perceived class differences in family emotionality involved definitions of mental cruelty as grounds for divorce, in United States law in the later nineteenth century. This was a catch-all category, of course, but it included arguments (mainly by wives complaining about their husbands) that the marriage had become emotionally cold, that the partner had withdrawn active affection (Phillips 1991). In the view of American courts this was a valid concern for middle-class plaintiffs, but not for working-class families who lacked the finely tuned sensitivities for mental cruelty to be an issue.

While unquestionably the push toward new family emotionality saw the middle classes taking the lead, there were signs of change in other classes as well. Middle-class standards could themselves have some influence in setting goals for others. Not only reformist propaganda but also the experiences of domestic help in middle-class households could spread awareness of the new goals of the affectionate family (McBride 1976). Even more important was the fact that the lower classes, as well, encountered important shifts in their own family contexts, which could generate emotional changes in response.

Most obviously, the framework for courtship shifted dramatically, with clear reactions emerging from the later eighteenth century onward. Population growth and industrialization combined to increase the number of lower-class families, both urban and rural, that lacked significant property. Little property, in turn, allowed individuals who were employed to think about serious courtship earlier in life than had been true previously (when it was normal to have to wait until the prospect of inheritance); and lack of dependence on inheritance also reduced parental voice in courtship decisions. Young people, in other words, became freer to act on their own. This meant, even more fully than with the middle class a bit later on, enhanced opportunities for real or imagined romance. Sexual activity definitely went up: we know this through dramatically rising rates of illegitimate pregnancy in what has been called the modern world's first sexual revolution. Premarital sex might of course substitute for, or even inhibit, actual romance, but surely the emotional and the physical often combined (Shorter 1977).

Later—in Western Europe, by the second half of the nineteenth century—working class families also reduced their birth rate, implicitly if not explicitly emulating middle-class behavior (Seccombe 1993). This was the point at which, thanks to declining child labor and rising school requirements, children in these families turned into economic liabilities. As with the middle classes, lower birth rates might increase emotional attachments to individual children.

Again, the unfortunate fact is that we know less about lower-class domestic emotionality than we do about the middle classes. Patterns of change and continuity were undoubtedly somewhat distinctive. But there were some common directions of change, and in some cases a degree of direct influence by middle-class standards as well.

Gender is far less problematic than social class in discussing the long nineteenth century as a period of rising family emotionality. Both males and females actively participated in the changing valuation of emotion and, as we have seen, women's domestic status improved in many ways as a result, as they became seen as the family's leading emotional agent.

By the same token, however, men and women encountered changes in family emotionality somewhat differently. Nineteenth-century middle-class culture tended to argue that women were naturally more attuned to appropriate family emotion than men were. Hence, respectable women could far more easily avoid anger than men, though men too, in principle, were supposed to keep their anger in check in family settings. Mothers had by nature a fund of deep love for children; men were more problematic in this regard.

Conventions of this sort had real impact. Diary evidence suggests that nineteenth-century women worried more about displays of anger in domestic settings than men did. Men had their own issues, however, in that they were supposed to retain the capacity for anger in public settings while curbing it in private; not an easy combination. Men, away from home at work, in any event, may well have had greater problems attuning their emotions to children than women did in this period, as the common wisdom suggested. Gender standards, in other words, could have a self-fulfilling quality (Stearns 1990).

Certainly the standards called for pronounced differences in the emotional socialization of children. Girls were held to much tighter temper control than were boys. They were encouraged to learn not only about love but also about grief, while boys were excused from so much attention. Dolls' kits for girls, by the 1870s and 1880s, not only included opportunities for displays of cuddling and affection but some of them also came with grief paraphernalia, like black armbands, so that their mistresses could practice this emotion as well. Toys for boys had far different, and less purely domestic, implications (Stearns 1994).

Gendered emotional life for the nineteenth-century middle classes embraced at least one other differential, less closely linked to the more familiar aspects of gender conventions. Both men and women formed emotionally intense friendships in their youth, prior to the age at which courtship was possible. The friendships were deeply important to many men, who for economic reasons had to wait longer for courtship than did women. Many men wrote passionate letters to each other, embraced frequently, and showed every sign of intense emotionality in friendship during their twenties—much as women did, in their late teens and early twenties. For both genders, a heightened emotionality in friendship during the nineteenth century both expressed intense emotions learned in the family during childhood, and prepared for the emotional intensity expected of adults. But there was a revealing difference. Men largely dropped their friendships when they began courtship, relying on wives and family for the emotional outlets they required from that point onward. Women, however, more commonly retained strong emotional ties with friends, either in addition to those formed with husbands and children or as compensations for disappointed emotional expectations once their families were formed (Rotundo 1989; Rosenzweig 1999; Smith-Rosenberg 1975).

In sum, while both genders actively shared in the emotional redefinitions of family life, they did so amid important distinctions in culture and in experience alike.

Finally, regional differences need attention, within the larger framework of transatlantic Western civilization—though here too, as with social class, further research and in this case explicit comparative analysis are still desirable.

The basic factors prompting family emotionality were widely shared across the West, in terms of common types of reading and other cultural prompts, and the impacts of early industrialization. Chronologies varied a bit, particularly in terms of industrialization's advent or the beginnings of birth rate decline, but common processes ultimately emerged. There was also a good bit of mutual influence, for example, in new ideas about children's innocence and lovability.

But specific regions also showed some variability. Catholic countries like France, on the whole, placed somewhat lower emphasis on women's emotional leadership in the family, though even here there was substantial new emphasis on maternal warmth (Smith 1981; Yeo 1999). New emphasis on familial grief was also more muted, in favor of greater reliance on established rituals. While interest in emotional happiness rose everywhere, the attachment to manifestations of cheerfulness and a hope for cheerful children accelerated more rapidly in the United States than in Europe, at least after 1800, as European travelers themselves routinely noted (Stearns 2012a). In this case, prior cultural traditions were not clearly involved; in the eighteenth century, Americans had been at least as likely to apologize for undue levity as had Europeans, though it was in the New United States that a right to happiness was first politically enshrined. Possibly a desire to please children, also noted by European observers, contributed to the devotion to familial cheer. Again, there are a variety of comparative issues that await additional analysis.

THE KEY CHANGES

The central change, within the overall intensification of the family as emotional center, obviously involved the growing emphasis on love in virtually all aspects of familial relationships, from courtship to grandparenthood. But the centrality of love had other implications, at least as commonly interpreted, spilling over into redefinitions of domestic anger and fear, but also into a heightened experience of grief. The new emphasis on guilt had some distinct bases in reconsiderations of discipline more generally, but was clearly tied to love as well through the threat of emotional deprivation. Finally, the push for happiness, though also linked to familial love, also touched on other facets of family change, such as a historic reevaluation of the importance of children's obedience.

Love

New interest in love began to emerge from the later eighteenth century onward. Already in the 1750s law courts in some places, such as Neufchatel, Switzerland, began to rule in favor of young people, particularly women, who contested a parentally arranged marriage on grounds that they could never love the mate that had been selected (Trumbach 1978). Christian law had long contended, in principle, that marriages must involve the consent of the partners, so this kind of ruling was not a total innovation. But basing arguments on emotional expectations was a new element, both reflecting and encouraging novel expectations in this arena.

New interest in mother-love also emerged in the eighteenth century, but it was carried much further from the early nineteenth century onward. Here was an emotion, Victorian advice-givers argued, that could sustain the family as a whole, for from it a host of loving relationships could develop. Thus in the United States a Protestant minister, John Todd, argued in 1839, that "God planted this deep, unquenchable love for her offspring in the mother's heart." From it, children's reciprocal love would automatically develop. Love and morality intertwined in this new family context: "It is the province of the mother [both] to cultivate the affections [and] to form and guard the moral habits of the child." Catharine Sedgwick, one of the most influential prescriptive writers in the early nineteenth century in the United States, drove the point home. "The mother holds, as it were, the hearts of her children in her hand." She offers "disinterested love ... ready to sacrifice everything at the altar of affection." *Mother's Magazine* gushed, "Love —flowing from

FIGURE 7.1: Mother love. Courtesy of Library of Congress.

the hidden spring in a mother's heart . . . [flows] deeper and wider as it goes, till neighborhood, friends and country are refreshed by its living waters." The mother "teaches our hearts the first lesson of love," and children of a loving mother inevitably "revere her as the earthly type of perfect love . . . they cannot but desire to conform themselves to such models." The qualities of mother-love, in this new vision, knew no bounds: it was "untiring," "imperishable," "unquenchable," and "irrepressible" (Stearns 1994; Lewis 1989).

Not surprisingly, this almost religious treatment of mother love suggested an enduring emotional power. A popular style of fiction, by the mid-nineteenth century, both in Britain and the United States, involved a young man who strays from righteousness, causing great pain to his mother. But the wayward youth retains a deep impression of his mother's love—"the only humanized portion of my heart"—which ultimately rights the ship, bringing the youth back to the bosom of family and righteous living alike (Arthur 2004; Lewis 1989).

While mother love served as an emotional core, the power of family love more generally had many branches. The new portrait of family emotionality included assumptions of deep affection among siblings (an aspect of the new family emotionality that deserves greater attention from historians) (Hemphill 2011). Middle-class fiction—*Little Women* is an obvious example—often emphasized the deep love among sisters, but brothers and sisters were also linked by emotion. Stories for boys often featured a brother saving a sister from some disaster, demonstrating proto-manly courage but also love, simultaneously.

Love between spouses both followed from the new criteria for courtship, and completed the circle of affection within the mature family itself. Here, marriage advice writers specifically noted the role of family emotionality in contrast to the competitive public world. "Men find so little sincere friendship abroad, so little true sympathy in the selfish world, that they gladly yield themselves to the influence of a gentle spirit at home" (Lystra 1989).

Emphasis on romantic love—and some Victorians found "romantic" too superficial a term for the emotion involved—took on additional importance and intensity from the mid-nineteenth century onward, particularly in the United States and Britain. Middle-class families and their advisors were trying to resolve a new, or at least heightened, tension. They believed in love, they sought courtships that would allow young people to find love as the basis for subsequent marriage, and without too much parental interference. But they also, somewhat desperately, wanted to avoid premarital sex (particularly for women), out of genuine moral conviction but also from a realization of the growing need

FIGURE 7.2: Courtship in the early nineteenth century. Courtesy of Library of Congress.

to limit birth rates at a time when restraint seemed to provide the only sure method of birth control. And while the problem was greatest in courtship, it affected marital relations as well, where periods of sexual abstinence were increasingly essential to achieve the desired family size. A particular definition of love was the only way to square this circle.

Thus advice givers increasingly wrote of a love that, while it might ultimately include sexuality, would have other primary sources. "Is it not possible that there may be a love strong enough and abiding enough, untinged by (sexual) passion, to hold a husband and wife firm and fast in its bonds, and leave them little to desire? I believe it; I know it." Or as a popular medical advisor put it: "But while we speak of pure and passionate love, we may refer to the animal passion, which in no ways is akin to love." "Pure love . . . appertains mainly to . . . this cohabitation of soul with a soul. . . . It is this spiritual affinity of the mental masculine and feminine with each other." Because it was widely preached and met real needs of couples who sought passion without, initially, an explicitly sexual element, this idea of deep, ethereal love caught on widely, and really came to describe a key aspect of emotional life in many middle-class courtships (Lystra 1989; Stearns and Knapp 1993; Dana 1822: 22; Saunders 1868: 105, 143; Montegazza 1896: 217; Arthur 1888).

REDEFINING OTHER FAMILY EMOTIONS

The central emphasis on love as the core of family emotionality generated several other emotional redefinitions, widely adopted in the prescriptive literature.

Fear, for example, had to be reexamined. If the primary bond between parent and child was a deep affection, fear must be rethought as an element in family discipline. The review of fear corresponded more generally with the decline of traditional Christian preoccupation with sin, hell, and damnation—in itself a huge change in cultures like the French, not to mention New England Protestantism (Delumeau 1990). Explicit injunctions against uses of fear emerged in the early nineteenth century, with explicit recognition that a traditional disciplinary ploy was being attacked. Innocent children, the new argument went, had no reason to fear unless the idea was put into their heads by conniving adults. Scary stories or invocations of imminent death or bogeymen should be abandoned, in this new emotional culture, because they would needlessly disrupt emotional tranquility within the family. There was a real battle over this issue within American Protestantism, in the 1820s and 1830s, when whole congregations might abandon ministers who refused to go along with the new belief in children's innocence and the primacy of love over fear (Stearns and Haggerty 1989).

With time, the continued campaign against the use of fear in managing young children was combined with a characteristic Victorian interest in making sure that boys, at least, were also taught the importance of courage. (Girls, of softer emotional stuff, were exempt from this requirement.) But this challenge was to be met by uplifting stories or experiences outside the family—in sports, for example. There was no contradiction of the ongoing belief that fear should be purged from the emotional lexicon of the family itself.

Anger also came under attack, another emotion that seemed incompatible with a loving atmosphere at home. Much ink was spilled over the importance for parents of subduing any anger, lest again it needlessly complicate childish innocence. "A mother must have great control over her own feelings, a calmness and composure of spirit not easily disturbed." Children's anger must also be controlled, lest it disrupt the family or damage their own character for later life. And anger between spouses was equally to be avoided, with much attention going to issues such as avoiding or at least minimizing the "first fight"—a theme that would persist into the marital advice of the twentieth century. Here, too, gender differences were significant, but only outside the domestic arena. Boys and men must expect to have the capacity for anger as a spur to achievement in business or political life, whereas respectable women had no need for the emotion in any context. But males had a responsibility equal to that of females of disciplining their temper within the confines of family (Stearns and Stearns 1986).

Jealousy was less widely discussed than fear or anger, though commentary made it clear that this emotion, also, was incompatible with the purity of family love. A few high-profile court cases in the United States successfully argued that male jealousy, in the case of unfaithful spouses, was an understandable but temporarily uncontrollable emotion that might even excuse murder—but this was not the stuff of standard emotional advice (Ireland 1988; 1989). Generally, jealousy was seen as primarily a woman's issue which, like anger, must be kept under control.

If the new family emotional lexicon called for new levels of restraint for types of emotions viewed as incompatible with family life, the approach to grief was quite

FIGURE 7.3: The new poignancy of grief. Courtesy of Library of Congress.

FIGURE 7.4: A husband's grief. Courtesy of Library of Congress.

different. Here, as with love, was another illustration of how the emotional functions of the family took on new importance. Indeed, as many observers noted, the two emotions were twinned. If the family existed to provide love and emotional support, so the loss of a family member must become the occasion for unprecedented emotional response. And while the new levels of grief were painful—in principle and for many in actual fact—they confirmed in their own way the family's emotional importance, helping to bind family members together in the face of death or even the absence of a beloved. Victorians could revel in the emotion far more elaborately than had been true in the past, with children actively involved as well as adults. An American Protestant put the emotional puzzle together this way, in 1882: "It may truly be said that no home ever reaches its highest blessedness and sweetness of love and its richest fullness of joy till sorrow enters its life in some way" (Stearns 2007).

Open grief, at this new level, not only reflected the emphasis on love but also an equally novel sense of the inappropriateness of death—particularly of course the death of a child or a sibling but also other common outcroppings such as maternal death in childbirth. Actual mortality rates would not drop sharply until after 1880, but emotional opposition to death was prepared well before this. Songs, fiction, and new rituals and cemetery arrangements all confirmed the increased emotional attention paid to death. Grief could soar, just as love did. It was revealing that, as one means of assuaging grief, many Christian groups began to introduce the idea of family reunion in heaven (a decidedly untraditional notion from a theological standpoint). Family emotionality was becoming so important that it reshaped the conception of the afterlife.

Finally, the emphasis on love, and the attacks on traditional disciplinary mechanisms such as fear, placed a new premium on guilt as the family emotion most involved in responses to inappropriate behavior. Public shaming and even physical discipline were increasingly downplayed, in favor of emotional reactions that depended heavily, at least in their initial formation, on family ties. The new normal, at least at the level of recommendations, for dealing with a misbehaving child involved calmly isolating the child from daily loving family interactions—without anger or threat. A period alone was intended to promote self-reflection but also an active desire to return to the warmth of the family circle, with repentant apology the badge of admission. Guilt, and its initial basis in family emotional relationships, clearly linked to the other new emotional goals (Demos 1988).

THE CHEERFUL FAMILY: ANOTHER NEW HOPE

The idea that families should be cheerful entities was of course not brand new. The Protestant encouragement to new satisfactions in family life, as early as the seventeenth century, might have pointed in that direction, and there were earlier injunctions for wives to be cheerful as well. But a thorough embrace of the idea of familial cheerfulness awaited the nineteenth century, and it is just now being explored. Cheerfulness and love might seem to be emotional soulmates, but cheer had its own characteristics and might separate to some extent from the most intense renderings of love and grief (Lewis 1985).

A cheerful family atmosphere was certainly part of what was supposed to make a middle-class home a refuge from the tensions of business and public life. This was another assignment for wives and mothers, part of their responsibility for an appropriate emotional rendering of the family. Cheerfulness helped link the family to the newly explicit quest for happiness that the Enlightenment had introduced—the domestic translation of this new goal, in fact (Lasch 1977).

But cheerfulness also emerged, less predictably, in injunctions for children, beginning early in the nineteenth century in Britain and even more the United States. A crucial development in Victorian childrearing standards, going beyond emotional life but with clear relevance to it, involved a reassessment of the importance of obedience—which had been a standard assumption in previous commentary. With more emphasis on love and positive emotional interaction, and less need to condition children for work, it was probably inevitable that obedience would come in for some critical comment. Reconsideration of the role of fear in discipline pointed in the same direction. And, indeed, as part of the recasting of the idea of original sin in the early nineteenth century, obedience was widely discussed for several decades, only to decline, as a topic, subsequently (see Figure 7.6) as parental interest turned more to seeking creativity and affection in children (Stearns 2012).

FIGURE 7.5: The happy family. Courtesy of Library of Congress.

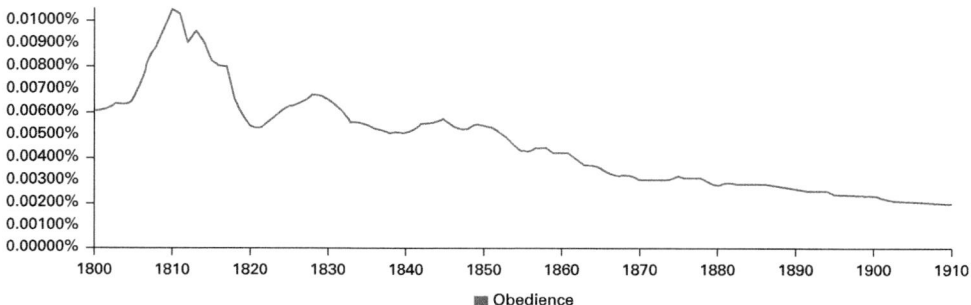

FIGURE 7.6: Relative frequency of obedience references in the United States. Source: Google Books (American English) Corpus. http://googlebooks.byu.edu

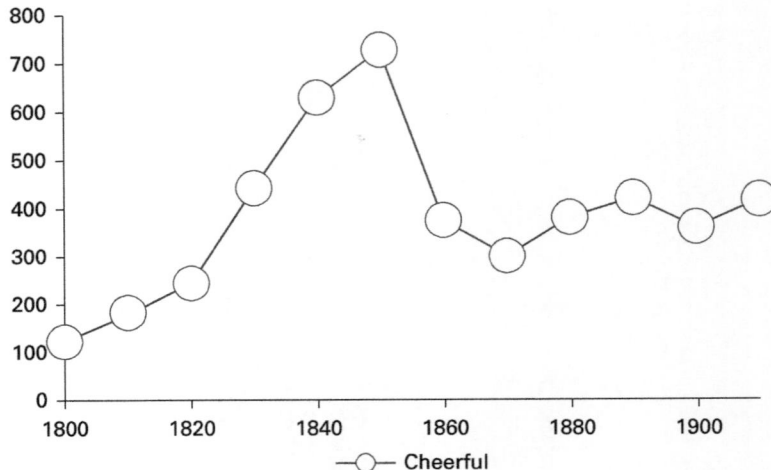

FIGURE 7.7: Cheerful obedience: U.S. data. Source: Google Books (American English) Corpus. http://googlebooks.byu.edu

A key part of this transition, however, involved several decades in which obedience was still widely sought, but now accompanied by a new expectation of cheerfulness—clearly an effort to make traditional requirements more compatible with the more modern hopes that the family would be a loving and emotionally pleasant environment. Opportunities to use digitized data show the new association quite clearly, both in Britain and the United States. Links between obedience and cheerfulness were almost nonexistent in 1800, but they surged forward rapidly thereafter, with phrases such as "cheerful acquiescence in parental demands." Insistence on obedience, itself traditional, was now redefined to make it more compatible with the new tone of family emotionality—and the emotional demands on children clearly increased in the process. Not surprisingly, such a complex combination required much discussion. British linkages between obedience and cheerfulness doubled between 1820 and 1840, while in the United States the increase was more than sevenfold between 1800 and the 1860s (see Figure 7.7). New terminology was also introduced to designate children who did not cooperate. The word sulky, new to the language in 1744, was increasingly applied to children; its use in published works in the United States increased by 1,000 percent between 1830 and 1900 (Google Books 2013).

By the second half of the century, again particularly in the United States, a further evolution increasingly reduced attention to obedience altogether—new attacks in fact directly targeted the undesirability of "unreasoning obedience," in favor of a more uniform insistence on good cheer. Independent references to the importance of cheerful children exploded in the United States from the 1870s onward (see Figure 7.8; British trends were similar in direction but consistently lower in volume). Disgruntled children, so the argument now went, could "destroy the peace and happiness of a home." To avoid this, parents should understand that "a child should be helped and urged and joked into cheerfulness"—a state now seen as essential to family emotionality and also a vital step in building appropriate adult character (Stearns 2012; Kotchemidova 2005).

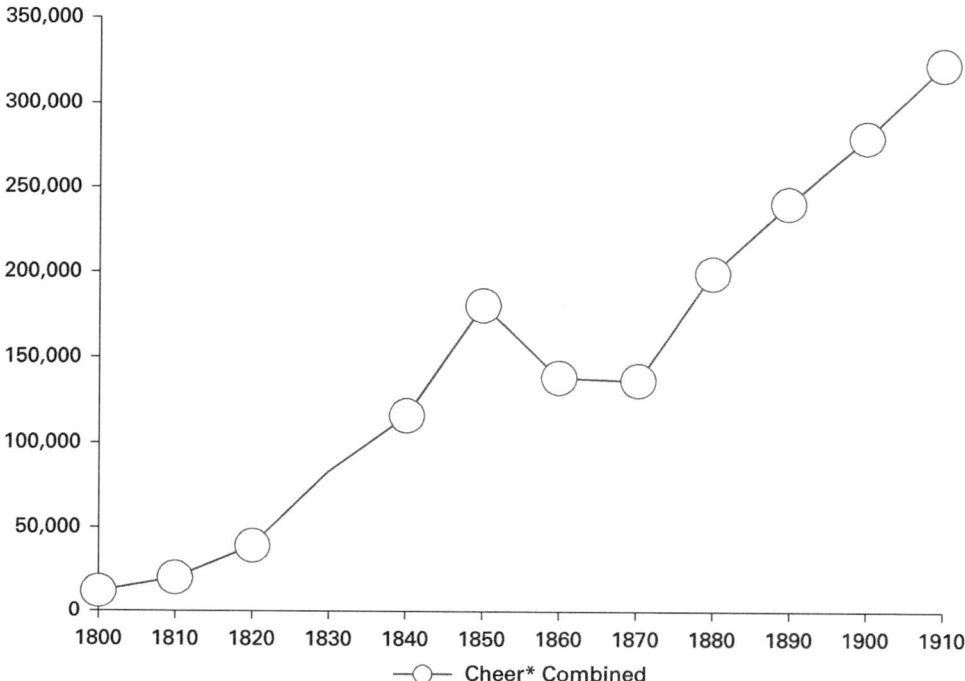

FIGURE 7.8: Cheer combined references: U.S. data (cheerful, etc.). Source: Google Books (American English) Corpus. http://googlebooks.byu.edu

THE IMPACTS OF CHANGE: EMOTIONAL EXPERIENCES AND WIDER RESPONSE

The marked changes in family emotional culture that were crafted in advice literature and other outlets from the late eighteenth century onward obviously raise questions about impact. Dominant cultures almost always produce important results, but rarely as uniformly as their advocates intend. And evidence about emotional experience remains far more elusive and contested than the sources for the culture itself.

Unsurprisingly, many middle-class people clearly worked to conform to the new standards, in personal assessments of emotion and in wider behaviors. Women's diaries often chronicled concerns about controlling anger and jealousy, while recognizing the importance of love and cheerfulness. They often reflected acknowledgment that they, at least, were not as anger-free as gender conventions urged, but they worked to achieve placidity. Many children certainly came to identify their mothers as sources of deep affection: from another diary, "We all loved mother with all our hearts, with all our souls and with all our bodies" (Spencer 1983).

Letters, both in Britain and the United States, easily show the internalization of ideals of intense but spiritual love in courtship. "[True love] is to love with all one's soul what is pure, what is high, what is eternal," one young man wrote to his beloved, noting the distinction of his feelings from the "mere surprise of the senses." Or from a young woman, later an ardent feminist: "Why do I feel in my inmost soul that you, you only, can fill the deep void that is there." Whatever the combination—childhood emotional intensity now transferring to adult goals, the prod of pervasive romantic literature, some degree of sexual sublimation—deep love was clearly a reality for many (Lystra 1989).

Grief, too, was experienced intensely, though of course there were personality variations and not everyone felt that they measured up to expectations (Wells 2000). Expressions of sorrow and lament and outright weeping, affected men as well as women. Deaths of children provoked new intensity, at least in rhetoric. A great deal of nineteenth-century etiquette was arranged around the appropriate recognition of the depths of grief on the death of a family member.

Beyond records of personal experience, there is other evidence of change. An intriguing article contends that Southern men, by the early nineteenth century, gained awareness of the dangers in their wives' pregnancy through a new combination of deeper love and a realization of the potential pains of grief—in marked contrast to more cavalier attitudes in the eighteenth century (Dye and Smith 1986; Lewis 1985). On another front: grief rituals unquestionably deepened in the nineteenth century, reflecting expectations if not consistent inner realities. More elaborate tombs, including now separate commemorations of dead children, and other funeral apparatus attempted to translate the new emotional standards (Stannard 1977). Laws changed, and not only for divorce. A new torts category targeted "alienation of affections," and while this reflected a proprietary attitude toward one's spouse it also specifically attempted to capture the pain of lost love. Breach of promise suits were another innovation, reflecting an attempt to enforce sincerity of affection during courtship—obviously revealing that real love was not always present but also reflecting the common expectation that it should be. The growing legal acceptance of mental cruelty arguments also recognized the change involved: as a Kansas court intoned, "The tendency of modern thought is to elevate the marriage relationship and place it on a higher plane, and to consider it as a mental and spiritual relation, as well as a physical relation" (Griswold 1986). On yet another front: the monetary value of children increased greatly at the end of the nineteenth century, as evidenced in the costs of insurance policies and also the initiation of monetary allowances for children themselves, a tribute to the belief in their emotional importance even as their economic contributions declined (Zelizer 1985). Again, there is substantial and varied evidence of wide awareness of the new emotional standards for family life, and substantial acceptance.

ASSESSMENT: SOME DOWNSIDES OF THE NEW CULTURE

Any widely accepted set of emotional standards will present some mixture of advantages and disadvantages. Contemporary Western audiences are still sufficiently conditioned by key nineteenth-century patterns to discern advantages without too much difficulty: pressures on parents and other adults to reduce anger and fear in dealing with children surely still seem desirable (with concerns mainly about lack of compliance). Invocations of family love still resonate, and demonstrably contemporaries in many Western societies continue to list the family first when they think about happiness (World Values Survey 2012).

But there were some drawbacks to the new culture, and it was a revealing indication of the real impact of the standards that some of these drawbacks became quite noticeable in a number of Western societies, particularly by the later nineteenth century.

The new culture could easily encourage expectations about family emotional performance that surpassed actual achievements. There were many reasons for the increase in divorce rates in the later nineteenth century (with levels depending on particular national cultures and legal systems), but emotional disappointment clearly entered the mix. In the United States, the mental cruelty category, which could extend to cover lack of affection, was a clear extension of the idea of the family as a loving center (Friedman and Percival 1982: 79; Griswold 1986).

Two diseases, both increasing during the nineteenth century, also suggested emotional strains. The surge in hysterical paralysis, in which for no physical reasons patients—usually women—were confined to the home, distorted but built upon the new distinction between family as emotional haven and a cruel external world. The late nineteenth-century rise in anorexia nervosa responded to a number of causes, but among them was the new difficulty many middle-class girls faced in seeking to protest parental authority while also recognizing the loving, cheerful atmosphere that conscientious parents now sought to provide: it was hard to rebel directly in this new climate, so getting sick could be an essential option (Brumberg 1988; Shorter 1988). More generally, of course, the increasing concern about the emotional state of adolescents—the term was coined in the nineteenth century—reflected another characteristic tension between dominant family emotional goals and the realities of adjustments to puberty (Kett 1978).

There is abundant room for further analysis of the complexities involved in dealing with the new standards, including of course tracing relationships between the late nineteenth-century concerns about guilt and repression and now-widespread patterns of family emotionality (Gay 1999). Most generally, potential strains in living up to expectations of love and happiness, and the dwindling room for sadness (aside from outright grief) in family life, deserve wider attention.

CONCLUSION: THE 1920s AS THE END OF A PERIOD

We have traced a new domestic emotional culture that began to take shape in the eighteenth century and in most respects steadily intensified, while widening the relevant audience in Western society, into the twentieth century. Choosing 1920 as an end point for this development is valid in many ways, so long as several more durable continuities are understood.

Some of the goals of the new emotional culture were widely realized by 1920, allowing some relaxation of effort. Parenting manuals in this decade, at least in the United States, stopped issuing the routine warnings against the use of fear in child discipline. Obviously, some individuals and subcultures remained committed to fear, but in the American middle class, the new wisdom had been widely assimilated. The emotional goal continued to be valid, but explicit warnings had become unnecessary (Stearns 1998).

At the same time, several signals began to change in the 1920s, significantly altering Victorian familial emotional culture. Intense emphasis on spiritual love, amid courting couples, gave way to greater acknowledgement of a sexual component, as American adolescents and young adults also shifted from courtship to dating (Bailey 1989). Love was still a valid and expected goal—though perhaps more for women than for men, as French data suggested (Segalen 1981)—but it was no longer so ethereally defined. Victorian language here began to seem a bit silly. At the same time, more open mixing of the sexes, amid heightened sexuality, raised jealousy to new problem levels, in contrast to the fairly low-keyed discussions of the previous century. It was more important than before to defend true affection from possessiveness (Stearns 1990a). Gender standards changed amid new concerns about the effects of anger—now commonly labeled aggression, though the idea of defending the family setting against anger persisted. The most important shift involved a concerted attack on nineteenth-century grief standards and rituals. The dramatic reduction of infant and maternal mortality in the Western world, between 1880 and 1920, made grief both less fashionable and less necessary, and this aspect of familial emotional intensity was substantially revisited. Whether actual familial grief declined as much is open to question, but prescriptive commentary shifted (Stearns 2007).

With all this, however, basic elements persisted; there was no wholesale recasting. The importance of trying to assure familial happiness remained a vital component of Western emotional culture, again with the United States in the lead. It was in the 1920s and 1930s that "happy birthday" ceremonies became central to family life, first in the United States and then more widely. The related notion of the emotional importance of children—the idea, ironic as children's costs mounted, that a child was increasingly "priceless"—continued to be a central pillar of emotional culture and family values alike (Zelizer 1985; Stearns 2012). Assumptions of love in marriage, and disappointments at its lack of intensity, hardly changed despite the shifts in specific vocabulary. Connections between family emotionality and consumer culture intensified as well, building on what was now a longstanding linkage (Cross 2004).

The emergence, in sum, of a substantially emotional definition of the family, with the recasting of supportive and negative emotions in response to this evaluation, has not been reversed, despite important shifts in detail. This creation of the long nineteenth century, in turn a core response to the changes in family function associated with industrialization, retained its basic value, complicating the relationship of the most recent decades to their arguably more fundamentally creative Victorian predecessor. One further change emerging in the 1920s really confirmed the importance of key Victorian standards: what had been middle-class emotional goals were now applied increasingly to society more generally, in what added up to a complex process of emotional democratization (Wouters 2004; 2007).

CHAPTER EIGHT

In Public

Emotional Politics

UTE FREVERT

Considering Europe during the long nineteenth century, politics strikes us as the field where change was probably most salient and fundamental. In the beginning, there was the 1789 revolution that profoundly transformed the political landscape in France, with strong repercussions in other parts of Europe and beyond. In 1848, many countries experienced considerable revolutionary turmoil, and even though political activists failed to reach their ambitious goals, they still managed to leave a long-lasting imprint on political structures and processes. Even tradition-bound monarchies gradually learned to accept constitutions that forced them to share power with self-assertive citizens. Rather than being confronted with passive and (more or less) obedient subjects, European kings and queens increasingly had to come to terms with a citizenry that was pleading for a new political contract between rulers and ruled. Political buzzwords such as parliamentary representation, universal suffrage, and democratization were swiftly gaining momentum, and so were notions of national identification. New political players entered the field as parties, associations, and the media attempted to mobilize and organize those who felt empowered to voice political opinions and take part in political deliberations. Such attempts included novel forms of addressing the public and reaching out to people whose backgrounds and interests were hard to gauge. At the same time, "old" players had to get accustomed to new rules and competitive claims as to who could legitimately participate in political debates and decision-making. In short, politics were to be redefined as a multi-layered process with a growing multitude of participants whose expectations were as diverse as their experiences.

What role, if any, did emotions play in this development? Although this question has rarely been asked, there is plenty of evidence to help answer it. Revolutionaries of 1789 and 1848 zealously talked about new feelings engendered by the overthrow of the Ancien Régime; liberal activists somewhat ambivalently agonized over politics becoming an arena of passionate party struggles; conservatives evoked traditions of loyalty and dynastic reverence and monarchs engaged in sophisticated emotional politics in order to uphold those bonds of faithful adherence. Republicans in turn invented their own emotional mechanisms to foster political allegiance and took great care to create emotionally charged national symbols and material culture. All in all, it can be argued that processes of politicization and democratization brought about and mobilized collective emotions that had hitherto not played a significant role on the political stage. Even if early modern kings and princes had been keen to proclaim their intention to rule by love instead of fear, their concept of loving relations was light-years away from what the nineteenth century witnessed as a manifestation of love of country, king/queen, and nation. In a similar vein, trust entered the political lexicon as a new and powerful term that was accompanied by tight restrictions and conditions and, in many ways, replaced or curtailed older notions of loyalty and fidelity.

To analyze how and why emotions became ever more important in politics during the long nineteenth century, one has to distinguish between various political actors, spaces, and media. Revolutionaries followed a different agenda than embattled monarchies, thinking out strategies to win (back) the hearts of citizens in (post-)revolution times. Citizens of different social classes and political leanings harbored their own ideas on how to define relations with the state and its personnel. As for political spaces, palaces elicited other types of emotions and emotional practices than city squares and streets, as much as party meetings nurtured other emotional styles compared with parliamentary sessions. The media, finally, underwent an equally strong tide of change that affected both the quantity and quality of political information and opinion-making. If one only considers the huge proliferation of newspapers (with often more than one daily edition) around 1900, the extent to which they were able to influence the mass market politically becomes apparent.

Politics, on the whole, learned to experiment with diverse languages of emotions, in oral and written form, with visual as well as audible repercussions. The more political actors reached out to citizens in the age of ongoing franchise reform, the more they relied on enlisting emotions in order to attract and retain public support. When in 1919 the German sociologist Max Weber (1994: 353) warned that politics "is an activity conducted with the head, not with other parts of the body or soul," he found himself in the midst of a new revolution with passions rising high on all sides. But Weber was far from eschewing passion altogether, since he knew from first-hand experience that dedication to politics "can only be generated and sustained by passion." This held true for both the men, and, to a lesser extent, the women, who held or sought political office, as well as for the far larger constituencies that discovered politics not as a personal fate, but as a civic commitment.

1789—EMOTIONAL POLITICS BEFORE, DURING, AND AFTER THE REVOLUTION

In the effort to trace emotions in politics, one might start with Ancient Greece and Aristotle's reflections on how to move an audience through emotional rhetoric. Considering the participatory structure of Athenian politics, orators were indeed well advised to create "suitable temperaments" and steer emotional energy towards certain objects and goals (Rorty 1996; Calhoun and Solomon 1984: 48; Harris 2001). With the democratic element lost in later times, rulers no longer had to make engaging speeches in order to rally support and consent. Nevertheless, as the Florentine politician, diplomat, and political philosopher Niccolò Machiavelli pointed out in the early sixteenth century, princes should strive to be both loved and feared by their subjects; in case both could not be achieved, fear generally proved to be a more stable mechanism of rule than love (Machiavelli 2005: 90–93).

During the era of absolutism, European monarchs increasingly chose to disregard Machiavelli's recommendation, at least in theory. Prussia's Frederick II, who became king in 1740, wrote long treatises to refute him. Fear, he claimed, would only produce crowds of slaves who would do no more than what was requested. Love, instead, could incite subjects to bring about "great achievements" that enhanced the state's power and glory. As a matter of fact, however, he did very little to put this theory into practice. Even though he graciously accepted his subjects' tokens of reverence, his rule relied on strict obedience rather than on emotional compliance and commitment (Frevert 2012: 50, passim; for France, see Reddy 2000: 110).

Frederick II died three years before the French Revolution violently turned the tables of emotional politics. Obedient subjects reinvented themselves as self-confident citizens who took pride in claiming political rights and asserting sovereign power over their own—the nation's—fate and well-being. *La volonté de la nation*, the Paris-based writer Germaine de Staël spoke so highly of in 1789, was not only expressed with *un enthousiasme sincère et désintéressé*, it also went hand in hand with *sentiments généreux* that aimed to engender a new solidarity or *fraternité* among citizens (Reddy 2000: 110, 134). Fraternal bonds and feelings were henceforth to unite the French people regardless of social class and religion, with the exception of women and slaves, who were initially omitted from the national project.

Efforts to imagine and present the nation as a band of brothers who had emancipated themselves from an omnipotent father drew on a variety of conceptions of fraternity circulating at the time: monastic, pietistic, and masonic. They all placed great emphasis on brotherly love and friendship as the glue that bound men of different social origins together and that was capable of forming a new unity of companions who thought and felt alike (Schieder 1972: 554–566; Hunt 1992: 12–13, ch. 3). Politicized during the revolutionary events of 1789, fraternity became the rallying cry of civic assemblies and was demonstrated by emotional practices such as walking arm in arm or publicly embracing each other (Schieder 1972: 565–566; Reddy 2000: 140). Such practices were widely appreciated by those who fervently sought to put revolutionary achievements on safe and stable grounds. Remodeling free citizens' sentiments, habits, principles, and actions proved to be a major task.[1] Robespierre even called it the *chef d'œuvre de la société* to create a rapid "instinct" in men that told them how to do the morally (or rather, politically) good without having to appeal to protracted reasoning (Wahnich 2011: 32; Wahnich 2009). Emotions, so to speak, were supposed to do the job of directing people's political opinions and judgments. But how could one instill such emotions and intuitions? And how to make sure that they remained aligned with revolutionary politics, especially since the latter became widely and ferociously contested among the various groups of self-proclaimed revolutionaries? New symbols (for instance, the cockade), hymns, cults, and festivals seemed to be as helpful as were political assemblies, speeches, and rallies, which were, however, in increasing danger of being fractured along party lines (Ozouf 1988).

To avert such danger, republicans placed a strong emphasis on national identification and patriotic feelings. After Abbé Sieyès famously proclaimed that the third estate—i.e. those not belonging to the clergy and the aristocracy—was the nation itself, it became the deliberate focus of patriotism and related propaganda efforts. When the Jacobin deputy Joseph Fouché visited the provinces in 1793, he reported on the strong emotional appeal of the "happy festival of a general and fraternal reunion around the tree of liberty": "Such sweet tears ran from every eye, because the love of the fatherland lives in every heart." The following sentence was equally telling: "Send arms to the citizens of Clamecy, they are ready to shed their blood in its defense" (Reddy 2000: 140).

This outspoken love of nation and fatherland was not only materialized in joyous, tearful outbursts of fraternal feeling for other members of the nation; it was also expressed in acts of sacrifice such as going to war and protecting the nation from outside enemies. The nation here acquired a quasi-religious aura; it was clearly more than the sum of its parts and promised transcendence and progress. By embodying the cherished values of liberty and equality, it assumed a historical mission to serve humanity and foster social improvement. To be a citizen of the French nation, therefore, meant to commit oneself without restraint to this kind of universal service. Anyone who lacked commitment and maintained a distance was suspected of treason and faced severe sanctions that ranged from public humiliation to radical exclusion (Walton 2009: 3–9, 193–225).

Such expectations exercised a great deal of emotional pressure on men as well as on the smaller number of women who, despite widespread male resistance, strove to be active members and participants of the political nation. Especially during the Reign of Terror, accusations of treason were omnipresent, and the fanatic moralization and emotionalization of politics did much to turn even the most eager *ami du peuple* into an alleged enemy of the nation's cause. With the immediate threat of foreign military invasion, which had rallied citizens in a concerted action of collective sacrifice, receding, Robespierre's camp attempted to purify and regenerate the nation through violent purges sold as radical justice. Having vastly overplayed their hand, the Jacobins quickly lost out to more moderate factions that reduced the pressure on displaying (and questioning) heart-felt, utterly sincere emotions towards the revolutionaries' societal goals. Depoliticizing the streets and clubs went along with handing politics back to those who were more concerned with citizens' private fortunes than with the *bonheur commun* and the republic of virtue. From then on, happiness was to be found in a calm family life and the pursuit of self-interest rather than in public agitation (Reddy 2001: 190–210).[2]

Yet there was no way back to the old times of the Ancien Régime, when politics had been largely monopolized by the absolutist ruler and his councils. Even under Napoleon's authoritarian rule, citizens were summoned to voice their opinions in plebiscites and did so in the millions (Crook 2000). After the Bourbon monarchy was restored in 1815, the constitution limited the right to elect parliamentary representatives to a small group of wealthy taxpayers. Although the franchise was extended after the July Revolution of 1830, it was still far from including the majority in the world of politics. Fear of the *classes dangereuses*—mainly workers, whose numbers were growing rapidly during the industrial revolution—prompted liberals and conservatives to restrict political deliberation to so-called reasonable and responsible citizens. Reason was associated with property and education. Elections, thus, were held to select those *notables* who had the political capacity to hold enlightened opinions and make logical judgments. In no way were they supposed to open the doors to the passionate agitation of radical demagogues who preached emotional excess and fostered social fracture.

Instead, the "bourgeois" monarchy installed in 1830 sought to engage citizens in a thoroughly pacified form of family romance.[3] Assuming the title "King of the French" instead of "King of France," Louis Philippe deliberately reached out to the people. He portrayed himself as a monarch whose habits, behavior, and morals were those of a "citizen king." Portraits showed him in the midst of his family, which was supposed to resemble the prototypical French family with its caring patriarch, loving mother, and cheerful children. The message was clearly stated: The king was the true representative of the French nation and embodied its fundamental virtues. If such a monarch bore responsibility for the nation's fate, politics would return to shallow waters and citizens would be able to rejoice in the peaceful conduct of their private affairs (Price 2007).

THE EMOTIONAL CHARM OF ROYALTY

Louis Philippe was not alone in sending this message. Earlier in the century, Prussia had seen similar tendencies of royal embourgeoisement and popularization. Before her untimely death in 1810, Queen Luise had been heralded as the heroine of middle-class mores and an intimate family life at the Berlin court. Together with her husband, Frederick William III, she stood at the center of public attention, and local guilds and civic associations competed jealously to host the couple for "coffee and cake." Even though she readily complied and promised to "earn and deserve the love of our subjects with politeness, attentiveness, and gratefulness," she quipped at the inverted expectation of the monarch "courting" citizens (Büschel 2006: 261; Schwengelbeck 2007: 121).

Shortly after the French royal couple had been guillotined, such inversions actually seemed to make a lot of sense. Although local magistrates vowed that Prussians would never emulate their neighbors' insolent example, there was widespread concern that even Prussians might turn against their king. As the officer von Gneisenau (1939: 175) wrote to Frederick William in 1811, the monarchy needed the "love of a people enthusiastic for its ruler" in order to be secure. Such love was to be nurtured and sustained by, for example, emphasizing the active role of subjects in "protecting throne and state." Due to long-lasting official neglect, such conservative forces were lying dormant. Once awakened, they would "amaze the world."

Defeated and humiliated in 1807 by Napoleon and his seemingly invincible army, the Prussian king took the advice to heart, albeit reluctantly. In 1813, he emphatically appealed to "my people" to defend the fatherland and assert Prussian honor (Hagemann 2015). While honor had hitherto been the exclusive property of the prince and the state he represented, it now stood out as a collective good in which each Prussian participated, for better or worse. Even if Frederick William surely did not intend to go so far, his offer to extend honor to all subjects and citizens was the first step on the long path to political democratization. Moreover it was a move that not only used highly emotional language but also targeted a crucial emotional concept and practice. Contemporaries held the belief that honor, whether socially or politically defined, was firmly "rooted in the heart," i.e. in the very organ from which emotions sprang (quoted in Frevert 2011: 41). To let citizens partake in the honor of state and prince thus created emotional ties that went far beyond the affection subjects were traditionally expected to harbor towards their dynastic rulers. Furthermore, it promised citizens a far larger share of active responsibility and pride than they had previously enjoyed.

In many European countries, citizens proved eager to bear such responsibility. They were no longer satisfied with being treated as children by an omnipotent father who claimed to know what was best for them. At the same time, very few went so far as to exile or kill the father. Even liberals who insisted on the necessity of a constitution did not want to abolish monarchical order. Rather, they promoted the iconic image of a citizen king and queen who consented to share power and cooperate with the "nation" on grounds of mutual respect and adherence to the rule of law. Britain served as a role model here, especially after the young Queen Victoria ascended the throne in 1837. As a constitutional monarch, her influence on government decisions was limited; she only had the "right to be consulted, the right to encourage, the right to warn," as Walter Bagehot (1995: 112) summed up in 1867. Her symbolic power, however, was immense.

Especially after her marriage to Prince Albert in 1840, Queen Victoria's popularity grew enormously. With nine children, the royal household appeared as the incarnation of middle-class morality and family values: loving, caring, burden-sharing, reasonably thrifty, responsible. Court scandals became a thing of the past; instead, heart-warming portraits of the royal family flooded the country, reproduced on postcards and other objects. Even though the monarchy was not uncontested, republican criticism remained on the margins

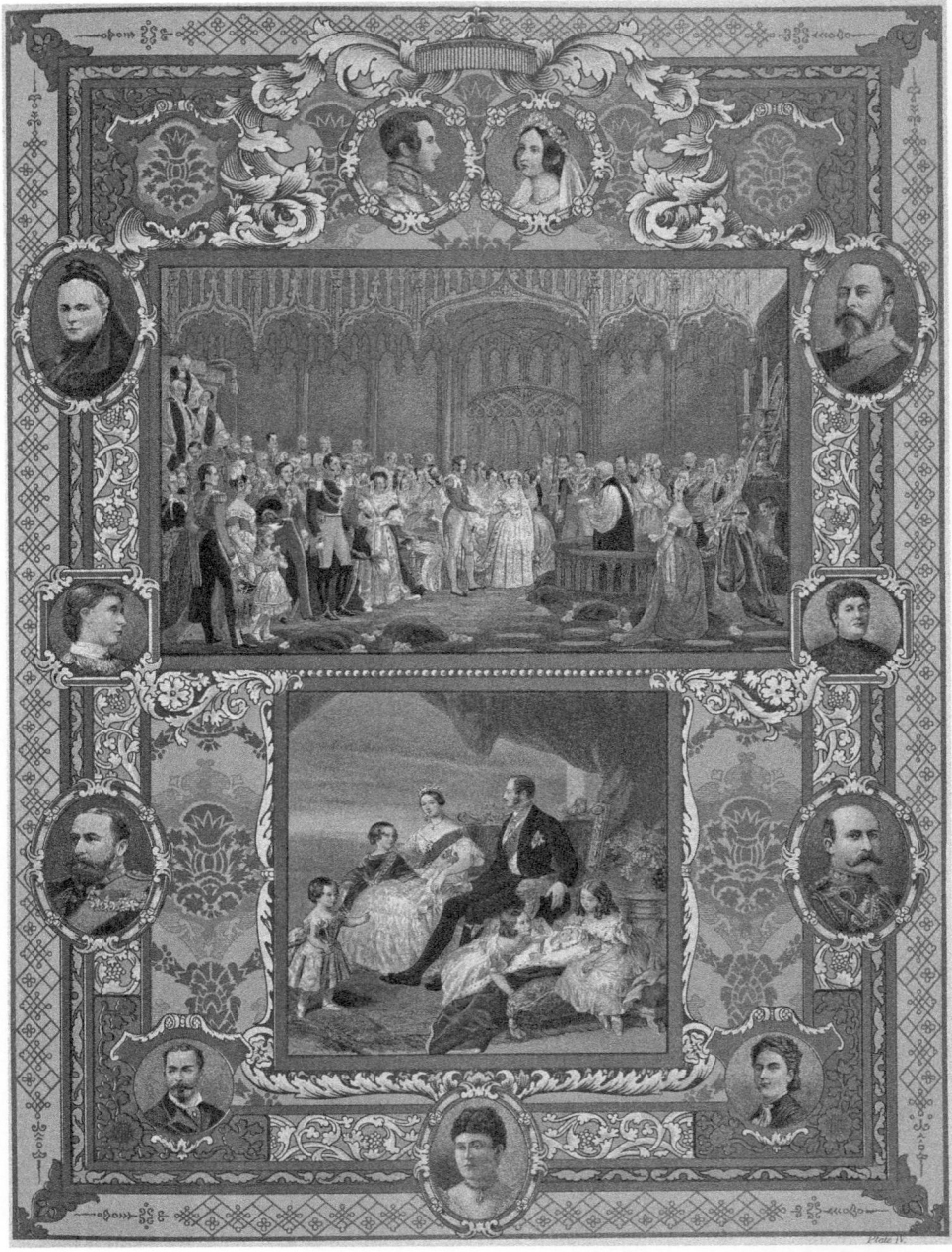

FIGURE 8.1: Queen Victoria's Jubilee, 1887, Queen's marriage to Prince Albert of Saxe-Coburg and Gotha, February 10, 1840, royal family in 1846. Photo by DEA PICTURE LIBRARY.

of public discourse. The middle-class press, in particular, actively propagated a sense of reverence that met with widespread approval. As the "first media monarch," Victoria was depicted, in an increasingly emotional language, both as the matriarchal center of a well-ordered family and as a romanticized fairytale figure. Each member of the growing family received ample attention; births were celebrated as much as weddings (Plunkett 2003; Williams 1997; Taylor 1999). Multiple assassination attempts served to further strengthen the nation's attachment to the Queen who, in Benjamin Disraeli's (1844: 101) words, was regarded as "the proper leader of the people."

The people who sent Victoria tokens of love and loyalty and took an eager interest in even trivial details of the royal household were by no means apolitical or, as republicans believed, "sick." In their eyes, the Queen was not removed from politics but at its very center. Her direct political power limited by the constitution, she was attributed with an affective power that helped to integrate diverse political opinions. Furthermore, it served the larger goal of epitomizing the global achievements and claims of the British Empire. Her jubilees, above all the "golden" and "diamond" in 1887 and 1897, respectively, marked the heyday of British glory and were deliberately staged as triumphant events. The millions of citizens who witnessed the royal procession or read about it in the newspapers were invited to feel included and to genuinely participate in that glory. Victoria personified everything that was laudable about British civilization, which was to be generously exported to other regions of the world.

Personification was a crucial part of what the constitutional monarch did in and for politics. At a time when political life was becoming ever more complicated, multi-layered, and bureaucratic, the focus on Queen or King offered a way for people to access politics without getting lost in procedural intricacies and complexities. In positive terms, it allowed emotions to be bound to abstractions like monarchical rule, empire, or national missions that by themselves could hardly be "loved," adored, or worshiped. Personified by the royal "leader," such abstractions were brought to life and embraced by large parts of the population, especially by those who shied away from getting tied up in the more mundane operations of the political process. With Victoria's character it was particularly easy to present her as the immaculate figurehead of British politics and as the embodiment of the Empire's "moral responsibility" (Times 1897: 13). But even when a monarch's personality was deemed to be less agreeable, it could, with the help of the press, acquire an air of serenity and gravitas that sold well to the national public.

Such public image production became more and more important in all European countries during the long nineteenth century. It proved particularly indispensable in newly founded nation states like Italy, where the monarchy actively participated in constructing national identities (Brice 2010). But it was equally essential in traditionally multi-ethnic empires like Austria-Hungary, which was experiencing increasing bouts of nationalist strife and the ongoing threat of secession after 1848. In this situation, Emperor Franz Joseph, who reigned between 1848 and 1916, played a crucial role. Having ascended to the throne in the midst of a revolution that strove to end absolutist rule in Vienna, the young emperor, who harbored strictly anti-constitutional views, was never popular among liberal-minded citizens, let alone the growing social-democratic movement. But he soon became iconic for bridging the rift between the various regions of the Habsburg Empire. Emphasizing his strong attachment to Catholicism and his position as the commander of a multi-national army, Franz Joseph sought to strengthen the two major forces that could fight nationalism and prevent the breakup of the Empire. The cult of personality that developed during the last decades of his long reign expressed itself in quasi-religious forms. In 1908, 80,000 children from all parts of the country were sent to Schönbrunn palace to congratulate the "lonely" Kaiser on the sixtieth anniversary of his reign. Having lost many members of his own family to death and assassinations, Franz Joseph was venerated as the uncontested father of the fatherland who worked incessantly for the unity and well-being of his "children." Even social democrats could not but acknowledge (albeit grudgingly) that monarchical sentiments had perhaps never been stronger and more pervasive: "It is altogether false to assume that our era bears a levelling tendency and minimizes monarchical grandeur and sublimity through parliamentary and constitutional mechanisms. When, in all times, have princes ever been worshiped in such devout humility as today?" (quoted in Wolf 2004: 172; see Cole and Unowsky 2007; Unowsky 1998).

What was new about the modern "worship" of princes was not the amount of humility, but the number of people who openly and voluntarily showed it. Nineteenth-century archives store hundreds of thousands of letters that were sent to kings and queens. They spoke of love, gratitude, and devotion, and they were written by men and women of all ages and from all social classes. Those who wrote letters or sent poems and presents did not do so for any material gain; if at all, they asked for a signed photograph to proudly put on display in the family's living-room (Giloi 2010; 2011). Such outpouring of "dynastic sentimentality" (Bismarck 1990: 222, 224) was indeed a novel experience that was by no means a self-explanatory given. After the revolutions of 1848 had been crushed in Vienna, Budapest, Munich, Berlin, and elsewhere, monarchical rule lost some of its unquestioned legitimacy and recognition. To the extent that it had become openly politicized by the king taking sides and dispatching troops against liberal and democratic forces, it no longer stood above politics and the urgent "question how the state should be governed in the future." Instead, as the German political economist Lorenz von Stein (1855: 12) observed in the 1850s, the monarchy had become, "even among the masses, an object of reflection, discussion, and investigation."

While von Stein spoke and wrote in favor of a bipartisan social monarchy that cared particularly for the lower classes and would in turn attract their strong support, organized labor was less enthusiastic. Even though some of its leaders approved of monarchical rule (albeit bound and limited by a constitution), most did not. Still, in their private homes, social democrats sometimes chose to hang portraits of Ferdinand Lassalle and August Bebel, the founders of the party, next to a picture of the Kaiser. In Bavaria or Saxony, allegiance to local dynasties outranked that to the Prussian rulers, who, despite ascending the imperial throne in 1871, never quite succeeded in presenting themselves as all-German (Blessing 1978).[4]

Nevertheless, even the house of Hohenzollern gradually learned how to deal with popular sentiment in post-revolutionary times. For William I, German emperor from 1871 to 1888, the learning curve was particularly steep. Widely despised and exiled as a military firebrand during the 1848 revolution, he later turned into a beloved fatherly figure whose death at the age of 91 was mourned by millions. His favorite blue cornflower became an emblem of personal attachment worn and given by citizens to one another on the king's birthday. When he was seriously wounded by an assassin in 1878, the palace was flooded with telegrams, letters, and presents from all parts of the population who wished him well. William then jokingly called the assassin his "best doctor," referring not to his physical health, but to the surge in popularity that he enjoyed as a result of the assassination attempt. Rather than being heralded as the martial hero and military commander-in-chief, his vulnerability and frailty won people's hearts (Dietze 2007; Giloi 2011: 157–185, 209).

That these hearts had to be won in order to sustain monarchical rule was the lesson learned against the background of what William (1906: 30, 39, 41) had earlier condemned as "misleading press" and "party fervor." Public opinion had to be recaptured by the throne, and this could be accomplished by means of emotional politics. As a Prussian king, William renounced traditional forms of collective homage and invented new ceremonies like the coronation. His birthday was made into both a local and national event, celebrated by middle-class dignitaries as well as by the army and in schools. Textbooks invariably included personal interest stories about the king and his queen; all students knew the poem "The Emperor is a kind and decent man," which was not only recited but also sung to a popular melody and thus stuck in everybody's memory. The words called up a recurring motive of monarchical sentiments: to be close to the king, to see him face-to-face and possibly hold his hand (John 2007).

Such "learned" longings were not limited to children. Many adults of both genders and all ages shared the desire to entertain a "personal relationship" with the monarch. While conservatives saw this as confirming the "indissoluble loyalty" of subjects, liberals emphasized the voluntary attachment of a "free citizenry" (Schwengelbeck 2007: 267–268). But freedom always harbored the possibility of a change of opinion, which is why the historian and public intellectual Heinrich von Treitschke repeatedly warned that "the intimate trust of a people in its rulers must constantly be earned afresh" (1916: 75).

To do this, the monarch and his councilors happily drew on the support of new channels of communication and media. Following in his English grandmother's footsteps, the German emperor William II (who ruled from 1888 to 1918) deployed photography and film to reach out to the public and to portray himself as a monarch in close touch with his people.

He was constantly in the news, inaugurating patriotic monuments, visiting cities, opening military celebrations, or meeting with other monarchs. And he incessantly gave speeches. Nicknamed the "talking emperor," he used every opportunity to address diverse

FIGURE 8.2: Photomontage postcard showing William II in front of the Berlin Cathedral. Courtesy of Eva Giloi.

audiences in highly emotional language. Sometimes he forgot that journalists were present, who had their own agenda and interests. The press, as he soon found out, could by no means be relied on as an obedient tool of monarchical politics. Liberal, Catholic, and socialist dailies that had been rapidly multiplying since the 1880s often selectively quoted the Emperor's speeches to pinpoint political flaws and rebuke offensive views. Scandalizing strategies proved a convenient way to sell more copies and win over readers. Even though they refrained from directly insulting the monarch, many newspapers carefully maintained their distance or, if they aligned with liberal or left-wing party politics, openly attacked William's behavior and politics (Kohlrausch 2005; 2010; Requate 1995).

MASS MOBILIZATION AND PARTY POLITICS

The press was one of several factors that thoroughly influenced the emerging political mass market during the long nineteenth century. As that market expanded with the extension of the franchise, new forms of political mobilization and organization emerged. They created further opportunities for emotional politics and put emotions center stage.

In many continental European countries, mass mobilization started in 1848. Revolutionary news from Paris traveled fast and sparked off a wave of popular protests and petitions to kings and parliaments (at least in places where they already existed). People gathered at local squares and in the streets, listened to self-proclaimed orators, and continued debating in pubs and assemblies of all kinds. New associations were formed every day, and older ones became highly politicized spaces where men, and sometimes women, too, expressed opinions and fought to defend them against competing ones. Millions of people were suddenly initiated into political life and set out to redefine and transform politics.

Constant communication was at the heart of the politicizing process. People talked and listened, read leaflets and newspapers, passed on rumors, wrote letters and articles. In cities like Berlin and Vienna, speeches were being held on every corner at every hour. It was the time of the orator whose rhetoric decided over success or failure. To capture people's attention, appeals to their emotions proved particularly helpful. How the audience was addressed—as brothers, fellow-citizens, friends—set the tone for what was to follow. One strategy was to empower listeners and spectators as political actors and whip up public spirit. The newborn citizen was supposed to cast off his passive status as subject and proudly voice his own views, thoughts, and feelings. Imbued with patriotic fervor, he would then seek like-minded others with whom he could collaborate and form a movement to bring about change. Another strategy aimed at emotionally dividing the political field into friends and enemies. While friends could be trusted and loved, enemies had to be suspected, feared, despised, or even hated. On both extremes, such strategies could, and did, verge on the fanatic. While fanaticism had hitherto been defined as a religious phenomenon, it now extended to politics.

This became evident not only in spontaneous gatherings, but also in parliamentary assemblies, which were institutionalized during the constitutionalist phase of the revolution. As had happened in France sixty years earlier, competing factions quickly put on oratory steam and fought each other with strong words and emotional zeal. Parliamentarians did not shy away from insulting each other, and more than once they provoked duels in order to honorably settle a case. They shouted, screamed, threatened, and sought to seduce. They hammered their fists, waved their arms, rose from their seats, and rushed to the rostrum. They shed tears, they were enraged, they jubilated. And they were watched in their emotional outbursts: by journalists who later reported on what they had seen and heard, and by spectators who had come to witness first-hand how the new politics was practiced. Rather than silently observing from the gallery what was happening downstairs, however, visitors chose to be vocal and either cheer or howl down the speakers. Parliamentary assemblies thus resembled and were perceived as battlefields, with words and voices as sharp as weapons, supported by body language that not only expressed strong emotions but also helped to impress them on others.[5]

At times, passions ran so high that violence broke out, and assassination attempts were not unheard of. Even elderly gentlemen, professors, and businessmen felt emotionally overwhelmed, and were deeply troubled by the heated style of political communication. They tended to blame democrats and socialists for kindling political passions and stoking social discontent. But this was only half true. Even though left-wingers were more closely attuned to popular moods and movements and were better able to use them to boost their political claims, liberals and conservatives quickly learned to reach out to the wider public as well. Especially during elections, they developed increasingly sophisticated strategies to mobilize voters, again by issuing fervently emotional appeals and promises.

"Practicing democracy" by attracting citizens to the ballot box and persuading them to support a party's political program demanded passionate campaigning on behalf of those who wanted to be elected (Anderson 2000). Winston Churchill, who went on his first campaign in 1899, thoroughly enjoyed "the succession of great halls packed with excited people until there was not room for one single person more—speech after speech—meeting after meeting—three even four in one night—intermittent flashes of Heat & Light & enthusiasm—with cold air and the rattle of a carriage in between." He always appreciated a "splendid fight" that should, however, stick to the rules and be fought with words rather than with fists. When Conservative supporters in Birmingham turned in fury

FIGURE 8.3: Political meeting, sketches, agitation in Ireland (1879). Photo by DEA PICTURE LIBRARY.

against the Liberal politician David Lloyd George in 1902 and physically threatened him, Churchill was outraged (Gilbert 2006: 16, 25).[6]

The emotionalization of politics as it occurred in parliamentary sessions as well as during election campaigns was not applauded by everybody. When the republican lawyer Léon Gambetta took the floor of the French National Assembly in the 1860s and 1870s and swept away friends and foes with his passionate oratory, he was widely criticized for the omnipresence of emotions in his speeches. Detractors reprimanded him for behaving irresponsibly, and felt threatened by the prospect of Gambetta becoming a plebiscitary tribune of the people. Those who favored his politics tried hard to defend him against such allegations, maintaining that reason and emotion were not, in his case, opposed but rather that they strategically complemented each other (Cossart 2003; Déloye 2000). Politics needed both careful reasoning and strong passions. Politicians, as Max Weber (1994: 353) put it, had to be passionate as well as responsible, and act with a sense of proportion. They thus faced the problem of how to merge "hot passion and cool judgement . . . together in a single soul" without privileging one over the other.

In the popular opinion of the times, this problem could only be solved, if at all, by men. A majority of people, including women, held politics to be a male affair. It demanded strong nerves and equally sturdy egos that would not break under emotional pressure. This is why, they thought, it would be better if women were not involved at all. Considered as emotionally frail and delicate, they were not deemed capable of participating in the "passionate battles" fought over political affairs. If they did they would either be defeated by more passionate and determined men, or lose their "sweet femininity" and turn into despicable viragos. Politics, too, would suffer from women participating in party strife and verbal sparring matches. Since women were considered to be strong in sentiments but weak in passions, they would temper down politics to a babbling brook rather than elevate it to an energetic, powerful stream. Great deeds, as conventional wisdom had it, came out of "great passions" and thus demanded genuinely passionate men rather than overly sensitive women (Frevert 2011: 115–119).

For this and other reasons, women were allowed neither to vote in political elections nor to participate in party politics. Party membership, which rose constantly during the latter half of the nineteenth century, generally remained an exclusively male privilege and was zealously guarded against feminist demands for inclusion. On the other hand, parties increasingly learned to integrate and enlist their members' wives, sisters, and daughters, albeit on allegedly non-political grounds. Socialist and social-democratic parties in particular evolved into complex organizations with a myriad of branches and activities open to families, from cradle to grave. Getting children and wives involved in party festivals, choirs, and volunteer work in fact meant politicizing even those who could not and would not be part of direct political deliberation and decision-making. And it formed lasting emotional bonds between the families, who viewed each other as parts of a fast growing and ultimately victorious political movement. Such bonds were fostered by common symbols and practices, such as flags and songs that were emotionally charged and that connected the individual person to the higher goals of the political community (Ritter and Tenfelde 1992: 818–835; Ruppert 1986: ch. 4).

From its very beginning, the labor movement had invented and employed strong emotional language in order to strengthen internal cohesion and provide shelter against external repression. Robert Owen's cooperative movement was no less keen on emphasizing warm fraternal relations among its members than the friendly societies that played a significant role in the making of the English working class. Labor's first political

FIGURE 8.4: SPD banner commemorating the 10th anniversary of the General German Workers' Foundation, May 23, 1873. Courtesy of Archiv der sozialen Demokratie/Friedrich-Ebert-Stiftung.

organization in Germany, formed in 1848, carried fraternity in its very name and chose two clasped brotherly hands as their main (and lasting) emblem.

As brothers, party members were not only supposed to love and help, but also trust each other. As an organizer warned in 1862, if workers did not learn to overcome mutual suspicion and establish "fraternal trust" with one another, they would never achieve their ambitious political goals (Thompson 1968: 456–488, 857–887; Balser 1962; Frevert 2013: 172).

Trust, defined as the ability to believe in, and rely on, the cooperating person's goodwill, kindness, and benevolence, became a major political buzzword alongside the development of constitutionalism, party politics, and democratization. Trust, in liberal opinion, was supposed to govern the relations between rulers and ruled and to allow for power-sharing: Rulers trusting their former subjects, who were becoming self-assertive citizens, citizens trusting the government that they had themselves helped to install by sending elected representatives to parliament. Unlike traditional notions of loyalty, modern trust was considered to be mutual, conditional, and relatively short-term. In order for the people to trust the government, certain prerequisites had to be in place, above all parliamentary control. And in order for voters to trust their representatives, the latter had to stick to their political program and keep the promises they had made before and during the elections. Periodically, such compliance had to be tested and affirmed (or not) in new elections. Even hereditary monarchs were well advised, as Treitschke reminded them, to bid for the people's trust, which, in the age of political mass mobilization and participation, was no longer a given.

Trust thus proved to be both a highly attractive and utterly deceptive emotional disposition. It was positively charming because it secured the smooth functioning of political cooperation and communication. Its downside lay in the fact that trust was inherently unstable and constantly endangered. When betrayed, trust could and would be withdrawn, with profoundly negative consequences for the trusting and the trusted alike. This is why political parties and associations were so keen on building multiple layers of trust with and among their members and supporters. Integrated networks of mutual trust not only stabilized and streamlined organizational structures; they also helped, through the constant practice of trust-building rituals, to bind people more permanently to the organization. Even if political goals and dreams, as in the socialist case, would not be achieved during a person's lifetime, and even if members were disappointed with their leaders' performance, such networks and practices were able to hold their own.

In an age that was becoming increasingly obsessed with the image of allegedly unbound and unstructured "masses," the task was not a trivial one. As much as liberals and conservatives had feared the *classes dangereuses* in the early decades of the nineteenth century, later decades witnessed a growing anxiety about political masses. In 1895, Gustave Le Bon published a treatise on *La psychologie des foules*, which was immediately translated into English and German, among other languages. The book drew on Le Bon's observations of what had happened in the French capital under military siege in 1870–71, especially during the times of the Paris Commune. For Le Bon, this had been a lesson in demagoguery that emotionally manipulated and channeled the discontent widespread among working-class "masses." In Le Bon's view, masses were easy prey for gifted orators who knew how to excite them. Emotional contagion traveling fast, masses behaved in a "feminine" way with exaggerated feelings that often triggered violent actions. Especially when masses were anonymous, as in demonstrations or spontaneous gatherings, they proved highly suggestible and reacted strongly to visual incentives like flags, banners, and posters (Le Bon 2003; Barrows 1981; van Ginneken 1992).

On the one hand, such anonymous masses posed a threat to a civil society that had developed a close-knit web of diverse groups, associations, and parties to organize and integrate the newly empowered citizens. On the other hand, they provided the dynamic base from which emerging social and political movements recruited their followers. This held particularly true for the new brand of nationalism that had flourished in many European countries since the 1870s. In Britain, it bore the name of jingoism, referring to a popular song in which "true Britons" pledged to take up arms and fight the Russian Bear, if necessary. As could already be witnessed during the revolutionary and Napoleonic era, wars had become highly politicized events intimately bound up with patriotic feelings and national interest (Colley 1992; Kennedy and Nicholls 1981). Even in countries like Great Britain, which did not have compulsory conscription and relied on a professional army, military conflict usually sparked off a fire of popular enthusiasm that increasingly verged on openly chauvinistic attitudes. "Sentiments of national honour," as Lord Cromer (1908: 110), Britain's strong man in Egypt after 1883, put it, were "stung to the quick" whenever colonial or intra-European conflicts arose. And politicians were well advised not "to run absolutely counter to the impulse of the national imagination." Instead of "attempting an impossible task," they should seek to march ahead of the crowd and "guide it."[7]

This is what the French general Georges Boulanger attempted in the 1880s. Seeking revenge for the defeat France had suffered at the hands of the German forces in 1870–71, the highly decorated officer and war minister put himself at the top of a fast growing political movement that sought to restore national honor and return the country to monarchical rule. Parading on a black horse through the streets of Paris, Boulanger was the chosen idol of many who were disappointed by the Third Republic. *Boulangisme*, as the movement was called, drew on mass popular feeling that converged on the exaltation of the French nation as the most cherished object of identification.

Several songs hailed and admired the general as the nation's savior, and tens of thousands of Parisians joined in the refrain *C'est Boulanger qu'il nous faut* (Hutton 1976).

The idealized hero guiding the misled nation back to honor and glory could be associated both with traditional monarchy and with the modern form of charismatic leadership that was gaining momentum in the process of nineteenth-century politicization. As Max Weber (Weber 1978: 241–242) observed first-hand, charisma held even more affective power than dynastic sentimentalism. It drew on personal trust and the belief that the charismatic leader embodied values, feelings, and visions of the future similar to those of the people he ruled. At the same time, the leader depended on his followers, who added collective force to his ideas and ensured that they had a chance to be put into action. In return, charismatic men speaking in the name of the nation offered citizens the chance to actively participate in the national project of self-purification and self-elevation. Ultimately, everybody would benefit and feel honored.

CONCLUSION

Socializing national honor was one important way to emotionally rally citizens behind a political agenda. Once the nation found itself ennobled as sovereign during the French Revolution, each citizen theoretically had a part in its newly ascribed honor and glory. Patriotism, the love of the fatherland, became redefined as the love of the nation. Such love stemmed from, and was translated back into, fraternal feelings that male citizens were supposed to espouse for one another as free and equal members of the united and indivisible nation. Fraternity implied mutual assistance and solidarity, and was accompanied by strong bonds of trust. Trust, however, was not a given but had to be built and stabilized through cooperation and communication.

Although it depended on a multitude of prerequisites, trust proved to be another influential means of emotionally enriching the world of politics as it developed during the long nineteenth century. Gradually replacing older notions of subjects' unconditional loyalty, trust became the buzzword of a political system that was based on a novel calibration of power. Even in those European countries where monarchical power was less bound by constitutional constraints, politics was no longer confined to what was decided in palaces and cabinets. As citizens demanded and eventually succeeded in being politically represented, parliamentary politics gained in visibility and importance. Parties and other political associations sought to organize and channel political opinion, and they achieved this by enlisting members and followers through intensely emotional rhetoric and social practices. Warm and trusting relations within the organization stood side by side with deep distrust towards those outside whose interests and motives were deemed hostile and treacherous.

FIGURE 8.5: Claude Monet, Rue Saint-Denis, Celebration of June 30, 1878. Source: The Yorck Project on Wikimedia Commons.

As much as politicization was accompanied by a growing sense of political fragmentation and exclusionary polarization, inclusive reminders of the "nation" as one and indivisible gathered momentum. Monarchy, which had persisted in almost all European countries, here took on new tasks. First, it reinvented itself as an integrative element of politics that stood above party factions and embodied the nation as a whole. From Louis Philippe, who ascended the French throne in 1830 to William II, the last German Emperor, virtually all monarchs imagined and portrayed themselves as *roi citoyen* or *Volkskaiser*. They tried or pretended to be in close touch with citizens and the people, and took great care to endear themselves to the hearts of those who would otherwise be driven apart by political strife and controversy. With the help of new forms of media presence, they made themselves both visible and approachable; people were offered the chance to follow, in all intimate detail, their Queen's or King's or Emperor's actions. And they were supposed to feel invited to address the royals, send them poems and presents, congratulate them on their birthdays, and mourn their passing.

Second, this kind of intense communication served the task of rendering government "intelligible," as Walter Bagehot (1995: 78, 81–82) phrased it in 1867. While "the nature of a constitution, the action of an assembly, the play of parties, the unseen formation of a guiding opinion, are complex facts, difficult to know and easy to mistake," the actions of the monarch were "easy ideas" that effortlessly captured the "attention of the nation." Rather than embracing complicated "impersonal" laws and mechanisms, people felt personally attached to the man or woman on the throne. Such attachment was further strengthened as a monarchy, third, "appeals to diffused feeling." By contrast, Bagehot saw republics "appeal to the understanding" and thus lose the "vacant many" who were neither able nor interested in comprehending what politics was about and how it functioned. The best of all monarchical worlds that the English journalist observed in his time was "a *family* on the throne" that "brings down the pride of sovereignty to the level of petty life," and "sweetens politics" by speaking to men's and women's "bosoms."

Sweetening politics, however, was not equivalent to abolishing the taste for participatory politics altogether. While nineteenth-century monarchies fared rather well in mastering their complex emotional tasks they stopped short of depoliticizing citizens and turning them into passive spectators of royal weddings and state visits. The limits of political legitimacy and dynastic attachment became obvious during and after the First World War. By the 1920s, many continental European countries had abolished monarchical rule. Revolutions in St. Petersburg, Berlin, Munich, Vienna, and Budapest once again turned the tables of politics by either having royal families executed or sent into exile. Even if monarchical sentiment survived in some niches of society (as it had done before in republican France), it could no longer mobilize or integrate larger parts of the population.

This did not mean that citizens became indifferent to affective and personalized politics. The more politically fragmented and polarized the political culture was, and the more a nation had suffered from military defeat and alleged dishonor, the more citizens were attracted by charismatic leaders promising new glory and national regeneration. Such leaders based their appeal not on traditional sources of legitimacy, but on strong affective ties to those who trusted them and shared their visions of the future. In Italy, Benito Mussolini set the precedent of novel populist politics. Dismantling the constitution, outlawing parties, and abolishing parliament, the self-proclaimed Duce quickly installed himself as the single focus of political allegiance (Duggan 2012; Gundle, Duggan, and Pieri 2013). Meanwhile in Germany, the 26-year-old journalist Joseph Goebbels still despaired about the fate of his country and longed for someone to save it from further humiliation. Such a man would have to generate "enthusiasm and complete devotion" (1987: 34) on his path to fortifying the nation and helping it overcome internal decomposition and external weakness. In Goebbels' imagination, such a man would resemble the late Otto von Bismarck rather than the kings and emperors Bismarck had served as Prussian prime minister and German chancellor. A few months later, the young man met his new hero, Adolf Hitler, who would soon open another chapter of emotional politics (Frevert 2015).

NOTES ON CONTRIBUTORS

Rob Boddice is a Marie-Skłodowska-Curie Global Fellow, based at Freie Universität Berlin and McGill University. He worked at the "Languages of Emotion" Excellence Cluster in Berlin and was for five years a guest researcher at the Center for the History of Emotions, Max Planck Institute for Human Development. He has published extensively in the fields of history of medicine, history of science, and the history of emotions. His recent books include *The Science of Sympathy: Morality, Evolution and Victorian Civilization* (University of Illinois Press, 2016), *Pain: A Very Short Introduction* (Oxford University Press, 2017), and the first comprehensive textbook on history-of-emotions theories and methods, *The History of Emotions* (Manchester University Press, 2018).

Gregory Eiselein is the Donnelly Professor of English and University Distinguished Teaching Scholar at Kansas State University, where he also serves as the Director of the first-year experience program, K-State First. His research focuses on Louisa May Alcott, Emma Lazarus, and the intersections of literature and emotion in nineteenth-century America. He is the author of *Literature and Humanitarian Reform in the Civil War Era* and numerous articles on American literature and culture. He is also the editor or co-editor of seven books including the Norton Critical Edition of *Little Women*. The winner of multiple teaching awards, he was named the 2013 CASE/Carnegie Kansas Professor of the Year.

Aileen Forbes received her PhD in English Literature from Princeton University, where she studied British Romanticism and critical theory. Her research interests focus on the intersection between literature and philosophy, nineteenth-century women authors, and the history and philosophy of emotion. She has taught courses on British Romanticism, psychoanalytic theory, and George Eliot at Princeton, Bryn Mawr, and Swarthmore. Currently, she teaches at Columbia University in New York City.

Ute Frevert is Director at the Max Planck Institute for Human Development and Scientific Member of the Max Planck Society. Between 2003 and 2007 she was Professor of German History at Yale University and prior to that she taught history at the Universities of Konstanz, Bielefeld, and the Free University in Berlin. Her research interests include the history of emotions, social and cultural history of modern times, gender history, and political history. She is honorary professor at the Free University in Berlin, a member of the Berlin-Brandenburg Academy of Sciences and Humanities, the German Academy of Sciences Leopoldina, and the British Academy, and serves on several scientific boards. She was awarded the prestigious Leibniz Prize in 1998.

Susan J. Matt is Presidential Distinguished Professor of History at Weber State University. She is the author of *Homesickness: An American History* (Oxford University Press, 2011), *Keeping Up with the Joneses: Envy in Consumer Society, 1890–1930* (University of

Pennsylvania Press, 2003), and co-editor of *Doing Emotion History* (University of Illinois Press). She co-edits the history of emotions series for University of Illinois Press. With Luke Fernandez she is co-author of *Bored, Lonely, Angry, Stupid: American Feelings about Technology, from the Telegraph to Twitter* (forthcoming, Harvard University Press). Her essays have appeared in the *Journal of American History*, *the New York Times*, and the *Wall Street Journal*. She received her BA from the University of Chicago and her MA and PhD from Cornell University.

Julius H. Rubin is a Professor of Sociology, Emeritus at the University of Saint Joseph in Connecticut. He is the author of interdisciplinary studies of religion in America and Native American Studies. His books include: *Religious Melancholy and Protestant Experience in America*, *The Other Side of Joy: Religious Melancholy Among the Bruderhof*, *Tears of Repentance: Christian Indian Identity and Community in Colonial Southern New England*, and *Perishing Heathens: Stories of Protestant Missionaries and Christian Indians in Antebellum America*.

Peter N. Stearns is University Professor of History at George Mason University. Professor Stearns has written widely on world and emotions history, including two popular textbooks. Recent books include *Shame: A Brief History*, *Tolerance in World History*, *The Industrial Turn in World History*, *Doing Emotions History*, and *Childhood in World History*, among many others. He also edited the *Encyclopedia of World History*, 6th edition. Before coming to George Mason University, Professor Stearns taught at the University of Chicago, Rutgers University, and Carnegie Mellon University. He served as vice president of the American Historical Association, Teaching Division, from 1995 to 1998. He was also founder and editor of the *Journal of Social History* from 1967 to 2015.

Kerstin Thomas has been full professor for Modern and Contemporary Art History at Stuttgart University since April 2016. From 2010 to 2015 she was director of the research group *Form and Emotion*, at Johannes Gutenberg-University Mainz. She studied Art History, Philosophy, and Western Archaeology at the Goethe-University Frankfurt, receiving her PhD with a dissertation on the notion of mood in post-impressionist painting, published in 2010. Between 2006 and 2009, Kerstin was scientific assistant at the *Centre Allemand d'histoire de l'Art* in Paris. She specializes in nineteenth-century French art, while her research is focused on emotions in art, on which she has published several books and articles. Currently she works on the concept of form in twentieth-century art theory.

Wiebke Thormählen is the Area Leader in History at the Royal College of Music in London. Recently awarded a three-year collaborative research grant from the Arts and Humanities Research Council (*Music, Home and Heritage: Sounding the Domestic in Georgian Britain*), she explores the interaction of the domestic with the public in musical arrangements, in devotional music, and in the relationship between music as domestic social activity and the development of amateur choral societies in Britain. She is co-editor of the *Routledge Companion to Music, Mind and Wellbeing: Historical and Scientific Perspectives* (forthcoming); her current book project exposes layers of meaning behind different forms of "musical engagements" in early nineteenth-century London.

NOTES

Chapter One

1. The best introduction to the scientific appropriation of the passions and their transformation into modern emotions is T. Dixon (2006), *From Passions to Emotions: The Creation of a Secular Psychological Category*. See also T. Dixon (2008); R. Boddice (2016).
2. For this development in medicine see Weisz (2005), Maehle, (2009), Weindling (1991: 198–223). The most compendious account of the professionalization of scientific practice, with profound implications for the place and meaning of emotions in scientists, is Daston and Galison (2007). This is complemented ably by White (2009).
3. On physiology see Geison (1978), Romano (2002), Cunningham and Williams (1992), Dror (1999; 1999a). On psychology see Rylance (2000), Rieber and Robinson (2001), Woodward and Ash (1982), Richards (1989).
4. See Richards (1989) for the classic study.
5. See, for example, More (1834, vol. 6, pp. 295–308).
6. See Arnaud (2015), Stirling (2010), Scull (2009), Showalter (1985), Micale (1995), Furst (2008), Gilman (1993, pp. 345–452).
7. The classic studies were undertaken by Charcot (1877) at the Salpêtrière Hospital.
8. The classic formulations are Beard (1881) and Freud (2002). See also Killen (2006), Kenny (2015), Lutz (1991).
9. For more on the psychological ordering of species see Boddice (2011: 321–40). For Darwin's racial and intellectual ordering of types of humanity, see Darwin ([1871] 2004: 86, 114–116, 118, 119, 125, 133), for typical examples.
10. Darwin built this idea on Adam Smith, but departed from him in his understanding of natural origins, the influence of public opinion on emotional development, and the intrinsic morality of instinctive sympathy (Smith, and later the Utilitarians, would stress the need for intentionality). See Boddice (2016, chapter 2). For the proto-biological ideas about emotions that both Bell and then Darwin drew upon, see Frazer (2012), Csengei (2011), Goring (2004), Mercer (1972). See also Smith ([1759] 2009).
11. The principles of acquired habit and inheritance are laid out in the first chapter of Darwin (1872: 27–49).
12. The archetypical misunderstanding and extension thereof is Ekman and Friesen (1971: 124–129).
13. A notable example would be Vogt (1864: 80–82). For a full survey see Boddice (2011: 330–333).
14. See Conklin (2013: 19–57), Sera-Shriar (2016: 109–146). See also, Gould (1993: 84–115).
15. See Boddice (2011), Conway (1972: 140–154), Russett (1989).
16. For a general introduction, see Thomson (1998). The key biometrist was Karl Pearson. See Pearson (1910).
17. See also Bain (1894: 3).

18. Bain (1894: 423–424).
19. Danish physician Carl Lange (1887) arrived independently at the same point, arguing for the physiological basis of emotions. It came to be known as the James–Lange theory of emotion.
20. See esp. Dror (1999a). Some of the classic studies include Mosso (1896), originally under the title of *Sulla paura* in 1884, Cannon (1915), Ribot (1896), Sherrington (1899–1900: 390–403).
21. *"les sentiments . . . plongent au plus profond de l'individu; ils ont leurs racines dans les besoins et les instincts, c'est-à-dire dans des mouvements."*

Chapter Three

1. "We remarked with pain that the indecent foreign dance called the Waltz was introduced (we believe, for the first time)" (*The Times* 1816: 2).

Chapter Eight

1. As the Temporary Commission on Republican Surveillance put it in 1793: "There is nothing, absolutely nothing in common between the slave of a tyrant and the inhabitant of a free state; the customs of the latter, his principles, his sentiments, his action, all must be new" (quoted in Hunt 1984: 29).
2. The *bonheur commun* was proclaimed as the "goal of society" in the Jacobin Constitution of 1793.
3. Hunt (1992) makes use of Freud's concept to analyze the power games of 1789 in terms of filial and parental/maternal relations.
4. As for the republican city of Hamburg, see the police reports on workers' opinions about the monarchy: Evans (1989: 322–340).
5. See, f.ex., the first-hand account by Laube (1978).
6. See also, for Britain, O'Gorman (1992); for the United States, Bensel (2004).
7. For the United States, see Eustace (2012).

REFERENCES

Ablow, R. (1991), "Victorian Feelings," in D. David (ed.), *The Cambridge Companion to the Victorian Novel*, 2nd ed., Cambridge: Cambridge University Press.
Adorno, T. W. and Horkheimer, M. (1947), *Dialektik der Aufklärung: Philosophische Fragmente*, Amsterdam: Querido.
Albanese, C. (1990), *Nature Religion in America from the Algonkian Indians to the New Age*, Chicago, University of Chicago Press.
Aldrich E. (1991), *From the Ballroom to Hell: Grace and Folly in Nineteenth – Century Dance*, Evanston: Northwestern University Press.
Amiel, H. ([1883]1915), *Fragments d'un journal intime*, 2 vols, 12th ed., Geneva: Georg.
Amiel, H. (1894), *Amiel's Journal. The Journal intime of Henri-Frédéric Amiel*, 2nd ed., trans. H. Ward, London and New York: Macmillan.
Anderson, A. (2001), *The Powers of Distance: Cosmopolitanism and the Cultivation of Detachment*, Princeton: Princeton University Press.
Anderson, M. (1985), *Approaches to the History of the Western Family, 1500–1914*, London: Macmillan Studies in Economic and Social History.
Anderson, M. (2000), *Practicing Democracy: Elections and Political Culture in Imperial Germany*, Princeton: Princeton University Press.
Andrews, W., ed. (1986), *Sisters of the Spirit: Three Black Women's Autobiographies of the Nineteenth Century*, Bloomington, Indiana University Press.
Appleby, J. (2010), *The Relentless Revolution: A History of Capitalism*, New York: W.W. Norton, 2010.
Applegate, C. (2005), *Bach in Berlin: Nation and Culture in Mendelssohn's Revival of the St. Matthew Passion*, Ithaca, NY: Cornell University Press.
Aristotle (1987), *Poetics*, trans. R. Janko, Indianapolis: Hackett Publishing.
Arnaud, S. (2015), *On Hysteria: The Invention of a Medical Category between 1670 and 1820*, Chicago: University of Chicago Press.
Arthur, T. (1888), *The Mother's Rule: Or, The Right Way and The Wrong Way*, New York: Lovell.
Arthur, T. (2004), "The Mother's Promise," in *Home Lights and Shadows*, Whitefish, Montana: Kessinger Publishing.
Audoin-Rouzeau, S. (1992), *Men at War, 1914–1918: National Sentiment and Trench Journalism in France during the First World War*, Providence, RI: Berg.
Bagehot, W. (1995), *The Collected Works of Walter Bagehot*, vol. 4: *The English Constitution*, ed. F. Morgan, London: Routledge.
Bailey, B. (1989), *From Front Porch to Back Seat: Courtship in Twentieth-Century America* Baltimore, MD: Johns Hopkins University Press.
Bailey, C. (2014), "Social Emotions," in U. Frevert et al. (eds), *Emotional Lexicons: Continuity and Change in the Vocabulary of Feeling 1700–2000*, Oxford: Oxford University Press.
Baillie, J. ([1798]2001), *Plays on the Passions*, ed. Peter Duthie, Ontario: Broadview.
Bain, A. (1859), The *Emotions and the Will*, London: John W. Parker and Son.

Bain, A. (1865), *The Emotions and the Will*, 2nd ed., London: Longmans, Green.
Bain, A. (1894), *The Senses and the Intellect*, 4th ed., London: Longmans, Green.
Bainbridge, W. S. (1984), "Religious Insanity in America: The Official Nineteenth Century Theory," *Sociological Analysis*, 45(3): 223–240.
Baker, J. (2011), "'Strange Contrarys': Figures in Melancholy in Eighteenth-Century Poetry," in E. A. Allan (ed.), *Melancholy Experience in Literature in the Long Eighteenth Century, Before Depression, 1660–1800*, Ingram Hampshire: Palgrave MacMillan, 83–113.
Baldwin, J. (1909), "La Mémoire affective et l'art," *Revue Philosophique*, 67(5): 449–460.
Baldwin, J. (1949), "Everybody's Protest Novel," *Partisan Review*, 16: 578–585.
Ball, J. ([1925]1997) "Autobiography of John Ball, 1794–1884, compiled by his daughters: Kate Ball Powers, Flora Ball Hopkins, Lucy Ball" in J. Appleby (ed.), *Recollections of the Early Republic: Selected Autobiographies*, Boston: Northeastern University Press.
Balser, F. (1962), *Sozial-Demokratie 1848/49–1863: Die erste deutsche Arbeiterorganisation "Allgemeine Arbeiterverbrüderung" nach der Revolution*, Stuttgart: Klett.
Barker, E. (2005), *Greuze and the Painting of Sentiment*, Cambridge: Cambridge University Press.
Barker-Benfield, G. (1992), *The Culture of Sensibility: Sex and Society in Eighteenth-Century Britain*, Chicago: The University of Chicago Press.
Barrows, S. (1981), *Distorting Mirrors: Visions of the Crowd in Late Nineteenth-Century France*, New Haven: Yale University Press.
Bashford, C. (1999), "Learning to Listen: Audiences for Chamber Music in Early-Victorian London," *Journal of Victorian Culture*, 4: 25–51.
Bätschmann, O., Eisenman, S., and Gloor, L. (1987), *Ferdinand Hodler: Landscapes*, exh. cat. Wight Art Gallery, University of California, Los Angeles, Zurich: Schweizer Verlagshaus.
Baudelaire, C. ([1846]1976), *Salon de 1846*, in C. Baudelaire, *Œuvres complètes*, C. Pichois (ed.), 3 vols, vol. 2, Paris: Gallimard, 415–496.
Baudelaire, C. ([1846]1981), "The Salon of 1846," in C. Baudelaire, *Art in Paris 1845–1862, Salons and Other Exhibitions*, trans. and ed. J. Mayne, 2nd ed., Oxford: Phaidon, 41–120.
Baudelaire, C. ([1859]1976), *Salon de 1859*, in C. Baudelaire, *Œuvres complètes*, C. Pichois (ed.), 3 vols, vol. 2, Paris: Gallimard, 608–682.
Baudelaire, C. ([1859]1981), "The Salon of 1859," in C. Baudelaire, *Art in Paris 1845–1862, Salons and Other Exhibitions*, trans. and ed. J. Mayne, 2nd ed. Oxford: Phaidon 144–216.
Baudelaire, C. ([1859]2006), *Salon de 1859: texte de la Revue française*, W. Drost (ed.), Paris: Champion 2006.
Baudelaire, C. ([1863]1976), *Le peintre de la vie moderne*, in C. Baudelaire, *Œuvres complètes*, C. Pichois (ed.), 3 vols, vol. 2, Paris: Gallimard, 683–724.
Baxmann, I. (1989), *Die Feste der Französischen Revolution. Inszenierung von Gesellschaft als Natur*, Weinheim/Basel: Beltz.
Baxter, R. (1806), *A Call to the Unconverted*, Northampton: S.E. Butler.
Beard, G. (1881), *American Nervousness: Its Causes and Consequences, a Supplement to Nervous Exhaustion (Neurasthenia)*, New York: G.P. Putnam's Sons.
Becq, A. (1994), *Génèse de l'esthétique française moderne: De la Raison classique à l'Imagination créatrice, 1680–1814*, Paris: Albin Michel.
Beer, G. (1983), *Darwin's Plots: Evolutionary Narrative in Darwin, George Eliot, and Nineteenth-Century Fiction*, London: ARK.
Bell, C. (1806), *Essays on the Anatomy of Expression in Painting*, London: Longman, Hurst, Rees, and Orme.
Bell, C. (1824), *Essays on the Anatomy and Philosophy of Expression*, London: John Murray.

Bell, M. (2000), *Sentimentalism, Ethics and the Culture of Feeling*, Houndmills: Palgrave Macmillan.

Bensel, R. (2004), *The American Ballot Box in the Mid-Nineteenth Century*, Cambridge: Cambridge University Press.

Benson, T. ed. (2014), *Expressionism in Germany and France, From Van Gogh to Kandinsky*, exh. cat. Los Angeles County Museum of Art, Munich: Prestel.

Berlant, L. (1992), "The Female Woman: Fanny Fern and the Form of Sentiment," in S. Samuels (ed.), *The Culture of Sentiment: Race, Gender, and Sentimentality in Nineteenth-Century America*, New York: Oxford University Press.

Berlin, I. (1999), *The Roots of Romanticism*, London: Chatto & Windus.

Bernier, M.-A. (2012), "De l'expression des passions à celle d'une 'impression de sentiment': la rhétorique du siècle des Lumières à l'école de la philosophie sensualiste," in L. Desjardins and D. Dumouchel (eds), *Penser les Passions à l'âge classique*, Paris: Hermann, 213–231.

Beus, Y. (2003), "Alfred de Musset's Romantic Irony," *Nineteenth-Century French Studies* 31: 197–209.

Bismarck, O. v. (1990), *Gedanken und Erinnerungen. Mit einem Essay von Lothar Gall*, Berlin: Propyläen.

Blauvelt, M. (2007), *The Work of the Heart, Young Women and Emotion 1780–1830*, Charlottesville: University of Virginia Press.

Blessing, W. (1978), "The Cult of Monarchy, Political Loyalty and the Workers' Movement in Imperial Germany," *Journal of Contemporary History*, 13: 357–375.

Boddice, R. (2011), "The Manly Mind? Re-visiting the Victorian 'Sex in Brain' Debate," *Gender and History*, 23: 321–340.

Boddice, R. (2016), *The Science of Sympathy: Morality, Evolution and Victorian Civilization*, Urbana-Champaign: University of Illinois Press.

Boehm, G. (1988), *Paul Cézanne: Montagne Sainte-Victoire*, Frankfurt/M: Insel.

Bogucki, M. (2010), "Echo Sign: J.M. Synge and Naturalist Theatricality," *Modern Drama*, 53: 516–532.

Böhme, G. (2006), *Architektur und Atmosphäre*, Munich: Fink.

Bolufer, M. (2016), "Reasonable Sentiments: Sensibility and Balance in Eighteenth-Century Spain," in L. Delgado, P. Fernández and J. Labanyi (eds), *Engaging the Emotions in Spanish Culture and History*, Nashville: Vanderbilt University Press.

Booth, M. (1965), *English Melodrama*. London: H. Jenkins.

Booth, M. (1995), "Nineteenth-century Theater," J. Brown (ed.), *The Oxford Illustrated History of Theatre*, Oxford: Oxford University Press.

Borchmeyer, D. (2008), "Critique as Passion and Polemic: Nietsche and Wagner," in T. Grey (ed.), *The Cambridge Companion to Wagner*, Cambridge: Cambridge University Press, 192–202.

Börsch-Supan, H. and Jähnig, K. (1973), *Caspar David Friedrich: Gemälde, Druckgraphik und bildmäßige Zeichnungen*, Munich: Prestel.

Bouillon, J.-P. (1989), *La Critique d'art en France, 1850–1900*, conference proceedings Clermont-Ferrand 1987, Saint-Étienne: Université de Saint-Étienne.

Bouillon, J.-P. (1993), *Maurice Denis*, Geneva: Skira.

Bound Alberti, F., ed. (2006), *Medicine, Emotion and Disease, 1700–1950*, Basingstoke, New York: Palgrave Macmillan.

Bound Alberti, F. (2010), *Matters of the Heart: History, Medicine, and Emotion*, Oxford: Oxford University Press.

Bourke, J. (1996), *Dismembering the Male: Men's Bodies, Britain and the Great War*, London: Reaktion.
Bourke, J. (2014), "Phantom Suffering: Amputees, Stump Pain and Phantom Sensations in Modern Britain," in R. Boddice (ed.), *Pain and Emotion in Modern History*, Houndmills: Palgrave.
Bower, B. (2016), *The Crystal Palace Saturday Concerts, 1865–1879: A Case Study of the Nineteenth-Century Programme Note*, PhD Diss. Royal College of Music, London.
Bowler, P. (1989), *The Mendelian Revolution: The Emergence of Hereditarian Concepts in Modern Science and Society*, London: Athlone.
Brendel, F. ([1859]2008), *Neue Zeitschrift fuer Musik*, trans. P. Weiss in *Music in the Western World*, ed. P. Weiss and R. Tarsukin, Boston: Schirmer Cengage Learning.
Brice, C. (2010), *Monarchie et Identité Nationale en Italie (1861–1900)*, Paris: Editions EHESS.
Brissenden, R. (1974), *Virtue in Distress: Studies in the Novel of Sentiment from Richardson to Sade*, New York: Barnes & Noble.
Brooks, P. (1976), *The Melodramatic Imagination: Balzac, Henry James, Melodrama, and the Mode of Excess*. New Haven: Yale University Press.
Broomhall, S., ed. (2017), *Early Modern Emotions: An Introduction*, Routledge, London.
Brown, T. (1822), *Lectures on the Philosophy of the Human Mind in Three Volumes, Vol. 1* Andover: Mark Newman.
Bruhm, S. (1994), *Gothic Bodies: The Politics of Pain in Romantic Fiction*, Philadelphia: University of Pennsylvania Press.
Brumberg, J. (1988), *Fasting Girls: The Emergence of Anorexia Nervosa as a Modern Disease* Cambridge, MA: Harvard University Press.
Brunetière, F. (1888), "Revue littéraire. Symbolistes et décadens," *Revue des deux mondes*, 90: 213–226.
Buckley, J. (1883), "Faith Cures," *Christian Advocate*, May 31, 1883.
Buckley, M. (2006), *Tragedy Walks the Streets: The French Revolution in the Making of Modern Drama*. Baltimore: Johns Hopkins University Press.
Buckster, A. and Glazier, S., eds (2003), *The Anthropology of Religious Conversion*, New York: Rowman & Littlefield.
Bunyan, J. (2010a), *The Pilgrim's Progress*, Boston, MobileReference.
Bunyan, J. (2010b), *Grace Abounding to the Chief of Sinners*, Boston: MobileReference.
Burke, E. (1958), *A Philosophical Enquiry into the Origin of our Ideas of the Sublime and Beautiful*, ed. J. Boulton, Notre Dame: University of Notre Dame Press.
Burke, E. ([1790]2009), *Reflections on the Revolution in France*, Oxford: Oxford University Press.
Burke, E. (2015), *A Philosophical Enquiry into the Origin of Our Ideas of the Sublime and Beautiful*, Oxford: Oxford University Press.
Burney, C. (1785), *An Account of the Musical Performances in Westminster Abbey and the Pantheon, May 26, 27, 29 and June 3, and 5, 1784*, London: T. Payne and Son.
Burnham, S., ed. and trans. (2006), *Musical Form in the Age of Beethoven: Selected Writings on Theory and Method*, Cambridge: Cambridge University Press.
Burroughs, C. (1997), *Closet Stages: Joanna Baillie and the Theater Theory of British Romantic Women Writers*. Philadelphia: University of Pennsylvania Press.
Burton, R. ([1621]1927), *The Anatomy of Melancholy*, New York: Farrar and Rinehart.
Burwick, F. (2009), *Romantic Drama: Acting and Reacting*, Cambridge: Cambridge University Press.

Busch, W. (1993), *Das sentimentalische Bild: die Krise der Kunst im 18. Jahrhundert und die Geburt der Moderne*, Munich: Beck.

Büschel, H. (2006), *Untertanenliebe: Der Kult um deutsche Monarchen 1770–1830*, Göttingen: Vandenhoeck & Ruprecht.

Bushnell, H. ([1847]1904), *Christian Nurture*, New York: Charles Scribner's Sons.

Butler, M. (1992), *Romantics, Rebels and Reactionaries: English Literature and Its Background, 1760–1830*, Oxford: Oxford University Press.

Byron, Lord ([1818]1986), "Mazeppa," in *Lord Byron, The Complete Poetical Works*, J. McGann (ed.), 7 vols, vol. 4 (no. 327), Oxford: Clarendon Press, 173–200.

Byron, Lord (1996), *Selected Poems*, eds S. Wolfson and P. Manning, London and New York: Penguin.

Byttebier, S. (2014), "'None of the Effect of an Invalid': The Trials of Empathy in Henry James's *The Wings of the Dove*," *The Henry James Review*, 35: 157–174.

Calhoun, C. and Solomon, R., eds (1984), *What is an Emotion?* New York: Oxford University Press.

Campbell, C. (2005), *The Romantic Ethic and the Spirit of Modern Consumerism*, rev. ed., York: Alcuin Academics.

Cannell, F., ed. (2006), *The Anthropology of Christianity*, Durham: Duke University Press.

Cannon, W. (1915), *Bodily Changes in Pain, Hunger, Fear and Rage: An Account of Recent Researches into the Function of Emotional Excitement*, New York and London: D. Appleton and Co.

Carey, B. (2005), *British Abolitionism and the Rhetoric of Sensibility: Writing, Sentiment, and Slavery, 1760–1807*, Houndmills: Palgrave Macmillan.

Carones, L. (1987), "Noverre and Angiolini: Polemical Letters," *Dance Research*, 5(1): 42–54.

Carpeaux, J.-B. ([1861]1912), Letter to Louis Dutouquet, March 1861, in J.-B. Carpeaux, *Lettres et nombreux documents inédits*, ed. E. Florian-Parmentier, Paris: Louis-Michaud, 159–160.

Carrà, C. ([1913]1978), "La pittura di suoni, rumori, odori: Manifesto futurista," *Lacerba*, 1 September 1913, in C. Carrà, *Tutti gli scritti*, M. Carrà (ed.), Milan 1978, 16–21.

Carus, C. ([1815–1824]2002), *Nine Letters on Landscape Painting, Written in the Years 1815–1824; with a Letter from Goethe by Way of Introduction*, ed. O. Bätschmann, trans. D. Britt, Los Angeles: Getty Publications.

Carus, C. ([1835]1992), *Neun Briefe über Landschaftsmalerei, geschrieben in den Jahren 1815 bis 1824*, in F. Apel (ed.), *Romantische Kunstlehre. Poesie und Poetik des Blicks in der deutschen Romantik*, Frankfurt/M: Dt. Klassiker-Verlag, 203–279.

Catteau, J. (1989), *Dostoyevsky and the Process of Literary Creation*, Cambridge: Cambridge University Press.

Caylus, Conte de (1757), *Tableaux tirés de l'Illiade et de l'Odyssée d'Homère et de l'Énéide de Virgile* Paris: Tilliard.

Charcot, J. (1877), *Leçons sur les maladies du système nerveux faites a la Salpêtrière*, Paris: Adrien Delahaye.

Chaussard, P. (1806), *Le pausanias français : État des Arts du dessin en France, à l'ouverture du XIXe siècle—Salon de 1806*, Paris: Buisson.

Chazin-Bennahum, J. (2011), "Jean-Georges Noverre: Dance and Reform," in M. Kant, (ed.), *The Cambridge Companion to Ballet*, Cambridge: Cambridge University Press, 87–97.

Chekhov, A. (1997), *Plays*, trans. P. Schmidt. New York: Harper Collins.

Chenique, B. (1998), *Les cercles politiques de Géricault, 1791–1824*, Lille: ANR Thèses.

Christensen, T., ed. (2006), *The Cambridge History of Western Music Theory*, Cambridge: Cambridge University Press.

Clark, S., and Rehding, A. (2001), *Music Theory and Natural Order from the Renaissance to the Early Twentieth Century*, Cambridge: Cambridge University Press.
Clarke, S. (1991), *Sentimental Modernism: Women Writers and the Revolution of the World*, Bloomington: Indiana University Press.
Clarkson, J. (2010), *Constable*, London and New York: Phaidon.
Clebsch, W. (1964), *Pastoral Care in Historical Perspective*, New York, Harper and Row.
Cogeval, G., ed. (2003), *Édouard Vuillard*, exh. cat. Washington, National Gallery of Art, New Haven and London: Yale University Press.
Cole, L. and Unowsky, D., eds (2007), *The Limits of Loyalty: Imperial Symbolism, Popular Allegiances, and State Patriotism in the Late Habsburg Monarchy*, New York: Berghahn.
Coleridge, S. ([1797]1880), "Remorse, A Tragedy in Five Acts," *The Poetical and Dramatic Works of Samuel Taylor Coleridge*, vol. 4, London: Macmillan and Co.
Colley, L. (1992), *Britons: Forging the Nation 1707–1837*, New Haven: Yale University Press.
Cone, E., ed. (1971), *Hector Berlioz, Fantastique Symphony*, New York: W.W. Norton & Co.
Conklin, A. (2013), *In the Museum of Man: Race, Anthropology, and Empire in France, 1850–1950*, Ithaca: Cornell University Press.
Constable, J. ([1830]1970), "Letterpress to English Landscape," in R. Beckett (ed.), *John Constable's Discourses*, Ipswich: Suffolk Records Society, 12–27.
Conway, J. (1972), "Stereotypes of Femininity in a Theory of Sexual Evolution," in M. Vicinus (ed.), *Suffer and Be Still: Women in the Victorian Age*, Bloomington: Indiana University Press.
Coontz, S. (2006), *Marriage, A History: How Love Conquered Marriage*, New York: Penguin.
Corot, C. ([1856]1924), "Sketchbook of 1856, Paris, musée du Louvre, département des Arts graphiques," in É. Moreau-Nélaton, *Corot raconté par lui-même*, 2 vols, Paris: Henri Laurens, 105–106.
Corrigan, J. (2002), *Business of the Heart, Religion and Emotion in the Nineteenth Century*, Berkeley, University of California Press.
Cossart, P. (2003), "L'émotion: un dommage pour l'idée républicaine. Autour de l'éloquence de Léon Gambetta," *Romantisme*, 119: 47–60.
Cott, N. (1997), *The Bonds of Womanhood: 'Woman's Sphere' in New England, 1780–1835*, 2nd ed., New Haven, CT: Yale University Press.
Cowper, W. (1984), *The Letters and Prose Writings of William Cowper*, Oxford: Clarendon.
Cox, J. (1990), "The French Revolution in the English Theater," in S. Behrendt (ed.), *History and Myth: Essays on English Romantic Literature*, Detroit: Wayne State University Press.
Cox, J. (1992), *Seven Gothic Dramas, 1789–1825*, Athens: Ohio University Press.
Cromer, E. (1908), *Modern Egypt*, vol. 2, London: Macmillan.
Crook, M. (2000), "The Uses of Democracy: Elections and Plebiscites in Napoleonic France," in M. Cross and D. Williams (eds), *The French Experience from Republic to Monarchy, 1792–1824*, New York: Palgrave, 58–71.
Cross, G. (2004), *The Cute and the Cool: Wondrous Innocence and Modern American Children's Culture*, Oxford and New York: Oxford University Press.
Csengei I. (2011), *Sympathy, Sensibility and the Literature of Feeling in the Eighteenth Century*, Houndmills: Palgrave Macmillan.
Cunningham, A. and Williams, P., eds (1992), *The Laboratory Revolution in Medicine*, Cambridge: Cambridge University Press.
Cunningham, R. (1993), "From Holiness to Healing: The Faith Cure in America 1872–1892," in M. Marty (ed.), *Varieties of Religious Expression*, New York, K. G. Saur, 3–17.
Daemmrich, I. (1973), "Alfred de Musset's View of the Poet," *Revue des Langues Vivantes*, 39: 5–10.

Dahlhaus, C. (1978), *Die Idee der absoluten Musik*, Munich: Deutscher Taschenbuchverlag.
Dahlhaus, C. (1989), *Nineteenth-Century Music*, trans. J. Bradford Robinson, Berkeley: University of California Press.
Dahms, S. (2010), *Der konservative Revolutionär: Jean Georges Noverre und die Ballettreform des 18. Jahrhunderts* (vol. 4). Munich: Epodium.
Dalle Pezze, B. and Salzani, C., eds (2009), *Essays on Boredom and Modernity*, Amsterdam: Rodopi.
Damasio, A. (1999), *The Feeling of What Happens: Body and Emotion in the Making of Consciousness*. New York: Harcourt Brace.
Dames, N. (2005), "'The withering of the individual': Psychology in the Victorian Novel," in F. O'Gorman (ed.), *A Concise Companion to the Victorian Novel*, Oxford: Blackwell.
Dana, R. (1822), *The Idle Man*, New York: Wiley and Halsted.
Darwin, C. ([1871]2004), *The Descent of Man, and Selection in Relation to Sex*, London: Penguin.
Darwin, C. (1872), *The Expression of the Emotions in Man and Animals*, London: John Murray.
Darwin, C. (1998), *The Expression of the Emotions in Man and Animals*, 3rd ed., Oxford: Oxford University Press.
Dassas, F., ed. (2002), *L'invention du sentiment: aux sources du romantisme*, exh. cat. Paris Musée de la musique, Paris: Réunion des musées nationaux.
Daston, L. and Galison, P. (2007), *Objectivity*, New York: Zone Books.
Dauvois, D. and Dumouchel, D., eds (2015), *Vers l'esthétique. Penser avec les "Réflexions critiques sur la poésie et sur la peinture" de Jean-Baptiste Du Bos, 1719*, Paris: Hermann.
Davies, M. (2002), *Graceful Reading, Theology and Narrative in the Works of John Bunyan*, Oxford, Oxford University Press.
Davis, P. (2002), *The Oxford English Literary History, Volume 8. 1830–1880: The Victorians*, Oxford: Oxford University Press.
Davis, T. and Holland, P., eds (2007), *The Performing Century: Nineteenth-Century Theatre's History*. Houndmills: Palgrave Macmillan.
Dawson, M. (2008), "Ruiz de Burton's Emotional Landscape: Property and Feeling in *The Squatter and the Don*," *Nineteenth-Century Literature*, 63: 41–72.
Dawson, M. (2015), *Emotional Reinventions: Realist-Era Representations Beyond Sympathy*, Ann Arbor: University of Michigan Press.
Degler, C. (1980), *At Odds, Women and the Family in America from the Revolution to the Present*, New York, Oxford University Press.
DeJean, J. (1997), *Ancient Against Moderns: Culture Wars and the Making of a Fin de Siècle*, Chicago and London: University of Chicago Press.
Déloye, Y. (2000), "Le charisme contrôlé. Entre grandeur et raison: la posture publique de Léon Gambetta," *Communications*, 69: 157–172.
Delumeau, J. (1990), *Sin and Fear: The Emergence of the Western Guilt Culture, 13th–18th Centuries*, New York: Palgrave Macmillan.
Demos, J. (1988), "Shame and Guilt in Early New England," in C. Stearns and P. Stearns (eds), *Emotion and Social Change: Toward a New Psychohistory*, New York: Holmes & Meier, 69–85.
Demos, J. (2000), *A Little Commonwealth: Family Life in Plymouth Colony*, 2nd ed., Oxford and New York: Oxford University Press.
Denby, D. (1994), *Sentimental Narrative and the Social Order in France, 1760–1820*, Cambridge: Cambridge University Press.
Denis, M. ([1907]1993), Cézanne, *L'Occident*, 70, September 1907, 118–133, in J.-P. Bouillon (ed.), *Le ciel et l'arcadie*, Paris: Hermann, 129–150.

De Sousa, R. ([1987]1999), *The Rationality of Emotion*. Cambridge, MA: MIT Press.
De Vries, J. (2008), *The Industrious Revolution: Consumer Behavior and the Household Economy, 1650 to the Present*, New York: Cambridge University Press.
Dickson, L. and Ingraham, A., eds (2012), *Depression and Melancholy, 1660–1800*, London: Pickering & Chatto.
Diderot, D. ([1763]2003), *Salon de 1763*, in D. Diderot, *Essais sur la peinture, Salon de 1759, 1761, 1763*, eds J. Chouillet and G. May, 2nd ed, Paris: Hermann, 171–255.
Diderot, D. ([1767]1995), *Salon de 1767*, in D. Diderot, *Ruines et paysages, Salons de 1767*, eds E. Bukdahl, M. Delon, and A. Lorenceau, Paris: Hermann.
Dietze, C. (2007), "Terror in the Nineteenth Century: Political Assassinations and Public Discourse in Europe and the United States, 1878–1901," *Bulletin of the German Historical Institute*, 40: 91–97.
Disraeli, B. (1844), *Coningsby*, vol. 3, 2nd. ed., London: Colburn.
Dixon, T. (2003), *From Passions to Emotions: The Creation of a Secular Psychological Category*, Cambridge: Cambridge University Press.
Dixon, T. (2006), *From Passions to Emotions: The Creation of a Secular Psychological Category*, Cambridge: Cambridge University Press.
Dixon, T. (2008), *The Invention of Altruism: Making Moral Meanings in Victorian Britain*, Oxford: Oxford University Press.
Dixon, T. (2012), "Emotion: The History of a Key Word in Crisis," *Emotion Review*, 4(4):338–344.
Dixon, T. (2015), *Weeing Britannia: Portrait of a Nation in Tears*, Oxford: Oxford University Press.
Donne, J. (1929), *Complete Poetry and Selected Prose*, Bloomsbury: Nonesuch Press.
Dorra, H. ed. (1994), *Symbolist Art Theories: A Critical Anthology*, Berkeley and Los Angeles: University of California Press.
Douglas, A. (1977), *The Feminization of American Culture*, New York: Knopf.
Dowling, L. (1996), *The Vulgarization of Art: The Victorians and Aesthetic Democracy*, Charlottesville and London: University Press of Virginia.
Draper, J. and Papet, É., eds (2014), *The Passions of Jean-Baptiste Carpeaux*, exh. cat. New York, Metropolitan Museum of Art, Paris, Musée d'Orsay, New Haven and London: Yale University Press.
Dror, O. (1999), "The Scientific Image of Emotion: Experience and Technologies of Inscription," *Configurations*, 7: 355–401.
Dror, O. (1999a), "The Affect of Experiment: The Turn to Emotions in Anglo-American Physiology, 1900–1940," *Isis*, 90: 205–237.
Dror, O. (2014), "What is an Excitement?" in F. Biess and D. Gross (eds), *Science and Emotions After 1945: A Transatlantic Perspective*, Chicago: University of Chicago Press.
Drummond, P. (2011), *The Provincial Music Festival in England*, Farnham: Ashgate.
Du Bois, J. (1719), *Réflexions critiques sur la poésie et sur la peinture*, 2 vols, vol. 1, Paris: Mariette.
Duchenne (de Boulogne), G. (1862), *Mécanisme de la physionomie humaine de analyse électro-physiologique de l'expression des passions*, Paris: Jules Renouard.
Duggan, C. (2012), *Fascist Voices: An Intimate History of Mussolini's Italy*, London: Bodley Head.
Duncan, B. (2003), "Sturm und Drang Passions and Eighteenth-Century Psychology," in D. Hill (ed.), *Literature of the Strum und Drang: The Camden House History of German Literature, Volume 6*, Rochester: Camden House.

Dye, N. and Smith, D. (1986), "Mother Love and Infant Death, 1750–1920," *Journal of American History*, 73 (1986): 329–353.

Edwards, J. ([1746]1821), *A Treatise Concerning Religious Affections: In Three Parts*, Philadelphia: James Crissy.

Ekman, P. and Friesen, W. (1971), "Constants across Cultures in the Face and Emotion," *Journal of Personality and Social Psychology*, 17: 124–129.

Elderfield, J. (1974), "Monet's Series," *Art International*, 18/9(28), 45–46.

Eliot, T. (1951), "Tradition and the Individual Talent," in *Selected Essays*, 3rd. ed., London: Faber and Faber.

Elkin, R. (1947), *The Annals of the Royal Philharmonic Society*, London: Rider and Company.

Ellison, J. (1999), *Cato's Tears and the Making of Anglo-American Emotion*, Chicago: The University of Chicago Press.

Enderwitz, A. (2015), *Modernist Melancholia: Freud, Conrad, and Ford*, Houndmills: Palgrave Macmillan.

Engelhardt, M. (2009), *Dancing out of Line: Ballrooms, Ballets, and Mobility in Victorian Fiction and Culture*, Athens: Ohio University Press.

Erichsen, J. (1867), *On Railway and Other Injuries of the Nervous System*, Philadelphia: Henry C. Lea.

Eustace, N. (2008), *Passion is the Gale: Emotion, Power, and the Coming of the American Revolution*, Chapel Hill: University of North Carolina Press.

Eustace, N. (2012), *1812: War and the Passions of Patriotism*, Philadelphia: University of Pennsylvania Press.

Evan Bonds, M. (1997), "Idealism and the Aesthetics of Instrumental Music at the Turn of the Nineteenth Century," *Journal of the American Musicological Society*, 50(2–3): 387–420.

Evan Bonds, M. (2009), *Music as Thought: Listening to the Symphony in the Age of Beethoven*, Princeton: Princeton University Press.

Evan Bonds, M. (2014), *Absolute Music: The History of an Idea*, New York: Oxford University Press.

Evans, R. J. (ed.) (1989), *Kneipengespräche im Kaiserreich: Die Stimmungsberichte der Hamburger Politischen Polizei 1892–1914*, Reinbek: Rowohlt.

Faucheur, N. (1886), *Mon histoire, à mes chers enfants et petits-enfants*, Lille: L. Danel.

Faulds, K. (2015), *"Invitation pour la danse": Social dance, dance music and feminine identity in the English country house c.1770–1860*, PhD Diss., University of Southampton.

Faust, D. (2008), *This Republic of Suffering, Death and the American Civil War*, New York, Alfred A. Knopf.

Ferber, M. (2010), *Romanticism: A Very Short Introduction*, Oxford: Oxford University Press.

Fisher, P. (1985), *Hard Facts: Setting and Form in the American Novel*, New York: Oxford University Press.

Fisher, P. (2002), *The Vehement Passions*. Princeton: Princeton University Press.

Flatley, J. (2008), *Affective Mapping: Melancholia and the Politics of Modernism*, Cambridge: Harvard University Press.

Flavel, J. (n.d.), *Keeping the Heart; or the Saint Indeed*. New York: American Tract Society.

Floerke, G. (1901), *Zehn Jahre mit Böcklin: Aufzeichnungen und Entwürfe*, Munich: F. Bruckmann.

de Font-Réaulx, D. (2002), "La Grâce d'une grande figure qui écoute en silence," in F. Dassas (ed.), *L'invention du sentiment: aux sources du romantisme*, exh. cat. Paris, Musée de la musique, Paris: Réunion des musées nationaux, 49–59.

Foster, T. (1813), *Researches about Atmospheric Phenomena*, London: T. Underwood.

Frank, H. (2004), *Aussichten ins Unermessliche. Perspektivität und Sinnoffenheit bei Caspar David Friedrich*, Berlin: Akademie-Verlag.

Franks, A. (1963), *Social Dance: A Short History*, London: Routledge and Kegan Paul.

Frazer, M. (2012), *The Enlightenment of Sympathy: Justice and the Moral Sentiments in the Eighteenth Century and Today*, Oxford: Oxford University Press.

Freud, S. (1919), "The Uncanny," in J. Strachey (trans. and ed.), *The Standard Edition of the Complete Psychological Works of Sigmund Freud, Volume XVII (1917–1919): An Infantile Neurosis and Other Works*, London: Hogarth Press.

Freud, S. ([1930]2002), *Civilization and Its Discontents*, London: Penguin.

Freud, S. (1961), *Beyond the Pleasure Principle*, James Strachey (trans. and ed.). New York: Norton.

Freud, S. and Breuer, J. ([1893–95]1974) *Studies on Hysteria*, London: Penguin.

Frevert, U. (2011), *Emotions in History—Lost and Found*, Budapest/New York: Central European University Press.

Frevert, U. (2012), *Gefühlspolitik: Friedrich II. als Herr über die Herzen?*, Göttingen: Wallstein.

Frevert, U. (2013), *Vertrauensfragen*, Munich: C.H. Beck.

Frevert, U. (2014), "Defining Emotions: Concepts and Debates over Three Centuries," in U. Frevert et al. (eds), *Emotional Lexicons: Continuity and Change in the Vocabulary of Feeling 1700–2000*, Oxford: Oxford University Press.

Frevert, U. (2015), "Faith, Love, Hate: The National Socialist Politics of Emotions," in W. Nerdinger and H.-G. Hockerts (eds), *Munich and National Socialism*, Munich: C.H. Beck, 479–486.

Frevert, U. (2017), "Wartime Emotions: Honour, Shame, and the Ecstasy of Sacrifice," *1914–1918 Online International Encyclopedia of the First World War*, https://encyclopedia.1914-1918-online.net/article/wartime_emotions_honour_shame_and_the_ecstasy_of_sacrifice accessed August 14, 2017.

Frevert, U. et al., eds (2011), *Gefühlswissen: Eine lexikalische Spurensuche in der Moderne*, Frankfurt/M and New York: Campus.

Frevert, U. et al., eds (2014), *Emotional Lexicons: Continuity and Change in the Vocabulary of Feeling 1700–2000*, Oxford: Oxford University Press.

Fried, M. (1980), *Absorption and Theatricality: Painting and Beholder in the Age of Diderot*, Berkeley: University of California Press.

Friedman, L. and Percival, R. (1982), "Who Sues for Divorce? From Fault through Fiction to Freedom," *Journal of Legal Studies*, 104: 79.

Friedrich, C. ([1809]2006), Letter to Johannes Karl Hartwig Schulze, 8 February 1809, in C. Friedrich, *Die Briefe*, ed. H. Zschoche, 2nd ed, Hamburg: ConferencePoint, 51–54.

Friedrich, C. (1999), *Äußerungen bei Betrachtung einer Sammlung von Gemählden von größtentheils noch lebenden und unlängst verstorbenen Künstlern*, G. Eimer (ed.), Frankfurt/M: Kunstgeschichtliches Institut.

Frye, N. (1963), "The Drunken Boat: The Revolutionary Element in Romanticism," in N. Frye (ed.), *Romanticism Reconsidered: Selected Papers from the English Institute*, New York and London: Columbia University Press, 1–25.

Fuhrmann, W. (2015), "'Alle inner Gefühle hörbar hervor in die Luft gezaubert': Wilhelm Heinse und die Theorie des musikalischen Ausdrucks nach dem Verblassen der Figurenlehre," in W. Thormählen, T. Irvine, and O. Wiener (eds), *Musikalisches Denken im Labyrinth der Aufklärung: Wilhelm Heinses Hildegard von Hohenthal*. Mainz: Are-Musik-Verlag.

Furst, L. (2008), *Before Freud: Hysteria and Hypnosis in Later Nineteenth-Century Psychiatric Cases*, Lewisburg: Bucknell University Press.

Gaehtgens, T. (2010), "'Cet ordre de sentiments confus [. . .] par les mots de Gemuth et de Stimmung': Böcklin aus französischer Sicht," in K. Thomas (ed.), *Stimmung: Ästhetische Kategorie und künstlerische Praxis*, Berlin and Munich: Deutscher Kunstverlag, 197–211.

Galton, F. (1878), "Composite Portraits," *Journal of the Anthropological Institute of Great Britain and Ireland*, 8: 132–142.

Gamboni, D. (1989), *La plume et le pinceau. Odilon Redon et la littérature*, Paris: Ed. de Minuit.

Gamboni, D. (2002), *Potential Images: Ambiguity and Indeterminacy in Modern Art*, London: Reaktion Books.

Garrison, L. (2001), *Science, Sexuality and Sensation Novels: Pleasures of the Senses*, Houndmills: Palgrave Macmillan.

Gauguin, P. ([1884–85]1962), "Notes synthétiques," in R. Cogniat and J. Rewald (eds), *Carnet de croquis*, New York: Hammer Galleries.

Gauguin, P. ([1885]1984), Letter to Émile Schuffenecker, January 14, 1885, in P. Gauguin, *Correspondance de Paul Gauguin: Documents, témoignages*, ed. V. Merlhès, Paris: Singer-Polignac, no. 65, 87–89.

Gauguin, P. ([1899]1946), Letter to André Fontainas, March 1899, *Lettres de Gauguin à sa femme et à ses amis*, 4th ed, ed. M. Malingue, Paris: Éd. Bernard Grasset, 286–290.

Gauguin, P. (1946), *Letters to his Wife and Friends*, ed. Maurice Malingue, trans. H. J. Stenning, London: Saturn Press.

Gautier, T. ([1857]1996), "Salon de 1857," *L'Artiste*, 25 October 1857, in T. Gautier, *Bonjour, Monsieur Corot*, ed. M. H. Girard, Paris: Séguier, 70–71.

Gay, P. (1999), *Pleasure Wars: The Bourgeois Experience: Victoria to Freud*, New York: W.W. Norton & Company, 1999.

Geertz, C. (1973), *The Interpretation of Cultures*, New York, Basic Books.

Geison, G. (1978), *Michael Foster and the Cambridge School of Physiology: The Scientific Enterprise in Late Victorian Society*, Princeton: Princeton University Press.

Gendron M. and Feldman Barrett, L. (2009), "Reconstructing the Past: A Century of Ideas about Emotion in Psychology," *Emotion Review*, 1(4): 316–339.

Géricault, T. (1819), Letter to Jean-Jacques de Montcimet de Musigny, August–September 1819, in *Chenique* 1998, vol. 2, 513–514.

Gianquitto, T. and Fisher, L., eds (2014), *America's Darwin: Darwinian Theory and U.S. Literary Culture*, Athens: University of Georgia Press.

Gilbert, M. (2006), *The Will of the People: Winston Churchill and Parliamentary Democracy*, Toronto: Vintage Canada.

Gilchrist, A. ([1863]1998), *Life of William Blake, "Pictor ignotus": With Selections from his Poems and Other Writings*, New York: Dover Publications.

Gill, M. (2015), "Self-Control and Uncontrollable Passion in Stendhal's Theory of Love," *French Studies* 69: 462–478.

Gillespie, J. (1991), "1795: Martha Laurens Ramsay's 'Dark Night of the Soul'," *William and Mary Quarterly*, 48 (January): 68–92.

Gillis, J. (1985), *For Better, For Worse: British Marriages, 1600 to the Present*, New York: Oxford University Press, 1985.

Gilman, S. (1993), "The Image of the Hysteric," in S. Gilman, H. King, R. Porter, G. Rousseau, E. Showalter (eds), *Hysteria Beyond Freud*, Berkeley and Los Angeles: University of California Press.

Giloi, E. (2010), "'So Writes the Hand that Swings the Sword': Autograph Hunting and Royal Charisma in the German Empire, 1861–1888," in E. Berenson and E. Giloi (eds), *Constructing Charisma*, New York: Berghahn, 41–51.

Giloi, E. (2011), *Monarchy, Myth, and Material Culture in Germany 1750–1950*, Cambridge: Cambridge University Press.

Gneisenau, A. v. (1939), *Ein Leben in Briefen*, K. Griewank (ed), Leipzig: Köhler & Amelang.

Goebbels, J. (1987), *Die Tagebücher von Joseph Goebbels*, ed. E. Fröhlich, vol. 1, Munich: Saur.

Goethe, J. (1988), *The Sorrows of Young Werther/Elective Affinties/Novella*, New York: Suhrkamp.

Goldman, H. (1988), *Max Weber and Thomas Mann, Calling and the Shaping of the Self*, Berkeley: University of California Press.

Goldman, M. (1999), *Ibsen: The Dramaturgy of Fear*. New York: Columbia University Press.

Goldwater, R. (1979), *Symbolism*, London: Lane.

Google Books (American English) Corpus, http://googlebooks.byu.edu

Goring, P. (2004), *The Rhetoric of Sensibility in Eighteenth-century Culture*, Cambridge: Cambridge University Press.

Gouk, P. (1999), *Music, Science and Natural Magic in Seventeenth-century England*, Yale: Yale University Press.

Gould, S. (1993), "American Polygeny and Craniometry before Darwin: Blacks and Indians as Separate, Inferior Species," in S. Harding (ed.), *The "Racial" Economy of Science: Toward a Democratic Future*, Bloomington and Indianapolis: Indiana University Press.

Gould, S. (2008), *The Mismeasure of Man*, New York: W.W. Norton.

Gourmont, R. (1892), "Le Symbolisme," *Revue blanche*, 2, June, 321–325.

Gowing, L. (1978), "The Logic of Organized Sensations," in W. Rubin and T. Reff (eds), *Cézanne: The Late Work*, exh. cat. Museum of Modern Art New York, 1977, 55–71, London: Thames and Hudson.

Gowland, A. (2006), *The Worlds of Renaissance Melancholy: Robert Burton in Context*, Cambridge, Cambridge University Press.

Gramit, D. (2002), *Cultivating Music: The Aspirations, Interests, and Limits of German Musical Culture, 1770–1848*, Berkeley; London: University of California Press.

Green, J. (1934), "The Emmanuel Movement," *New England Quarterly*, 7(3): 494–532.

Greiner, R. (2012), *Sympathetic Realism in Nineteenth-Century British Fiction*, Baltimore: Johns Hopkins University Press.

Greven, P. (1972), *Four Generations: Population, Land, and Family in Colonial Andover, Massachusetts* Ithaca: Cornell University Press.

Griswold, R. (1986), "The Evolution of the Doctrine of Mental Cruelty in Victorian American Divorce, 1790–1900," *Journal of Social History*, 20: 127–148.

Gross, D. (2010), 'Defending the Humanities with Charles Darwin's *The Expression of the Emotions in Man and Animals* (1872)', *Critical Inquiry*, 37: 34–59.

Guégan, S., ed. (2003), *De Delacroix à Renoir: l'Algérie des peintres*, exh. cat. Paris, Institut du monde arabe, Paris: Hazan.

Gundle, S., Duggan, C. and Pieri, G., eds (2013), *The Cult of the Duce: Mussolini and the Italians*, Manchester: Manchester University Press.

Hagemann, K. (2015), *Revisiting Prussia's Wars against Napoleon: History, Culture and Memory*, New York: Cambridge University Press.

Hall, T. (1994), *Contested Boundaries: Itinerancy and the Shaping of the Colonial American Religious World*, Durham: University of North Carolina Press.

Hallock, W. (1835), *Memoir of Harlan Page, or, The Power of Prayer and Personal Effort for the Souls of Individuals*, New York, American Tract Society.

Hanslick, E. ([1854]1986), *Vom musikalisch Schönen: ein Beitrag zur Revision der Ästhetik der Tonkunst*, G. Paysant, Leipzig.

Hansson, H. and Norberg, C. (2102), "Storms of Tears: Emotion Metaphors and the Construction of Gender in *East Lynne*," *Orbis Litterarum*, 67: 154–170.

Harbus, A. (2011), "Reading Embodied Consciousness in *Emma*," *SEL: Studies in English Literature, 1500–1900*, 51: 765–782.

Harmon, W. and Holman, C. (1996), *A Handbook to Literature*, 7th ed., Upper Saddle River: Prentice Hall.

Harris, W. (2001), *Restraining Rage: The Ideology of Anger Control in Classical Antiquity*, Cambridge: Harvard University Press.

Harrison, C. and Wood, P. in collaboration with Gaiger, J., ed. (1998), *Art in Theory: 1815–1900*, Oxford and Malden: Blackwell.

Harrison, C. and Wood, P. in collaboration with Gaiger, J., ed. (2000), *Art in Theory: 1648–1815*, Oxford and Malden: Blackwell.

Harvey, P. (2011), *Through the Storm, Through the Night: A History of American Christianity*, Lanham, MD: Rowman & Littlefield.

Hauptman, W. (1975), *The Persistence of Melancholy in Nineteenth Century Art: The Iconography of a Motif*, PhD Pennsylvania State University, 2 vols, Ann Arbor: UMI.

Hazlitt, W. (1818), *A View of the English Stage*, London: Robert Stodart.

Helme, D. (1985), *The Role of the Assembly Rooms in the Social Education of the Middle – Class in England, 1750–1840*, M.Ed, University of Manchester.

Hemphill, C. (2011), *Siblings: Brothers and Sisters in American History*, Oxford and New York: Oxford University Press.

Hendler, G. (2001), *Public Sentiments: Structures of Feeling in Nineteenth-Century American Literature*, Chapel Hill: University of North Carolina Press.

Herding, K. (1990), "Kunst aus hochgemuter Düsternis: Über Delacroix' Paradoxien," *Städel-Jahrbuch*, 12: 259–278.

Hibberd, S. and Wrigley, R. (2014), *Art, Theatre and Opera in Paris, 1750–1850*, Aldershot: Ashgate.

Hill, C. (1989), *A Tinker and a Poor Man, John Bunyan and His Church, 1628–1688*, New York: Random House.

Hill, D. (1985), *Constables's English Landscape Scenery*, London: John Murray.

Hirschman, A. (1997), *The Passions and the Interests: Political Arguments for Capitalism before Its Triumph*, Princeton: Princeton University Press.

Hodler, F. ([1885–86]1972–1973), *Physiognomie der Landschaft*, lost manuscript, transcript. C. Loosli, trans. J. Brüschweiler, *Physiognomy of Landscape*, in *Ferdinand Hodler*, exh. cat. Berkeley, University Art Museum, 111–112.

Hoeller, H. (2006), "From Agony to Ecstasy: The New Studies of American Sentimentality," *ESQ: A Journal of the American Renaissance*, 52: 339–369.

Hofmann, W. (1972), *Das irdische Paradies: Motive und Ideen des 19. Jahrhunderts*, 2nd ed, Munich: Prestel.

Hoffmann, E. ([1809–10]1989), "L. van Beethoven: Symphony no.5," *Allgemeine musikalische Zeitung*, xii: 630–642, 652–659, trans. and ed. D. Charlton, *E.T.A. Hoffmann's Musical Writings: "Kreisleriana"—"The Poet and the Composer"—Music Criticism*, Cambridge: Cambridge University Press.

Holcroft, T. (2007), *The Novels and Selected Plays of Thomas Holcroft*, Gen. Ed. W. Verhoeven, vol. 5, ed. P. Cox, London: Pickering & Chatto.

Hoozee, R. (ed) (2007) *British Vision*, exh. cat. Gent, Museum vor Schoonen Kunsten, Brussels: Fonds Mercator.

Hosler, B. (1981), *Changing Aesthetic Views of Instrumental Music in 18th Century Germany*, Epping: Bowker.

Howard, L. ([1803]1865), *Essay on the Modifications of Clouds*, 3rd ed, London: John Churchill & Sons.

Hughes, W. (2001), *The Maniac in the Cellar: Sensation Novels of the 1860s*, Princeton: Princeton University Press.

Hui, A. (2013), *The Psychophysical Ear: Musical Experiments, Experimental Sounds, 1840–1910*, Cambridge: MIT Press.

Hulbert, A. (2003), *Raising America; Experts, Parents, and Century of Advice about Children*, New York: Alfred A Knopf.

Hume, D. (1998), *Enquiry Concerning the Principles of Morals*, Oxford: Oxford University Press.

Hume, D. (1969), "Of the Passions," in E. Mossner (ed.), *A Treatise of Human Nature*, London: Penguin.

Hume, D. (2000), *A Treatise of Human Nature*, Oxford: Oxford University Press.

Hume, R. (1969), "Gothic Versus Romantic: A Revaluation of the Gothic Novel," *PMLA*, 84: 282–290.

Hunt, L. (1984), *Politics, Culture, and Class in the French Revolution*, Berkeley: University of California Press.

Hunt, L. (1992), *The Family Romance of the French Revolution*, Berkeley: University of California Press.

Huret, J. and Mallarmé, S. ([1891]1995), "Enquète sur l'évolution littéraire," *Echo de Paris*, March 3–July 5, in Stéphane Mallarmé, *Œuvres complètes*, ed H. Mondor and G. Jean-Aubry, Paris: Gallimard, 866–872.

Hurley. T. (2011), "Opening the Doors to a Fairy-tale World: Tchaikovsky's Ballet Music," in M. Kant (ed.), *The Cambridge Companion to Ballet*, Cambridge: Cambridge University Press, 164–174.

Hutton, P. (1976), "Popular Boulangism and the Advent of Mass Politics in France, 1886–90," *Journal of Contemporary History*, 11: 85–106.

Ireland, R. (1988), "Insanity and the Unwritten Law," *American Journal of Legal History*, 32: 157–172.

Ireland, R. (1989), "The Libertine Must Die: Sexual Dishonor and the Unwritten Law in the Nineteenth-Century United States," *Journal of Social History*, 23.

Jackson, S. (1986), *Melancholia and Depression: From Hippocratic Times to Modern Times*, New Haven, Yale University Press.

Jacobs, H. ([1861]2001) *Incidents in the Life of a Slave Girl*, Mineola, NY: Dover.

Jäger, L. (ed.), (1988), *Zur historischen Semantik des deutschen Gefühlswortschatzes. Aspekte, Probleme und Beispiele seiner lexikographischen Erfassung*, Aachen: Alano.

James, W. (1884), "What Is an Emotion?" *Mind*, 9(34): 188–205.

James, W. ([1890]1910), *The Principles of Psychology*, London: MacMillan.

James, W. (1961), *The Varieties of Religious Experience, A Study in Human Nature*, New York, Collier Books.

Jann, R. (1994), "Darwin and the Anthropologists: Sexual Selection and its Discontents," *Victorian Studies*, 37: 287–306.

Jauß, H.-R. (1970), *Literaturgeschichte als Provokation*, Frankfurt/M: Suhrkamp.

Ji, W. (1989), "Significance of *Tentatio* in Luther's Spirituality," *Concordia Journal*, 15(2): 181–189.

Jobert, B. (2002), "Romantisme, préromantisme: quelques propositions," in *Dassas 2002*, 43–48.

Jobert, B. (2004), "The French Romantic Generation: Passion and Sentiment," in K. Herding and B. Stumpfhaus (eds), *Pathos, Affekt, Gefühl: Die Emotionen in den Künsten*, Berlin: de Gruyter, 419–432.

John, E. (2007), "'Der Kaiser ist ein lieber Mann': Schulische Liedsozialisation im Kaiserreich," in B. Stambolis and J. Reulecke (eds), *Good-bye Memories?*, Essen: Klartext.

Johnson, C. (1995), *Equivocal Beings: Politics, Gender, and Sentimentality in the 1790s—Wollstonecraft, Radcliffe, Burney, Austen*, Chicago: University of Chicago Press.

Johnson, J. (1995), *Listening in Paris: A Cultural History*, Berkeley: University of California Press.

Jonas, U. (2015), "On the Church, the State, and the School: Grundtvig as Enlightenment Philosopher and Social Thinker," in J. Hall, O. Korsgaard, and O. Pedersen (eds), *Building the Nation: N.F.S. Grundtvig and Danish National Identity*, Copenhagen: Djøf Publishing, 169–191.

Jones, E. and Wessely, S. (2014), "Battle for the Mind: World War 1 and the Birth of Military Psychiatry," *The Lancet*, 384(9955): 1708–1714.

Kant, I. ([1790]1990), *Kritik der Urteilskraft*, ed. K. Vorländer, 7th ed., Hamburg: Meiner.

Kant, I. (1951), *Critique of Judgment*, trans. J. Bernard. New York: Hafner Press.

Kant, M. (2011), "The Soul of the Shoe," in M. Kant (ed.), *The Cambridge Companion to Ballet*, Cambridge: Cambridge University Press.

Kaufman, P. (1996), *Prayer, Despair, sand Drama: Elizabethan Introspection*, Urbana, University of Illinois Press.

Kearns, J. (1989), *Symbolist Landscapes: The Place of Painting in the Poetry and Criticism of Mallarmé and his Circle*, London: Modern Humanities Research Association.

Keane, W. (2007), *Christian Moderns, Freedom and Fetish in the Mission Encounter*, Berkeley, University of California Press.

Kemp, W. (1983), *Der Anteil des Betrachters: Rezeptionsästhetische Studien zur Malerei des 19. Jahrhunderts*, Munich: Mäander.

Kemp, W. (2016), *John Ruskin: 1819–1900, Leben und Werk*, Frankfurt/M: Fischer.

Kennaway, J. (2012), *Bad Vibrations: The History of the Idea of Music as Cause of Disease*, Farnham and Burlington, VT: Ashgate.

Kennedy, P. and Nicholls, A., eds (1981), *Nationalist and Racialist Movements in Britain and Germany before 1914*, London: Macmillan.

Kenny, N. (2015), "City Glow: Streetlights, Emotions, and Nocturnal Life, 1880s–1910s," *Journal of Urban History*, 43(1): 91–114.

Kern, S. (1983), *The Culture of Time and Space, 1880–1918*, Cambridge, Massachusetts: Harvard University Press.

Kernbauer, E. (2011), *Der Platz des Publikums: Modelle für Kunstöffentlichkeit im 18. Jahrhundert*, Köln: Böhlau.

Kett, J. (1978), *Rites of Passage: Adolescence in America 1790 to the Present*, New York: Basic Books.

Killen, A., (2006), *Berlin Electropolis: Shock, Nerves, and German Modernity*, Berkeley: University of California Press.

King, J. (1983), *The Iron of Melancholy, Structures of Spiritual Conversion in American from the Puritan Conscience to Victorian Neurosis*, Middletown: Wesleyan University Press.

Kirchner, T. (1991), *L'expression des passions: Ausdruck als Darstellungsproblem in der französischen Kunst und Kunsttheorie des 17. und 18. Jahrhunderts*, Mainz: Zabern.

Kirchner, T. (2001), *Der epische Held: Historienmalerei und Kunstpolitik im Frankreich des 17. Jahrhunderts*, Munich: Fink.

Kitson, P. (1998), "Beyond the Enlightenment: The Philosophical, Scientific, and Religious Inheritance," in D. Wu (ed.), *A Companion to Romanticism*, Oxford: Blackwell.

Kleinman, A. (1980), *Patients and Healers in the Context of Culture, An Exploration of the Borderland between Anthropology, Medicine, and Psychiatry*, Berkeley: University of California Press.

Kleist, H. v. (1810), "Empfindungen vor Friedrichs Seelenlandschaft," *Berliner Abendblätter*, 12, 13 October 1810, 47–48.

Knabe, P.-E. (1972), *Schlüsselbegriffe des kunsttheoretischen Denkens in Frankreich von der Spätklassik bis zum Ende der Aufklärung*, Düsseldorf: Schwann.

Knott, S. (2004), "Sensibility and the American War for Independence," *American Historical Review*, 109(1): 19–40.

Knowles, C. (2013), *Sensibility and Female Poetic Tradition, 1780–1860*, Farnham: Ashgate.

Knox, R. (1962), *Enthusiasm, A Chapter in the History of Religion*, London: Oxford University Press.

Kohlrausch, M. (2005), *Der Monarch im Skandal: Die Logik der Massenmedien und die Transformation der wilhelminischen Monarchie*, Berlin: Akademie Verlag.

Kohlrausch, M. (2010), "The Workings of Royal Celebrity: Wilhelm II as Media Emperor," in E. Berenson and E. Giloi (eds), *Constructing Charisma*, New York: Berghahn, 52–66.

Koselleck, R., Conze, W. and Brunner, O. (1972–1997), *Geschichtliche Grundbegriffe: Historisches Lexikon zur politisch-sozialen Sprache in Deutschland*, 9 vols, Stuttgart: Klett-Cotta.

Kotchemidova, C. (2005), "From Good Cheer to 'Drive by Smiling': A Social History of Cheerfulness," *Journal of Social History*, 39: 5–38.

Krämer, F., ed. (2013), *Schwarze Romantik*, exh. cat. Frankfurt/M, Kunsthalle Schirn, 2012–2013, Ostfildern: Hatje Cantz.

Kuchar, G. (2012), *The Poetry of Religious Sorrow in Early Modern England*, Cambridge: Cambridge University Press.

La Font de Saint-Yenne, É. ([1754]1970), *Sentimens sur quelques ouvrages de Peinture, Sculpture et Gravure: Écrits à un Particulier en Province*, reprint Geneva: Slatkine.

Lamb, C. (1885), "The Tragedies of Shakspeare, Considered With Reference to Their Fitness for Stage Representation," *The Art of the Stage as Set Out in Lamb's Dramatic Essays*. London: Remington & Co.

Lambert, F. (1999), *Inventing the "Great Awakening"*, Princeton: Princeton University Press.

Lange, C. (1887), *Ueber Gemüthsbewgungen. Eine Psycho-Physiologische Studie*, Leipzig: Theodor Thomas.

Lasch, C. (1977), *Haven in a Heartless World*, New York and London: W.W. Norton & Company.

Laube, H. ([1849]1978), *Das erste deutsche Parlament*, 3 vols, Aalen: Scientia.

Le Bon, G. (1895), *Psychologie des foules*, Paris: Germer Baillière.

Le Bon, G. ([1896]2003), *The Crowd: A Study of the Popular Mind*, Whitefish: Kessinger.

Lebensztejn, J.-C. (1989), *Chahut*, Paris: Hazan.

Lecomte, G. (1892), "L'Art contemporain," *Revue indépendante*, 23(66), April : 1–29.

Leed, E. (1979), *No Man's Land: Combat & Identity in World War I*, Cambridge: Cambridge University Press.

Leen, F. (2004), *Fernand Khnopff, 1858–1921*, exh. cat. Brussels, Musée Royaux des Beaux-Arts, Schoten : BAI.

Leidner, A. (1994), *The Impatient Muse: Germany and the Strum und Drang*, Chapel Hill: University of North Carolina Press.

Leites, E. (1995), *The Puritan Conscience and Modern Sexuality*, New Haven: Yale University Press.

Lessing, G. ([1766]1982), *Laokoon: oder über die Grenzen der Malerei und Poesie*, in Gotthold Ephraim Lessing, *Werke*, ed. Herbert G. Göpfert, 3 vols, Munich: Hanser, vol 3, 9–188.

Levine, G. (1989), *Darwin and the Novelists: Patterns of Science in Victorian Fiction*, Cambridge: Harvard University Press.

Levinger, M. (2000), *Enlightened Nationalism: The Transformation of Prussian Political Culture, 1806–1848*, New York: Oxford University Press.

Lewes, G. (1874), *Problems of Life and Mind*, 1st series, 1, London: Trübner & Co.

Lewes, G. (1879), *Problems of Life and Mind*, 3rd series, 1, London: Trübner & Co.

Lewis, J. (1985), *The Pursuit of Happiness: Family and Values in Jefferson's Virginia*, Cambridge: Cambridge University Press.

Lewis, J. (1989), "Mother's Love: The Construction of an Emotion in Nineteenth-Century America," in A. Barnes and P. Stearns (eds), *Social History and Issues in Human Consciousness*, New York: New York University Press.

Lewis, M. ([1798]1990), *The Castle Spectre*, Oxford: Woodstock Books.

Lipps, T. (1903–1906), *Ästhetik*, 2 vols, Hamburg and Leipzig: Voss.

Lobstein, D. (2006), *Les Salons au xixe siècle: Paris, capitale des arts*, Paris: La Martinière.

Lochnan, K., ed. (2004) *Turner, Whistler, Monet*, exh. cat. Toronto, Musée des Beaux-Arts de l'Ontario; Paris, Musée d'Orsay; London, Tate Britain, Paris: Réunion des musées nationaux.

Lombroso, C. ([1872]1882), *Genio e follia, in rapporto alla medicina legale, alla critica ed alla storia*, Rome: Bocca.

Lombroso, C. ([1897]2013), "Affetti e passioni dei delinquenti," *L'uomo delinquent*, 5th ed., Milan: Bompiani.

Loughran, T. (2012), "Shell Shock, Trauma, and the First World War: The Making of a Diagnosis and Its Histories," *Journal of the History of Medicine and Allied Sciences*, 67 (1): 94–119.

Lovejoy, A. (1924), "On the Discrimination of Romanticisms," *PMLA*, 39: 229–53.

Lövgren, S. ([1959]1971), *The Genesis of Modernism: Seurat, Gauguin, van Gogh and French Symbolism in the 1880s*, London: Bloomington.

Lund, M. (2010), *Melancholy, Medicine and Religion in Early Modern England, Reading The Anatomy of Melancholy*, Cambridge: Cambridge University Press.

Lutz, T. (1991), *American Nervousness, 1903: An Anecdotal History*, Ithaca: Cornell University Press.

Lynch, K. (2003), *Individuals, Families and Communities in Europe, 1200–1800*, Cambridge: Cambridge University Press.

Lystra, K. (1989), *Searching the Heart: Women, Men, and Love in Nineteenth-Century America*, New York: Oxford University Press.

MacDonald, M. and Murphy, T. (1981), *Mystical Bedlam*, Cambridge: Cambridge University Press.

Machiavelli, N. (2005), *The Prince*, ed. W. J. Cornell, Boston: Bedford.

Maehle, A. (2009), *Doctors, Honour and the Law: Medical Ethics in Imperial Germany*, Houndmills: Palgrave.

Maffly-Kipp, L., Schmidt, L. and Valeri, M., eds, (2006), *Practicing Protestants, Histories of Christian Life in America 1630–1965*, Princeton: Princeton University Press.

Malinar, A., and Basu, H. (2008), "Ecstasy," in J. Corrigan (ed.), *The Oxford Handbook of Religion and Emotion*, New York: Oxford University Press, 241–258.

Mallarmé, S. ([1863]1959), Letter to Henri Cazalis, London, 24 July 1863, in S. Mallarmé, *Correspondance*, ed. H. Mondor, 6th ed., vol. 1, Paris: Gallimard.

Mallarmé, S. (1956), *Selected Prose Poems, Essays, & Letters*, B. Cook (ed.), Baltimore: Johns Hopkins Press.

Mandell, L. (2017), "Enlightenment," in S. Broomhall (ed.), *Early Modern Emotions: An Introduction*, London: Routledge, 269–272.

Manheim, R. (1986), "'Expressionismus', Zur Entstehung eines kunsthistorischen Stil- und Periodenbegriffes," *Zeitschrift für Kunstgeschichte*, 49(1): 73–91.

Marciuk, C. (1991), *Mazeppa: ein Thema der französischen Romantik; Malerei und Graphik 1823–1827*, Munich and Vienna: Profil.

Marshall, D. (1988), *The Surprising Effects of Sympathy: Marivaux, Diderot, Rousseau, and Mary Shelley*. Chicago: University of Chicago.

Martin Moruno, D. (2014), "Feeling Nature: Emotions and Ecology. The Legacy of Romanticism," *Archives Internationale d'histoire des Sciences*, 64(172–173): 195–203.

Martinsen, L. (2015), "Monarchism and Emotion in Denmark in the 19th Century: The Case of Frederick VI," Weber State University Symposium on Emotions and European Politics, September 9, 2015.

Marx, A. B. (1852), *The Universal School of Music: A Manual for Teachers and Students in Every Branch of Musical Art*, trans. A.H. Wehrman, London: Robert Cocks and Co.

Marx, A. B. (i 1837, ii 1838, iii 1845, iv 1847), *Die Lehre von der musikalischen Komposition, praktisch-theoretisch*, Leipzig.

Mathew, N. & Walton B., eds (2013), *The Invention of Beethoven and Rossini: Historiography, Analysis, Criticism*, New York: Cambridge University Press.

Matisse, Henri ([1908]2009), "Notes d'un peintre," *La Grande Revue*, 52, 25 December 1908, in D. Fourcade (ed.), *Henri Matisse, Écrits et propos sur l'art*, Paris: Hermann, 40–74.

Maturin, C ([1816]1992), *Bertram: or, the Castle of St. Aldobrand*, Oxford: Woodstock Books.

Marty, M., ed. (1993), *Varieties of Religious Expression, Modern American Protestantism and its World, Historical Articles on Protestantism in American Religious Life*, New York: K.G. Saur.

Matt, S. (2003), *Keeping Up with the Joneses: Envy in American Consumer Society, 1890–1930*, Philadelphia: University of Pennsylvania Press.

Matt, S. (2011), *Homesickness: An American History*, New York: Oxford University Press.

Matt, S. (2015) "The Myth of the Rational Actor," *History News Network*, February 22, 2015, http://historynewsnetwork.org/article/158361

Mayne, J. (1981), *Art in Paris: 1845–1862; Salons and Other Exhibitions*, Oxford: Phaidon.

McBride, T. (1976), *The Domestic Revolution: The Modernisation of Household Service in England and France, 1820–1920*, Teaneck NJ: Holmes & Meier Publishers.

McGann, J. (1983), *The Romantic Ideology: A Critical Investigation*, Chicago: University of Chicago Press.

McMahon, D. (2006), *Happiness: A History*, New York: Atlantic Monthly Press.

McMahon, L. (2012), "'So Truly Afflicting and Distressing to Me His Sorrowing Mother': Expressions of Maternal Grief in Eighteenth-Century Philadelphia," *Journal of the Early Republic*, 32(1): 27–60.

Meier, F. (1999), "A Book of Etiquette for Sufis," *Essays in Islamic Piety and Mysticism*, trans. J. O'Kane, Leiden: Brill.
Menand, L. (2001), *The Metaphysical Club*, New York: Farrar, Straus, and Giroux.
Mendel, G. (1901), *Versuche über Pflanzenhybriden. Zwei Abhandlungen (1865 und 1869)*, Leipzig: Wilhelm Engelmann.
Menninghaus, W. (2002), *Ekel: Theorie und Geschichte einer starken Empfindung*, Frankfurt/M: Suhrkamp.
Mercer, P. (1972), *Sympathy and Ethics: A Study of the Relationship between Sympathy and Morality with Special Reference to Hume's Treatise*, Oxford: Clarendon Press.
Micale, M. (1995), *Approaching Hysteria: Disease and Its Interpretations*, New Jersey: Princeton University Press.
Micale, M. (2008), *Hysterical Men: The Hidden History of Male Nervous Illness*, Cambridge: Harvard University Press.
Miles, J. (1965), *Pathetic Fallacy in the Nineteenth Century*, new ed., New York: Octagon Books.
Mill, J. (1844), "On the Definition of Political Economy; And on the Method of Investigation Proper to It," in *Essays on Some Unsettled Questions of Political Economy*, London: John W. Parker.
Minor, R. (2012), *Choral Fantasies: Music, Festivity, and Nationhood in Nineteenth-Century Germany*, Cambridge: Cambridge University Press.
Mintz, S. (2004), *Huck's Raft, A History of American Childhood*, Cambridge, Harvard University Press.
Mirbeau, O. ([1889]1993), "L'Exposition Monet-Rodin," *Gil Blas*, 22 June 1889, in *Combats esthétiques*, eds P. Michel and J.-F. Nivet, vol. 1, Paris: Séguier, 377–382.
Momigny, J.-J. de (1810), *Cours complet d'harmonie et de composition d'après une théorie neuve et générale de la musique*, Paris: chez l'auteur.
Montagu, J. (1994), *The Expression of the Passions: The Origin and Influence of Charles Le Brun's 'Conférence sur l'expression générale et particulière'*, New Haven and London: Yale University Press.
Montegazza, P. (1896), *The Art of Taking a Wife*, London: Gay and Bird.
Moody, J. and O'Quinn, D., eds (2007), *The Cambridge Companion to British Theatre, 1730–1830*, Cambridge: Cambridge University Press.
More, H. ([1778]1834), "On the Danger of Sentimental or Romantic Connexions," *Works*, vol. 6, London: Fisher, Fisher and Jackson.
Moréas, J. (1886), "Le symbolisme, Supplément littéraire," *Figaro*, 18 September 1886, 150.
Moreau-Nélaton, É. (1884), *Corot raconté par lui-même*, 2 vols, Paris: Henri Laurens.
Morgan, C. (1894), *An Introduction to Comparative Psychology*, London: W. Scott.
Morris, J. (1966), *Versions of the Self: Studies in English Autobiography from John Bunyan to John Stuart Mill*, New York: Basic Books.
Moscoso, J. (2012), *Pain: A Cultural History*, Houndmills: Palgrave.
Moss, A. (1973), *Baudelaire et Delacroix*, Paris: Nizet.
Mosso, A. (1896), *Fear*, London and New York: Longmans, Green, and Co.
Murfin, R. and Ray, S.M. (2003), *The Bedford Glossary of Critical and Literary Terms*, 2nd ed., Boston: Bedford/St. Martin's.
Nelson, B. (1964), "Actors, Directors, Roles, Cues, Meanings, Identities: Further Thoughts on 'Anomie'," *Psychoanalytic Review*, 64: 135–160.
Nelson, B. (1965), "Self-Images and Systems of Spiritual Direction in the History of European Civilization," S. Klausner, ed., *The Quest for Self-Control, Classical Philosophies and Scientific Research*, New York: Free Press.

Neubauer, J. (1986), *The Emancipation of Music from Language: Departure from Mimesis in Eighteenth-Century Aesthetics*, New Haven: Yale University Press.

Nietzsche, F. ([1884–85]1988), *Kritische Studienausgabe*, G. Colli and M. Montinari (eds), 15 vols, 2nd ed, Munich: dtv; Berlin and New York: De Gruyter, vol. 11: *Nachgelassene Fragmente 1884–1885*.

Noble, M. (2000), *The Masochistic Pleasures of Sentimental Literature*, Princeton: Princeton University Press.

Noll, M. (2002), *America's God, From Jonathan Edwards to Abraham Lincoln*, New York, Oxford University Press.

Noon, P., ed. (2003), *Constable to Delacroix: British Art and the French Romantics*, exh. cat. London, Tate Britain, London: Tate.

Nord, D. (2004), *Faith in Reading, Religious Publishing and the Birth of Mass Media in America*, New York: Oxford University Press.

Norris, F. (2012), "Zola as a Romantic Writer," in Nina Baym et al. (eds), *The Norton Anthology of American Literature, Volume C: 1865–1914*, 8th ed., New York: Norton.

Noverre, J. (1760, 2/1783), *Lettres sur la Danse et sur les Ballets*, enlarged 1803 as vol. I of *Lettres sur la danse, sur les ballets et les arts*, Lyons.

Nussbaum, M. (2001), *Upheavals of Thought: The Intelligence of Emotions*. Cambridge: Cambridge University Press.

O'Gorman, F. (1992), "Campaign Rituals and Ceremonies: The Social Meaning of Elections in England 1780–1860," *Past and Present*, 135: 79–115.

Oxenhandler, N. (1988), "The Changing Concept of Literary Emotion: A Selective History," *New Literary History*, 20: 105–121.

Ozment, S. (1985), *When Fathers Ruled: Family Life in Reformation Europe*, Cambridge, MA: Harvard University Press.

Ozment, S. (2011), *The Serpent and the Lamb: Cranach, Luther and the Making of the Reformation*, New Haven: Yale University Press.

Ozouf, M. (1988), *Festivals and the French Revolution*, Cambridge: Harvard University Press.

Palmer, P. (1998), *Selected Writing*, New York: Paulist Press.

Pascoe, J. (1997), *Romantic Theatricality: Gender, Poetry, and Spectatorship*. Ithaca: Cornell University Press.

Paulson, R. (1983), *Representations of Revolution, 1789–1820*, New Haven: Yale University Press.

Pearson, K. (1909), *On the Scope and Importance to the State of the Science of National Eugenics*, London: Dulau & Co.

Pearson, K. (1910), "Darwinism, Biometry and Some Recent Biology," *Biometrika*, 7: 368–85.

Pearson, K. (1912), *Social Problems: Their Treatment, Past, Present, and Future*, London: Dulau & Co.

Pederson, S. (1994), "A.B. Marx, Berlin Concert Life, and German National Identity," *19th Century Music*, 18(2): 87–107.

Pennsylvania Magazine (1776), "On Sensibility," 176–77.

Pernau, M. and Jordheim, H., eds (2015), *Civilizing Emotions: Concepts in Nineteenth-Century Asia and Europe*, Oxford: Oxford University Press.

Pernau M. and Jordheim, H. (2015a), "Introduction," in M. Pernau and H. Jordheim (eds), *Civilizing Emotions: Concepts in Nineteenth-Century Asia and Europe*, Oxford: Oxford University Press.

Persky, J. (1995), "Retrospectives: The Ethology of Homo Economicus," *Journal of Economic Perspectives*, 9: 221–231.
Pfister, J. and Schnog, N. (1997), *Inventing the Psychological: Toward a Cultural History of Emotional Life in America*, New Haven: Yale University Press.
Phillips, R. (1991), *Untying the Knot: A Short History of Divorce*, Cambridge: Cambridge University Press.
Pick, D. (1993), *Faces of Degeneration: A European Disorder, c.1848–c.1918*. Cambridge: Cambridge University Press.
Pigeaud, J. (2008), *Melancholia, Le Malaise de l' Individu*, Paris, Manuels Payot.
Pinch, A. (1996), *Strange Fits of Passion: Epistemologies of Emotion, Hume to Austen*. Stanford: Stanford University Press.
Pixerécourt, G. (1841), *Théatre Choisi*. Introduction par Ch. Nodier. Paris: Tresse.
Pizer, D. (2000), "Frank Norris's *McTeague*: Naturalism as Popular Myth," *ANQ*, 13: 21–26.
Plamper, J. (2015), *The History of Emotions: An Introduction*, trans. Keith Tribe, Oxford: Oxford University Press.
Plunkett, J. (2003), *Queen Victoria: First Media Monarch*, Oxford: Oxford University Press.
Pollock, L. (1983), *Forgotten Children: Parent–Child Relations from 1500 to 1900*, Cambridge and New York: Cambridge University Press, 1983.
Pomarède, Vincent (1996), *Corot*, Paris: Flammarion.
Porter, L. (2004), "The Art of Characterisation," in T. Unwin (ed.), *The Cambridge Companion to Flaubert*, Cambridge: Cambridge University Press.
Porterfield, A. (2005), *Healing in the History of Christianity*, New York, Oxford University Press.
Potkay, A. (2015), "Contested Emotions: Pity and Gratitude from the Stoics to Swift and Wordsworth," *PMLA*, 130: 1332–1346.
Pound, E. (1986), *The Cantos of Ezra Pound*, New York: New Directions.
Powell, L. (1909), *The Emmanuel Movement in a New England Town, A Systematic Account of the Experiments and Reflections Designed to Determine the Proper Relationship between the Minister and the Doctor in the Light of Modern Needs*, New York, G. P. Putnam's Sons.
Praz, M. (1930), *La carne, la morte e il diavolo nella letteratura romantica*, Milano: La Cultura.
Price, M. (2007), *The Perilous Crown: France between Revolutions, 1814–1848*, London: Macmillan.
Prince, R. (1985), "The Culture-Bound Syndrome: Anorexia Nervosa and Brain-Fag," *Social Science and Medicine*, 21(2): 197–203.
Pritchard, B. (1968), *The Music Festival and the Choral Society in England*, PhD. Dissertation, University of Birmingham.
Purton, V. (2012), *Dickens and the Sentimental Tradition*, London: Anthem Press.
Pykett, L. (1991), "Sensation and the Fantastic in the Victorian Novel," in D. David (ed.), *The Cambridge Companion to the Victorian Novel*, 2nd ed., Cambridge: Cambridge University Press.
Raboteau, A. J. (2004), *Slave Religion, the "Invisible Institution" in the Antebellum South*, New York, Oxford University Press.
Rabinowitz, R. (1989), *The Spiritual Self in Everyday Life, The Transformation of Personal Religious Experience in Nineteenth-Century New England*, Boston, Northeastern University Press.
Rable, G. (2010), *God's Almost Chosen Peoples, A Religious History of the Civil War*, Chapel Hill: University of North Carolina Press.

Radden, J. (2000), *The Nature of Melancholy: From Aristotle to Kristeva*, New York: Oxford University Press.

Radden, J. (2009), *Moody Minds Distempered, Essays on Melancholy and Depression*, New York: Oxford University Press.

Ramdohr, F. ([1809]1968), *Über ein zum Altarblatte bestimmtes Landschaftsgemälde von Herrn Friedrich in Dresden, und über Landschaftsmalerei, Allegorie und Mystizismus überhaupt*, S. Hinz (ed.), *Caspar David Friedrich in Briefen und Bekenntnissen*, Berlin: Henschel, 138–158.

Ramsay, D. (1811), *Memoirs of the Life of Martha Laurens Ramsay*, Philadelphia: James Maxwell.

Rapetti, R. (2005), *Le Symbolisme*, Paris: Flammarion.

Rapetti, R., Stevens, M., Zimmermann, M., and Goldin, M. (2003), *Monet*, conference proceedings Treviso 2002, Conegliano: Linea d'Ombra Libri.

Recchio, T. (2011), "Melodrama and the Production of Affective Knowledge in *Mary Barton*," *Studies in the Novel*, 43: 289–305.

Reddy, W. (2000), "Sentimentalism and Its Erasure: The Role of Emotions in the Era of the French Revolution," *Journal of Modern History*, 72: 109–152.

Reddy, W. (2001), *The Navigation of Feeling: A Framework for the History of Emotions*, Cambridge: Cambridge University Press.

Redon, O. ([1867–1915] 2000), *À soi-même, Journal 1867–1915: Notes sur la vie, l'art et les artistes*, Paris: José Corti.

Rehding, A. (2000), "The Quest for the Origins of Music in Germany circa 1900," *Journal of the American Musicological Society*, 53(2): 345–385.

Reicha, A. (1814), *Traité de Mélodie*, Paris.

Rendell, J. (2002), *The Pursuit of Pleasure: Gender, Space and Architecture in Regency London*, London: The Athlone Press.

Renoir, J. (1962/1981), *Pierre-Auguste Renoir, mon père*, Paris: Gallimard.

Requate, J. (1995), *Journalismus als Beruf*, Göttingen: Vandenhoeck & Ruprecht.

Ribot, T. (1896), *La psychologie des sentiments*, Paris: Alcan.

Richards, R. (1989), *Darwin and the Emergence of Evolutionary Theories of Mind and Behaviour*, Chicago: University of Chicago Press.

Richardson, A. (1988), *A Mental Theater: Poetic Drama and Consciousness in the Romantic Age*. University Park: Pennsylvania State University Press.

Richardson, P. (1960), *The Social Dances of the Nineteenth Century in England*, London: Herbert Jenkins.

Richter, V. (2011), *Literature After Darwin: Human Beasts in Western Fiction, 1859–1939*, Houndmills: Palgrave Macmillan.

Rieber, R. and Robinson, D., eds (2001), *Wilhelm Wundt in History: The Making of a Scientific Psychology*, New York: Kluwer Academic.

Riegl, A. ([1899]1929), "Die Stimmung als Inhalt der Modernen Kunst," *Graphische Künste*, 22, in A. Riegl, *Gesammelte Aufsätze*, ed. K. Swoboda, Augsburg and Vienna: Filser, 28–39.

Riis, O. and Woodhead, L. (2010), *A Sociology of Religious Emotion*, New York: Oxford University Press.

Riley, M. (2004), *Musical Listening in the German Enlightenment*, Aldershot: Ashgate.

Riskin, J. (2002), *Science in the Age of Sensibility: The Sentimental Empiricists of the French Enlightenment*, Chicago: University of Chicago Press.

Ritter, G. and Tenfelde, K. (1992), *Arbeiter im Deutschen Kaiserreich 1871–1914*, Bonn: Dietz.

Roche-Pézard, F. (1983), *L'aventure futuriste, 1909–1916*, Rome: École Française de Rom.
Rodenbach, G. ([1892]1903), *Bruges-la-Morte. A Romance*, trans. T. Duncan, London: Swan Sonnenschein & Co.
Rodenbach, G. ([1892]1998), *Bruges-la-Morte*, J. Bertrand and D. Grojnowski (eds), Paris: Flammarion 1998.
Rohe, M. (1912), "Von Ausstellungen und Sammlungen: München," *Die Kunst für Alle*, 27(12), 290.
Romanes, G. (1883), *Animal Intelligence*, 1882; 3rd ed., London: Kegan Paul, Trench, & Co.
Romanes, G. (1883a), *Mental Evolution in Animals*, London: Kegan Paul, Trench, & Co.
Romanes, G. (1888), *Mental Evolution in Man: Origin of Human Faculty*, London: Kegan Paul, Trench & Co.
Romano, T. (2002), *Making Medicine Scientific: John Burdon Sanderson and the Culture of Victorian Science*, Baltimore: Johns Hopkins University Press.
Rookmaaker, H. (1959), *Synthetist Art Theories. Genesis and Nature of the Ideas on Art of Gauguin and his Circle*, Amsterdam: Swets & Zeitlinger.
Rorty, A., ed. (1996), *Essays on Aristotle's Rhetoric*, Berkeley: University of California Press.
Rosen, C. (1998), *The Romantic Generation*, Cambridge, MA: Harvard University Press.
Rosenbaum, A. (1998), *Shout Because You're Free, The African American Ring Shout Tradition in Coastal Georgia*, Athens, GA: University of Georgia Press.
Rosenberg, A. (1894), *Geschichte der Modernen Kunst*, 3 vols, Leipzig: Grunow.
Rosenblatt, P. (1983), *Bitter, Bitter Tears: Nineteenth-Century Diarists and Twentieth-Century Grief Theories*, Minnesota: University of Minnesota Press.
Rosenzweig, L. (1999), *Another Self: Middle-Class American Women and Their Friends in the Twentieth Century*, New York and London: New York University Press.
Rosenzweig, L. (2005), "If They Have any Orders, I Am Theirs to Command: Indulgent Middle-Class Grandparents in American Society," in P. Stearns (ed.), *American Behavioral History: An Introduction*, New York and London: New York University Press.
Rosenzweig, R. (1985), *Eight Hours for What We Will: Workers and Leisure in an Industrial City, 1870–1920*, Cambridge: Cambridge University Press.
Rotundo, A. (1989), "Romantic Friendship: Male Intimacy and Middle-Class Youth in the Northern United States, 1800–1900," *Journal of Social History*, 23(1): 1–25.
Rousseau, J. J. ([1782]1959–), *Rêveries du promeneur solitaire*, in J. J. Rousseau, *Œuvres complètes*, B. Gagnebin and M. Raymond (eds), vol 1, Paris: Gallimard, 993–1099.
Rousseau, J. ([1754]2011), *The Basic Political Writings*, 2nd ed., D. Cress (trans. and ed.), Indianapolis: Hackett Publishing.
Rubin, J. (1979), *Mental Illness in Early Nineteenth Century New England and the Beginnings of Institutional Psychiatry as Revealed in a Sociological Study of the Hartford Retreat, 1824–1843*, PhD Diss., New School for Social Research.
Rubin, J. (1994), *Religious Melancholy and Protestant Experience in America*, New York: Oxford University Press.
Rubin, J. (2000), *The Other Side of Joy: Religious Melancholy Among the Bruderhof*, New York: Oxford University Press.
Rubin, J. (2008), "Melancholy," in J. Corrigan (ed.), *The Oxford Handbook of Religion and Emotion*, New York: Oxford University Press: 290–309.
Rubin, J. (2013), *Tears of Repentance: Christian Indian Identity and Community in Colonial Southern New England*, Lincoln: University of Nebraska Press.
Ruppert, W. ed. (1986), *Die Arbeiter*, Munich: C.H. Beck.

Ruprecht, L. (2011), "The Romantic Ballet and Its Critics: Dance Goes Public," in M. Kant (ed.), *The Cambridge Companion to Ballet*, Cambridge: Cambridge University Press, 175–183.

Ruskin, J. (1860), *Modern Painters*, 5 vols, London: Smith, Elder and Co.

Russett, C. (1989), *Sexual Science: The Victorian Construction of Womanhood*, Cambridge: Harvard University Press.

Ryan, M. (1983), *Cradle of the Middle Class: The Family in Oneida County, New York, 1790–1865*, Cambridge: Cambridge University Press.

Rybczynski, W. (1986), *Home: A Short History of an Idea*, New York: Viking.

Rylance, R. (2000), *Victorian Psychology and British Culture, 1850–1880*, Oxford: Oxford University Press.

Saada, E. (2015), "France: Sociability in the Imperial Republic," in M. Pernau and H. Jordheim (eds), *Civilizing Emotions: Concepts in Nineteenth-Century Asia and Europe*, Oxford: Oxford University Press.

Saunders, F. (1868), *About Women, Love and Marriage*, New York: G.W. Carleton.

Scheer, M. (2014), "Topographies of Emotion," in U. Frevert et al. (eds), *Emotional Lexicons: Continuity and Change in the Vocabulary of Feeling 1700–2000*, Oxford: Oxford University Press.

Schieder, W. (1972), "Brüderlichkeit," in O. Brunner, W. Conze and R. Koselleck (eds), *Geschichtliche Grundbegriffe*, vol. 1, Stuttgart: Klett-Cotta, 552–581.

Schiller, F. ([1792]1989), *The Robbers*, Oxford: Woodstock Books.

Schlegel, F. (1991), "On Goethe's *Meister*," J. Bernstein (ed.), *Classic and Romantic German Aesthetics*, Cambridge: Cambridge University Press.

Schmalenbach, F. ([1961]1972), "Das Wort 'Expressionismus'," *Neue Zürcher Zeitung*, 12 March 1961, in F. Schmalenbach, *Studien über Malerei und Malereigeschichte*, Berlin: Mann, 40–44.

Schmidt, J. (2007), *Melancholy and the Care of the Soul*, Burlington, Ashgate.

Schnog, N. (1997), "Changing Emotions: Moods and the Nineteenth-Century American Woman Writer," in J. Pfister and N. Schnog (eds), *Inventing the Psychological: Toward a Cultural History of Emotional Life in America*, New Haven: Yale University Press.

Schuster, D. (2011), *Neurasthenic Nation: America's Search for Health, Happiness, and Comfort, 1869–1920*, New Brunswick: Rutgers University Press.

Schwengelbeck, M. (2007), *Die Politik des Zeremoniells: Huldigungsfeiern im langen 19. Jahrhundert*, Frankfurt: Campus.

Scull, A. (2009), *Hysteria: The Biography*, Oxford: Oxford University Press.

Séailles, G. (1888), "Peintres Contemporains: Puvis de Chavannes (I, II, III)," *Revue bleue*, 25(5): 140–144; 25(6): 179–185.

Seccombe, W. (1993), *Weathering the Storm: Working-class Families from the Industrial Revolution to the Fertility Decline*, London: Verso.

Segalen, M. (1981), *Sociologie de la famille*, Paris: Armand Colin.

Semler, C. (1800), *Untersuchungen über die höchste Vollkommenheit in den Werken der Landschaftsmalerey*, Leipzig: Schäfer.

Sena, J. (1973), "Melancholic Madness and the Puritans," *Harvard Theological Review*, 66(3): 292–309.

Sennett, R. (1977), *The Fall of Public Man*, New York: Alfred A. Knopf.

Sera-Shriar, E. (2016), *The Making of British Anthropology, 1813–1871*, London: Routledge.

Seurat, G. ([1890]1991), Letter to Maurice Beaubourg, 28 August 1890, in F. Cachin and R. Herbert (eds), *Seurat*, exh. cat. Paris, Musée d'Orsay, Paris: Réunion des musées nationaux, 429–431.

Shaftesbury, A. Third Earl of ([1711]2001), *Characteristicks of Men, Manners, Opinions, Times*, D. Den Uyl (ed.), Indianapolis: Liberty Fund.
Sharpe, L. (1991), *Friedrich Schiller: Drama, Thought and Politics*, Cambridge: Cambridge University Press.
Shepherd, S. and Womack P. (1996), *English Drama: A Cultural History*. Oxford: Blackwell.
Sherrington, C. (1899–1900), "Experiments on the Value of Vascular and Visceral Factors for the Genesis of Emotion," *Proceedings of the Royal Society of London*, 66: 390–403.
Shiff, R. (1984), *Cézanne and the End of Impressionism: A Study of the Theory, Technique, and Critical Evaluation of Modern Art*, Chicago and London: University of Chicago Press.
Shiff, R. (1991), "Cézanne's Physicality: the Politics of Touch," in S. Kemal and I. Gaskell (eds), *The Language of Art History*, Cambridge: Cambridge University Press, 129–180.
Shorter, E. (1977), *The Making of the Modern Family*, New York: Basic Books.
Shorter, E. (1988), "Paralysis: The Rise and Fall of a 'Hysterical' Symptom," in P. Stearns (ed.), *Expanding the Past: A Reader in Social History*, New York: New York University Press: 215–248.
Showalter, E. (1985), *The Female Malady: Women, Madness and English Culture, 1830–1980*, London: Virago.
Siddons, H. (1807), *Practical Illustrations of Rhetorical Gesture and Action, Adapted to the English Drama*, London: Richard Phillips.
Siddons, H. (1822), *Practical Illustrations of Rhetorical Gesture and Action, Adapted to the English Drama*, 2nd ed. London: Richard Phillips.
Slagle, J., ed. (1999), *The Collected Letters of Joanna Baillie*, Volume 1. Madison, NJ: Fairleigh Dickinson University Press.
Smith, A. ([1759]2009), *The Theory of Moral Sentiments*, London: Penguin.
Smith, A. (2000), *The Theory of Moral Sentiments*, Amherst: Prometheus Books.
Smith, A. (2002), *The Theory of Moral Sentiments*, Cambridge: Cambridge University Press.
Smith, B. (1981), *Ladies of the Leisure Class: The Bourgeoisies of Northern France in the Nineteenth Century*, Princeton, NJ: Princeton University Press.
Smith, M. (2011), "The Orchestra as Translator: French Nineteenth-Century Ballet," in M. Kant (ed.), *The Cambridge Companion to Ballet*, Cambridge: Cambridge University Press, 138–150.
Smith-Rosenberg, C. (1975), "The Female World of Love and Ritual: Relations between Women in Nineteenth-Century America," *Signs*, 1(1): 1–29.
Souriau, P. (1893), *La suggestion dans l'art*, Paris: Alcan.
Spacks, P. (1995), *Boredom: The Literary History of a State of Mind*, Chicago: University of Chicago Press.
Spencer, E. (1983), *The Spencers of Amberson Ave: A Turn-of-the-Century Memoir*, Pittsburgh, PA: University of Pittsburgh Press.
Stachniewski, J. (1991), *The Persecutory Imagination: English Puritanism and the Literature of Religious Despair*, Oxford: Clarendon Press.
Staël, A. ([1810]1845), *De l'Allemagne*, Paris: Firmin Didot Frères.
Staël, H., de ([1810]1813), *Germany*, 3 vols, London: John Murray.
Stannard, D. (1977), *The Puritan Way of Death: A Study in Religion, Culture and Social Change*, New York and Oxford: Oxford University Press.
Stansell, C. (1987), *City of Women: Sex and Class in New York, 1789–1860*, Urbana: University of Illinois Press.
Starling, E. (1905), "The Croonian Lectures. I. On the Chemical Correlation of the Functions of the Body," *Lancet*, 166: 339–341.

Starobinski, J. (1966), "The Idea of Nostalgia," *Diogenes*, 14(54): 81–103.
Stearns, C. (1988), "'Lord Help Me Walk Humbly': Anger and Sadness in England and America, 1570–1750," in C. Stearns and P. Stearns (eds), *Emotions and Social Change: Toward a New Psychohistory*, New York: Holmes and Meier.
Stearns, C. and Stearns, P. (1986), *Anger: The Struggle for Emotional Control in America's History*, Chicago: University of Chicago Press.
Stearns P. (1990), *Be a Man! Males in Modern Society*, 2nd ed., Teaneck, NJ: Holmes & Meier Publishing.
Stearns. P. (1990a), *Jealousy: The Evolution of an Emotion in American History*, New York: New York University Press.
Stearns, P. (1994), *American Cool: Constructing a Twentieth-Century Emotional Style*, New York: New York University Press.
Stearns, P. (2006), *Consumerism in World History: The Global Transformation of Desire*, 2nd edition, New York: Routledge.
Stearns, P. (2007), *Revolutions in Sorrow: The American Experience of Death in Global Perspective*, Boulder: Paradigm Publishers.
Stearns, P. (2012), "Obedience and Emotion: A Challenge in the Emotional History of Children," presented to Conference on Childhood, Youth and Emotions in Modern History, Max Planck Institute for Human Development, Berlin, Germany.
Stearns, P. (2012a), *Satisfaction Not Guaranteed: Dilemmas of Progress in Modern Society*, New York and London: New York University Press.
Stearns, P. and Haggerty, T. (1989), "The Role of Fear: Transitions in American Emotional Standards for Children, 1850–1950," *American Historical Review*, 96(1): 63–94.
Stearns, P. N. and. Lewis, J. (1998), *An Emotional History of the United States*, New York: New York University Press.
Stearns, P. and Knapp, M. (1993), "Men and Romantic Love: Pinpointing a Twentieth-Century Change," *Journal of Social History*, 26: 769–796.
Stein, L. v. (1855), *Das Königthum, die Republik und die Souveränetät der französischen Gesellschaft seit der Februarrevolution 1848*, 2nd ed., Leipzig: Wigand.
Stewart, A., ed. (2012), *Handbook of Pentecostal Christianity*, DeKalb, Ill, Northern Illinois Press.
Stirling, J. (2010), "Hystericity and Hauntings: The Female and the Feminised," *Representing Epilepsy: Myth and Matter*, Liverpool: Liverpool University Press.
Stone, L. (1983), *Sex and Marriage in England 1500–1800*, New York: Harper Perennial.
Sulzer, J. (1771–1799), *Allgemeine Theorie der schönen Künste: in einzelnen, nach alphabetischer Ordnung der Kunstwörter aufeinanderfolgenden Artikeln abgehandelt*, Leipzig: Weidmannsche Buchhandlung. (Leipzig, 1771–4, 2/1778–9, enlarged 3/1786–7 by F. von Blankenburg, 4/1792–9/R).
Sykes, S. (2005), "Wonders in the Deep: William Cowper, Melancholy and Religion," in C. Saunders, and J. Mcnaughton (eds), *Madness and Creativity in Literature and Culture*, New York: Palgrave MacMillan.
Synan, V. (1997), *The Holiness-Pentecostal Tradition: Charismatic Movements in the Twentieth Century*, Grand Rapids, Michigan: W.B. Eerdmans Publishing Company.
Taine, H. (1870/1878), *De l'intelligence*, 2 vols, 3rd ed, Paris: Hachette.
Tait, P. (2015), "Love, Fear, and Climate Change: Emotions in Drama and Performance," *PMLA*, 130: 1501–1505.
Taves, A. (1999), *Fits, Trances, & Visions, Experiencing Religion and Explaining Experiences from Wesley to James*, Princeton: Princeton University Press.

Taylor, A. (1999), *"Down with the Crown": British Anti-Monarchism and Debates about Royalty since 1790*, London: Reaktion Books.
Taylor, C. (1975), *Hegel*, Cambridge: Cambridge University Press.
Taylor, C. (1989), *Sources of the The Self: The Making of the Modern Identity*, Cambridge: Harvard University Press.
Taylor, M. and Fink, M. (2007), *Melancholia: The Diagnosis, Pathophysiology and Treatment of Depressive Illness*, New York, Cambridge University Press.
Thomas, K. (2007), "Heroen der Moderne: Zur kollektiven Konstruktion von Heldenbildern—Ablösung oder Umwertung eines traditionellen Konzeptes in der französischen Kunst des 19. Jahrhunderts?," *Acta Historiae Artium*, 48: 305–315.
Thomas, K. (2010), *Welt und Stimmung bei Puvis de Chavannes, Seurat und Gauguin*, Berlin: Deutscher Kunstverlag.
Thomas, K. (2012), "Corot und die Ästhetik der Rêverie," in D. Schäfer and M. Stuffmann (eds), *Camille Corot: Natur und Traum*, exh. cat. Karlsruhe, Staatliche Kunsthalle, Heidelberg: Kehrer, 363–373.
Thomas, K. (2014), "Aufruhr der Malerei. Das Ereignis als synästhetischer Schock in Carlo Carràs Begräbnis des Anarchisten Galli," in U. Fleckner (ed.), *Bilder machen Geschichte: Historische Ereignisse im Gedächtnis der Kunst*, Berlin: Akademie Verlag, 293–304.
Thomas, K. (2016), "Grau als Farbe des Gefühls in der symbolistischen Malerei," in M. Bushart and G. Wedekind (eds), *Die Farbe Grau*, Berlin: de Gruyter, 219–234.
Thomson, M. (1998), *The Problem of Mental Deficiency: Eugenics, Democracy, and Social Policy in Britain, c. 1870–1959*, Oxford: Oxford University Press.
Thomson, R., Rapetti, R., Fowle, F., and von Bonsdorff, A. M. (eds) (2012), *Symbolist Landscape in Europe 1880–1910*, exh. cat. Edinburgh, National Galleries of Scotland, London: Thames & Hudson.
Thompson, E. (1968), *The Making of the English Working Class*, Harmondsworth: Penguin.
Thormählen, W. (2014), "Physical Distortion and Mental Imbalance: Musical Virtuosity between Body and Mind," in *Music and the Nerves, 1700–1900*, J. Kennaway (ed.), Houndsmill, Basingstoke, Hampshire: Palgrave Macmillan, 191–215.
Thormählen, W. (forthcoming), "Framing emotional responses to music: music-making and social well-being in early nineteenth-century England," in P. Gouk, J. Kennaway, J. Prins and W. Thormählen eds. *The Routledge Companion to Music, Mind and Well-Being*, Oxon and New York: Routledge.
Thormählen, W. (in press), 'Sound, Music and Narrative: The Disenchantment of Music in the Twentieth Century', in J. Damousi and J. Davidson (eds), *Bloomsbury Cultural History of Emotions*, vol. 6, *The Twentieth Century*, London: Bloomsbury, 77–122.
Thrailkill, J. F. (2006), "Emotive Realism," *Journal of Narrative Theory*, 36: 365–388.
Thrailkill, J. F. (2007), *Affecting Fictions: Mind, Body, and Emotion in American Literary Realism*, Cambridge: Harvard University Press.
Times (1816), *The Times Digital Archive*, 16 July, Issue 9888. Available online: http://tinyurl.galegroup.com/tinyurl/5GDBS1 (accessed 4 October 2017).
Times (1897), "The Queen and Her People". 17 July.
Todd, J. (1986), *Sensibility: An Introduction*, London: Methuen.
Tompkins, J. (1985), *Sensational Designs: The Cultural Work of American Fiction, 1790–1860*, New York: Oxford University Press.
Treitschke, H. v. (1916), *Politics*, New York: Macmillan.
Trumbach, R. (1978), *The Rise of the Egalitarian Family*, Amsterdam: Academic Press.

Tucker, P., ed. (1989), *Monet in the '90s: The Series Paintings*, exh. cat. Boston, Museum of Fine Arts, New Haven and London: Yale University Press.
Tzara, T. (1977), *Seven Dada Manifestos and Lampisteries*, London: John Calder.
Tzara, T. (1995), "Zurich Chronicle February 1916," in J. Rothenberg and P. Joris (eds), *Poems for the Millennium: The University of California Book of Modern and Postmodern Poetry, Volume One: From Fin-de-Siecle to Negritude*, Berkeley: University of California Press.
Unowsky, D. (1998), "Creating Patriotism: Imperial Celebrations and the Cult of Franz Joseph," *Österreichische Zeitschrift für Geschichtswissenschaften*, 9: 280–293.
van Ginneken, J. (1992), *Crowds, Psychology, and Politics, 1871–1899*, New York: Cambridge University Press.
Vilain, J., ed. (1989), *Claude Monet—Auguste Rodin. Centenaire de l'exposition de 1889*, exh. cat. Paris, Musée Rodin, Paris: Musée Rodin.
Vischer, R. (1873), *Über das optische Formgefühl: Ein Beitrag zur Ästhetik*, Leipzig: Hermann Credner.
Vlaminck, M. (1943), *Portraits avant décès*, Paris: Flammarion.
Vogel, J. (1902), *Toteninsel und Frühlingshymne: Zwei Gemälde Boecklins im Leipziger Museum*, Leipzig: Seemann.
Vogt, C. (1864), *Lectures on Man: Place in Creation, and in the History of the Earth*, London: Longman, Green, Longman and Roberts.
Wackenroder (1797), *Herzergiessungen eines kunstliebenden Klosterbruders*, Berlin.
Wackenroder (1799), *Phantasien über die Kunst für Freunde der Kunst*, Hamburg: F. Perthes.
Wacker, G. (2001), *Heaven Below: Early Pentecostals and American Culture*, Cambridge: Harvard University Press.
Wagner, R. ([1849]1895), "The Art Work of the Future," in *Richard Wagner's Prose Works*, trans. W. Ellis, London: Kegan, Paul. Trench, Träuner.
Wahnich, S. (2009), *Les Émotions, la Révolution française et le present*, Paris: CNRS Éditions.
Wahnich, S. (2011), "Sentiments et émotions dans l'élaboration des savoirs politiques instinctifs," *Revue Suisse d'Histoire*, 61: 22–38.
Wakefield, D. (2007), *The French Romantics: Literature and the Visual Arts 1800–1840*, London: Chaucer Press.
Walton, C. (2009), *Policing Public Opinion in the French Revolution: The Culture of Calumny and the Problem of Free Speech*, New York: Oxford University Press.
Watkins, O. (1972), *The Puritan Experience: Studies in Spiritual Autobiography*, New York: Schocken Books.
Weatherill, L. (1996), *Consumer Behaviour and Material Culture in Britain, 1660–1760*, 2nd ed. London: Routledge.
Weber, M. (1958), *The Protestant Ethic and the Spirit of Capitalism*, New York: Charles Scribner's Sons.
Weber, M. (1963), *The Sociology of Religion*, Boston: Beacon Press.
Weber, M. (1978), *Economy and Society*, G. Roth and C. Wittrich (eds), vol. 1 Berkeley: University of California Press.
Weber, M. (1994), "The Profession and Vocation of Politics," in P. Lassman and R. Speirs (eds), *Weber: Political Writings*, Cambridge: Cambridge University Press, 309–369.
Weber, W. (1989), "The 1784 Handel Commemoration as Political Ritual," *The Journal of British Studies*, 28(1): 43–69.
Weber, W. (2008), *The Great Transformation of Musical Taste: Concert Programming from Haydn to Brahms*, Cambridge: Cambridge University Press.

Wedekind, G. (2007), *Le portrait mis à nu: Théodore Géricault und die Monomanen*, Berlin and Munich: Deutscher Kunstverlag.

Wedekind, G. (2010), "Metaphysischer Pessimismus: Stimmung als ästhetisches Verfahren bei Caspar David Friedrich," in K. Thomas (ed), *Stimmung: Ästhetische Kategorie und künstlerische Praxis*, Berlin and Munich: Deutscher Kunstverlag, 31–49.

Wedekind, G. (2013), *Géricault: Images of Life and Death*, G. Wedekind and M. Hollein (eds), exh. cat. Frankfurt/M, Schirn Kunsthalle, Munich: Hirmer.

Wedekind, G. (2014), "Schiffbruch des Zuschauers: Théodore Géricaults 'Floß der Medusa' als Dekonstruktion des Historienbildes," in U. Fleckner (ed.), *Bilder machen Geschichte: Historische Ereignisse im Gedächtnis der Kunst*, Berlin: Akademie Verlag, 235–252.

Weindling, Paul (1991), "Bourgeois Values, Doctors and the State: The Professionalization of Medicine in Germany, 1848–1933," in D. Blackbourn and R. Evans (eds), *The German Bourgeoisie: Essays on the Social History of the German Middle Classes from the Late Eighteenth to the Early Twentieth Century*, New York and London: Routledge.

Weisz, G. (2005), *A Comparative History of Medical Specialization*, Oxford: Oxford University Press.

Wellek, R. (1949), "The Concept of Romanticisms in Literary Scholarship," *Comparative Literature*, 1: 1–23 and 147–172.

Wells, R. (1985), *Uncle Sam's Family: Issues in and Perspectives on American Demographic History*, New York: State University of New York Press.

Wells, R. (2000), *Facing the "King of Terrors": Death and Society in an American Community, 1750–1990*, Cambridge: Cambridge University Press.

White, P., ed. (2009), "Focus: The Emotional Economy of Science," *Isis*, 100.

White, R. (2017), "Romanticism," in S. Broomhall (ed.), *Early Modern Emotions: An Introduction*, London: Routledge, 273–276.

Wigger, J. (1998), *Taking Heaven by Storm, Methodism and the Rise of Popular Religion in American*, New York: Oxford University Press.

Wiley, R. (1985), *Tchaikovsky's Ballets: Swan Lake, Sleeping Beauty, Nutcracker*, Oxford: Oxford University Press.

[William, German Emperor] (1906), *Kaiser Wilhelms des Großen Briefe, Reden und Schriften*, E. Berner (ed.), vol. 2, Berlin: Mittler und Sohn.

Williams, R. (1997), *The Contentious Crown: Public Discussion of the British Monarchy in the Reign of Queen Victoria*, Aldershot: Ashgate.

Wilson Bareau, J. ed. (1993), *Goya. El capricho y la invención*, exh. cat. Madrid, Museo del Prado, Madrid: Museo del Prado.

Wimsatt Jr., W., and Beardsley, M. (1949), "The Affective Fallacy," *The Sewanee Review*, 57: 31–55.

Winckelmann, J. (1754/1756), *Gedanken über die Nachahmung der griechischen Werke in der Malerey und Bildhauerkunst*, 2nd ed, Dresden and Leipzig: Walther.

Wolf, C. (2004), "Monarchen als religiöse Repräsentanten der Nation um 1900?," in H.-G. Haupt and D. Langewiesche (eds), *Nation und Religion in Europa*, Frankfurt: Campus, 153–172.

Wölfflin, H. (1886), *Prolegomena zu einer Psychologie der Architektur*, Munich: Wolf.

Wölfflin, H. (1898), "'Arnold Böcklin': Festrede gehalten am 23. Oktober 1897," *Basler Jahrbuch*, 45–47.

Wolfgang, M. (1961), "Pioneers in Criminology: Cesare Lombroso (1825–1909)," *Journal of Law and Criminology*, 52: 361–391.

Woods, M. (2014), *Emotion and Sectional Conflict in the Antebellum United States*, New York: Cambridge University Press.

Woodward, W. and Ash, M., eds (1982), *The Problematic Science: Psychology in Nineteenth-century Thought*, New York: Praeger.

Woodworth, S. (2001), *While God is Marching On, The Religious World of Civil War Soldiers*, Lawrence: University Press of Kansas.

Woolf, V. (1919), "Modern Novels," *Times Literary Supplement*, 10 April 1919: 189–190.

Wordsworth, W. (1969), "The Borderers, A Tragedy," *Poetical Works*, ed. T. Hutchinson, London: Oxford University Press.

Wordsworth, W. ([1800]2010), "Preface to *Lyrical Ballads, with Pastoral and Other Poems*," in V.B. Leitch et al. (eds), *The Norton Anthology of Theory and Criticism*, 2nd ed., New York: Norton.

Wordsworth, W. and Coleridge, S. T. (1991), *Lyrical Ballads*, eds R. Brett and A. Jones, London: Routledge.

World Values Survey, retrieved December 3, 2012 from http://www.wvsevsdb.com/wvs/WVSData.jsp

Wouters, C. (2004), *Sex and Manners: Female Emancipation in the West 1890–2000*, London and Thousand Oaks, CA: SAGE Publications.

Wouters, C. (2007), *Informalization: Manners and Emotions since 1890*, London and Thousand Oaks, CA: SAGE Publications.

Wright, N. (2015), "Tendering Judgment?: Vying Prototypes of 'Judicial Sensibility' in Later Eighteenth-Century British Narratives of Justice," *Eighteenth-Century Studies*, 48: 329–352.

Wundt, W. (1864), *Vorlesungen über die Menschen und Tierseele*, Leipzig: Voss.

Wundt, W. (1874), *Grundzüge der physiologischen Psychologie*, Leipzig: Engelmann.

Yaraman, S. (2002), *Revolving Embrace: The Waltz as Sex, Steps, and Sound*. Hillsdale: Pendragon Press.

Yeo, E. (1999), "'The Creation of 'Motherhood' and Women's Responses in Britain and France, 1750–1914," in *Women's History Review*, 8(2): 201–218.

Yousef, N. (2013), *Romantic Intimacy*, Stanford: Stanford University Press.

Zelizer, V. (1985), *Pricing the Priceless Child: The Changing Social Value of Children*, New York: Basic Books.

Zimmermann, M. (1991), *Seurat: Sein Werk und die kunsttheoretische Debatte seiner Zeit*, Antwerpen and Weinheim: Mercatorfonds and VCH, Acta Humaniora.

Zola, E. (1964), "The Experimental Novel," *The Experimental Novel and Other Essays*, trans. B. Sherman, New York: Haskell House.

INDEX

Italic numbers are used for illustrations.

Abandoned City (Khnopff) 113, *113*
Ablow, Rachel 129, 134
absolute music 70–1
acedia (sloth) 35
Adorno, Theodor 104
Adventures of Huckleberry Finn (Twain) 133
aesthetic assessment of music 55–6, 59–60, 65, 71
aesthetics of dance 68
affections 2, 34, 39–40, 50
affective disorders 18
affective distance in literature 129
affective memory 118–19
Affekt (emotions of the body) 4
African American Methodism 42, *43*, 44
Age of Sensibility 7, 11
Ahnung (premonition) 58
Albanese, Catherine L. 51
Alcott, Louisa May 132
allusion and indeterminacy in art 112
amateur music 66–7
American Civil War 50–1
American Jerusalem 44
American Revolution 5–6
American Tract Society (ATS) 47–50
Amiel, Henri-Frédéric 114
anger
    in family life 138, 143, 147–8, 155
    of men 13, 148
    as resource for change 6
animals, emotions of 26–7, 32, 131, *131*
animals, humans as 134
anorexia nervosa 155
anthropology 23
antisentimentalism in literature 128
antislavery texts 125–6, *126*
appetites 1
art market and social change 95–6
artists and passions 110–11
arts and music, purpose of 57
assurance of election (*certitudo salutis*) 37

attentive listening 59, 60–1
audiences for music 59, 67–8, 71–2
Austen, Jane 124
Ayer, Sarah Connell 47

Bagehot, Walter 161, 173
Baillie, Joanna 81, 87, 88, 90–1
Bain, Alexander 3, 27–8, 29
Baldwin, James Mark 119, 123
Ball, John 13
Ballanche, Pierre-Simon 11
ballet 68, 72–3
Baptist revivals 33
Baudelaire, Charles 109, 110
Beethoven, Ludwig van 61, 64, 69–70, 71
Bell, Charles 3, 19–20, *20*
Bell, Michael 123
Berlioz, Hector 70
Bertram (Maturin) 80
biological determinism 22
birth rates 140, 142, 146–7
Blair, James 9
Blake, William 106, 128
Blauvelt, Martha Tomhave 46
Böcklin, Arnold 114
Bogucki, Michael 133
Böhme, Gernot 116
Booth, Michael 82
boredom 11–12
Boulanger, Georges 171
Bound Alberti, Fay 4–5
brains, measurement of 22
Brendel, Franz 70
Brissenden, R. F. 123
British qualities in literature 128
Broca, Paul 22
Brooks, Peter 76, 78
Brown, Thomas 2–3
Brunetière, Ferdinand 114
Brutus (David) 97, *98*
Buckley, James 52

Buckley, Matthew 77
Bunyan, John 38–9
Burke, Edmund 76–7, 83, 84, 85, 124
Burroughs, Catherine 88
Burton, Robert 37
Bushnell, Horace 9
Businessman's Revival 50
Byron, George, 6th Baron 92, 108, 109
Byttebier, Stephanie 133

Calvinism 36–7
Cane Ridge Revival, Kentucky 33
capitalism 6–7, 9
Carey, Brycchan 125–6
Carpeaux, Jean-Baptiste 107–8, *107*
Carrà, Carlo 116, *117*
Carus, Carl Gustav 102
Castil-Blaze, Francois 59, 68
Castle Spectre (Lewis) 81
Chahut (Seurat) 118, *119*
charisma of politicians 171, 173
Chaussard, Pierre Jean-Baptiste 99
cheerful families 150–2, *151–3*
Chekhov, Anton 93, 133
childhood 140, 142, 147, 150, *151–3*, 152, 154, 156
Chodowiecki, Daniel Nikolaus 99, *99*
choral music 66–7
Churchill, Winston 167–8
citizenship 14
city paintings 115–16
civilization, stages of 13–14
Clarke, Suzanne 135–6
class differences in family emotionality 141–3
class identities 13
closet drama 76, 86–93
Coleridge, Samuel Taylor 75, 83–4, 86
color, use of in art 109–10, 113, 114
communal solidarity 5
comparative psychology 27
Constable, John 100, *101*
consumerism 139, 141
Corot, Camille 104–5, *104*
Corrigan, John 50
courage 146, 147
courtship 140, 141, 142, 146–7, *146*, 155
criminality, appearance of 24–6, *25*
Cromer, Evelyn Baring, 1st Earl of 170–1
cues in religious culture 34
Cullis, Charles 52
cultural changes and family life 139–40

Dada poetry 134–5, *135*
Dalle Pezze, Barbara 11–12
Damasio, Antonio 78, 81, 92
dance 57, 59, 67, 68, 72–3
dark romanticism 106
Darwin, Charles 3, 4, 20–3, 26, 131, *131*, 133–4
David, Jacques-Louis 97, *98*
Davis, Philip 130–1
Dawson, Melanie 129, 131–2
De Sousa, Ronald 81, 82, 83, 86
death 149–50
 See also grief
Death of Sardanapalus (Delacroix) 109, *110*
Debussy, Claude 74
DeJean, Joan E. 95
Delacroix, Eugène 109–10, *110*
demographic changes 140, 142
Denby, David 95, 123
Denis, Maurice 118
Denmark 9–10
Desastres de la Guerra (Goya) 105
De Sousa, Ronald 75
devotionalism 45, 47, 48
Dickens, Charles 130–1, *130*
Diderot, Denis 91, 97–8
Die Meistersinger von Nürnberg (Wagner) 55
Die Räuber (Schiller) 84–5
differentiation of people 12–15, 20–1, 22–4
divorce in America 142, 154–5
Dixon, Thomas 1, 2
dogs, emotions of 27
domestic life 9
domestic music 66
domestication in work of Darwin 21
Dostoyevsky, Fyodor 131
drama 75–93
 closet drama 76, 86–93
 melodrama 76–83
 mental theater 76, 92–3
 realist 133
 romantic tragedy 76, 83–6
Dror, Otniel 3, 31
Du Bos, Jean-Baptiste 96
Dubois, W. E. B. 42, 44
Duchenne de Boulogne, Guillaume-Benjamin-Amand 21, 22
Duncan, Bruce 124
dynastic sentimentality 164

East Bergholt, Suffolk (Constable) 100
economic life, emotions in 6–7, 13

ecstasy 34, 39–40, 41–4
Edwards, Jonathan 39–40
Elaw, Zilpha 42
electoral franchise in France 159
Eliot, George 133
Eliot, T. S. 135
Ella, John 60
Emma (Austen) 124
Emmanuel Movement 52–3
emotion, definitions of 1–4
Emotional Reinventions (Dawson) 131–2
Enderwitz, Anne 135
England, politics in 6
English landscape painting 100–2, *101*
English Landscape Scenery (Constable) 100
Enlightenment
    emotions 95–6, 140
    literature 121–4
    philosophy 5
Eustace, Nicole 5, 6, 9–10
evangelical pietism 35, 36, 45
evangelical revivals 40
evolution 20–1, 23, 26–7, *26*, 29
existential situations in art 107–8
Expression of Emotion in Man and Animals (Darwin) 3, 22, 131, *131*, 133
Expressionism 120
expressions 3, 19–26, 88, 90, 131

faith healing 52
family life. *See* private life
family love 9, 144–7
fanaticism 166
Faust, Drew Gilpin 51
fear 15, 51, 79, 83, 147, 158
Finney, Charles Grandison 33, 50
Fisher, Philip 82, 84, 91, 126
Flatley, Jonathan 135
Flaubert, Gustave 133
Flavel, John 48
Floerke, Gustav 114
Fouché, Joseph 159
Franz Joseph I, Emperor of Austria 163–4
fraternity of the French 159, 171
Frederick II, King of Prussia 158–9
Frederick William III, King of Prussia 161
French landscape painting 103–5
French Revolution 6, 76–8, 159–60
French territories 14
Freud, Sigmund 18
Freudian psychoanalysis 4
Frevert, Ute 1, 4, 6, 95

Fried, Michael 97
Friedrich, Caspar David 102–3, *103*
friendships, same-sex 142, 143
Füssli, Johann Heinrich 105–6
Futurism 116

Galenic humors 17–18
Galton, Francis 24
Gambetta, Léon 168
Gamboni, Dario 112
Gaskell, Elizabeth 129
Gauguin, Paul 118
Gefühl (feeling associated with the soul) 4
Geist of music 61, 64
gender differences 12–13
gendered emotional life 142–3
genre painting 98
Géricault, Théodore 107, 108–9, *108*, 111
German landscape painting 102–3
Germany 3–4, 6
gestures in drama 78–9, *79–80*, 88, 90
Gilchrist, Alexander 106
Gill, Miranda 128
Gillespie, Joanna Bowen 46
Girodet, Anne-Louis 99
Giselle (ballet) 72
Goebbels, Joseph 173
Goethe, Johann Wolfgang von 124–5, *125*
gothic literature 123–4
Gourmont, Remy de 117
Goya, Francisco de 105, *106*
Grace Abounding to the Chief of Sinners (Bunyan) 38–9
grandparents 140
Great Awakenings 40
Great War 14–15, 18–19
Greiner, Rae 129
Greuze, Jean-Baptiste 98
grief
    display of 10, 97
    in family life 148–50, *148–9*, 154, 156
    practice of by girls 143
    regional differences 144
Grove, George 60
Grundtvig, N. F. S. 10
guilt 138, 150

Habsburg Empire 163–4
Hall, Timothy D. 40
Handel, George Frederick 66–7
Hanslick, Eduard 55–6, 64–5

happiness 11, 140, 144, 156
Harbus, Antonina 124
Hazlitt, William 88
healing cults 52
hearing of music 58–61, 64–5, 66, 74
Heinse, Wilhelm 58
Helmholtz, Hermann 70
Hendler, Glenn 126–7
heroes and antiheroes 108–9
Hirschman, Albert O. 7
history painting 96–7
Hodler, Ferdinand 119–20, *120*
Hofer, Johannes 10
Hoffmann, E. T. A. 61, 64
Hofmann, W. 100
Holcroft, Thomas 78–9, 82
Holiness movement 44, 52
homesickness 10, 13, 15
Horkheimer, Max 104
hormones 30, *31*
Howells, William Dean 132
human beasts 134
humanitarian reform 125–6
Hume, David 87–8, 122
Hume, Robert 124
humors 17–18
Huret, Jules 111
hysteria 18–19
hysterical paralysis 155

Ibsen, Henrik 133
identity and the self 36
imperialism 13–14
Impressionism 114
individualism 5, 6, 8, 12
industrialization 8, 140–1
inner worlds in art 111–14, 118–19
inner worlds in literature 133
insanity, religious 44
instrumental music 57, 58
intimacy in literature 128–9

Jackson, John Hughlings 5
Jackson, Stanley W. 35
Jacobs, Harriet 13
Jäger, Ludwig 95
James, Henry 133
James, William 3, 4, 22, 30, 31, 51–2
Janin, Jules 68
Jauß, Hans Robert 109
jealousy 148
jingoism 170

Johnson, Claudia 123
Jordheim, Helge 13–14
Joyce, James 134
judges, literature of 124

Kant, Immanuel 56, 83, 85
Kaufman, Peter Iver 37
Kean, Edmund 88, 90
Kemp, Wolfgang 102
Khnopff, Fernand 113–14, *113*
Kiesewetter, Raphael 69
King, John Owen 39
Kleist, Heinrich von 102
Knabe, Peter-Eckhard 96
Knowles, Claire 127
Knox, R. A. 40
Koch, Heinrich Christoph 61
Koselleck, Reinhart 95

La bête humaine (Zola) 134
La Font de Saint-Yenne, É. 97
labor movement 168–9
Laclos, Choderlos de 121
Lake Thun (Hodler) *120*
Lamb, Charles 90, 92
Lambert, Frank 40
landscape painting 100–5, 114–15
Lange, Carl Georg 3
Le Bon, Gustave 170
Le Brun, Charles 96, 97
Lecomte, Georges 116
Lee, Jarena 42, *43*
legal processes 124, 154
Leichentritt, Hugo 65
Les liaisons dangereuses (Laclos) 121
Lessing, Gotthold Ephraim 105
level ubiquity of emotion 75
Lewes, George Henry 28–9
Lewis, Matthew 81
Lincoln, Abraham 11
listening to music 58–61, 64–5, 66, 74
Liszt, Franz 68–9, *69*, 71
literature 121–36
 sentimentalism 121–3
 legacies of sentimentalism 123–7
 Romanticism and revolutionary emotions 127–9
 Realism, Darwin, naturalism 129–34
 modernism 134–6
lithographic art 108–9
Lombroso, Cesare 24, *25*, 111
Loughran, Tracey 15

Louis Philippe, King of the French 159
love
    and civilization 13–14
    in family life 9, 144–7
    of monarchs 158, 161
    of mothers 9, 144–5, *145*
    nationalistic 9–10
    romantic 8–9, 146–7, 153–4
    sexual 155
lower class families 141–2
Luise, Queen of Prussia 160–1
Lyrical Ballads (Wordsworth) 83
Lystra, Karen 8

Machiavelli, Niccolò 158
Madame Bovary (Flaubert) 133
madness in painting 106–7, 111
Mallarmé, Stéphane 111, 116
Manfred (Byron) 92
marriage 138, 142, 144
Marshall, David 86
Martín Moruno, Dolores 8
Marx, Adolph Bernhard 64
Mary Barton (Gaskell) 129
mass media in America 50
mass mobilization and party politics 166–71
Maturin, Charles 80
Mazeppa (Byron) 109
Mazeppa (Géricault) 108–9, *108*
McTeague (Norris) 134
medical and scientific understanding 4, 12, 17–32
    emotional upheaval 17–19
    evolution and psychology 26–9
    expressions 19–26
    measuring and physiology 29–32
melancholy 34–41, 46–8, 49, 53, 113
melodrama 76–83
mémoire affective 118–19
Mendel, Gregor 30
mental cruelty and divorce 142, 154–5
mental theater 76, 92–3
Methodism in America 33, *34*, 41–2, 44
middle-class emotions 13
middle-class families 141–3, 146, 150, 153
Miles, Josephine 129
Mill, John Stuart 7
mimetic understanding of music 58
mind and body in musical performance 68–9
mind and emotion 3–4, 15, 18, 26–7
mind cure 51–2

Mirbeau, Octave 115
modern identity 36
modernism 134–6
Momigny, Jérôme-Joseph de 61, *62–3*, 64
monarchy 158, 160–6, 173
Monet, Claude 114–15
Monk by the Sea (David) 102, *103*
Monomaniacs (Géricault) 107, 111
mood in painting 100–5, 114–16
morals in the Enlightenment 122
Moréas, Jean 111
Morgan, Conwy Lloyd 30
mother love 9, 144–5, *145*
mourning. *See* grief
Muir, John 51
music and dance 55–74
    ballet 72–3
    festivals 66–7
    the language of emotions 56–7
    listening to music 58–61, 64–5, 66, 74
    musical form 61, 64–5, 70, 74
    musical performance 68–9, *69*, 71–2
    Schoenberg and Debussy 73–4
music and melodrama 82
Musical Union 60, *60*
Musset, Alfred de 128
Mussolini, Benito 173
mutes in melodrama 78–9

nationalism
    in Austro-Hungary 163
    in France 159–60, 171
    in Great Britain 170–1
    and love 9–10
    and music 66, 70
    and race 14–15
natural listening 59
natural selection 20–1, 23, 26–7, *26*, 29
naturalism
    of actors 88
    of Charles Darwin 131
    in literature 133–4
nature religion 51
Natürliche und affectirte Handlungen des Lebens (*Natural and Affected Acts of Life*) (Chodowiecki) 99, *99*
Nebukadenzar (Blake) 106
neurasthenia 12, 15, 18
New England Way 39
Nietzsche, Friedrich 71, 109
Nightmare (Füssli) 105–6
Noble, Marianne 127

Nocturne in Blue and Gold (Whistler) 115, 116
Nodier, Charles 77–8
Noll, Mark A. 40
Norris, Frank 134
nostalgia (*heimweh*, homesickness) 10, 13, 15
novels 121–4, 129–34, 139
Noverre, Jean-Georges 57, 59, 68

obedience of children 150, *151–2*, 152
obedience of subjects 158–9
Old Curiousity Shop (Dickens) 130, *130*
Old Sarum (Constable) 100, *101*
opera 55–6, 59, 67, 68, 72
outer worlds in art 114–17

Page, Harlan 48–9, *49*
pain and gothic literature 124
pain and hysteria 19
Paine, Thomas 6
painting 96–9, 100–7, 109–11, 112–20
Palmer, Phoebe 44
pantomime 57
parliamentary assemblies 166–7
party politics 166–71
passions
    and artists 110–11
    of color 109–10
    and dance 68
    definition of 18
    in drama 87–8, 90–1
    and music 58
    and self-control 128
    and the sublime 84–5
    and time 82
    views on 2
pathetic fallacy 129
pathos 99
patriotism 9–10, 159–60, 166, 170, 171
Pentecostalism in America 44
perception, theories of 116
Pernau, Margrit 13–14
Petipa, Marius 73
physiological study of emotions 4, 30–2
Pilgrim's Progress (Bunyan) 38
Pinch, Adela 87
pity in literature 128
Pixerécourt, Guilbert de 77–8
Plamper, Jan 4
Plater, Felix 37
plays. *See* drama

poetry
    and art 111
    modernist 135
    romanticist 105, 109, 127, 128
politicians 166–8
politics. *See* public life
Poor Fisherman (Puvis de Chavannes) 112, *112*
Poor Folk (Dostoyevsky) 131
Pope, Alexander 11
Potkay, Adam 128
Powell, Lyman P. 53
Praz, Mario 106
premarital sex 146–7
premonition 58
primativization of emotions 4–5
printed religious materials in America 49–50
private life 137–56
    assessment of change 154–5
    baseline for change 137–9
    causes of change 139–41
    cheerful families 150–2
    complexities 141–4
    conclusion and 1920s 155–6
    domestic life 9
    impacts of change 153–4
    key changes and love 144–7
    of monarchs 160–1
    redefining family emotions 147–50
Protestantism in America 34, 45–50
Prout, Ebenezer 65
Prussia 10
psychoanalysis and emotions 4
psychological study of emotions 4, 14, 26–9
public life 5–6, 157–74
    before during and after the 1789 revolution 158–60
    charm of royalty 160–6
    mass mobilization and party politics 166–71
Puritanism in England 36–7
Purton, Valerie 130
Puvis de Chavannes, Pierre 112, *112*

Rabinowitz, Richard 45
racial differentiation 13
Raft of the Medusa (Géricault) 107
railway spine 18
Railway Station (Carrà) *117*
Rain, Steam, Speed—the Great Western Railway (Turner) 101
Ramsay, Martha Laurens 45–6, 47–8
rationalism in the Enlightenment 122

Realism and literature 129–32, 133
reason
   and emotion 2
   inexplicability of music 58
   and morals 122
   in politics and economy 6–7, 160, 168
Recchio, Thomas 129
Reddy, William M. 2, 6, 7, 95, 121
Redon, Odilon 111–12
reform movements 125–6
Reicha, Anton 61
religion and spirituality 33–53
   evangelical religion in the Civil War 50–1
   Methodism, holiness, and African American religious experience 41–4
   Protestant identity and religious experience 45–50
   religious melancholy and Protestantism 35–41
   secularization of spirituality 51–3
religion of music 59–61
religious affections 34, 39–40, 50
religious personality 35–6
Remorse (Coleridge) 75, 83–4, 86
Renoir, Auguste 115
republicanism 159
Rêverie 102, 104
revivals, religious 33, 40, 50
Ribot, Théodule 31, 116, 118
Richardson, Alan 92
Riegl, Alois 114
Riemann, Hugo 65
Rimsky-Korsakov, Nikolai 73
Riskin, Jessica 122
Rite of Spring (ballet) 73
Robespierre, Maximilien 159
Rodenbach, Georges 113–14
Romanes, George John 26–7, *26*
romantic love 8–9, 146–7, 153–4
romantic tragedy 76, 83–6
Romanticism 7–12
   and arts 99–105, *106*, 108
   and drama 83–6
   and literature 127–9
   and music 58, 59
Rosenzweig, Roy 13
Rossini, Gioachino 69–70
Rousseau, Jean-Jacques 57, 79, 86–7, 102
Ruiz de Burton, María Amparo 129–30
Ruskin, John 101
Ryan, Mary 9
Rybczynski, Witold 9

sadness 10–11
salience of melodrama 82
Salzani, Carlo 11–12
sanctification, process of 41, 42, 44
Saturn (Goya) 105, *106*
Scenes of the Flood (Girodet) 99
Scheer, Monique 3–4
Schiller, Friedrich 84–5
Schlegel, Friedrich 127
Schnog, Nancy 35, 132
Schoenberg, Arnold 73–4
Schumann, Robert 70
scientific and medical understanding 4, 12, 17–32
   emotions and passions 17–19
   evolution and psychology 26–9
   expressions 19–26
   measuring and physiology 29–32
sculpture 107
Séailles, Gabriel 112
secularization of spirituality 51–3
secularization of western societies 8
Sedgwick, Catharine 144
self-control and passion 128
sensation novels 132
sensibility 2, 12, 60, 70
sentiment 2, 96–9
sentimentalism in literature 121–7
Series of Plays (Baillie) 87, 88, 90–1
Seurat, Georges 118, *119*
sex, premarital 146–7
sexual desire 105–6, 155
sexual tension of dancing 67
Seymour, William J. 44
Shadow of the Glen (Synge) 133
Shaftesbury, Anthony Ashley-Cooper, 3rd Earl of 96
Sharpe, Lesley 124
shell shock 15, 19
shipwrecks in art 107
Shouting Methodists 42, *43*
sibling relationships 146
Siddons, Henry 79–*80*, 88, *89*
singing. *See* opera; vocal music
skulls, measurement of 22
slavery 11, 13
sloth, sin of 35
Smith, Adam 88, 122
Smith, William Russell 11
social theatricality 86–7
soldiers in the Civil War 50–1
sorrow song spirituals 42, 44

Sorrows of Young Werther (Goethe) 124–5, *125*
Souvenir of Riva (Corot) *104*
Spacks, Patricia Meyer 11
Spain, politics in 6
spiritual pilgrimages 38–9, 45–9
Squatter and the Don (Ruiz de Burton) 129–30
Stachniewski, John 36–7
Staël, Madame de (Anne-Louise-Germaine) 99, 159
stagecraft of melodrama 81–2
standardization of emotions 4
Starling, Ernest 30, *31*
Stearns, Peter 10
Stein, Lorenz von 164
Stendhal 128
stream of consciousness 133
Sturm und Drang movement in German literature 124–5
subjectivity 69, 73–4, 128
sublime experience of music 59
sublime in literature 124
sublime, use of in romantic tragedies 83–6
suffering in art 106–9
Sulzer, Johann 57, 58, 59
Symbolism 111, 115, 117
sympathy 20–1, 87–8, 90–1, 122, 129, 132
synaesthesia in art 116
Synge, J. M. 133
synthesis in art 117–20

Taglioni, Marie 68
Taine, Hippolyte A. 116
Tait, Peta 133
Tale of Mystery, A (Holcroft) 78–9, 82
Taves, Ann 41
Taylor, Charles 36
Tchaikovsky, Peter Ilich 73
terror in gothic literature 123–4
thinking and feeling in literature 128
Thrailkill, Jane 133
Three Sisters (Chekhov) 133
time and melodrama 82
Todd, Janet 128
Todd, John 144
Tompkins, Jane 126
tragedies, romantic 83–6
Treatise Concerning Religious Affections (Edwards) 39–40
Treitschke, Heinrich von 165
trust, in politics 169–70, 171
truthfulness of painting 98, 101, 103

Turner, J. M. W. 101
Twain, Mark 133
Tzara, Tristan 135, *135*

Ugolino (Carpeaux) 107–8, *107*
United States of America
  American Revolution 5–6
  Civil War 50–1
  divorce in 142, 154–5
  religion in 33–4, 41–50
universality of emotions 4

vapors, attacks of 18
verbal expression in melodrama 80
Victoria, Queen 161, *162*, 163
violence in art 105
virtuoso performances 69–70
visual arts 95–120
  the artist 110–11
  Enlightenment and emotions 95–6
  inner worlds 111–14
  mood in painting 100–5
  outer worlds 114–17
  passion of color 109–10
  Romanticism and emotions 99–105, 108
  sentiment 96–9
  suffering, madness, death 107–9
  synthesis 117–20
  violence, eros, agony 105–6
visuality of melodrama 81–2
vocal music 66–7
  See also opera
Vogel, Julius 114
Vuillard, Édouard 113

Wackenroder, W. H. 58, 59
Wagner, Richard 55, 71–2, 72
waltz, dangers of 67
Weber, Max 35–6, 41, 158, 168, 171
Wedekind, Gregor 102
weeping 10–11
Weltshmerz (world suffering) 10–11
Werthersfieber (Werther's fever) 10
Whistler, James McNeill *115*, 116
Wigger, John H. 42
wilderness experience 51
William I, Emperor of Germany 164–5
William II, Emperor of Germany 165–6, *165*
Winckelmann, Johann Joachim 105
Wings of the Dove (James) 133
Wölfflin, Heinrich 114

women
    brains, measurement of 23
    emotions of 12–13
    and family life 140–1, 143, 144
    maladies of 18, 155
    and politics 168
    religious experiences of 42, 44–8, 52
    weaknesses of 24
    writing of 124, 126–7, 129–30, 132, 133, 136
Woods, Michael 11
Woolf, Virginia 134

Wordsworth, William 83, 127, 128
working-class emotions 13, 24
working-class families 141–2
World War I 14–15, 18–19
Wright, Nicole 124
Wundt, Wilhelm 4, 27

Young Woman Attacked by a Tiger (Delacroix) 109
Yousef, Nancy 128

Zola, Émile 134